The Distinguished Charity of Mete

Frontispiece by Jesse Peper

BAPHOMET
The Temple Mystery Unveiled

By Tracy R. Twyman
And Alexander Rivera

BAPHOMET

The Temple Mystery Unveiled

By Tracy R. Twyman
And Alexander Rivera

ISBN # 978-0-692-58076-9

© 2005-2015

All Rights Reserved

2nd Edition (errors corrected)

12/9/2015

Front and Back Cover:
Artwork by Jesse Peper
Jesse-Peper.org

No part of this publication may be reproduced in any form or by any means, electronic or mechanical, including photocopying, recording, or by any information storage or retrieval system, without permission in writing from the publisher.

Other Books by Tracy R. Twyman

Clock Shavings

Money Grows on the Tree of Knowledge

Solomon's Treasure: The Magic and Mystery of America's Money

The Merovingian Mythos and the Mystery of Rennes-le-Chateau

Mind-Controlled Sex Slaves and the CIA

The Arcadian Mystique: The Best of Dagobert's Revenge Magazine

Hocus Pocus: The Magical Power of St. Peter

The Judas Goat: The Substitution Theory of the Crucifixion

The Choice Vine: Mary Magdalene, the Sacred Whore, and the Benjamite Inheritance

The Cutting of the Orm: The Secret Calendar of the Priory of Sion

Dead But Dreaming: The Great Old Ones of Lovecraftian Legend Reinterpreted as Atlantean Kings

Read more from the authors at:

TracyRTwyman.com and TheAeonEye.com

[P]ower and dominion

over all that is on earth,

both that which is above

and that which is beneath,

are in my hand.

—Melek Taus,

from *Al-Jilwah* (*The Revelation*),

Yezidi scripture

Contents

Preface 1

Chapter 1: Pacts with the Devil ………………………….. 5

Chapter 2: Seed of the Serpent …………………………… 22

Chapter 3: The Goat-Faced Wild Man ………………… 68

Chapter 4: The Three Hermeses ………………………… 108

Chapter 5: Divine Knowledge ……………………………. 140

Chapter 6: The Head of Prophecy ……………………… 199

Chapter 7: The Baptism of Wisdom …………………… 292

Chapter 8: Abraxas: Secret of the Temple ………………… 370

Chapter 9: Riding the Goat Current ……………………… 458

Preface

. . . I believe the despite its cerebral dementia and its alvine madness, this book, by virtue of its very subject, rendered a service. It refocused attention on the machinations of the Evil One who had succeeded in making people disbelieve his existence; it was the starting-point for all the renewed studies of the eternal advance of Satanism. By revealing the hateful practices of necromancy it has helped to annihilate them. . . .

J-K Huysmans, Preface to the Second Edition of *Against Nature*, regarding his book *The Damned*

What you are about to read is the product of over ten years of obsession and sacrifice. While I first wrote on the subject of Baphomet in 1999 for *Dagobert's Revenge* (the magazine I published at the time), my true obsession started when I was contacted by this entity through the Ouija board after a series of encounters with other spirits. This contact subsequently happened dozens of times over the course of several years, as it aided the research I was doing on the Holy Grail and the sacred bloodlines of Europe. Through those conversations (detailed in my 2014 book *Clock Shavings*) I got to know this personality well, and became intrigued by the complexity of its nature. I decided to research the subject of Baphomet itself: where it came from, what it meant, and how it had influenced history.

This led to the writing of my first book on the esoteric history of money, 2005's *Solomon's Treasure*. The subject of that book is, believe it or not, intimately connected with that of Baphomet, as the book itself explains. This was a bit of a detour from my main goal, but my research of

Baphomet had led me there, so I went with it. Then in 2007 I started in earnest writing a book on the topic of Baphomet alone.

This has proved to be the most challenging effort I have ever made. The subject defies exact interpretation. The clues lead down tortuous footpaths deep into labyrinthine forests where one becomes easily lost. "Facts" that seem to be taken for granted by most other authors fall apart under scrutiny, with no evidence pointing to where the real truth is, or how and why the lie was constructed and perpetuated. In addition, both I and several of the people I ended up working with on this project found that a sense of fogginess would descend upon the brain whenever a serious attempt was made to sort out the details. It seemed as if Baphomet was playing hard to get. He wanted to be seen and credited for his influence, but never pinned down.

It required the help of a partner to complete this task. My mind simply could not display all of the conflicting information about Baphomet on a single desktop for analysis. That is why I was very grateful when in 2014, Gnostic writer Alexander Rivera joined me in this quest. From that point on, things quickly began to take shape. Throughout the process, it seemed like our efforts were both helped and hindered by forces from without: like there was a supernatural entity putting us in the right place at each step to receive the information we needed next, yet at the same time unexpected obstacles would come along to thwart our efforts.

A crucial element of the research, the translation of Joseph von Hammer-Purgstall's *Mysterium Baphometis Revelatum* from Latin into English, almost didn't happen for numerous reasons. First the translator suffered a sudden and severe decline in his health, requiring him to finish the rest of the work with an assistant to help in the typing of the words. Then he almost quit near the end because of spiritual attacks he endured involving disturbing mental images and poltergeist activity. Even his assistant experienced the haunting. Finally, the discovery of the artifacts in the British Museum was a fluke, particularly the second casket, which I wasn't even looking for because I didn't know it existed. (All of this is covered thoroughly in the final chapter of this book.)

I must stress that, although my obsession with Baphomet began because of an encounter on the Ouija board (which I did not ask for, mind you, as I was simply trying to contact a dead French artist at the time), and some of my early research was inspired by clues given to me in this manner, all of the information that you find here was discovered and analyzed the old-fashioned way, pouring through books in various languages, some over two thousand years old, utilizing inter-library loan programs, and purchasing (at great expense) rare out-of-print volumes. We also utilized the plethora of old material scanned into Google Books, as well as the catalogues of display listings for several museums. Of course, we made good use of our network of friends all over the world, many of whom truly went out of their way to help, including, notably, Karl James Smith and Christopher Knowles.

It goes without saying that we could not have done this without our mysterious translator (who wishes to be anonymous). We are also forever indebted to Philip Gonzalez, who tracked down a copy of the Hammer-Purgstall book, scanned the images, helped us find a translator, helped us with analysis, and in the end provided crucial proofreading and fact-checking of the final manuscript. The people at the British Museum have been extremely helpful as well, including Parveen Sodhi in the Images Department, and Virginia Smithson in the Department of Britain, Europe & Prehistory. Also, thanks must go to the talented Jesse Peper for providing the cover art and frontispiece.

Today "Baphomet" is almost a household name, thanks to the prevalence of conspiracy theories that have spread widely on the internet. It is even pre-loaded into the dictionary on my smartphone, unlike a lot of normal English words that I am surprised to find missing. Nevertheless, despite the great many words being written about Baphomet, very few seem to understand it as anything more than a symbol of Satan. It may be that, but it is a lot more also. In fact, as Masonic writers have hinted in the past, it may be the preeminent mystery of the Western spiritual tradition. Understanding Baphomet sheds light not only on the motivations of the Devil, but on the mind of God as well. I hope you find reading this book to be almost as enlightening as it was for us to write it.

    Tracy R. Twyman

    Vancouver, Washington

    October 2015

Chapter 1: Pacts with the Devil

It is established from their monuments that three capital crimes brought against them by the Articles of Accusation— the crimes of apostasy, idolatry and pederasty—are foundation teachings of the Ophitic doctrine of which the Templars were followers. . . .

—Baron Joseph von Hammer-Purgstall, *Mysterium Baphometis Revelatum*

It was, in many ways, the greatest political scandal of European history, and certainly the most bizarre. The charges included sodomy, infanticide and other murders, kissing a goat's behind, spitting and urinating on the cross, invoking the Devil, and worshipping a demonic idol, as well as denying Christ, the Virgin, the Saints, and God himself. The alleged perpetrators were the members of one of the richest and most powerful entities on the continent, an enormous transnational business enterprise that had begun as a holy order of fighting monks receiving its authority directly from the Pope, largely responsible for the success, and then the failure, of the Crusades to capture Jerusalem for Christendom. After 200 years, their power and wealth had swelled to the point where it seemed they feared no one, not even the king of France himself. That was about to change.

At dawn on Friday the 13th, 1307, the Knights Templar in France were arrested *en masse* by King Philip IV's seneschals. Philip was out to get the order. He owed them a lot of money, and they had embarrassed him by refusing him membership to their club. Now he planned to use his influence on the papacy to have them disbanded. He had already sent in spies to join the order and see if there was any truth to the rumors: that there was something unholy about the Templar initiation ceremony. What his spies reported back would make anyone's hair stand on end.

When the stories of the spies are combined with the confessions of the tortured knights, a remarkably cohesive, if horrific, pattern begins to form. The Templars apparently had a secret Rule, different than the one given to them by their patron, Saint Bernard of Clairvaux. Outwardly, they were Christian warrior-monks, pledged to fight for the protection and expansion of Christendom, and to adhere to an extremely ascetic lifestyle. Inwardly though, it seemed, they practiced anti-Christian rites.

It was said that at initiation new recruits were forced to kiss the naked behind of one of their new brothers, although sometimes the backside of a goat or a cat was substituted. They were made to spit upon the Cross, revoke their Christian baptism, and denounce Jesus. They were then introduced to their new savior, whom they were to worship. It was a "head" of some sort named "Baphomet." None of the inquisitors knew what that meant at the time, and no translation was offered by any of the confessors.

This "Baphomet" head was variously said to be that of a bearded man, a woman, a goat, or a demon with leathery skin. Some said that it had two or three faces, or that it had "feet." While it was generally described as a mummified flesh-and-blood relic of some sort, others said that it was a skull, or that it was made of brass or gold, or that it was merely a painting of a head. All witnesses agreed that it was terrifying to behold. They said that the head "prophesied" to them during the ceremonies, and gave them "wisdom." They believed that it "made them rich" and "caused the land to germinate."

Pacts with the Devil 7

By November 1307, even the Grand Master of the Templars himself, Jacques de Molay had confessed to these charges, and more. Pope Clement had heard enough. He issued a bull ordering the arrest of all Templars in eight countries, including England, Ireland, Portugal, Italy and Germany. On August 12, 1308, he drew up a list of 127 offenses with which they were charged. In addition to the various acts of blasphemy, heresy, sodomy and murder already discussed, they were also accused of treasonous dealings with the Muslim enemy during the Crusades, the Saracens. Trials dragged on for another five years. Many recanted their confessions, including that of the Grand Master, and those knights who did so were put to death in brutal ways. As he burned at the stake in 1314, Grand Master Jacques De Molay uttered a curse against Pope Clement and King Philip, prophesying that they would both die within a year. They did.

Other knights stuck to their confessions, and were rewarded with lenient sentences of monastic penance not much different from the ascetic lifestyle they were already used to. The order was officially disbanded by the Pope, its property given over to other monastic orders. So ended what was once the greatest military and economic power in Europe.

How could things have gone so horribly wrong? In the beginning, nobody could have imagined this. The Templars were thought of as the Special Forces of their day, the elite fighting force at the forefront of the Crusades. The order began when a 22-year-old French knight named Hughes de Payens and eight of his friends took a vow of obedience to the Patriarch of Jerusalem, pledging to live in poverty and chastity. They dedicated themselves to the protection of pilgrims *en route* to the Holy Land. The knights were given lodging by Baldwin II, King of Jerusalem, who stationed them at the al-Aqsa Mosque next to the Dome of the Rock, site of the original Temple of Solomon. Thus they were named "the Poor Knights of the Temple of Solomon," which was rendered "Knights Templar" in common usage.

Soon the knighthood was adopted by Saint Bernard of Clairvaux, leader of the Cistercian order of monks. Membership blossomed. In 1128 the knights assembled at the papal Council of Troyes in France, where they were given an official rule and assigned a plain white robe as their uniform. A red equilateral cross was added to the outfit in 1147. The Templar Rule consisted of 72 paragraphs detailing every aspect of life in the monastery and on the battlefield. At most meals they were allowed only bread with no water, although meat was served three times a week. Scriptures were read aloud during meal times, but all other talking was forbidden. New members had to give up their wives and donate all of their property to the order, so as to live in perfect poverty and chastity. They slept on the floor communally, always with a candle left burning to discourage "immoral acts" at night.

In battle the Templars were forbidden to retreat, required to fight to the death of their last man. This made the Templars very formidable foes at war. Because of this, they were feared and respected by their Muslim Saracen enemies. In 1148, as the Second Crusade commenced, King Louis VII of France put the Templars in command of all European armies, and they led every major battle of the Crusades from then onward.

However, the most important moment for the Templars had come in March of 1139, when Pope Innocent II issued a papal bull entitled "Omne Datum Optimum" (usually translated "Every Best Gift," although a "datum" is actually a "fact" or "object of knowledge" more than a "gift."). In it, the Knights Templar were declared the "true Israelites," and the Pope's private army, answerable to him alone. No other king, bishop or nobleman had any ultimate authority over them. They were granted the right to form their own priesthood, with full authority to forgive sins and to raise tithes. They were also given the right to lend money with interest, something that the Church's anti-usury policy forbade all other Christians from doing.

The Templars began to amass wealth and power quickly. Their membership was taken from the cream of European aristocracy, so each new initiate remitted to the order what was often considerable money and property. Wealthy families from all over Europe also donated lands and money as the Second Crusade mounted. The Templars set up "preceptories" throughout the continent. These were conducted like semi-autonomous city-states, where the knights farmed their own food, ran their own hospitals, and engaged in the manufacture of arms, textiles, and other goods. They also ran their own banks. This network of preceptories created ideal routes of travel for European pilgrims seeking the Holy Land, whom the Templars had sworn to protect at their inception.

Indeed it was the way these preceptories operated, particularly their banking operations, which provided a form of protection for the pilgrims. Instead of loading themselves down with gold and provisions, which were likely to be stolen, the pilgrims would simply deposit some money in the form of gold or silver at the Templar preceptory nearest to their point of departure. From there they would make their way to Jerusalem, traveling from one preceptory to another. At each stop the pilgrim would present the banker with a "chit"—a piece of paper that was encoded with ciphered information regarding the pilgrim's deposit at the originating bank. The pilgrim's account would then be charged for all the accommodation he received while staying at that particular preceptory, and he could also make cash withdrawals if he wished. A new chit, encoded with his new balance, would then be given to him to present at the next preceptory. In this way the word "check" or "cheque" entered into the French and English languages.

It was thus by donations, money-lending and industrial trade that the Templars were able to expand their empire to become Europe's most powerful economic influence. They were able to maintain this even after the Holy Land was finally lost in the Eighth Crusade in 1271. But now they were without a cause. Some of Europe's kings and nobles, and well as many within the Church, began to wonder what the Templars were going to do next. They had money, property, authority, horses, weapons, and a standing army with nothing to do. Many European crown heads were heavily indebted to the Templars financially, and since they were also banned by papal decree from exercising any political authority over the knights, many of these kings understandably felt threatened.

There was another potential threat as well, of a more metaphysical nature. Not everyone understood exactly how the Templars had become so wealthy and powerful. It was rumored that there must have been a secret to this. One rumor popular now, which may have circulated at the time, was that the original nine founding Templars had discovered a treasure within or beneath the Al-Aqsa Mosque in Jerusalem, perhaps a cache of King Solomon's fabled wealth. After the arrests, King Philip had the Templar properties in France turned upside down looking for treasure, but found very little money at all, something that has always puzzled Templar scholars (as noted in the book *The Warriors and the Bankers* by Alan Butler and Stephen Dafoe).

Theories of a secret Templar treasure have been the subject of hundreds of books throughout the years, and this idea is even at the heart of some rituals performed by modern Freemasons. It is often suggested that the knights might have found the lost Ark of the Covenant underneath the Temple Mount. How this would have made the order wealthy, however, is something that really remains unexplained by the theorists. Some suggest that it would have given them negotiating power with the Church, which would have been eager to possess such a relic.

Another rumor floating around at the end of the 13th century was that the Templars acquired their wealth because their founders had made a pact with the Devil. According to this theory they allegedly kept the Pope under their control and compelled others to give them money through the power of witchcraft. Stories had begun to leak from disgruntled ex-knights about the secret initiation rituals. Word was getting around about the idol worship, the obscene kisses, the homosexual orgies, and the desecration of the Cross. Why would men in such important, respectable positions do such things, unless they were benefiting from it in some tangible way?

It would be so easy to dismiss these rumors as typical tall tales of the Middle Ages. But in their confessions the knights admitted that they did these horrible things in their rituals. They said it was all part of the worship of their demonic idol, a head named Baphomet. As Michael Baigent, Richard Leigh and Henry Lincoln put it in *Holy Blood, Holy Grail*:

> Subjected to interrogation by the Inquisition . . . a number of knights referred to something called "Baphomet"—too many, and in too many different places, for Baphomet to be the invention of a single individual or even a single preceptory.

The knights also voluntarily proclaimed that it was the worship of the head which made them wealthy. Is this the "secret of the Templar treasure" for which King Philip was looking? Did he perhaps think that by forcing the knights to describe their rituals in detail, he would discover a method of getting rich through witchcraft?

When Philip's police raided the Templar properties in France, they found very little gold or silver bullion. They certainly did not find the Ark of the Covenant. But they did find, in the Paris Temple, the large bust of a female figure made out of silver. It was hollow. Inside were two head bones wrapped in white and red cloths, with a label attached that, according to the authors of *Holy Blood, Holy Grail*, quoting, in translation, Raymond Oursel's French language *Le Proces des Templiers*, 1955) read "Caput LVIIIm"—"Head 58m." Another source, Jules Michelet's *History of France, Volume 1* (as translated by GH Smith, 1860), says that the head was labeled "LIII," meaning "53." From this evidence, we can presume that there were at least 52 other heads somewhere that the police did not find. So what was the true purpose of all these heads? What does the name "Baphomet" actually mean?

The Oxford English Dictionary says that the first appearance of the name "Baphomet" in English text was in the May 12th edition of the *Classical Journal*, Volume 5, published in 1812, in an article by Charles Villers called "Some Account of the Researches of the German Literati on the Subject of Ancient Literature and History." There, in a footnote on page 88, a French scholar referred to only as "M. Lentz" is quoted, from an essay of his entitled "On the goddess of Paphos as represented on ancient monuments and on the Baphomet." This referred to a goddess worshipped in the coastal city of Paphos on the island of Cyprus, where the Templars were stationed. Idols of the goddess were used as land markers, just as statues of Hermes, the Greek wisdom god, were also used in ancient times. These images of the goddess had gradually combined with and then transmuted into images of Hermes himself. M. Lentz suggested that the name of these markers—*metae*—got fused with that of Paphos to form "Paphometa," and thus, Baphomet. Jules Michelet referred to Francois Just-Marie-Raynouard's *The Templars: Tragedy in Five Acts* (1805) regarding the origin of the word:

> M. Raynouard considers the word Baphomet in these two depositions, as an alteration of that of Mahomet, mentioned by the first [Templar] witness; and sees in it a desire on the part of the examiners to confirm the charges of a good understanding with the Saracens, so generally reported of the Templars. . . . [In their depositions] the Templars admit nothing more serious than that they have felt alarm, that they have fancied they saw a devil's head, a *mauffe*'s head, that in these ceremonies they have seen the devil himself under the shape of a cat, or of a woman. . . .

The word "Mauffe" appears to originate in French as a way of spelling this alleged alteration of Mahomet, the name of the Muslim prophet, more frequently spelled "Mohammed" or "Muhammad," which supposedly morphed into the word Baphomet. Variations seen in print also include "Maufe," Mauffez," and "Maphumet" (according to the

Bulletin de la Societe Academique de Laon, Vol. 21, 1876). In the book *The View of the State of Europe During the Middle Ages* by Henry Hallam, published in 1818, the author concurs that the word is "an early French corruption of 'Mahomet.'" This goes along with the reports, mentioned by Raynouard and Michelet, that the Templars were suspected at the time of their trials of having been secret converts to Islam, and secret friends of their supposed enemies, the Saracens. In one knight's confession he mentioned that he had been taught to exclaim the word "Yallah" during the blasphemous ceremonies, which he said was "a word of the Saracens." Also, according to the Online Etymology Dictionary, "Mahomet" was used in the Middle Ages as a generic word for "idol."

But there have been other interpretations as well. The writer responsible for our modern understanding of Baphomet was a mid-nineteenth-century occult author named "Eliphas Levi." Born Alphonse Louis Constant, he was the son of a shoemaker in Paris, and had studied in the Seminary of St. Sulpice, a known hotbed of occultism and heretical thinking. He eventually dropped out, got married, and began writing books about ritual magic that were published in the 1850s under the Hebraicized version of his name.

Levi's main thesis was that all forms of occultism and mysticism held a common, secret doctrine. Ritual magic, he said, utilized the existence of what he called the "Astral Light," defined in *Magic: A History of Its Rites, Rituals, and Mysteries*, as:

> . . . a natural and divine agent, at once corporeal and spiritual, a universal plastic mediator, a common receptacle for vibrations of movement and

images of form, a fluid and a force which may be called, in a sense at least, the imagination of nature.

It was this agent which, he said, reflected the magician's will, expressed during a ritual, and actualized it into existence. He illustrated this concept with a hieroglyphic form which he called "Baphomet," claiming that this was the spiritual principle secretly revered by the Templars. Levi used this picture as the frontispiece for a number of his books.

At first glance Levi's Baphomet looks like the Devil himself. That is partially because the most common modern depiction of the Devil is based on the card of the same name in the popular Rider-Waite tarot deck, and this card is itself based on Levi's depiction of Baphomet. (In other words, the modern conception of the Devil has been influenced by Levi's illustration.) Certainly the creature presented by Levi looks demonic and evil, with the head and legs of a goat, along with a human torso sporting both male and female sexual organs. On its forehead is that foremost symbol of witchcraft, the pentagram, and between its horns issues forth an inflamed torch.

Levi repeatedly stated that Baphomet was not the same as the Devil, however. Rather it was a symbol of a transcendental power beyond good and evil, man and beast, or male and female energies. Baphomet was in Levi's view the synthesis of all energy, both on Earth and in Heaven, forming something greater than the sum of its parts, capable of performing any transformation of matter which the human mind could conceive. As for the meaning of the word, Levi suggested it was a code, made up of abbreviations for the Latin words *Templi omnium hominum pacis abhas*, meaning "abbot of the temple of universal peace (or 'understanding') among men."

Eliphas Levi wrote many books in which he proclaimed the virtues of Baphomet, and of the universal agent which he said the figure represented. His writings, translated into English by AE Waite, helped to spread the occult revival which swept Europe in the mid-1800s. His ideas contributed greatly to the type of magic that was practiced by the Hermetic Order of the Golden Dawn. Later, at the turn of the twentieth century, one Golden Dawn student, Aleister Crowley, not only adapted many of Levi's ideas, but saw himself as a reincarnation of Levi. He took on "Baphomet" as his own initiatory name in the magical order he headed: the Order of Oriental Templars (a.k.a. "Ordo Templi Orientis," or "OTO") Interestingly (for reasons which will soon become obvious), Crowley also chose to use Islamic terminology when he proclaimed himself the "Caliph" of the OTO

Towards the end of his life, Eliphas Levi himself had come to question his dabblings in the occult. When he had quit the seminary as a young man, his mother had actually committed suicide, perhaps because of her disappointment in her son's life choice. Levi had apparently carried that guilt with him his whole life, and as he neared death, he converted back to Catholicism. His final book, *Magic: A History of Its Rites, Rituals and Mysteries*, was a sad attempt to reconcile the faith of his family with the occult ideas he had promoted all along. The text is full of statements which contradict those found in his previous works. He came to describe Baphomet as a false idol, and the Templars as practitioners in Black Magic:

> For their better success, and in order to secure partisans, they fostered the regrets of every fallen worship and the hopes of every new *cultus*, promising to all liberty of conscience and a new

orthodoxy which should be the synthesis of all
persecuted beliefs. They even went so far as to
recognize the pantheistic symbolism of the grand
masters of Black Magic, and the better to isolate
themselves from obedience to a religion by which
they were condemned beforehand, they rendered
divine honors to the monstrous idol Baphomet,
even as of old the dissenting tribes had adored the
Golden Calf of Dan and Bethel. Certain monuments
of recent discovery and certain precious documents
belonging to the thirteenth century offer abundant
proof of all that is advanced here. Other evidences
are concealed in the annals and beneath the
symbols of Occult Masonry.

There are two very interesting lines in this last quote. The first is his description of the secret Templar doctrine as "the synthesis of all persecuted beliefs." This indicates the exact same thing that our own investigation came to reveal: that, just as the figure of Baphomet is formed by a conglomerate of occult symbols, the Templar belief system (represented by Baphomet) is a conglomerate of all the most noteworthy of the heretical beliefs that plagued the early days of the Christian church. Or it could be seen as the other way around: all Christian heresies are corruptions of the original Baphometic wisdom that the Templars somehow tapped into.

The second interesting point in the above-quoted passage from Levi is his claim that "monuments of recent discovery" and "precious documents belonging to the thirteenth century" proved that the Templars were guilty of worshipping this demonic idol. This may indicate where Levi got his idea of the Baphomet image from. After all, the Templar confessions described Baphomet mainly as a head.

True, some of them told of rituals in which the behind of a goat was kissed. But where did Levi get the idea for a winged half-human, half-goat androgyne? According to various writers, Levi based his depiction of Baphomet on a gargoyle that he found on a former Templar property, either in Saint Bris le Vineux in Burgundy, Lanleff in Brittany, or St. Merri in Paris.

The "certain precious documents belonging to the thirteenth century" refer to the Templars' alleged "secret rule," which we will discuss in a later chapter. The "monuments of recent discovery" that he was referring to were undoubtedly those documented by nineteenth-century Austrian Orientalist scholar Joseph, Baron von Hammer-Purgstall, and his book *Mysterium Baphometis Revelatum* (*Mystery of Baphomet Revealed*), published in 1818, about 30 years before Levi's first writing on Baphomet. In it he documented a number of objects discovered at former Templar properties throughout what are now Austria, Germany, Hungary, and the Czech Republic. This curious document, written in Latin, is part of a larger book entitled *Fundgruben des Orients* (usually translated "Treasures of the Orient").

Although a great many writers have leaned upon Purgstall-Hammer's work on the subject in the last two centuries, most have merely consulted other books that mention him, rather than actually looking at what he wrote. We found that in order to complete our study of Baphomet, we really needed to find out what the book actually says. Therefore, we hired as a translator an excellent, well-rounded scholar in Latin who wishes to take no credit, but who painstakingly worked through the text over a period of several months (with the help of Philip Gonzalez). We can now present the world's first English translation of

Mysterium Baphometis Revelatum, which will be published shortly after the book you are currently reading.

Hammer-Purgstall's "Baphometic Idols," as they were later called by other authors, consisted mostly of statuettes, coffers and cups presenting strange images of inhuman figures. Seven of the images show only a head, and in two of these cases it is a head with two faces, much akin to the descriptions given by some Templars of the Baphomet head. Many of them were decorated with scenes of bizarre sexual ceremonies of a seemingly religious nature. The figures presented were in some cases covered all over their bodies with multiple eyes, or with serpents.

One image that Hammer-Purgstall found used repeatedly was said by him to represent Baphomet, or, rather, "Mete," as he decoded it. The images he found show an androgynous figure wearing a cape, often crowned with towers *a la* the goddess Cybele of the ancient world, though sometimes with horns instead. In several versions this person is holding in each hand a chain connected to the sky. While the figure appears female in one version, in the others it is shown with a beard, making it quite clear that it was meant to be taken as androgynous. Other items found by Hammer-Purgstall in the form of statues, which he called "idols" of Mete, also depict a bearded and horned figure with breasts. This, then, may have been why Eliphas Levi chose to depict Baphomet in this way.

Arabic, Greek, and Latin inscriptions were found among these images too. One in particular brings to mind the confessions of the Knights Templar about Baphomet. Hammer-Purgstall translated it into Latin, and then 1865, Thomas Wright, in his book *Worship of the Generative Powers*, translated it thusly:

Let Mete be exalted, who causes things to bud and blossom! He is our root; it is one and seven; abjure (the faith), and abandon thyself to all pleasures.

You will recall that some confessing Templars said Baphomet "caused the land to germinate." Hammer-Purgstall believed that the Templars had been secret practitioners of a fringe religious movement called "Ophite Gnosticism." The word "Mete" in the translation above was a Greek word for "wisdom." He believed "Baphomet" was an allusion to a Gnostic rite of "Bapho Metis," a "Baptism of Wisdom."

The root syllable "met" in "Baphomet" has also been connected by some linguists to the name of the sun god Mithras, worshipped by some Gnostics as an incarnation of divine wisdom. Thus Aleister Crowley's alternative interpretation of Baphomet as meaning "Father Mithras" can be considered part of the same family of translations. More recently Dr. Hugh Schonfield, known for his work on the Dead Sea Scrolls, also proffered an interpretation that again led back to this concept of divine wisdom or Gnosis. He said that "Baphomet," when transliterated into Aramaic and fed through the Atbash cipher (in which the value of the alphabet is inverted, it yields the word "Sophia," another Greek word meaning "wisdom." In a similar vein, Sufi scholar Idries Shah has suggested that the Templars were influenced by Islamic Sufism, and that the word "Baphomet" came from the Arabic *abufihamat*, meaning "father of understanding." This, again, connects to Eliphas Levi's interpretation of Baphomet's name, involving the code that supposedly yields the words "father of universal understanding among men" (in Latin).

It seems as if all of these translations and interpretations of Baphomet, although arrived at in entirely different ways, all yield the same sort of meaning. So exactly what is this hidden "wisdom" principle that Baphomet has always been associated with, which the Templars allegedly venerated and utilized? It will take the rest of this book for us to unravel this for you as best we can. Our story starts where, supposedly, time and space began: at the Tree of Knowledge of Good and Evil in the Garden of Eden.

Chapter 2: The Seed of the Serpent

Notwithstanding, the devil entered into a wicked serpent and seduced the angel that was in the form of the woman, and he wrought his lust with Eve in the Song of the serpent. And therefore are they called sons of the devil and sons of the serpent that do the lust of the devil their father, even unto the end of this world. And again the devil poured out upon the angel that was in Adam the poison of his lust, and it begetteth the sons of the serpent and the sons of the devil even unto the end of this world.

—Interrogatio Johannis (a.k.a. *The Secret Supper* or *The Book of John the Evangelist*)

In *The Book of Genesis* there are a number of mysteries that have always puzzled scholars and vexed religious apologists. One of the most bothersome issues occurs right in the first two chapters. It appears that there are two separate tellings of the creation of the human race!

The first version can be found in Chapter 1: 26-28 (KJV), where on the sixth day of creation, after he created the heavens and the earth, the flora and the fauna, God says:

> Let us make man in our image, after our likeness: and let them have dominion over the fish of the sea, and over the fowl of the air, and over the cattle, and over all the earth, and over every creeping thing that creepeth upon the earth. So God created man in his own image, in the image of God created he him; male and female created he them.
>
> And God blessed them, and God said unto them, Be fruitful, and multiply, and replenish the earth, and

subdue it: and have dominion over the fish of the
sea, and over the fowl of the air, and over every
living thing that moveth upon the earth.

The use of a plural possessive pronoun here by the supposedly singular "God" is telling, and indicates that there was more than one creative being involved. This is another mystery often explained away by Christian apologetics as unimportant, but, as we will see, it tends to corroborate the Gnostic or Ophite view of creation being a joint process.

Yet that isn't the only deliberate misinterpretation of the text commonly made by Christian apologetics. A key detail of this first creation story is when the Lord informs the newly created mankind that all vegetation has been created for their consumption, and they are free to eat whatever they want, as we read in verses 29-31 of the same chapter (KJV):

And God said, Behold, I have given you every herb
bearing seed, which is upon the face of all the earth,
and every tree, in the which is the fruit of a tree
yielding seed; to you it shall be for meat. And to
every beast of the earth, and to every fowl of the
air, and to every thing that creepeth upon the earth,
wherein there is life, I have given every green herb
for meat: and it was so. And God saw every thing
that he had made, and, behold, it was very good.
And the evening and the morning were the sixth
day.

So it would appear then that God created man on the sixth day. Furthermore, he apparently created man and woman at the same time. It is unspecified whether there is only one human couple created at first or several, but let us just assume there was only one. Why, then, does God seem to re-create mankind later in Chapter 2? That chapter starts out with a description of God resting on the seventh day. Then in verses 4-9 of the second chapter (KJV) we are told:

> And the LORD God formed man of the dust of the ground, and breathed into his nostrils the breath of life; and man became a living soul. And the LORD God planted a garden eastward in Eden; and there he put the man whom he had formed. And out of the ground made the LORD God to grow every tree that is pleasant to the sight, and good for food; the tree of life also in the midst of the garden, and the tree of knowledge of good and evil.

This is the first mention of the Tree of Knowledge and the Tree of Life. A few verses later (2: 15-17, KJV) Adam is given charge of tending the garden and also told specifically not to touch the fruit of one of those two trees:

> And the LORD God took the man, and put him into the garden of Eden to dress it and to keep it. And the LORD God commanded the man, saying, Of every tree of the garden thou mayest freely eat: But of the tree of the knowledge of good and evil, thou shalt not eat of it: for in the day that thou eatest thereof thou shalt surely die.

It is only at this point in verses 18-25 (KJV), in this second version of the story of mankind's creation, that the female is mentioned at all:

> And the LORD God said, It is not good that the man should be alone; I will make him an help meet for him. . . . And the LORD God caused a deep sleep to fall upon Adam, and he slept: and he took one of his ribs, and closed up the flesh instead thereof; And the rib, which the LORD God had taken from man,

made he a woman, and brought her unto the man.

And Adam said, This is now bone of my bones, and flesh of my flesh: she shall be called Woman, because she was taken out of Man.

So in the first creation, man and woman were created at the same time. They were apparently created the same way, from the dust of the Earth. In the second creation, the man was created first and then the female was created secondly out of Adam's rib. In the first version, God created man "in his own image." In the second creation, God breathes into Adam "the breath of life," something not mentioned in the first version. In the first creation, there is no mention of a garden, and no mention of forbidden fruit. Rather mankind is specifically told to eat whatever they want—that all vegetation had been created for that purpose—and it is all "good" in the Lord's eyes.

Perhaps most importantly, since only the creatures of the second creation are given rules to follow, only they can transgress those rules. The first mankind is blessed and told to "be fruitful and multiply." It is only the second mankind that experiences the fall from grace after eating from the Tree of Knowledge, and it is only after this that they begin to breed, seemingly as a result of the sexual awareness that they gain after the Fall.

The rabbinical school known as the Pharisees believed that the first creation was of Adam Kadmon, the perfect Primordial Man, a mirror image of the divine Logos ("the Word"), and a hermaphroditic being. Philo wrote that Adam Kadmon, whom he also called "heavenly man" or "original man" was "born in the image of God" with "no participation in any corruptible or earthlike essence; whereas the earthly man is made of loose material, called a lump of clay." The second creation, they teach, was when the female half was split apart from the whole, to become Adam and Eve.

The Pharisees thought that the Primordial Adam was created and destroyed prior to the actual creation of the universe. The cabalistic text known as *The Zohar* says that within his body were contained all of the elements of creation. That text even indicates that God patterned existence after the image of Adam Kadmon, and that perhaps God himself was made in Adam's image, not the other way around. Or perhaps Adam Kadmon is God, in this view, and the creator of Adam and Eve. As *The Zohar* says, "The form of man is the image of everything that is above and below; therefore did the Holy Ancient select it for His own form." This seems to agree with what the apostle Paul wrote in *1 Corinthians* 15:45-47 (KJV):

> And so it is written, The first man Adam was made a living soul; the last Adam was made a quickening spirit. Howbeit that was not first which is spiritual, but that which is natural; and afterward that which is spiritual. The first man is of the earth, earthy: the second man is the Lord from heaven.

Paul referred to Adam Kadmon as the "second man" because he thought that, although he was conceived as a spirit prior to the creation of the earthly Adam, he wasn't created in the flesh until afterwards. This is because Paul believed that Adam Kadmon incarnated for the first time as Jesus Christ. In a similar vein, members of the Judeo-Christian Gnostic sect known as the "Elcesaites" believed that when Adam Kadmon split in two, the male side became the Messiah, and the female part the Holy Ghost.

This may all be a bit confusing. However, the most important points, for our current inquiry, are these:

The Seed of the Serpent

1. There were forms, primordial entities, and events that took place between them prior to what we consider the actual creation of our present universe

2. These primordial entities were hermaphroditic, and split apart into male and female entities during creation.

3. Creation was a fall from the perfection of the prior state.

Herein lies the key to our investigation about Baphomet: to hear many cabalists tell it, the first pair was not Adam and Eve, but rather Adam and Lilith. The story of Lilith is an epic saga all its own, and it all takes place prior to the events of *Genesis*, in a time before time, in what is referred to in Yiddish as "Yenne-volt" (the Other World). Lilith's name means "spirit of night," which is undoubtedly connected to the darkness of the "Great Supernal Abyss" (the nothingness prior to creation) out of which she is said to have sprung spontaneously.

Lilith and Adam allegedly quarreled over sex, specifically about who would be on top. When Adam insisted on being on top, Lilith left him. She is said to have disappeared from Paradise by pronouncing the secret and sacred name of God (the "Tetragrammaton" of cabalistic lore), which bestows godlike power on those who can speak it. Some legends even state that she obtained the divine name from God himself by seducing him! According to one version of the story, upon speaking the name, she shape-shifted into an owl and flew away to the Red Sea, which, according to the legend, has been her abode ever since.

Nocturnal emissions were believed by Jews to be evidence that the man had been visited by Lilith in the form of a succubus. It is said that she is cursed to give birth to children continuously, but that they are malformed half-demons who die at birth. As a way of getting revenge for that against the sons of Adam, they said that Lilith also visited infant boys in their sleep to suffocate them. Thus, every instance of the mysterious malady known as "crib death" (which affects mostly boys) was attributed to Lilith, and superstitious Jews would leave magical amulets on the walls of their children's bedrooms to ward off these attacks. The word "lullaby" is believed to derive from the incantations that Jews would sometimes say over their children while putting them to bed, again to protect them from Lilith. This is also the origin of the Jewish and European custom of letting boys grow their hair long until age three: to trick Lilith into thinking that they are girls. Some even dressed their sons in girls' clothes during this vulnerable period in their lives.

Amazingly, Lilith is not just a figure in Jewish cabalistic demonology, but appears in the mythologies of other cultures as well. In ancient Sumer she was called "Lilitu," which means "Queen of the Night," and they believed that she preyed on people during their sleep, just like the Jews did. She was called by the Babylonians "Lamashtu," meaning "the Daughter of Heaven." Lamashtu was known for strangling babies and drinking their blood. In ancient Greece she was called "Lamia" and was said to have had an affair with Zeus. In jealousy, Zeus' wife Hera killed all of their children, so it retaliation, Lamia began to kidnap and murder human babies. This is similar to the Jewish Lilith's motivation to kill infants.

However, the real reason why Lilith desires the sons of Adam as sexual partners is actually because Adam wasn't her first consort, or the lover whom she is truly pining after. In fact, rabbinical sources maintain that the first hermaphroditic pair was not Lilith and Adam but Lilith and the demon Samael. The creature that they formed together was a monstrous serpent, apparently equivalent to the one that later tempted Adam and Eve in the Garden. The cabalists called this Lilith-Samael creature "the Beast" and "the Other God." (This is especially interesting because, as we will soon discuss, some Gnostics referred to the "Demiurge" who they believed had created physical reality by the name of "Samael" also.) It is clear from the cabalists' texts that they saw this Lilith-Samael monster as the serpent that tempted Adam and Eve in the Garden of Eden. They even saw it as the father of Eve's son Cain. *Treatise on the Left Emanation* by R. Isaac b. Jacob Ha-Kohen and Tr. Ronald C. Kiener describes Samael as evil, but specifies that this is:

> . . . not because of his nature but because he desires to unite and intimately mingle with an emanation not of his nature. . . .

A sigil (a magical insignia) designed for Baphomet by nineteenth-century occultist Stanislas de Guaita includes the names of the demons Samael and Lilith. The opposite side of this sigil shows the figure of a man, with the names "Adam" and "Eve" written around it. We read in *Treatise on the Left Emanation* that:

> In this tradition it is made clear that Samael and Lilith were born as one, similar to the form of Adam and Eve who were also born as one, reflecting what is above.

In this instance the text seems to be saying that Adam Kadmon—the Adam-Eve hermaphrodite being—cast a reflection (or perhaps more appropriately, a shadow) that created the monstrous hermaphrodite entity of Lilith-Samael. However, while the human pair are described as "above" (and therefore, presumably, superior to) the serpent pair, cabalistic writings suggest that the serpents represent something older and more primordial, as the Abyss (nothingness or chaos) that they come from is considered older than creation.

It appears that the fathers of Western occultism were well aware of the legends about Lilith and Samael. Why else would their names have been included on De Guaita's Baphomet sigil (particularly with the names of Adam and Eve included on the other side of the sigil)? We also can presume that it is these two snakes who are being represented by the caduceus staff that Eliphas Levi depicted rising from Baphomet's crotch region. The caduceus (the ancient symbol of a pole encoiled with two snakes) has been connected not only to Hermes and alchemy (both things associated with Baphomet), but also with the image of a crucified serpent, and of the snake coiled around the Tree of Knowledge in the Garden of Eden. Now we know why!

The fact that the Baphomet sigil is also presented frequently with the word "Leviathan" indicates that some occultists have been aware that this is also another name for the same figure. Leviathan, described in the Old Testament as a giant sea dragon capable of encircling the Earth, is said to be either female, or part of a hermaphroditic beast just like Lilith and Samael. Sometimes Leviathan's male counterpart is said to be Behemoth, a land beast. Sometimes the pair is just referred to in the plural as "the leviathans."

Very similar things are said about Leviathan and her consort as are said about Lilith and Samael. They are clearly just different names for the same figures. In both cases, it is said that they were once together physically, but that God separated them, because the act of their mating was somehow dangerous to the well-being of the universe. So, in

The Seed of the Serpent 31

both cases, they were cleaved apart, castrating the male, and preventing them from ever uniting sexually again. With both sets of characters, it is written that if they ever come together again, all of existence will somehow be annihilated.

In the case of the leviathans, it is said numerous times in the Bible that at the End of Times, God will slaughter them and feed their flesh to the righteous among men. This will take place at a feast with the messiah in the New Jerusalem, inside of a tent made from the monsters' skin. This is what the Jewish festival known as the "Feast of the Tabernacles" is meant to celebrate, and it is probably why the early Christians adopted the fish as their symbol.

Because Samael and Lilith (a.k.a. Leviathan and Behemoth) are constantly longing for each other, they found a way to mate via an "intermediary" called "Tanin'iver" ("Blind Dragon") or "the Groomsman." We read about it in *Treatise on the Left Emanation*:

> You already know that evil Samael and wicked Lilith are like a sexual pair who, by means of an intermediary, receive an evil and wicked emanation from one and emanate to the other. . . . The heavenly serpent is a blind prince, the image of an intermediary between Samael and Lilith. Its name is Tanin'iver. The masters of tradition said that just as this serpent slithers without eyes, so the supernal serpent has the image of a spiritual form without color—these are "the eyes." The traditionists call it an eyeless creature, therefore its name is Tanin'iver. He is the bond, the accompaniment, and the union between Samael and Lilith. If he were created whole in the fullness of his emanation he would have destroyed the world in an instant.

Now this is getting really kinky! This Tanin'iver is a "slithering serpent" without eyes who somehow enables the castrated Samael to have sex with Lilith. But if he were to "manifest fully," then the destruction of the universe, which happens whenever these two "truly" mate, would come about anyway. So whatever Tanin'iver does for them, it has the capability of being just as good as the real thing. But mercifully, right now, it is not, or else we would all be dead.

More detail on this subject comes from *The Zohar* (I.152b-153a, as quoted by Andrei Orlov in *Dark Mirrors*), where the "intermediary" is described as none other than "Azazel," the goat demon who figures so prominently in the Old Testament (as we will explain shortly):

> Now observe a deep and holy mystery of faith, the symbolism of the male principle and the female principle of the universe. . . . [T]here is the line where the male and female principles join, forming together the rider on the serpent, and symbolized by Azazel.

So here the Tanin'iver is likened to a "line" that unites the two creatures, and is said to be "riding" them, and to be symbolized by the goat-demon Azazel. Another passage from *The Zohar* (Vayetze 116, as quoted by Mark Biggs in *The Case for Lilith*) goes on further with the same language:

> The unholy filth grasps the male above and the female below. Here, male and female join together. They are the rider on the serpent. . . . This is the secret of Azazel, which includes the male and female of defilement.

This exact same role—riding shotgun in-between a male-female pair that were formerly one hermaphroditic creature—was played by Azazel in another sacred text as well: the Slavonic pseudepigraphal *Apocalypse of Abraham*. Here he is described doing this with Adam and Eve. A vision is related of Adam and Eve standing under the Tree of Knowledge, entwined with each other physically, and with Azazel between them, feeding them both grapes. In his book *Dark Mirrors: Azazel and Satanael in Early Jewish Demonology*, Andrei A. Orlov compares this to a sexual *menage a trois*, and suggests that it may be an allusion to the first couple being "ridden" via demonic possession.

Is this, then, what the work of the Tanin'iver really entails? Is his function to facilitate the possession of human bodies by demons so that the spirits can "hook up" with each other sexually? Couldn't it be that Baphomet is the Tanin'iver, the Azazel that joins the serpent? Isn't he then like the "Philosophical Mercury"—the "Azoth"—of the alchemists which, they said, could bind any chemical marriage, no matter how unlikely? The product of alchemical marriage has always been represented as a Frankenstein chimera monstrosity like Baphomet, composed of many different types of animals and people. But, we must wonder: is it that the ultimate "chemical wedding" is between angels or spirits and men, like what the cabalists seem to be saying has happened between Adam, Eve, Samael and Lilith?

In addition to being the primordial sex goddess, Lilith, is a path to divine wisdom—the forbidden wisdom of the Tree of Knowledge of Good and Evil, which, according to *Genesis*, opens the eyes of a person and allows them to see things like God does. The thirteenth century Spanish Kabbalist R. Isaac Hacohen said that Lilith is "a ladder on which one can ascend to rungs of prophecy." Similarly, we read in *Left Emanation*:

> Concerning this point there is a received tradition from the ancient Sages who made use of the Secret Knowledge of the Lesser Palaces, which is the manipulation of demons and a ladder by which one ascends to the prophetic levels.

There are many other parallels as well between the cabalistic legends of Lilith-Samael in the Garden of Eden and the creation stories of the Gnostics. Gnostic cosmology describes creation as happening in a series of "aeons" (just as in *Genesis* it happens over a period of "days.") However, the word "aeon" not only means a lengthy span of time, but can also be thought of as a universe unto itself, with a living intelligence of its own too. Each aeon is generated by a "syzygy," a hermaphroditic male-female pair of intelligences. In the beginning, all of the primordial intelligences were together inside uncreated totality, which was called the "Pleroma."

However, just as Lilith wanted to be "on top" of Adam sexually, Sophia refused to submit to the dominance of a sexual partner. Instead, she tried to generate an aeon parthenogenically, on her own. The result was a deformity, an "abortion," that was "cast outside of the Pleroma" because of its hideousness, like a teen mother might discard her baby in a trash can or a toilet.

As the story goes, after Sophia's "abortion," the real "Father" of all made a new pair, called "Christos-Holy Spirit," to clean up the mess that had been made outside of the Pleroma. He then created a new, unpaired aeon named "Jesus," and he formed the abortion into the new entity, "Sophia Achamoth" (the lesser Sophia). Her name is related to the Hebrew word for wisdom, "Hokmah." Her pain at being separated from the Pleroma actually became the substance that Jesus then used (according to the Gnostics) to form the physical matter of the cosmos.

Achamoth, then, created the Demiurge out of that, and made him king of everything outside of the Pleroma, as well as the chief artificer in charge of rearranging matter. Then the Demiurge created the seven heavens below him, each with a god in charge of it. These seem to correspond with the planetary intelligences.

Note that, in this case, just as in Judaism, the "Fall" from perfection is caused by knowledge (which the cabalists say created a false universe of "shells" represented by the infernal "Qlipoth" tree), in Gnosticism the Fall is caused by wisdom (Sophia) giving birth to a malformed creation. Sophia's "abortion" can be thought of as parallel to the fact that, after being cast out of the Garden of Eden, Lilith was cursed to continue giving birth to demonic children (with no father, apparently) who would die as soon as they were born. Lilith is described in *The Zohar* as a "husk" covering divine light, just as Gnostics said we are divine light trapped inside husks (our physical bodies).

Just as the Gnostics had stories about Sophia and the "aeons," cabalists have stories about hermaphroditic beings (Lilith-Samael and Adam-Kadmon) that personified primordial forces existing in a netherworld of chaos prior to the present creation. The cabalists infer that the Fall occurred when the first male-female pair was split apart. The Gnostics said it was when the female Sophia tried to be independent without her male half.

In Mesopotamia, Lilith's companion was the screech-owl. In the Old Testament, references to this animal are used to denote Lilith. Note that owls are seen as symbols of wisdom in the West, as an owl was the sidekick of the

Above: Eliphas Levi's depiction of Baphomet.

Above: A "sigil of Baphomet" from Stanislas de Guaita's *La Clef de la Magic Noire*. Below: *Burning of Templars*, from Giovanni Boccaccio's *De casibus virorum illustrium*, 1450.

Above: A Templar initiate trampling on the cross. Left: The Seal of the Knights Templar, featuring two knights riding one horse. Opposite: *The Scapegoat*, by William Holman Hunt, 1854.

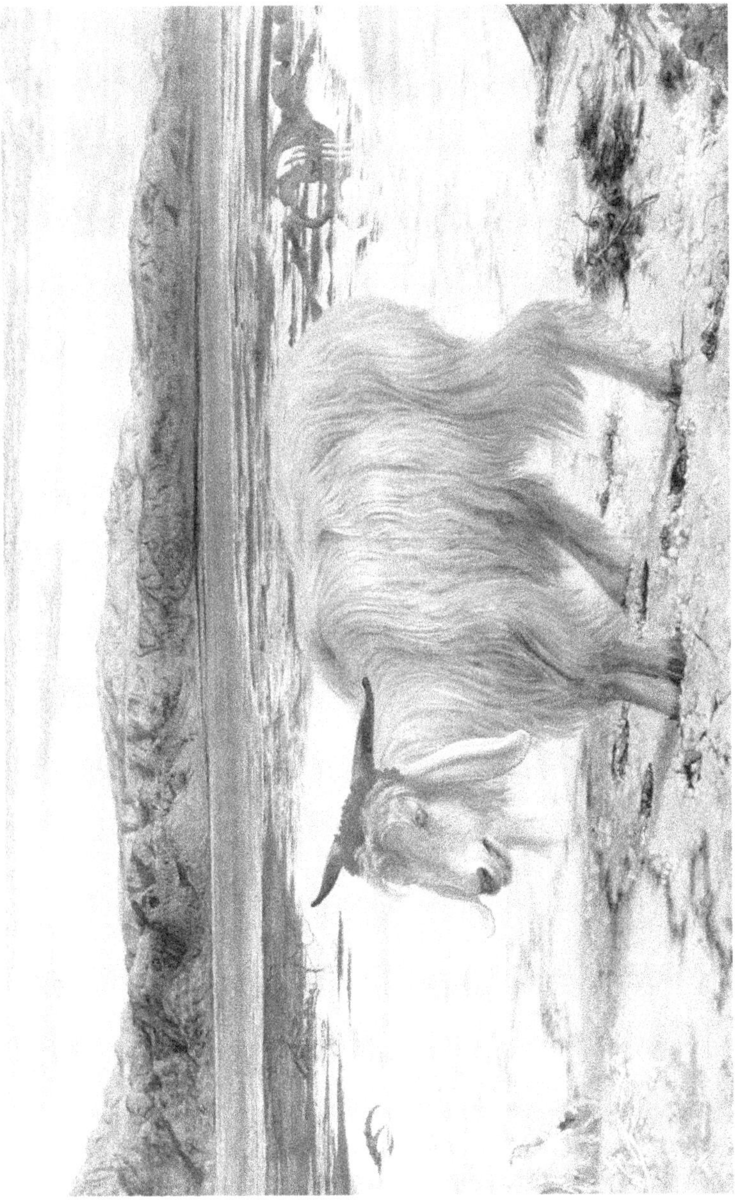

Above: "Mete" from *Worship of the Generative Powers* by Thomas Wright. This image does not actually appear in Hammer-Purgstall's *Mysterium Baphometis Revelatum*, though several others images of Mete are (see opposite page). We discovered the source of this image on a casket in the online catalogue of the British Museum (not on display).

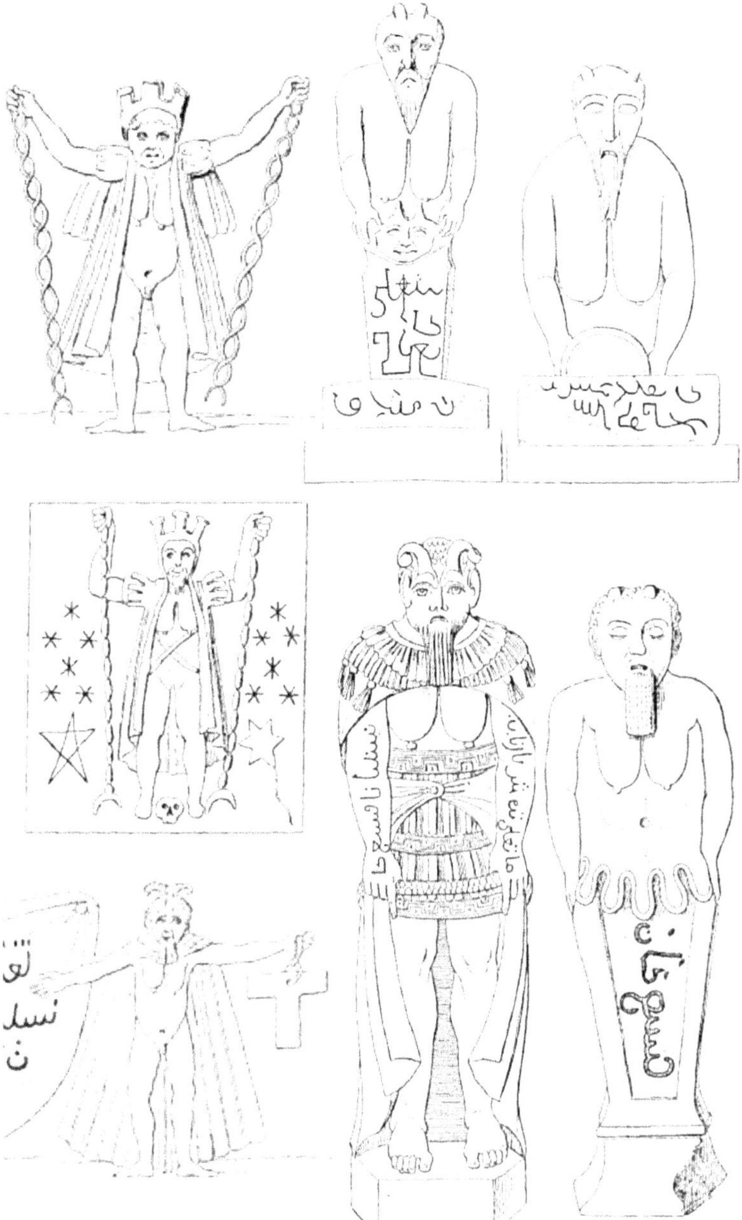

wisdom goddess Minerva (Athena to the Romans). You may recall that Minerva sprang spontaneously from the head of Zeus, just as Lilith is said to have randomly popped into existence from the Great Supernal Abyss. So Zeus fathered Minerva without a mate just like Sophia created the Demiurge in that same manner.

The legend of Lilith becomes even more complex when we learn that, according to cabalistic texts, there are in fact two Liliths: Lilith the Matron and Lilith the Maiden. The latter is described as the "slave" or "handmaiden" of the former. Lilith the Matron is said to be both the mate of Samael, and of God himself, seemingly the same as the Jewish concept of the Shekinah or "Matronit" as the bride of God. It also seems analogous to the idea of Sophia as the bride of Jesus that some Gnostics adhered to. Lilith the Maiden comes across as her dark doppelganger, and also subordinate, just like the relationship between Sophia and Sophia-Achamoth in the Gnostic system.

Another Jewish legend that seems to be connected with these concepts asserts that the Shekinah was for a time "exiled," while a slave woman, her "handmaiden," took her place. The "handmaiden" appears to be equated with the Egyptian kingly line. *The Zohar* (3:19a, as quoted by Alan Humm in his online article "Lilith in Kabbala: Zohar") tells us:

> One day the companions were walking with Rabbi Shim'on bar Yohai. Rabbi Shim'on said: "We see that all these nations have risen, and Israel is lower than all of them. Why is this? Because the King sent away the Matronit from Him, and took the slave woman in her place. Who is this slave woman? The Alien Crown, whose firstborn the Holy One, blessed be He, killed in Egypt. At first she sat behind the handmill, and now this slave woman inherited the

place of her mistress." And Rabbi Shim'on wept and said: "The King without the Matronit is not called king. The King who adhered to the slave woman, to the handmaid of the Matronit, where is his honor? He lost the Matronit and attached Himself to the place which is called slave woman. This slave woman was destined to rule over the Holy Land of below, as the Matronit formerly ruled over it. But the Holy One, blessed be He, will ultimately bring back the Matronit to her place as before. And then, what will be the rejoicing? Say, the rejoicing of the King and the rejoicing of the Matronit. The rejoicing of the King because He will return to her and separate from the slave woman, and the rejoicing of the Matronit, because she will return to couple with the King."

Occult writers Nigel Jackson and Michael Howard, in their book *The Pillars of Tubal-Cain*, equate the slave woman mentioned here with Lilith. The metaphor is commonly thought to refer to the time of destruction of the Temple of Solomon and the exile of the Israelites to Babylon in the 6th century BC. But why then the reference to the "Egyptian slave woman"? Although it was the Hebrews who were at one point the slaves of the Egyptians, several Egyptian women are depicted as slaves to important Old Testament figures, including Hagar, Abraham's slave and the mother of his disowned son Ishmael.

Interestingly, Hagar was said by cabalists R. Ya'aqov and R. Yitzhaq to "resemble" Lilith. Hagar and Ishmael were exiled to the desert to die of thirst after Abraham's wife Sarah became jealous of them. God miraculously saved them. This story of a slave woman as the mistress of the matron's husband, whom the legitimate wife is afraid of

44 Chapter 2

being displaced by implies the relationship of the younger Lilith as the slave or handmaiden of the elder.

Lilith the Maiden is said to be the consort of the demon Asmodeus. Her mother is purportedly a demoness named "Mehetabel," meaning "something immersed," which brings to mind the meaning of Baphomet's name, according to Hammer-Purgstall: "Baptism of Wisdom." *The Zohar* says that Lilith the Maiden incarnated in human form as Naamah, the daughter of the Cain's descendant Lamech (who accidentally killed Cain). Thus, the race of Lilith's human descendants are sometimes referred to by cabalists as the "sons of Naamah."

The Zohar further tells us that it was originally Naamah who first seduced the angels or "sons of God" referred to in *Genesis* Chapter 6 (which we will talk about soon), causing them to lust after human females and incur God's wrath. Lilith the Maiden/Naamah also allegedly incarnated as Moses' Egyptian wife, Zipporah. Both Liliths were said to have taken form as the two prostitutes who approached King Solomon to judge in their dispute over the parentage of a young child (for which he famously ruled that the child should be cut in half and shared between them).

Others see Lilith and Naamah as just two of a quartet of concubines for Samael. According to cabalist Nathan Nota Poira:

> Samael was given four kingdoms, and in each of them he has a concubine. The names of his concubines are: Lilith, whom he took as his consort, and she is the first one; the second is Naamah; the third, Even Maskit; and the fourth, Igrat daughter of Mahalath. and the four kingdoms are: first the kingdom of Damascus, in which is found the house

of Rimmon; the second, the kingdom of Tyre, which is opposite the land of Israel; the third, the kingdom of Malta, which formerly was called Rhodos; and the fourth, the kingdom called Granata, and some say that it is the kingdom of Ishmael. And in each of these four kingdoms dwells one of the four aforementioned concubines.

These four "concubines" are taken by other authors to be separate incarnations or emanations of the same goddess, Lilith. Besides Naamah and Lilith, the names of the other concubines vary according to the source. The above-quoted source names them as Even Maskit and Igrat. Other names that have been listed include Mahalath and Nega'. They appear to be demons like Lilith, but some of them also specifically correspond to women mentioned in the Bible.

Mahalath is the daughter of Abraham's son Ishmael, whom he sired by the daughter of Kasdiel, the Egyptian sorcerer. Ishmael's father disapproved of the marriage and successfully pressured him into divorcing her before the baby was born. Mahalath—who is also known as *Bashemath*, interestingly enough— is said to have performed "sorceries" in the desert with her mother, evoking a spirit named Igratiel, who had sex with Mahalath and conceived a daughter named Igrat. Mahalath later married Esau, the son of Isaac and brother of Jacob. Esau was the first of the kings of Edom.

Igrat went on to have sex with King David one night while he was sleeping, and conceived a child named Adad who was a duke of the nation of Edom. According to the cabalists, Adad is the same as the demon Asmodeus, or "Ashmodai," which comes from the Hebrew words "Sh'mi Ad, Ad Sh'mi," meaning "My name is Ad, Ad is my name." Of course, you will recall that Asmodeus was said to have been the husband of "Lilith the Maiden."

Asmodeus was the chief architect in a team of demonic stonemasons that Solomon allegedly enslaved to build his famous temple, according to Louis Ginzberg's *Legends of the Jews*. This makes him analogous to the figure of Hiram mentioned as the architect in the Bible, whom the Freemasons call Hiram Abiff and venerate in rituals. Another Jewish legend tells how Asmodeus took over King Solomon's throne for a while. If we consider the cabalistic legends mentioned above, this story could have been a memory of a real coup that occurred, as Asmodeus may have been, legitimately, the son and heir of David, and thus Solomon's brother and rival to the throne. To bring things full circle, although there were many historical kings of Edom named Adad (which was also the name of one of Ishmael's sons, and of an ancient storm god worshipped in that region), one in particular is said to have been married to a woman named Mehetabel. This, as we mentioned, is also the name of the mother of Lilith the Maiden.

Another human incarnation of Lilith was, allegedly, the Queen of Sheba, that mysterious woman described in *I Kings* Chapter 10 who came to visit King Solomon. "Sheba" is thought to correspond to the ancient kingdom of Saba in Southern Arabia, which included Eritrea, Ethiopia and Yemen. Allegedly this queen visited Solomon because she had heard of his renowned wisdom and wanted to test it, for she too was a wise woman. She arrived bearing an enormous tribute of gold, spices and precious stones. She presented Solomon with a series of riddles to assay his wisdom, all of which he answered easily. She was so awestruck by his sagacity that she decided to convert to Solomon's religion of worshipping one God. Solomon, quite enamored of her, presented her with loads of expensive gifts in return, which she took home with her when her visit was over.

But according to extra-biblical references, there was much more to the relationship between Solomon and the Queen of Sheba. All of these legends agree that they were lovers. Stories originating in Ethiopia say that Solomon sired a son with her named Menelik, or, according to Nigel Jackson and Michael Howard, Mardek (meaning "son of the wise"). Many scholars believe that the Song of Solomon or "Song of Songs" found in the Old Testament was meant to be a poem about Solomon and the Queen. The text of the poem is overtly sexual in nature. References to sexual organs, as well as human body fluids like semen, vaginal secretions, female ejaculate, and menstrual blood, are disguised as "spikenard," "wine," "myrrh," "living waters," "the Rose of Sharon," and "the Lily of the Valley." The "bride" in this poem describes herself as "black," which makes sense if she was an Ethiopian.

The Queen of Sheba is the subject of a number of bizarre folk tales, as related in *The Pillars of Tubal-Cain* by Jackson and Howard. One says that when she was a girl she was tied up in the branches of a tree as a sacrificial offering to a dragon. Seven "holy men" came to rescue her by slaying the dragon. Some of the dragon's blood splashed on her left foot and leg, turning it into that of a goat. Solomon first caught sight of the leg when she walked across a mirrored floor in his palace. As the authors relate, "Solomon decided that she must be one of the desert demons known as the *seirim*, who follow Azazel, or the demonic vampire Lilith." The goat imagery directly relates to Baphomet, and the goat-demon Azazel will be discussed in greater detail later on.

Other stories about the Queen of Sheba include one stating that Solomon gave her the emerald Grail stone that fell from Lucifer's crown, which was later carved into the cup used by Jesus at the Last Supper. The Grail legends tell us that Sheba built the "Ship of Solomon," which was made from timber taken from the Tree of Knowledge, and could travel through time. There is also a Masonic tradition that King Solomon had three of his stonemasons murder the Master Mason of his temple, Hiram Abiff, because the Queen of Sheba had fallen in love with him and Solomon was jealous.

Of course, we know that in Jewish folk tales, the architect of Solomon's Temple was the demon Asmodeus, consort of the lesser Lilith. So really, if the Queen of Sheba was actually a lesser Lilith figure incarnated, the personality whom Solomon might have been jealous of, then, was Asmodeus. The meaning of the story told in the paragraph above is that Sheba was of the bloodline of the Dragon (Lilith-Samael), and of Azazel the Goat. So that could have been why her body had features of that genetics (like a goat's legs).

Interestingly, many self-professed practitioners of witchcraft (which tended to run in families in Old Europe) considered Lilith to be their queen, and an ancestor. There were also rumors that she was the great ancestress of the fairy race. The Inquisition referred to Lilith as "the Mother of the Witches."

As Howard Schwartz demonstrates in his book *Lilith's Cave*, Jewish folk tales are full of stories about such demonic marriages to Lilith. In these stories, any man may fall prey to being seduced by Lilith and, once married to her, cannot betroth another without incurring her perpetual curse. The seduction of the young man is most likely to take place just when he is about to be wed, which is the origin for the superstition that a man cannot see his bride before his wedding day. He must be kept under watch during this vulnerable time, for Lilith may take the form of his bride and seduce him.

In one recurring version of the story, a boy who is about to be wed is walking through a forest with the wedding ring, and in jest slips the ring on the branch of a log, or on a stray finger found sticking out of a log, whilst saying the wedding vows. After saying the words, the log either comes to life as Lilith, or else the finger is revealed to belong to that of a corpse that was buried in the log. Either way, the boy is now married to a lady of the underworld, an incarnation of Lilith. This was dramatized in Tim Burton's film *Corpse Bride*. In most versions of the tale, Lilith curses the young man's family until they all agree to share him. He is condemned to spend half of his time in the underworld with his demon wife, and half of his time on the surface with his other wife.

What these stories represent is the idea that Lilith was the first wife of Adam, or of God. But she got supplanted by another woman, just like Eve became Adam's new lover, and like the cabalist stories where God let his wife go so that he could shack up with a slave woman. Of course, she could say that she has more right to her husband than the new interloper. But in the end, she has to share him with the new woman, because she is from the unreal kingdom of chaos. Her claim on him isn't entirely enforceable, but it isn't entirely dismissible either.

Isaiah 34:14 refers to Lilith as a screech-owl, and says that she lives "in the desolate wilderness with wild cats, jackals and satyrs for company." These satyrs are the seirim ("hairy ones"), descendants of the goat demon Azazel. A story from *The Epic of Gilgamesh* again suggests that Lilith can shape-shift into an owl. As retold in *The Pillars of Tubal-Cain*, the story is:

> . . . of the goddess Inanna, the Queen of Heaven, and how she found a sacred willow tree on the banks of the Euphrates that had been uprooted in a violent storm. The goddess rescued the fallen tree and replanted it in her garden. She planned to use the wood for a new bed and throne. However after it was planted the tree refused to grow because a snake had nested in its roots, the fierce Azu or Zu thunderbird was roosting in its branches and Lilith had built a house in its trunk. Inanna was distraught and tearfully enlisted the help of semi-divine hero Gilgamesh. He slew the snake and cut down the tree so Zu and Lilith lost their habitats. Lilith grew owl wings and flew off to the wilderness cursing the goddess and her champion.

This connection of Lilith to a serpent and a tree brings to mind the story of the Garden of Eden again. The cabalists say it was Lilith and Samael who combined to play the role of the adversarial serpent tempting the protoplasts, Adam and Eve, with the fruit of God-like knowledge. But what is really meant by this imagery?

Although Lilith (nicknamed by cabalists the "Woman of Whoredom") seduced Adam, and bred a race of demons with him, Samael allegedly seduced Eve as well. So according to the cabalists, Adam and Eve both had their first sexual experience at the hands of the hermaphroditic serpent. There would seem to be a connection between these occurrences and the act of disobedience that caused Adam and Eve to fall from grace. *Genesis* Chapter 3:1-7 (KJV) tells us:

> Now the serpent was more subtle than any beast of the field which the LORD God had made. And he said unto the woman, Yea, hath God said, Ye shall not eat of every tree of the garden?
>
> And the woman said unto the serpent, We may eat of the fruit of the trees of the garden:
>
> But of the fruit of the tree which is in the midst of the garden, God hath said, Ye shall not eat of it, neither shall ye touch it, lest ye die.
>
> And the serpent said unto the woman, Ye shall not surely die:
>
> For God doth know that in the day ye eat thereof, then your eyes shall be opened, and ye shall be as gods, knowing good and evil.
>
> And when the woman saw that the tree was good for food, and that it was pleasant to the eyes, and a tree to be desired to make one wise, she took of the fruit thereof, and did eat, and gave also unto her husband with her; and he did eat.
>
> And the eyes of them both were opened, and they knew that they were naked; and they sewed fig leaves together, and made themselves aprons.

It seems that, in part, the wisdom gained by eating the fruit of the Tree of Knowledge was awareness of their own sexuality, "carnal knowledge." Indeed the Hebrew word "yada," meaning "to know," also means "to have sex with," and is used in that sense dozens of times throughout the Torah. This was the wisdom that the Serpent wanted to share with Adam and Eve. Upon becoming aware of their separate bodies, and of their differing genitals, they became anxious to cover them, so they made clothes for themselves. But when God saw that they had realized their own nakedness, he knew that they'd eaten the forbidden fruit of knowledge. *Genesis* 3:8-11 (KJV) says:

> And they heard the voice of the LORD God walking in the garden in the cool of the day: and Adam and his wife hid themselves from the presence of the LORD God amongst the trees of the garden.
>
> And the LORD God called unto Adam, and said unto him, Where art thou?
>
> And he said, I heard thy voice in the garden, and I was afraid, because I was naked; and I hid myself.
>
> And he said, Who told thee that thou wast naked? Hast thou eaten of the tree, whereof I commanded thee that thou shouldest not eat?

In a way, the serpent was telling the truth when he told Eve that eating the fruit of knowledge would not kill her, at least not immediately, and that it would make her like unto a god. Not only did she and Adam gain the awareness that had heretofore been forbidden to them, but they also gained the godlike power to produce life "in their own image." But this transgression did bring death into the world for the first time as well.

The state of being that seems to have existed before the Fall was one of timeless eternity: the perfection of undifferentiated oneness. That is alluded to not only by the words of *Genesis*, but also by the interpretations of it found in the traditions of Gnosticism and the Cabala. Perhaps this is why the chronology of the events in the first three chapters of *Genesis* is hard to follow in linear time. This story is a representation of how our universe, including linear time, was created. Thus the events themselves did not occur inside of linear time, but outside of it.

Like the aeons of the Gnostic creation, the "six days" of creation as told in *Genesis* may represent the stages of development of a universe coagulating from a state of pure chaos. The first man, Adam Kadmon, existed prior to the creation we currently live in. Within this hermaphroditic being were all of the elements needed for the creation of the human race and maybe even the broader universe. The Garden of Eden could be thought of as a petri dish in which those elements were placed so that they could evolve into the first separate male and female. When the male and female elements separated into two distinct beings, they began to procreate, and that was when they were cast out of the Garden. That is when sexual generation, including life and death as we know it, began, as implied in the story of *Genesis*.

Perhaps this is why Eve is only given her name, which means "life," in Chapter 3, Verse 20, after they were cursed by God for their transgression. The verse says that Adam called her that "because she was the mother of all living." Later, in Chapter 4, after they are driven from the Garden, Adam "knows" his wife for the first time, and she conceives both Cain and Abel. God makes it pretty clear in Chapter 3 that sexual reproduction is one of the curses that will haunt their lives now that they have eaten of the Tree of Knowledge. Eve will now be burdened with the pains of childbirth.

By the same token, Adam is cursed to forever struggle to harvest food to eat from the ground. Prior to the fall, in the Garden of Eden, all of his needs had been provided for effortlessly. But in a world of birth and death, one must work hard in order to survive. *Genesis* Chapter 3: 16-19 (KJV) states:

> Unto the woman he said, I will greatly multiply thy sorrow and thy conception; in sorrow thou shalt bring forth children; and thy desire shall be to thy husband, and he shall rule over thee.

> And unto Adam he said, Because thou hast hearkened unto the voice of thy wife, and hast eaten of the tree, of which I commanded thee, saying, Thou shalt not eat of it: cursed is the ground for thy sake; in sorrow shalt thou eat of it all the days of thy life;

> Thorns also and thistles shall it bring forth to thee; and thou shalt eat the herb of the field;

> In the sweat of thy face shalt thou eat bread, till thou return unto the ground; for out of it wast thou taken: for dust thou art, and unto dust shalt thou return.

In the story of the Garden of Eden, the character known as "the serpent" (the hermaphroditic demon Lilith-Samael) appears to be an ancestral spirit that follows the bloodline of the Biblical patriarchs in order to mate with them and to be incarnated into the bodies of their children. The biblical texts allude to these clandestine demonic marriages and the children that resulted from them but do not overtly explain what happened, as the cabalistic interpretations try to do. Lilith-Samael seems to specifically represent a lineage that the authors of the biblical texts would rather not discuss.

As we have mentioned before, many witches see Lilith as one of their main spiritual patrons, an ancestral mother-goddess figure, from the distant past to modern times.

The Seed of the Serpent 55

These people believe that witches are essentially a race of humans with magical powers that have been passed down the generations through blood. The origin of these powers, they believe, comes from the demons of the underworld, which they actually see as their ancestors. For a look into this worldview, see *The Dragon Legacy* by Nicholas de Vere.

Just as Adam and Eve were cast out of the Garden and laden with various curses as punishment for their transgressions, the serpent was also cursed because of its role in the deed. *Genesis* 3:14-15 states:

> And the LORD God said unto the serpent, Because thou hast done this, thou art cursed above all cattle, and above every beast of the field; upon thy belly shalt thou go, and dust shalt thou eat all the days of thy life:
>
> And I will put enmity between thee and the woman, and between thy seed and her seed; it shall bruise thy head, and thou shalt bruise his heel.

One of the mysteries of *Genesis*, if it is taken by itself and at face value, is that there are people—the spouses of certain people, and entire bloodlines descended from them—that are mentioned or hinted at, but whose names, origins, and ultimate destinies are not specified. So when the text refers to the serpent's "seed," we have to look elsewhere for clues.

God told the serpent that he would put "enmity" between the serpent's "seed" and that of the "woman." What "seed" are we talking about? Well, again, Cain, destined to murder his brother Abel, is said, in cabalistic tradition, to have been the son of Eve seduced by Samael. So he was really half-human and half-demon. He and his descendants were the "seed" of the serpent, and there was indeed enmity between him and his brother Abel, presumably a child of Adam and Eve. The cabalists even said that Lilith drank the blood of Abel after Cain murdered him.

There was also a continuing blood feud, according to extra-biblical texts like *The Book of the Cave of Treasures*, between the children of Cain and those of his second brother, Seth, who was born after Cain murdered Abel. Seth's birth was mentioned at the end of *Genesis* Chapter 4, after the story of Cain and Abel is told. But then the conception and birth of Seth is told of again in Chapter 5. That chapter begins with a yet another reiteration of the story of man's creation, and it is mostly similar to the Chapter 1 version. *Genesis* 5: 1-2 states:

> This is the book of the generations of Adam. In the day that God created man, in the likeness of God made he him;
>
> Male and female created he them; and blessed them, and called their name Adam, in the day when they were created.

The third verse then tells us that when Adam conceived Seth, he begat him "in his own likeness, after his image." Clearly it is being indicated that Seth was conceived using a special creation process modeled on the way in which God created Adam "in His own image," for this phrase was not used regarding the conception of Cain and Abel. Seth went on to have children of his own. With what women, it isn't specified, but a Jewish legend recounted by Ginzberg states that each of Adam and Eve's sons were born with a twin sister, whom they married. The line of Seth eventually resulted in Noah and from him the rest of the biblical patriarchs, all the way up to Jesus Christ.

The Seed of the Serpent 57

Abel apparently died without progeny, while Cain, who was exiled to "the land of Nod," went on to bear children and established several cities. All of Cain's descendants were credited in *Genesis*, Chapter 4 with inventions key to civilization, including agriculture, animal husbandry, metalworking, and music. Now here's a strange thing though: the names of Cain's descendants and those of his brother Seth are almost identical. Cain's descendants are listed as Enoch, Irad, Mahujael, Methusael, and Lamech. Meanwhile, Seth's descendants are said to be Enos, Cainan, Mahalaleel, Jared, Enoch, Mathuselah, and Lamech. It appears that there is again an attempt by the author of *Genesis* to cover up something disturbing, while still leaving coded allusions to the truth for clever readers to pick up on. It would seem that the author has attempted to write off the descendants of Cain as extinct and historically insignificant.

The land of "Nod" to which Cain was banished seems like an imaginary parallel shadow-world, like the chaos that Lilith came from and lives in. *Genesis* makes it out to be a "wilderness." Jewish legend describes Cain's descendants as double-headed, dwarf-like creatures that literally live underground. Only six generations of Cain's descendants are given in *Genesis*. Lamech, the patriarch of the fifth generation after Cain, is said in Chapter 4 to have slain a "young man," with no further explanation. One has to look to extra-biblical Jewish legends to find out what this is about. As it turns out, there is a story stating that Lamech accidentally killed his ancestor Cain while hunting in the woods one day, mistaking him for an animal because for some reason he had horns on his head, like Baphomet.

After this brief reference to the slaying of the "young man," there is no further mention of the descendants of

Cain, and the text abruptly segues to the birth of Seth. The implication is that Cain's race died off. But none of Seth's descendants, with names so similar to those of Cain's, are mentioned in *Genesis* as having invented any of the primary arts of civilization, as Cain's children did. The next thing that happens in the narrative of *Genesis* is the Deluge. Seth's seed supposedly survived this through the family of Noah, while Cain's would have presumably been wiped out.

Who then passed on the crafts of farming, metallurgy, and music-making? Did Seth's descendants learn these from the Cainites before the Flood? Or is it true that the story of the births of Seth and his children was invented to cover up the fact that it was Cain's descendants on board the Ark— which the serpent's lineage continued after the Deluge? This possibility seems more likely when we realize that the whole purpose of the Flood was God's attempt to exterminate this controversial lineage in the first place.

The story of the allegedly global Deluge begins at Mount Hermon. This is on the border between Syria and Lebanon, the tallest peak in Syria and the summit of what is called the Anti-Lebanon Mountain Range. A UN base lovingly nicknamed "Hermon Hotel" is stationed there. This was the very place that *The First Book of Enoch* (a Jewish scripture dating back to 300 BC) refers to as "Ardis." According to this text, it was here that the group of 200 "Grigori" or "Watchers" descended for a meeting of what may have been the first secret society. There, they made a pact together, binding themselves with mutual "imprecations" (oaths or curses), swearing that they would all take wives from "the daughters of men" and breed children with them. The leader of the Grigori was said to be a figure named Samyaza.

From the descriptions in *The First Book of Enoch*, it seems that these Watchers are a form of angelic being from Heaven. Their act of seducing human women in this manner is portrayed as a transgression against God, just like the rebellion of Satan or Lucifer in Heaven is seen in the Christian tradition. Indeed, it seems that what is described here in *The First Book of Enoch* is an explanation of what caused the so-called "war in Heaven" of Christian theology, fought between the rebellious angels and those loyal to God. The actions portrayed here, corresponding to a shorter version of the story in *Genesis* Chapter 6, are shown as the real reason why God decided to cleanse the Earth by bringing about the Flood.

In *The First Book of Enoch*, the defiant angels are quite aware that their transgression will incur God's wrath. This is why they swear the oath to one another before they begin, promising to go through with the act. As it states:

> It happened after the sons of men had multiplied in those days, that daughters were born to them, elegant and beautiful. And when the angels, the sons of heaven, beheld them, they became enamoured of them, saying to each other, Come, let us select for ourselves wives from the progeny of men, and let us beget children.

> Then their leader Samyaza said to them; I fear that you may perhaps be indisposed to the performance of this enterprise; And that I alone shall suffer for so grievous a crime.

> But they answered him and said; We all swear; And bind ourselves by mutual imprecations, that we will not change our intention, but execute our projected undertaking.

> Then they swore all together, and all bound themselves by mutual execrations. Their whole number was two hundred, who descended upon Ardis, which is the top of mount Armon.
>
> That mountain therefore was called Armon, because they had sworn upon it, and bound themselves by mutual imprecations.

"Mount Armon," or Mt. Hermon, has been said to mean "Mount of the Curse," because the angels took their oath, and thus cursed themselves, upon that mountain. The word "Hermon" is also similar to the name of the Greek god "Hermes," who holds many mythological parallels to the Biblical figure of Enoch, the purported author of this text. There is another Enoch listed as the son of Cain in *Genesis*, as previously mentioned. Cain allegedly built a city that was named after this son. But the Enoch of the book that bears his name is said to be a descendant of Seth—grandson of Mahalaleel and great-grandfather of Noah.

The First Book of Enoch says that giants were born from the human-angel unions, and that they ravaged the earth with their ravenous appetites:

> And the women conceiving brought forth giants, Whose stature was each three hundred cubits. These devoured all which the labor of men produced; until it became impossible to feed them; When they turned themselves against men, in order to devour them; And began to injure birds, beasts, reptiles, and fishes, to eat their flesh one after another, and to drink their blood.

At this point in the story another figure enters the picture. He is named Azazel, and he is said to be guilty of teaching mankind forbidden knowledge. The text says:

Moreover Azazyel taught men to make swords, knives, shields, breastplates, the fabrication of mirrors, and the workmanship of bracelets and ornaments, the use of paint, the beautifying of the eyebrows, the use of stones of every valuable and select kind, and all sorts of dyes, so that the world became altered.

Another quote from *The First Book of Enoch* demonstrates that this forbidden teaching was offensive to God, and that people were not meant to know these things. Referring to the iniquity and rebellion that caused God to bring about the Flood, Enoch tells Noah:

They have discovered secrets, and they are those that have been judged; but not thou, my son. The Lord of Spirits knows that thou are pure and good, free from the reproach of discovering secrets.

As a punishment for his sins, Azazel is cast into a dark prison that is also described as "the desert," in a place named "Dudael" (Hebrew for "Cauldron of God.") We read:

Again the Lord said to Raphael, Bind Azazyel hand and foot; cast him into darkness; and opening the desert which is in Dudael, cast him in there. Throw upon him hurled and pointed stones, covering him with darkness; There shall he remain for ever; cover his face, that he may not see the light. And in the great day of judgment let him be cast into the fire.

Interestingly, even though the instigator of the sexual crimes committed by the angels is said to be Samyaza, the teaching of secrets was instigated by Azazel. So Jehovah decided to lay the blame most heavily upon him. *The First Book of Enoch* quotes God as saying:

All the earth has been corrupted by the effects of the teaching of Azazyel. To him therefore ascribe the whole crime.

As for the giants born of angels and men, God decided to bring about the Flood in order to rid the Earth of them. But he also decided to thin their population as much as possible first, by sending his angels to instigate violence amongst the giants, so that they killed each other off. As it states:

To Gabriel also the Lord said, Go to the biters, to the reprobates, to the children of fornication; and destroy the children of fornication, the offspring of the Watchers, from among men; bring them forth, and excite them one against another. Let them perish by mutual slaughter; for length of days shall not be theirs.

After the Watchers are forced to watch their children die, they are cast into the pit under the earth, where they are cursed to suffer and await the Final Judgment:

To Michael likewise the Lord said, Go and announce his crime to Samyaza, and to the others who are with him, who have been associated with women, that they might be polluted with all their impurity. And when all their sons shall be slain, when they shall see the perdition of their beloved, bind them for seventy generations underneath the earth, even to the day of judgment, and of consummation, until the judgment, the effect of which will last for ever, be completed.

Then shall they be taken away into the lowest depths of the fire in torments; and in confinement shall they be shut up for ever. Immediately after this shall he, together with them, burn and perish; they shall be bound until the consummation of many generations.

Although it is not told in so much detail, this same story is alluded to in *The Book of Genesis*. In Chapter 6 (KJV) we read:

And it came to pass, when men began to multiply on the face of the earth, and daughters were born unto them, that the sons of God saw the daughters of men that they were fair; and they took them wives of all which they chose. . . .

There were giants in the earth in those days; and also after that, when the sons of God came in unto the daughters of men, and they bare children to them, the same became mighty men which were of old, men of renown.

The Hebrew word that has been translated as "giants" is "Nephilim." What this word specifically means in Hebrew is "those who were cast down," "those who caused others to fall," or "those who battle" (i.e., "those who fall upon others"). The Deluge narrative is told in Chapter 6 also, immediately after the reference to the sons of God mating with human females. Suddenly God declares that he regrets mankind's creation because of its inherent "wickedness," and because "the Earth was filled with violence." He decides to destroy all life on Earth, except for Noah and the rest of the passengers chosen to board the Ark. Man was deemed wicked not because of sin in the ordinary sense (which had not actually been invented yet), but because they had interbred with angels and created a hybrid race, of which God did not approve.

The part about Azazel teaching forbidden knowledge to man is not specified in *Genesis*, as it is in *The First Book of Enoch*. Also, the picture of Azazel as an intermediary between Samael and Lilith, as described in *The Zohar*, is also not mentioned (nor are the names of Samael and Lilith). However, Azazel is mentioned in *Leviticus*. Here the temple rituals for the Israelites are specified. One of them involves the sacrifice of two goats on the holy day of "Yom Kippur," the Day of Atonement. In Chapter 6, God tells the high priest Aaron to "place lots upon two goats, one marked for the Lord, and the other marked for Azazel."

The Azazel goat was marked with a red string tied around his head. While the goat for the Lord was killed at the temple as an atonement sacrifice, the Azazel goat, or "scapegoat," as it is often termed, was forced, like Azazel in *The First Book of Enoch*, to bear the burden of everyone else's sin. The priest would confess the sins of the community with his hands placed on the head of the goat, laying the weight of those sins upon him. The goat was then led off into the desert and pitched over the side of a rocky cliff. A white cloth was also affixed to the door of the temple sanctuary, and it would supposedly turn red the moment the goat hit the bottom.

Azazel's name has been given several interpretations. These include "rugged and strong," which accurately describes the disposition of a mountain goat. Others are "he who is sent away," or "goat that disappears." The ceremony is clearly mimicking God's punishment of Azazel as related in *The First Book of Enoch*, by casting him in the desert prison of Dudael (or else *The First Book of Enoch* was written to explain the ritual). Parallels can also be seen with the story of Cain, cast into the land of Nod, which we described earlier as possibly a nebulous, ephemeral state of existence, or even non-existence. Indeed, the word "Nod" means "to wander" in Hebrew. Perhaps not coincidentally, "nod" means "to sleep" in English. So the land of Nod appears to represent a dream-like world of confusion and chaos, like the Abyss of the cabalists where the demons are said to live and which creation came out of.

In *The Case for Lilith*, author Mark Wayne Biggs makes the case that Samyaza in *The First Book of Enoch* is the same figure as Samael. He argues that Azazel is not one of the Watchers so much as a son of Lilith and Samael. He believes that before the angels could breed with humans, they needed to know how to speak the true name of God. This, as we mentioned, can purportedly be used to create magical effects, including bringing things to life, when pronounced correctly. Biggs theorizes that Samyaza/Samael gained his knowledge from Lilith, his lover, and then used it to bring their son Azazel to life by pronouncing it during their mating. This same process, writes Biggs, was then subsequently used by the rest of the Watchers when breeding the Nephilim giants with human women.

None of these connections seem far-fetched, although the idea of Azazel being Lilith and Samael's son doesn't entirely square with the idea that he is needed to facilitate their sexual union in the first place. At any rate, in a sexual union between a creature of flesh and a spirit, it seems reasonable that a magical process might be required to bring forth fleshly progeny. Note that both Azazel in *The First Book of Enoch* and the descendants of Cain in *Genesis* are credited with teaching mankind forbidden arts and crafts such as metallurgy. As noted, the descendants of Cain are a bloodline cast off into the wilderness by God's curses—just as Azazel was cast into the desert. This could also be said of Hagar, the slave woman and mother of

Ishmael through Abraham, who, as we said, were both were cast off by Abraham and left to die in the desert (but miraculously lived), and whose bloodline was disinherited. We know that Hagar is considered by cabalists to be an incarnation of Lilith.

Interestingly, there is a sect in Iraq called the Yezidis who worship and claim biological descent from a "half-angel" whom they alternately refer to as "Yazd," "Azazil," or "Melek Taus" ("Peacock King"). The Yezidi faith is an interesting mix of Jewish, Christian, Islamic, and seemingly satanic traditions. However, they believe that any enmity between the Peacock King and the Most High God will be reconciled at the Final Judgment, and the souls of the Yezidis will be forced into Heaven through the pronouncement of magical formulae that will somehow compel God's will. This can be gleaned from reading Isya Joseph's commentary on the Yezidi scripture called *The Black Book*, published as *Devil Worship: The Sacred Books and Traditions of the Yezidis*.

Twelfth-century Jewish scholars Nahmanides and Abraham ibn Ezra both wrote that Azazel was the chief of the *seirim*, or "goat demons." As previously mentioned, these beings are described as satyrs, the word for the half-goat creatures of Greek mythology, and they live in the desert. They are considered analogous to the jinn of Islamic legend, spirits of "smokeless fire," some of whom rebelled against God and now curse mankind with mischievous tricks. Among other things, the jinn possess people, seduce people, and sometimes even breed with them. Sometimes they are very malicious, causing harm to infants, for example. In these ways, the jinn, and thus the *seirim*, seem the same as the descendants of Lilith.

Indeed, in the word "jinn" there may be an etymological vestige of "Cain." Sumeriologist L.A. Waddell thought him to be the same figure as "Kan," "Gan" or "Gin," found on the kings lists of the Sumerians, Babylonians and Chaldeans. It may be also that this family of words is connected to the English words "king" and "kin." He describes him as one of the first kings on Earth. But the cabalists also saw him as part of a family of goat-demons, along with Azazel and the "serpent" Lilith-Samael. The political implications of this are interesting, for the Devil is considered the "Lord of the Earth." It would seem, perhaps, that the serpent, by possessing and seducing humans, was successful in not only penetrating the bloodline of Adam, but also putting his/her descendants in line to inherit the thrones of the world.

This is the real idea behind conspiracy theories, popular for centuries and now more so than ever, that the elite of the world serve the agenda of Satan, meeting in secret to plot the downfall of most of humanity. The fraternity most commonly associated with this plot is the Freemasons. It is to the symbolism of their mascot—not coincidentally, a goat—that we turn our attention to next.

Chapter 3: The Goat-Faced Wild Man

He [Satan] taught women the art of seduction, men to satisfy their feelings in their double sexual desires, he ran rim in color, discovered the flute and set the muscles in rhythmical movement, until the divine mania embraced the heart and the divine Phallus with its opulence sowed the fruitful womb.

—Stanislaw Przybyszewski, *The Cult of Satan's Church*

The relationship between the Freemasons and the Knights Templar is one of contention. Detractors of both organizations often accuse them of being part of a united anti-Christ conspiracy of occult secret societies spanning the last nine centuries. Meanwhile "debunkers" who wish to demystify the origins of Freemasonry claim that any connection is purely mythical, a product of a romantic imagination. Most scholars admit that the Masonic tradition received inspiration from the Templars, as they did from many old traditions. The rituals of the Freemasons pertain to the secrets of Solomon's Temple, the site of which the Templars originally called home, and which they named their organization after. The fact that there is a rank in York Rite Masonry explicitly called the "Knights Templar degree" makes the connection seem rather overt.

If the Freemasons are continuing the secret doctrine of the Templars, one would expect the rituals to Baphomet to have continued on in the Masonic order as well. Indeed the subject of Baphomet is addressed in the handbook for Scottish Rite Freemasons entitled *Morals and Dogma* by

The Goat-Faced Wild Man

Albert Pike. Echoing the thoughts of Eliphas Levi, he wrote of Baphomet as the magical force of the universe:

> There is in nature a most potent force, by means whereof a single man, who could possess himself of it, and should know how to direct it, could revolutionize and change the face of the world. . . .
>
> This force was known to the ancients. . . . If science can but learn to control it, it will be possible to change the order of the seasons, to produce in night the phenomena of day, to send a thought in an instant around the world, to heal or slay at a distance, to give our words universal success, and make them reverberate everywhere.
>
> This agent . . . is precisely what the adepts of the Middle Ages called the elementary matter of the great work. The Gnostics held that it composed the igneous body of the Holy Spirit, and it was adored in the secret rites of the Sabbat or the Temple, under the hieroglyphic figure of Baphomet or the hermaphroditic Goat of Mendes.
>
> There is a life-principle in the world, a universal agent, wherein are two natures and a double-current of love and wrath. This ambient fluid penetrates everything. It is a ray detached from the glory of the Sun, and fixed by the weight of the atmosphere and the central attraction. It is the body of the Holy Spirit, the universal agent, the serpent devouring its own tail. With this electro-magnetic ether, this vital and luminous caloric, the ancients and the alchemists were familiar. Of this agent, that phase of modern ignorance termed physical science talks incoherently, knowing naught of it save its

effects; and theology might apply to all of its pretended definitions of spirit. . . .

Far beyond the mere fertility of vegetation that most scholars have viewed Baphomet as a symbol of, Pike seems to be describing this figure as representative of the root of all physical powers and energies, now described, as Pike contemptuously states, according to the schematics of modern physics. While the prevailing model was by no means settled in Pike's day, we imagine he was saying that what we now describe as electromagnetism, as well as gravity and the strong and weak nuclear forces, are all derived from this root. We can understand, then, why occultists still think of the knowledge of how to master this power as the ultimate mystery, and the ultimate wisdom.

In the book *The American Quarterly Review of Freemasonry and Its Kindred Sciences, Volume 1* (1858), edited by Freemasonic scholar Albert Mackey, an article entitled "Horae Esotericae" by Giles F. Yates refers to an Arabic book called *Sun of Suns and Moon of Moons* that Yates found untranslated in the library of his Masonic lodge. There, he says, the author identifies an entity named "Bafumed or Karuf [*calf*]" symbolizing "the secrets of the nature of the world, or secret of secrets." This book apparently was known in the past, and may have been lost.

We know it existed because of the work of ninth to tenth-century alchemist Ibn Wahshiyya, most famous for translating the mysterious *Book of Nabathean Agriculture* into Arabic. He wrote a book called *Ancient Alphabets and Hieroglyphic Characters Explained*, which was translated into English by none other than Joseph von Hammer-Purgstall, who published his version in 1806, twelve years before his Baphomet essay. *Ancient Alphabets* also makes reference to "Bahumed," "Bahumed," or "Bahumet" and to the *Sun of Suns* book, which Ibn Wahshiyya claims to have translated from Nabathean into Arabic.

He says the subject of the book is "the discovery of the Hermesian alphabets," and then provides, presumably from that source, a hieroglyph of a beetle-like creature which he says is:

> ...expressive of the most sublime secret, called originally *Bahumed* and *Kharuf* (or calf), viz. *The Secret of the nature of the world*, or *The Secret of Secrets*, or *The Beginning and Return of every thing*.

This all-encompassing interpretation of the meaning of Baphomet as "the biggest thing ever," seemingly shared by so many revered Masonic scholars, may explain why, according to *Freemasons for Dummies* by Christopher Hodapp:

> Some early ritual books from the fraternity referred to God as "God of all Things" and abbreviated it as GOAT. That was quickly changed, and God is now referred to by Freemasons by the acronym GAOTU, for Grand Architect of the Universe.

The change was made because outsiders to the club viewed their use of the word "GOAT" to symbolize the creator God as blasphemous and satanic. But there is much more linking Freemasonry and goats. The animal is widely claimed by non-members to be part of the hazing rites for initiation into Freemasonry, during a ceremony supposedly called "Riding the Goat." Most Masonic literature on the subject makes it out to be a joke, based on the accusations of a secret doctrine of Satanism that have been made against the brotherhood by anti-Masons throughout the years. As we read from Albert Mackey's *Encyclopedia of Freemasonry and its Kindred Sciences* (1917):

The idea that "riding the goat" constitutes a part of the ceremonies of initiation of a Masonic lodge has its real origin in the superstition of antiquity. The old Greeks and Romans portrayed their mystical god Pan in horns and hooves and shaggy hide, and called him "goat-footed. When the demonology of the classics was adopted and modified by the early Christians, Pan gave way to Satan, who naturally inherited his attributes, so that to the common mind the devil was represented by the he-goat, and his best-known marks were the horns, the beard, and the cloven hoofs. Then came the witch stories of the Middle Ages, and the belief in the witch orgies, where, as it was said, the devil appeared riding on a goat. These orgies of the witches, where, amid fear of blasphemous ceremonies, they practiced initiation into their Satanic rites, became, to the vulgar and illiterate, the type of the Masonic mysteries; for, as Dr. [George] Oliver says, 'It was in England a common belief that the Freemasons were accustomed in their lodges 'to raise the devil.'

In Volume 14 of *The Short Talk Bulletin* of the Grand Lodge of New Brunswick in May 1936, the same argument was made, tracing the Masonic goat back to Pan via Satan, but also, back to Azazel. As it states:

The idea that the sins of the people might be transferred to a goat, which, driven into the wilderness to die, carried away the moral trespasses with which he was symbolically loaded, doubtless had much to do with the change which came over the complexion of the Great God Pan, when Christianity commenced to rewrite the ancient heathen mythology. Gently Pan, who harmed no one beyond creating terror, became first Satanic, and then, in the end, Satan himself.

A similar analysis is found in Thomas Wright's *Worship of the Generative Powers* (1865), one of the first works in English to examine Joseph von Hammer-Purgstall's "Baphometic Idols." In it, Wright demonstrates amazing similarity between the rituals that the Knights Templar were accused of doing, and the rites of the pre-Christian cult of Priapus. Also remarkably similar were the purported activities of many Gnostic groups, the Cathar heretics of France, and the European witch cults of the Middle Ages. We even see the same symbolism in the Satanic "Black Mass," allegedly celebrated throughout the centuries by the supposed "fifth column" of Satanist priests who purportedly lurk in secret within the upper echelons of the Catholic Church. Wright believed that the Christian image of "Satan" was in fact largely based on images of Priapus, and attempted to demonstrate that the traditions of underground "Satanist" and "witchcraft" cults were actually sublimated forms of Priapism.

After cataloging the widespread use of votive phalluses throughout Pre-Christian Europe, Wright describes how what he called the "cult of Priapus" spread deep into Europe. In Greek mythology, Priapus was of divine parentage (variously fathered by Pan, Hermes, or Zeus, depending on the story). He was cursed by Hera to be ugly and to have a dirty mind. He was so unpleasant to the other gods that they pitched him over the side of a cliff, like the Azazel goat on Yom Kippur. He landed on Earth and was raised by shepherds as one of their own.

Just as Hera cursed him to be, Priapus shared the stereotypical interests of pastoral Greek herdsmen: bestiality and the rape of passers-by. As part of his affliction,

Priapus had a giant penis with an almost-perpetual erection, which he would nonetheless lose at certain key moments, much to his frustration. For instance, as he was attempting to rape the sleeping nymph Lotis (or the goddess Hestia, in the version told by Ovid), a donkey brayed, waking the victim just in time and causing the loss of his erection. In retribution, Priapus is said to have raped the donkey to death, and the brutal sacrifice of these animals was part of his cult from that point onward.

It is interesting that Priapus was considered a symbol of fertility, despite his association with impotence as well. This is a problem that the she-demon Lilith was said by Jews to cause. The association of the Priapian cult with dildos also reminds us of Samael's need for an "intermediary" to simulate sex with his bride. One can see a parallel here between the unfulfilled lust of Priapus and the yearning that the castrated Samael has for Lilith. Perhaps his gigantic erection symbolizes potential energy unspoiled, stored up for future use, its magnitude only increased by repeated frustration of desire.

Statues of Priapus were traditionally placed in gardens, where they were believed to engender the crops. They also fulfilled a scarecrow-like function, protecting the crops not only from rapacious fowl, but also from people who might steal or otherwise tamper with them. Placards placed in gardens warned that Priapus would rape trespassers—vaginally, anally, or orally—if the crops were harmed in any way. The Priapian tradition was also related to the use of "herms," which consisted of the head of a satyr on top of a squared-off column with a large erect phallus jutting out the center. These were rubbed for good luck. Likewise, Thomas Wright documents the continuation of Priapism throughout Christian Europe with the use of amulets and coins featuring disembodied penises, sometimes with hands, feet, and even penises of their own. These were worn for good luck, or, rather, for the warding off of the evil eye.

Likewise the "fig" hand signal fulfilled a similar function, which could be performed either by making a fist with the thumb pushed between the middle and index finger, or else sticking the middle finger up alone, *a la* the modern "flipping off" gesture. The true meaning of this signal, then, is a curse, to say "May Priapus (that is, the Devil) fuck you." But originally, it was done to ward off evil, or bring good luck at a time of need, just like "crossing your fingers" is done now.

The Priapus statues called herms were so named because the features of Priapus and Hermes were in many ways conflated. For one thing, some genealogies had Hermes as the father of Priapus, or his grandfather via the half-goat, half-god-man known as Pan. All three of them have been depicted with horns and a goaty-looking beard in different instances—Pan most consistently, and Priapus quite often. Pan actually had the hairy legs and hooves of a goat, and was a full-blown satyr living in Arcadia, the unspoiled wilds where his father Hermes ruled. His mother and nurse were said to have fled in fear when they first saw him, because of the uncanny nature of his appearance. Despite this, they say, the gods of Olympus thought he was beautiful and may have named him "Pan" ("All") because to them he was perfect.

However, another, less flattering, origin of his name is given by Servius, a commentator on the writings of Virgil, who tells us that his mother was Penelope, wife of Odysseus. In this version of the story, she purportedly had sex with all 108 of her suitors and somehow conceived Pan from all of them. This fits with Pan's association with sexual promiscuity. But many other sources, including Herodotus,

Cicero, Apollodorus and Hyginus, claim that Pan's parents were Hermes and Penelope, which makes us wonder if the 108 suitors in Homer's epic were somehow symbolic of different aspects of Hermes. Either way it is obscene, as Hermes was said by Homer to be Odysseus' great-grandfather. After he killed the suitors, Hermes led their souls to Hades personally.

Pan was a physical embodiment of the spirit of the wilderness, and is invoked as such even today. He inspired wonder and lust, as well as madness. A visit from him—invited or unprovoked, usually in some wild or desolate place—would bring crazy visions, "panic attacks" (the word "panic" stemming from his name), and sometimes permanent insanity. It is the madness that comes upon seeing the raw, wild, and androgynous root of sexual energy—the undivided, unpolarized energy of life itself that divides and ignites creation. Weird horror author Arthur Machen described a vision of this entity in his short story *The Great God Pan*:

> Though horror and revolting nausea rose up within me, and an odour of corruption choked my breath, I remained firm. I was then privileged or accursed, I dare not say which, to see that which was on the bed, lying there black like ink, transformed before my eyes. The skin, and the flesh, and the muscles, and the bones, and the firm structure of the human body that I had thought to be unchangeable, and permanent as adamant, began to melt and dissolve.
>
> I know that the body may be separated into its elements by external agencies, but I should have refused to believe what I saw. For here there was

some internal force, of which I knew nothing, that caused dissolution and change.

Here too was all the work by which man had been made repeated before my eyes. I saw the form waver from sex to sex, dividing itself from itself, and then again reunited. Then I saw the body descend to the beasts whence it ascended, and that which was on the heights go down to the depths, even to the abyss of all being. . . .

Stories about frightening encounters with a Pan-like creature persist today with both urban and rural legends still being told about satyrs that rape, kill, and inspire madness. The deadly "Pope Lick Monster" of Kentucky is one such example. The flying, blood-sucking "Chupacabra" ("Goatsucker") of South America is another (although he mostly chooses livestock for victims). The Native North American figure of the Wendigo has a similar reputation, as he lives in the deep woods and drives his prey crazy before he kills them. But his horns are described as deer antlers.

Having heard such stories in our youth many times before, we were quite surprised to come across a far more ancient version in *The Book of Nabathean Agriculture*. Here a creature called "Al-Ghul" is described that sounds very similar to both Pan and Baphomet. It was said to be a human female from the waist up, with the legs and hooves of a donkey. Ghuls were described as living "in underground dens and dry, barren deserts, where people do not travel," just like Azazel and Lilith. The ghuls would only come out at night because the sun harmed them. Like the giant offspring of the Sons of God in *Genesis* or the Watchers in *The First Book of Enoch*, ghuls had a rapacious appetite for flesh and blood.

But their favorite prey was said to be humans. According to *Nabathean Agriculture*, ghuls can smell humans from far away, and "the utmost pleasure and lust of this animal is to get a human being in its power." Anyone who "looks attentively" at it for a while will die of fright. In particular, if anyone under the age of 20 looks a ghul in the face, it was said that "he will become paralyzed" upon seeing it and "will not be able to move until it takes him and cuts his throat and drinks his blood," after which the man, still living, had the horror of watching his penis and testicles get eaten by the creature, before it finally gobbles up his intestines. Arab astrologers identified a constellation in the heavens as "the head of the Ghul," and one of the blinking stars within as the eye with the deadly stare. The Greeks called this same constellation the head of the Gorgon monster, Medusa, a woman with a serpent's tale instead of legs (like Lilith), and serpents on her head, as well as a paralyzing stare like Al-Ghul.

Indeed, the whole story of the Gorgon and the "Aegis"—the magical shield that it was affixed to—has an interesting tie-in regarding the goat symbolism that we are examining. According to the Greeks, their highest God, Zeus, was raised in hiding, exiled on the island of Crete for fear of being eaten by his father, Kronos. His wet nurse during his infancy was a she-goat named Amalthea. Her name means "tender," specifically referring not to the financial term, but to that definition of "tender" as "a person who attends to or takes charge of someone or some thing" (*Webster's College Dictionary*, 1999). Some sources say the god Pan (also called "Aegipan") was nursed there alongside Zeus as well.

Having little thanks for the favors of Amalthea, Zeus had her slaughtered as soon as he was fully grown, and fashioned from her skin the "Aegis," an impenetrable shield.

The word "aegis" (or *aigis*) literally means "goat-skin." Zeus would shake this shield in the air in order to create thunder and lightning that could cause men to die of fright. Thus he earned the epithet "Aigiokhos," meaning "wielder of the goat-skin." He also made the "cornucopia" or "horn of plenty," from one of Amalthea's horns. This magical object contained an inexhaustible supply of fruits and flowers.

The Aegis is also the subject of other myths involving the figures of the bright-eyed wisdom goddess Athena, the cunning blacksmith god Hephaestus, and the Gorgon Medusa. Poet and mythographer Robert Graves believed that the Aegis originally belonged to Athena only, and that the myth was transposed onto Zeus at a later date. He also theorized that the reason why a goat was sacrificed at the Acropolis in Athens every year was because the Greeks saw the goat as a representation of Athena. He conjectured that the skin of the animal might have been placed on the shoulders of a statue of Athena after the sacrifice, as the Egyptians did with a ram skin to statues of their ram god Ammon. He thought that this may have been the origin of the ritual goatskin that would later be fashioned into the Aegis shield and associated with Zeus.

Eventually, the Aegis had the head of the Gorgon Medusa fixed to it, purportedly by Hephaestus, its real builder according to Homer. Euripides said that the Aegis was made from a goatskin that originally belonged to Medusa. You will recall that she had serpents on her head instead of hair and that one look at her face would turn a man to stone instantly. As we said, this was very similar to how the face of a ghul could cause mind-bending terror that paralyzed and sometimes even killed instantly. This was a property that was retained even after the head was severed by the hero Perseus, and affixed to the Aegis shield. The face was permanently frozen in a grimace of pain, its eyes rolling upward.

Could this unique state of madness and terror caused by things like Pan, Al-Ghul and Medusa be thought of as similar to that terrible "Baptism of Wisdom" which Baphomet is named for: a realization of the horror of existence, like the Knowledge of Good and Evil that the Serpent blessed and cursed Adam and Eve with? Traditionalist Julius Evola, in his classic book *The Mystery of the Grail*, gave us a relevant description of how the vision of Baphomet affected the Templars:

> The central ritual of Templar initiation was kept very secret. From one of the proceedings of the trial we learn that a knight who underwent it returned as pale as a corpse, and with a lost expression on his face, claiming that from then on he could never be happy again. Shortly after, the same knight fell into a state of invincible depression and died. . . What produces an extreme terror in some knights and causes them to flee. . . is the vision of an idol. . . the Baphomet.

Thomas Wright believed that the Knights Templar were practicing Gnostic rites of Priapism when they worshipped Baphomet, whom he saw as just another incarnation of Priapus. He found confirmation of this in the artifacts and images of Gnostic sex orgy rituals purportedly discovered by von Hammer-Purgstall on former Templar properties. These include images of the famous *osculum inflame*—the "obscene kiss" of the rear end of a statue of a goat-headed entity, corresponding to the accusation that the Templars "kissed the anus of a goat" during their rituals.

The Goat-Faced Wild Man 81

The Templar rites, as described by the knights under confession, were identical in many ways to the elements of the alleged "Witches' Sabbath" that accused witches have confessed to attending throughout centuries of persecution in the Christian world. From the Middle Ages of Europe, to sixteenth century England, to colonial America, the descriptions of the Sabbath in these confessions are remarkably uniform. These ceremonies were officiated by a dark figure, usually described as a man dressed in black with a goat's head, or a man who could transform into a goat. There was a mock Eucharist with a black Host, blaspheming of God, and ritual trampling upon the Cross (just as the Templars are said to have done). New initiates were made to sign a black book pledging their soul to him, and they received a mark from the goat god that tagged them as belonging to him.

These witches had a number of different nicknames for this figure. According to *The God of the Witches* by Dr. Margaret Alice Murray, these include: the Black Man (or Man in Black), the Antecessor, Robin Artisson (or Robinus Filius Artis), Christsonday, and Janicot (supposedly meaning "Little John" in Basque). Dr. Murray correctly connects this figure to a pre-Christian horned god:

> The great Gaulish god was called by the Romans Cernunnos, which in the English parlance was Herne, or more colloquially "Old Hornie." In Northern Europe the ancient Neck or Nick, meaning a spirit, had such hold on the affections of the people that the Church was forced to accept him, and he was canonised as St. Nicholas, who in Cornwall still retains his horns. Our Puck is the Welsh Boucca, which derives either directly from the Slavic Bog "God" or from the same root.

Puck and Cernunnos, along with the aforementioned Priapus, Pan, and Hermes (the Roman Mercury), all seem to be different versions of the same horned personality. To this we can also add the Greek Dionysus (the Roman Bacchus), the Roman Silvanus and Faunus, and the Celtic Green Man. What they have in common includes association with fertility, sexuality, luck, wealth, magical transformation, initiation, mischief, trickery, and the wilderness.

Puck (also related to *bucca*, a "male goat" in Old English) was a mischievous fairy (or "pixie," another word related to his name). He was known for his "merry jests." He could be invoked by witches to perform small tasks in exchange for food and drink. He could also show up uninvited and perform mischief, such as causing milk to spoil. Depictions of him show him looking very much like both Baphomet and Priapus, with a goat head and goat legs, a gigantic erect phallus, and protruding breasts. Witches are shown in some of these images dancing around him, and he does seem to have been the figure invoked at a Witch Sabbath. Shakespeare named him both "Puck" and "Robin Goodfellow" in *A Midsummer Night's Dream*, calling him a "Hobgoblin" and a "shrewd and knavish sprite."

As we mentioned, he was apparently known to witch covens as "Robin" as well. He seems to have influenced the stories of the thief Robin Hood and his Merry Men (thieves like Hermes), including "Little John" (whose name corresponds to Janicot, the Basque name for the goat god of the Witch Sabbath). Interestingly, a Robin Hood play was once performed at May Day (a witch holiday) every year by gypsies on the grounds of Rosslyn Chapel in Scotland (allegedly built by Templars who escaped persecution in France) under the patronage of the chapel's hereditary curators, the Sinclairs (a Templar-descended family).

Very similar goat man imagery is associated with several other figures, although their animal symbolism is not always that of a goat. For instance, the Roman Faunus eventually became amalgamated with Pan, as he was a wild god of the woods with horns and animal legs, but originally he was more of a wolf than a goat. There is also the horned Dionysus, the god of wine, who was more associated with the bull. To the Greeks, Dionysus was the god of divine madness, who revealed epiphanies to his followers when they were in a state of religious ecstasy. This was achieved through wild, drunken orgies in which sacrificial animals were torn to pieces by the teeth and claws of the worshippers. These rituals would have made the Priapists proud, undoubtedly setting the standard for the excesses of later Gnostic, Satanist, and witch cults. Dionysus was called "Eleutherios" ("the Liberator") and "Lyaeus" ("he who unties [the mind from worry]").

Purportedly, one of the items "revealed" to initiates of the cult of Dionysus was a giant dildo, supposedly crafted and *used anally* by the god himself! The story of its origin states that a shepherd named Prosymnus helped Dionysus rescue his mother Semele from the underworld on the promise that he and the god could have sex afterwards. However, the shepherd died before the promise could be consummated. As a way of making amends, Dionysus made a phallus out of fig wood (the tree associated with Priapus because its fruit was seen as symbolic of the penis). He then placed it on the shepherd's tomb and proceeded to sit upon it!

Dionysus was often depicted as an androgynous or even feminine youth. When he made his appearance at these rituals (as a manifested spirit), he was described as disheveled with a manic look in his eyes, as if returning from

Above: Bookplate from Frank C. Pape, 1920s.

Above: *Culte de Priape*, by Agostino Carracci.

Right: *A Greek Form of Hermes*, from *The Secret Teachings of All Ages* by Manly P. Hall, 1928.

Left: Image of a female satyr masturbating with a herm.

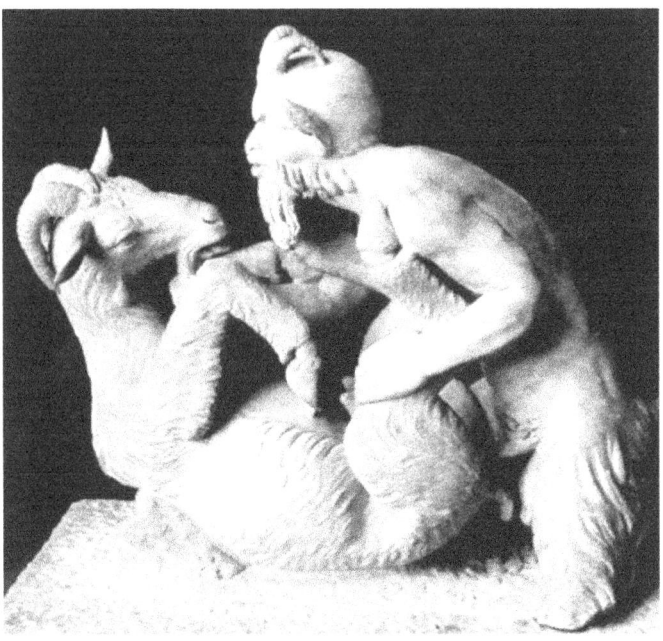

Above: Robin Goodfellow at a Sabbath. Below: Pan Copulating with Goat," from Herculaneum, now at National Museum of Naples.

Pan Teaching Olympus to Play the Syrinx. From the National Museum of Naples.

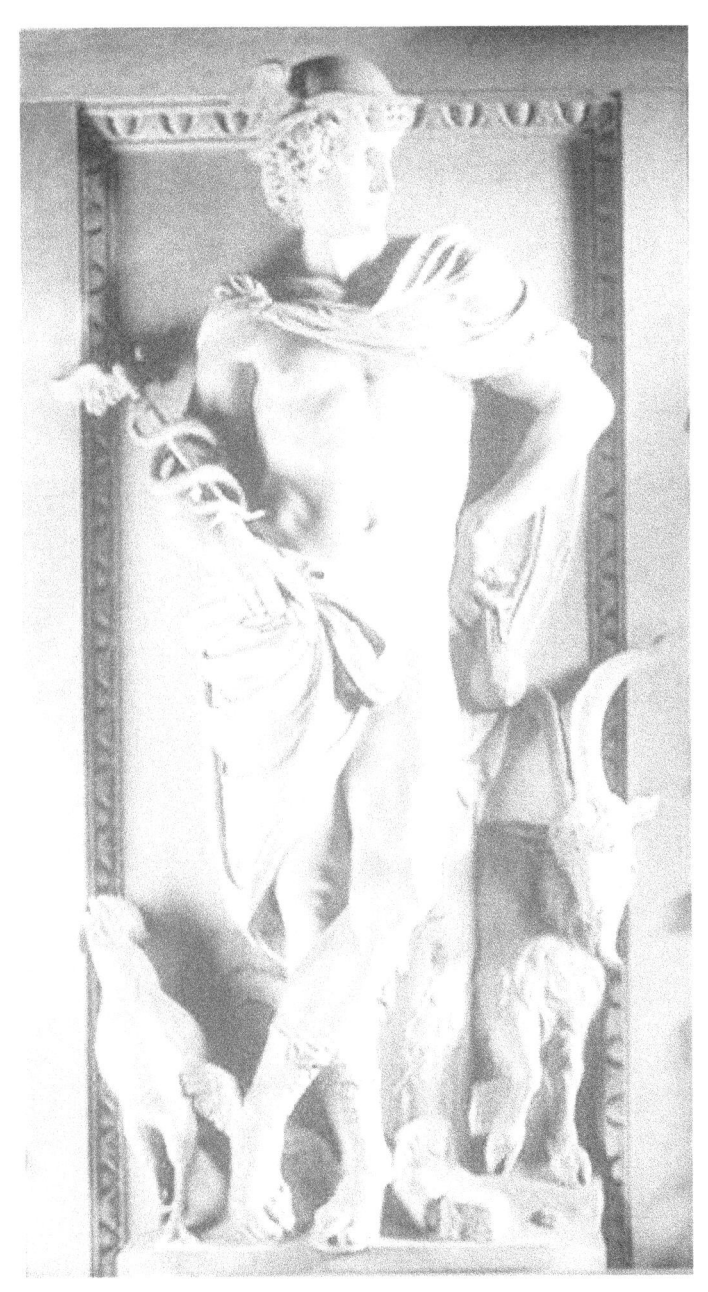

Hermes with Cock and Goat, by Artus Quellinus, from the Royal Palace in Amerstrdam.

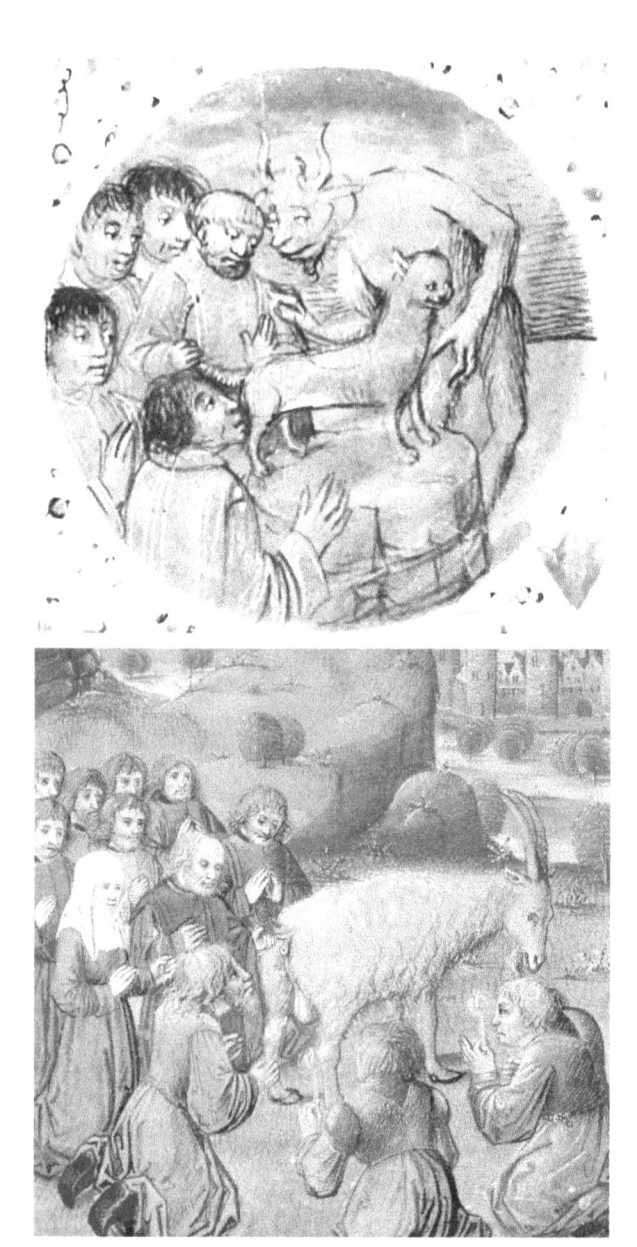

Waldensian heretics performing obscene kisses on beasts, from Jean Tinctor, *Traittié du crisme de vauderie*, from *Sermo contra sectam vaudensium* (*Sermon Against the Waldensians*), 1465.

Above: *The Ritual Kiss of the Sabbath*, from *Compendium Maleficarum*, 1608. Below: Priapus with caduceus.

From *Kitab al-Bulhan*, late 14th century. The Devil makes the cornu "goat horn" hand signal now popular with modern Satanists and fans of heavy metal music.

The Goat-Faced Wild Man 93

a realm beyond known existence. This was the true "wilderness" where he reigned, although it was symbolized by the forest, thus his epithet "dendrites" ("of the trees"). He was said to have come from the mythical "Mount Nysa," always described by the Greeks as someplace very far away and foreign to them. Just like the Gnostics and the witches of later times, the Dionysian mystery cults were at best just barely tolerated by the authorities, and frequently outlawed.

Other gods of the wilderness are usually shown as having a relationship to Dionysus. Silenus was one such figure, a wild man of the woods who is said in some myths to have raised Dionysus, or at least to have been in charge of finding him suitable foster parents. This happened after his mother was killed by the goddess Hera while he was still *in utero*, and his father Zeus had to carry him in his own testicles until he was ready to be born. Silenus was often portrayed as being part of the procession that would parade down the street during Dionysian festivals, along with satyrs and women with wild hair, their mouths still dripping blood from the brutal sacrifice.

Moving on to the myths of other cultures, the Celtic figure of Cernunnos is interesting for many reasons. He sits cross-legged like Eliphas Levi's Baphomet. His epithet "Herne the Hunter" sounds similar to Hermes. He was known as the "Lord of Wild Things." His name seems to mean "the Horned One." He has been connected by scholars to Mercury. Busts of his head showing two faces, back-to-back like the Roman Janus, have been found.

Cernunnos and Robin Goodfellow have both been connected to the Green Man, a.k.a. "Jack-in-the Green," whose foliage-sprouting face can be seen in gardens and greenery throughout Europe and the British Isles. Like the ritual phalli of Priapus, these fertility totems were omnipresent there at one time. They show the face of a man grimacing, seemingly almost under torture, as plants sprout from his face, and even from his nose and mouth. In a sense, it is reminiscent of the Gorgon head on the Aegis. He is frequently shown horned, and seems somewhat similar to the bearded faces of Bacchus or Dionysus that most of us have seen at one time decorating a garden gate. These Green Man masks are purported to ensure favorable circumstances to the crops nearby when given proper homage, just like the herms mentioned previously. The oldest known version has been found in France dated to 400 AD.

This "Green Man" is probably connected to several others in Celtic folklore. Most notably, the story of the "Green Man of Knowledge" is quite interesting. In this story, the title character, whose face is described as similar to that of the Green Man totem mask mentioned above, rules over a netherworld called "No Man's Land," which like the chaos that Lilith sprang from, doesn't really exist. He is, as a title implies, as wise man, but he uses his wisdom for ill, to keep the land enchanted under his spell, and rules as a tyrant.

Fascinatingly, there is a figure from Islamic legend that ties in with the Green Man mythos. His name, "Al-Khadir," is usually taken to be a misspelling of *al-akhdar*, and he is known for wearing green clothing. Like Hermes, he is a *psychopompus*. He shows up suddenly when worthy people need guidance, and imparts wisdom (usually strange wisdom against common logic). He will steer you into unforeseen luck, or away from danger, as he wishes. He is known to appear to pilgrims on the Hajj pilgrimage in Mecca, where he "gives power" to the holy Black Stone on display in the shrine called the Kaaba. Like Mercury, he can appear and disappear quite suddenly because his movements are very quick. He is said to look like a young man, but with a white beard. He features in many stories having to do with the Fountain of Youth and immortality. He lives at the junction of two rivers.

Al-Khadir is mentioned in *The Koran* as the "Servant of God" whom the deity granted divine wisdom to. Al-Khadir then met Moses at the crossing of two rivers, and taught him what he knew. He is also associated with the Prophet Elijah. According to a hadith, the spirit of Mohammed spends the month of Ramadan every year in Jerusalem with those of Al-Khadir and Elijah. Sufis also believe that Al-Khadir is the ruler of the *rijalu'l-gyab* ("the men of the unseen"), a panel of saints and angels who actually make some of the more important decisions regarding the fate of the universe and the things in it. This makes him part of the "Qutb," the spiritual pole of the universe that holds everything up properly, and around which everything rotates.

In addition to his connection to the European Green Man, Al-Khadir has been associated with the prophet Elijah, John the Baptist, St. George, Enoch and Metatron. As the personal "Servant of God," divine messenger, and patron of prophets, he is similar to the biblical figure of Enoch, who purportedly wrote 366 books based on his experiences traveling through various heavens, as well as the underworld. Enoch has been interpreted by some scholars as being the same personage as Hermes, as we will soon discuss. Enoch's body of written work, which includes details of how everything supposedly works, both on Earth and in the many heavens, has been compared to the famed "Emerald Tablet of Hermes," which likewise is said to contain the secrets of the universe. Al-Khadir supposedly had a staff that could turn into a snake, bringing to mind the caduceus of Hermes and the alchemical symbol of the crucified serpent (featured, among other places, on the "star jewels" worn by nineteenth-century members of the "Knights Templar" degree of York Rite Freemasonry). It is also reminiscent of the incident from *Exodus* Chapter 7, in which Moses and the Egyptian court magicians all turned their staves into snakes.

Al-Khadir had the secret of immortality, and could resurrect the dead as well. He was often depicted holding a golden goblet that contained the alchemical Elixir of Life, the drink of the immortals. He purportedly went on a mission with Alexander the Great (described as "Dhul-Qarnayn"—the "Man with Two Horns") in search of the Fountain of Youth (which Al-Khadir successfully found, they say). From that point on, according to legend, Al-Khadir had been the guardian of the fountain.

Just as he and Hermes were associated with immortality, Enoch did not die but was translated directly to Heaven, where he became the angel "Metatron." This figure was said to be a sidekick to God nicknamed "Little Jehovah" by rabbis because only God himself is comparable to him in power. In this way, the myths connect again to Hermes, who was not only the messenger and slave of the gods, but also the force that would perform miraculous transformations during alchemical operations and magical ceremonies. It also, in a way, confirms Plato's speculation that Thoth—equivalent to Hermes and thus to Enoch—was a deified human, although the deification is being said here to have been a supernatural act rather than, as Plato thought, a process of history.

Returning to Al-Khadir, we note that, as a patron of writers, poets and speakers, he is also in that respect like

Mercury, Thoth, and Hermes, as well as other gods of writing, poetry, rhetoric and prophecy from other cultures. These include the Babylonian Nebo, father of the Nabatean race. The related word *nabu* still means "prophet" in Arabic. It is at the root of the name of Nebaioth, the first-born son of Ishmael, progenitor of the Arabs and ancestor of Mohammed. Nebo's special fetish item was the stylus.

To ancient man, writing and speaking were powerful creative acts. Language was considered magical and of divine origin. The Jews thought that God had created the world through pronouncement. This is the concept of the Logos, the Divine Word. As *The Gospel of John* (KJV) states at its opening:

> In the beginning was the Word, and the Word was with God, and the Word was God.

This is why a divine messenger and teacher who can instruct in the holy arts of writing—incantations, law, poetry, mathematics, and all manner of recorded wisdom—is himself likened to a creator God, a "little Jehovah."

To the list of wisdom initiator figures we have to add the Babylonian figure of Oannes. The account of third century BC Babylonian writer Berossus on this topic (who himself actually purported to quote the writings of this "Oannes") was paraphrased first century BC Greek scholar Alexander Polyhistor, as quoted by *Cory's Ancient Fragments* from 1876:

> At Babylon there was (in these times) a great resort of people of various nations, who inhabited Chaldea, and lived in a lawless manner like the beasts of the field.

> In the first year there appeared, from that part of the Erythaean sea which borders upon Babylonia, an animal endowed with reason, by name Oannes, whose whole body (according to the account of Apollodorus) was that of a fish; that under the fish's head he had another head, with feet also below similar to those of a man, subjoined to the fish's tail. His voice, too, and language were articulate and human; and a representation of him is preserved even to this day.
>
> This being was accustomed to pass the day among men, but took no food at that season; and he gave them an insight into letters and sciences, and arts of every kind. He taught them to construct cities, to found temples, to compile laws, and explained to them the principles of geometrical knowledge. He made them distinguish the seeds of the earth, and showed them how to collect the fruits; in short, he instructed them in every thing which could tend to soften manners and humanize their lives. From that time, nothing material has been added by way of improvement to his instructions. And when the sun had set this being Oannes retired again into the sea, and passed the night in the deep, for he was amphibious. . . .

Images of this figure are abundant. They very much look like a person has cut open a large fish from tail to snout and then placed it on his head as a cap, with the body and tail of the fish then draped down his back like a cape. If that's how Oannes rolled, it must have been smelly indeed. Or maybe he really was a composite creature, as described, an animal endowed with reason and a human voice, a human face underneath his fish head, and feet beside his fish tail.

The Goat-Faced Wild Man 99

A similar mythological figure is the Mesopotamian Adapa, who also brought essential wisdom to mankind from the gods in Heaven. He too was depicted with a fish tail, but he also had goat horns on his head! Thus he is probably historically connected to the image of the constellation of Capricorn, which the Greeks portrayed as a goat-fish. Adapa was the son of Ea (a.k.a. "Enki," equivalent of the Philistine "Dagon"), the god of cunning wisdom and "Lord of the Flood." He lived in a house called the "Apsu" underground which was the source of the Tigris and Euphrates rivers. Like Enoch, Adapa was offered the food of the immortals while visiting Heaven, which would have made him immortal as well. However, he did not seem to realize this, as he had been warned by Enki not to eat anything while in Heaven, or he would die, so he passed on the opportunity.

This fish-god Ea was also said to have warned Uta-Napishtim, the hero of the Mesopotamian version of the Deluge story, about the catastrophe that was coming, and instructed him on how to build an ark to survive it. He was granted immortality, and lived at the mouth of two of the rivers of Paradise. Similarly, Hindu legend tells us that the god Vishnu (who in his incarnation as Matsya is depicted as a man with a fish-tail from the waist down) took the form of a giant fish and warned their Flood hero, Manu, about the Deluge. He told him how to build an ark, which Manu then attached to the fish's horn so that he could be towed safely to the place of landing.

In *The Natsarene and Hidden Gnosis*, Rene Salm writes about the Gnostic symbolism of the flood myth as well as Ea/Enki:

> In the flood story, secret knowledge protects the wise person against that which destroys the entire world. The flood was a divine judgment upon all

mankind, one which came suddenly. But god gave Noah secret knowledge in advance: to build an ark. The ark itself represents and symbolizes the secret saving knowledge of god. After all, it was the ark that saved Noah. Thus it is no surprise that in the Akkadian flood story the boat is named Natsirat Napishtim, "Preserver of Life," a phrase employing the root *n-ts-r*. It should also not surprise us that *netseru* in Akkadian means "secret knowledge," particularly that received from the moon god Ea/Enki.

Al-Khadir is also associated with fish. He is often shown in illustrations actually riding on the back of a very large fish. One of the miracles he is said to have performed was making a fish that was dead and already salted come back to life and jump into the river.

Another figure whom Al-Khadir is believed to be connected to is an Ugaritic god named Kothar-wa-Khasis, the bringer of "Hasisu," a special kind of wisdom. He was believed to have taught mankind writing, agriculture, and metal-working. He was also called a "servant" or "slave" of the god El, the etymological root of the Hebrew "Elohim" and the Arabic "Allah." So like Enoch-Metatron, he was second-in-command to the supreme creator God himself.

Also, like St. George (another form of the Green Man), Kothar famously slew a dragon. All stories of slaying a dragon are, perhaps, symbolic of the same thing as a crucified serpent in alchemy. It represents releasing the power of the *prima materia*, the original, undifferentiated chaos-matter of the universe. Serpents or dragons are seen as emblems of that chaos, like Samael and Lilith or the Leviathans are to the Cabalists. Stories of slaying a dragon to create a universe go back to ancient Sumer and the story of the dragoness Tiamat. The crucifying of a serpent for magical rituals is described in the ancient *Book of Nabathean Agriculture.*

The same role played by Al-Khadir in Arabic legend is played in a universal way in the Hermetic figure of the trickster-initiator Hermes, the fullest example of the archetype discussed in this chapter. When a character based on this archetype shows up in stories, both ancient and modern, he is often an agent sent by a hidden hierarchy to lure the protagonist down the path to his fate. He uses deceit to convince the hero of the tale to embark upon an adventure. He is often shown as playful and childish, enjoying his knavish pranks.

Although the earliest depictions of Hermes show him as old and wise with a beard, later renderings presented him as a youth, befitting his reputation. The word "capricious" means "wily," and comes from the Latin word for "goat." As we mentioned before, the Greeks sometimes showed Hermes as having partial goat features, especially in the early days, and he was frequently shown with a goat by his side, or being carried over his shoulders.

The satyr-like figure of Puck/Robin Goodfellow was certainly capricious, as were spin-off characters Peter Pan and Robin Hood. The theme of thievery, one of Hermes' areas of specialty, comes up quite often, as these stories often have the Hermes/Pan/Puck figure as a bandit. He was usually portrayed as having wings on his sandals and his hat, implying his swift-footed and slippery nature. He was always very sneaky, subtle, and hard to pin down, "the shrewdest and most cunning" of the gods, as Edith Hamilton wrote. This made him a natural master thief.

However, like Robin Hood, he would usually use his ill-gotten gain to help out an underdog, or he would sacrifice it to the gods, as he did with some of the cattle he stole from Apollo. This is why he is the patron of thieves as well as businessmen, because one of his first acts upon exiting the womb was to steal Apollo's cattle. When Hermes is caught, he proposes a deal with Apollo to keep the cattle in exchange for the lyre, a musical instrument he had just invented. One of his sons was Autolycus, literally called "the Prince of Thieves" (long before the Robin Hood movie). An ancient hymn to Hermes describes him as:

> . . . of many shifts (*polytropos*), blandly cunning, a robber, a cattle driver, a bringer of dreams, a watcher by night, a captain of raiders, a thief at the gates. . . .

Though he's sneaky and a bit dangerous, "Hermes Dolios" ("Tricky Hermes") is a necessary guide to realms beyond. He is the god of transitions, so just as in alchemy he is the bond which united unlikely pairs, in myth he builds bridges and opens portals between realms that are normally completely separated (such as Earth, Olympus, and the Underworld). In addition to the aforementioned title of "Psychopompus," his related epithets included "Oneiropompus" ("conductor of dreams," as he guided the soul through its nighttime adventures); "Hodios" ("patron of travelers"); and "Poimandres" ("shepherd of men"). He was also called "Hermes of the Ways," "Proopylaios" ("guardian of the gate"), "Pylaios" ("doorkeeper"), "Strophaios" ("standing at the door post") and "Stropheus" ("the socket in which the pivot of the door moves"), and was said to be "standing there at the crossroads." He was both a guardian of the borders (just as the herms and statues of Silenus were used to mark property boundaries in ancient times), and he was the key to open the gates between them.

One interpretation of the etymology of his name is that it comes from *hermai* ("boundary marker"). Likewise, his Roman name of Mercury might be related to the Proto-Indo-European *merg* (the root of the English "mark"). The other possible root for Hermes commonly given is *ermeneus* ("interpreter"), referring to his skills at speech and communication. He was the "Diactoros" or "Angelos" ("the messenger") and the "Logios" ("Speaker").

However, these things are not mutually exclusive, in our opinion, for as we know from reading motivational posters in corporate offices, "communication is the key." The most common interpretation of Mercury's name is that it is related to *merx* ("merchandise"), referring to his role as a tradesman, and maker of business deals as the master of persuasion. Also, written "marks" of words and numbers are vital in business, as is "communication," a word directly related to "commerce": the trafficking of goods and money. It's all about moving energy, words, and physical objects back and forth, between people and places, which it is the job of Hermes to facilitate.

Thus he was called "Agoraeus" ("of the market") and "Empolaios" ("engaged in traffic and commerce"). One of his fetish items was the purse, which served him as both a money pouch and a messenger bag or briefcase. He was also considered the benefactor responsible for arranging the receipt of unexpected boons such as gambling jackpots, inheritances, and other freaky fortunes, the "bringer of good luck" and "Ploutodotes" ("bringer of wealth"). All of this explains why images of him were often placed inside of people's money coffers and purses, as the Knights Templar did with images of Baphomet.

However, his most important piece of equipment was his snake-wrapped magic wand, the caduceus, identifying him as the chief of sorcerers and alchemists. With it he could open up a portal to the underworld and reanimate a dead body by reuniting it with its soul. He could pretty much do anything else as well. The wand was actually called the "Porta" in some cases. It was originally a stick with a figure 8 or infinity sign on top. Later the snakes were placed on the stick and arranged in the same configuration.

This image of the caduceus (the wand with dual serpents) seems connected to the story of Tiresias. According to Hyginus (a Latin author from around the time of Christ known for compiling Greek myths in his *Hygini Fabulae*), Tiresias was a prophet of Apollo in the court of Cadmus in Thebes. He was blind. One day when he was walking on Mount Cyllene in the Peloponnese, he came across a pair of snakes having sex. He disrespectfully hit them with his staff. This angered Hera, who punished him by turning him into a woman. Seven years later, the female Tiresias came upon snakes having sex once again. This time, she trampled them, which resulted in her being turned back into a man.

Several interesting associations come up in regard to the story of Tiresias. For one thing, the idea of a staff acting as an instrument of *coitus interruptus*, preventing the two snakes from mating, brings to mind the story of the demons Lilith and Samael, once a hermaphroditic being, now separated and segregated by God himself to prevent their unholy union. For another thing, Hyginus also brings up a similar story about Hermes. He said that while the god was traveling through Arcadia, he saw two snakes fighting, and used his staff to split them apart. He then prophesied that his staff would be used to bring peace from that moment forward.

Another important detail that comes to mind is the fact that the very word "hermaphrodite" comes from the name of the child that Hermes purportedly had with the goddess Aphrodite. Ovid wrote that their son was united permanently with the nymph Salmacis at her prayerful request, as she was in love with the boy and never wanted to part from him. From that point on, Hermaphroditus became a patron of marriage, as well as that of a certain sex cult operating in Cyprus in the seventh century BC (according to Yulia Ustinova's *The Supreme Gods of the Bosporan Kingdom*).

Edith Hamilton, in her collection of Greek myths published in 1940 (*Mythology: Timeless Tales of Gods and Heroes*), says of Hermes that "He appears oftener in the tales of mythology than any other god." This makes sense if you consider the fact that Hermes was the messenger and patron of writing, used by the gods on Olympus to bring messages to people on Earth. He was also the author of all wisdom, including poetry, philosophy, science and history. He would have thus been invoked to bring inspiration from the divine realm by anyone authoring a chronicle, a collection of myths, an epic poem, or a play. As the messenger, it is not hard to believe that he would have told the tale to those writing it down in such a way as to make him appear as the central figure.

Hermes was seen very much as a teacher and a mentor to those who invoked him. As such he was the grand "initiator," particularly of boys turning into young men. According to David Brooks Dodd's *Initiation in Ancient Greek Rituals and Narratives*, this is also related to Hermes' role as the lord of boundary crossings (such as passing from one age group or grade to the next, as well as his being traditionally called as a divine witness during the taking of oaths. He was invoked during initiation rites for young soldiers and hunters as well as for athletic youth training groups connected to the gymnasium, of which he was the patron. His feast time, called the "Hermaea," which started being celebrated at least as far back as the fourth-to-sixth century BC, was restricted to young boys only and involved athletic games. So it seems that Hermes was the original youth counselor and coach to pubescent males growing up in classical times.

These of course were the sort of initiation rites that most male citizens would have gone through. However, Hermes was also the patron of other, more arcane initiations. As Marie-Luise von Franz wrote in *Projection and Re-Collection in Jungian Psychology*, an astrological document from the third century BC, written for King Nechopso by a priest named Petosiris, states that Hermes is the teacher of secret wisdom, which:

> . . . can be experienced only in a state of ecstasy. This wisdom appears to the prophet as a 'voice' wrapped in a dark garment. As the follower prays, this voice points out to him the paths of the celestial bodies in the universe and reveals to him the wisdom of the cosmos.

This of course makes sense when you consider that, as the guardian of boundaries, one of Hermes' duties was to guide dead souls to the underworld, and those of the sleeping to the land of dreams. This earned him the epithet *psychopompus*: the one who guides the psyche. It follows, then, that the spirit of Hermes would also guide souls reaching for enlightenment from the realms beyond.

As it came to pass, that is what Hermes is currently most well-known for. But rather than being remembered as merely a nebulous spirit, Hermes came to be regarded as a flesh-and-blood person who ruled as a king and brought civilization to the rude masses over which he ruled. In this guise, he became known as Hermes Trismegistus: the "Thrice-Greatest." Alchemists claimed him as their patron, using the Caduceus as their symbol. Fittingly, the substance most quintessential to the transformation of elements in alchemy is mercury (a.k.a. "quicksilver"), named after the Roman name for this fleet-footed god with winged sandals. But how these associations came about is a story in itself.

Chapter 4: The Three Hermeses

The vice of ignorance floods the whole earth and utterly destroys the soul shut up in the body, preventing it from anchoring in the havens of deliverance. Surely you will not sink into this great flood? Those of you who can will take the ebb and gain the haven of deliverance and anchor there. Then, seek a guide to take you by the hand and lead you to the portals of knowledge.

—Hermes Trismegistus, *Corpus Hermeticum* VII

In Egypt, the god in the pantheon who most resembled the Greek Hermes and the Roman Mercury was Thoth. He was the inventor of the stylus, as well as all alphabets and other forms of writing. He was also the patron and initiator of priests into the closely-connected craft of magic. As such, under the Ptolemaic dynasty (the last royal family of ancient Egypt, who ruled from 305 to 30 BC, during the Hellenistic period), Hermes and Thoth became combined into the hyphenated entity of "Thoth-Hermes." Then the legend grew from there. As Garth Fowden writes in *The Egyptian Hermes*, *The Greek Magical Papyri* came to "present the new syncretistic Hermes as a cosmic power, creator of heaven and earth and almighty world-ruler."

Sometime between then and the second or third century AD (during which time, Egypt went from being in the Greek Hellenic empire into the hands of the Romans), certain works published in Egypt began to be attributed to Hermes as a *prophet*. This continued throughout the next four centuries as well, as the Roman Empire gave way to Byzantium and everyone began to (ostensibly) convert to

The Three Hermeses 109

Christianity (until vanquished by Islamic armies in 642). During this time of religious and philosophical "syncretism," as it has come to be called (influenced by the diverse intellectual milieu of Alexandria), mystic forms of Christianity, Judaism and paganism, along with Persian cults, mixed with the doctrines of classical Greek Philosophers like Plato, Aristotle, and even Pythagoras. Plato had already questioned whether or not Thoth was a deified human rather than an immortal god. Now Hermes came to be thought of as one of the philosophers, in the same camp as the aforementioned, and yet more than that as well.

Already there were a few works written about or attributed to Hermes that are now considered part of the broad category of "Hermetica." These include fragments (assembled about 500 AD) that were published in John of Stobi's *Anthologium* and three Coptic texts that were part of the Nag Hammadi library discovered in 1945 in Egypt. There were also several magical, astrological, and alchemical texts from this time, attributed to Hermes (such as *Liber Hermetis*, *The Picatrix*, and *The Emerald Tablets*).

The Picatrix (actually titled *Ghayat al-Hakim*, or *Goal of the Wise*) was an Arabic work that talked about the concept of a "Hermetic Man": one who, through training and practice in controlling the powers of the planets and stars, could become "the magus, the sage, the master of Heaven and Earth." This was possible, it posited, due to the notion that man contained within his own body a microcosm of the universe. Thus through the manipulation of his own mind and body he would purportedly effect the outer world correspondingly, via what anthropologist James Frazer has called "sympathetic magic." The name notion was inherent in the alchemical formula cryptically laid out in the *Emerald Tablet*, which described a process for uniting the powers of the reflective "above" and "below" realms of man and macrocosm. "As above, so below" has become the most quoted maxim from this text.

However, it was only later that the full figure emerged of the philosopher-king "Hermes Trismegistus"—the latter term generally interpreted to mean "thrice-greatest," or "triplicate in wisdom" when it was written in Arabic (*al-mutallat bi-l-hikma*). According to Kevin van Bladel, the title is thought to be derived from an older Egyptian epithet of Thoth as the "greatest and greatest great god." References to Trismegistus can be traced back to the earliest known texts of Christian philosophy from the second and third centuries.

These were mostly written either by Christian authors seeking antecedents for their new world-view with the wisdom of ancient "pagan philosophers" (like Plato and Aristotle), or else arguing against and distinguishing Christian thought from these older systems. Christian theologian Tertullian, writing during this time, called Hermes "the master of all natural philosophers." Just at the start of the fourth century, Arnobius, another Christian author, argued against the pagan philosophies of "Mercurius" (the Latin name for Hermes), among others. In the seventh century, Jacob of Edessa's *Hexameron* proclaimed that Hermes' philosophy was compatible with Christianity. As Kevin van Bladel writes: ". . . Hermes was considered a bearer of a primordial philosophy more ancient and closer to God than that of Plato."

However, when most writers talk about the "Hermetica" today, they are usually referring more specifically to a collection of philosophical dialogues between Hermes the philosopher-king and his disciples, most notably "Asclepius" (named after the Greek god of medicine), "King

Ammon," and Hermes' "son," named "Tat." (Whether there is any connection between the names "Tat" and "Thoth" is unknown.) These writings were obtained as part of a collection of Greek texts by a monk named Leonardo in 1460. They were brought to patron of the Renaissance Cosimo de Medici and translated by Marsilio Ficino, then published in Latin in 1471.

The Corpus Hermeticum was thought at this time to represent a "primordial philosophy" from before the Flood, or at least from Moses' time. In 1614, Isaac Casaubon proved they were derived from the early Christian era, but by that time the Latin version had already gone through twenty-five editions, with a considerable amount of influence on the philosophy of the day. Garth Fowden summarized the view of the universe purported in the *Corpus* in his book *The Egyptian Hermes* as:

> God is one . . . the sun, which is the demiurge around which revolve the eight spheres of the fixed stars, the planets and the earth. From these spheres depend the daemons, and from the daemons Man. . . .

Let us now shift our focus from the Greek Hermetica that was translated into Latin at the time of the Renaissance to the considerable number of Hermetic texts (that is, material written about and/or attributed to Hermes) in the Arabic language. Some of these were translated from the Greek originals, but many of them came as texts written in Middle Persian. Only recently has any of this material been properly catalogued and analyzed, such as the mammoth work done on the subject by Kevin van Bladel in his book *The Arabic Hermes: From Pagan Sage to Prophet of Science*. (Most of the Arabic material, as the author points out, has yet to be studied at all by modern scholars). These works had a hand in the transformation and magnification of the image of Hermes Trismegistus that eventually emerged from the evolutionary process of history. As Van Bladel states:

> Hermes is cited as an ancient authority already in the eighth century in some of the earliest known Arabic scientific works, the writings of Iranian court astrologers of the Abbasids. In the ninth century, Hermes came to be considered in Arabic literature as not just an ancient scientific authority, but an antediluvian prophet whose revelation formed the very beginnings of science. His works were therefore thought to have been transmitted from the extremely distant past. . . . The European concept of Hermes Trismegistus as a very ancient sage was derived from Arabic tradition as well as from the Church Fathers.

But well before that, during the start of the Sassanid dynasty (the last pre-Islamic Iranian/Persian empire, which ruled from 224-651 AD), a translation of ancient Iranian writings was commenced that included works supposedly written by "Hermes the Babylonian, who had been king over Egypt." This perhaps accords with the references made in the first century AD text *Carmen Astrologicum* by Dorotheus (originally written in Greek, then translated into Middle Persian before ultimately surviving only in Arabic), which mentions both "Hermes Trismegistus, King of Egypt," and a "Babylonian Hermes." At that time, the territory known as "Babylon" was part of the Persian Empire.

It would seem that the Persians had their own tradition of Hermes, which was influenced by the original Greek Hermetica, but which was also uniquely added to by them. It formed part of the basis for the traditions later proliferated in Arabic-language works. As Van Bladel put it:

What is certain is that the earliest appearance of Hermes in Arabic, in the eighth century, is from the Middle Persian tradition, not the Greek.

These traditions include the ones reflected in the *Kitab an-Nhmt'n*, translated into Arabic by Ibn Nawbaht. This text tells a story where a panel of twelve scholars corresponding to the houses of the zodiac is appointed by a tyrannical king to help govern the people from a group of twelve citadels situated in Iraq. When eventually their rule was rejected by the people, the sages scattered, and found new lands to rule over. One of these sages was Hermes. As it states:

> He was among them one of the most perfect in intellect, most accurate in knowledge, and most subtle in investigation. He went down to the land of Egypt and ruled its people as king, civilized it, improved the conditions of its inhabitants, and revealed his knowledge there.

Indeed, the legend of Hermes was well-known in Iraq during Sasanian times. A magical amulet found in Nippur and dated from this time is dedicated to "Hermes, Lord of the Universe."

When most scholars think of Arabic and Hermetics, they think of Harran, a city once in Upper Mesopotamia, the remains of which are now in Turkey. This is because, as Van Bladel put it, "they are the only special group credited with possessing works attributed to Hermes and transmitting them into Arabic." The Abbasid caliph Al-Ma'Mun (from 813 -833), demanded that the inhabitants of the city either claim themselves as one of the "People of the Book" or convert to Islam. Non-Islamic "People of the Book" included all Torah-based Abrahamic religions (such as Christianity and Judaism), as well as a group mysteriously referred to in the

114 *Chapter 4*

Koran as the "Sabians." It is implied that the latter group might not be strictly monotheists, but are still close enough in their beliefs to be part of the family. Instead of being forced to submit to conversion, People of the Book simply submitted to a social status called "dhimmitude," which involved paying a special tax. Other terms sometimes applied in Islamic Arabic texts to the "Sabians" mentioned in *The Koran* are "Magi" and "Hanifa." Seemingly in order to avoid religious persecution, the people of Harran were declared "Sabians" and were spared.

So what exactly was the religion of the Harranians? This is a problem that Van Bladel decided to take up for himself, as, shortly after this Sabian declaration, the Harranians also began to proclaim that the prophet of their religion was none other than Hermes. This claim has been taken at face value, so that through the years, much has been written about the role of the Harranians in the spread of Hermeticism. Van Bladel has taken a critical view of this, and so has taken pains to show exactly what association if any the Harranians actually had with Hermes, and how these "Hermetic" traditions clashed with what is considered today "Hermetic" doctrine.

Author Michel Tardieu has written that from the sixth to tenth centuries, a Platonic academy was there, founded by Hellenic philosophers and then later maintained by Harranian Sabians. Scholar Jan Hjarpe also says that later a group of Harranian Neoplatonists moved to Baghdad. They were headed by Tabit ibn Qurra, an astronomer and translator attached to the court of Abbasid Caliph al-Mu'tadid. He translated many Greek scientific and philosophical works into Arabic. Hjarpe has suggested that what is thought of as the "Hermetic doctrines of the pagan Sabians of Harran" were actually the beliefs of this one family and their followers. Writer Isetraut Hadot purported that by this time, the Harranian form of "Platonism" had become one and the same with "Hermeticism." John Walbridge, in an article from 1998 in *The Journal of the History of Ideas* entitled "Explaining Away the Greek Gods in Islam," wrote: "It seems that the ancient moon cult of Harran had evolved into a Hermetic sect that worshipped the planets. . . ."

The notion that the Harranians worshipped the heavenly bodies is echoed repeatedly by many writers. Theodore Abu Qurrah, an Orthodox Christian Bishop living in Harran in the ninth century, stated:

> They claim that they worship the seven planets—the sun, the moon, Saturn, Mars, Jupiter, Mercury, Venus—and the twelve zodiacal houses, because they are the ones that create and govern this creation and give good fortune and prosperity in the lower world, and ill fortune and suffering. They said that their prophet in that is Hermes the Sage.

In more modern times, HE Stapleton, GL Lewis, and F. Sherwood Taylor, in their 1949 work *The Sayings of Hermes Quoted in the Ma' Al-waraqi of Ibn Umail*, said: "The influence of the star-worshipping Sabaeans of Harran, to whom Thoth-Hermes was the god of all civilizing inventions, was widespread in the Islamic world."

Another popular idea is that the Harranians were responsible for "disseminating" Hermeticism around the global Muslim *ummah* (community). Seyyed Hossein Nasr, writing in 1967's *Hermes and Hermetic Writings in the Islamic World*, had the Harranians in mind when he said: "'Hermeticism was propagated by the Sabaeans who made known to the Islamic world the writings that were attributed to Hermes." The 1968 book *The Thousands of Abu Ma'shar*

116 *Chapter 4*

by David Pingree tells us that the aforementioned account of the Babylonian Hermes from Ibn Nawbaht was influenced by "Harranians," and that the Harranians held Hermes, along with his colleague teacher, "Agathodaemon," as their "prophets."

Even Sir Walter Scott, in his English translation and commentary on *The Corpus Hermeticum*, wrote of his belief that the text of the Corpus had appeared suddenly in Constantinople after 1000 years in obscurity just after the "Sabians" (i.e., the Harranian immigrants practicing paganism) had left Baghdad under Muslim persecution. As he put it:

> Is there not something more than chance in this? It may be that one of the Sabians of Bagdad, finding that his position under Moslem rule was becoming unendurable, migrated to Constantinople, and brought in his baggage a bundle of Greek *Hermetica*—and that our *Corpus* is that bundle. . . . The Pagans of Harran almost certainly possessed the whole collection of *Hermetica* (including many documents that are not now extant) in Greek, at the time when they adopted these writings as their Scriptures, in AD 830. . . .
>
> Moreover, if we choose to indulge in further conjectures, there is nothing to prevent us from supposing that it was the arrival in Constantinople of a few such Sabian Neoplatonists from Baghdad, and the writings brought with them, that first started the revival of Platonic study.

The image of the Sabians of and from Harran that has been presented for historians to document indicates that they indulged in rituals to stellar and planetary bodies (which would seem, ostensibly, pagan), and held Hermes to be their prophet (who is spoken of as a wise sage and historical king figure but still has everything in common with the old Greek pagan deity as well). Yet they are still somehow monotheists and "People of the Book" acceptable to Muslim society. The way that Al-Mubassir ibn Tatik's *Kitab Muhtar al-hikam* (written in Fatamid Egypt) described the religion taught by Hermes certainly sounds compatible with this. As Van Bladel tells us:

> It included feasts at astrological conjunctions and at the sun's entry into a new zodiacal sign, as well as sacrificial offerings to the planets at the appropriate times. Hermes is also said to have commanded them 'to perform prayers that he stated for them in ways that he described.' On the other hand, the religious laws of Hermes given here bear close resemblance to Islamic law: they require ritual purity, abstinence from intoxication, *gihad* against the enemies of the religion, . . . and prescribe most of the punishments called *hadd* punishments in Islamic law. All this leads me to conclude that the "religion of Hermes" described here was developed and described well after the establishment of Islam and Islamic law.

Van Bladel implies that perhaps the entire misfitted conglomeration of Islam, Platonism, and star-worshipping, as well as the claiming of Hermes as a religious prophet, was concocted (originally, perhaps, by Tabit ibn Qurra, his family, and their followers) to make the Harranians' religious practices seem acceptable to their Islamic rulers. However, one very interesting detail put forward by the *Kitab Muhtar al-hikam* is the suggestion that the name "Sabian" comes from "Sab," one of the nicknames or epithets of Hermes' son, Tat, to whom many of the Hermetic discourses are addressed. This notion is echoed by Al-Masudi (tenth century historian), by Al-Mubassir (eleventh century), and by Ibn Abi Usaybia (twelfth century scholar).

The question of whether the prophet Hermes should be considered identical to the deity on the Greek pantheon, or to the Egyptian god Thoth whose name was compounded with his, seems to be a matter on which none of the authors agree. Kevin van Bladel, whilst making a distinction between the two concepts (Hermes the God and Hermes the Prophet), nonetheless acknowledges that over time one became the other in the public mind, and in the opposite order than one would expect. Normally, historians write about the "deification" of a historical figure through myth-morphing, or a leader being worshipped like a god by his people, not the other way around. But we could imagine that when Ibn Nawbaht wrote in the *Kitab an-Nhmt'n* of Hermes being one of twelve ancient ruling sages, corresponding to the twelve houses of the Zodiac, he might have been tapping into some underlying truth behind the myths of the twelve Olympic gods.

The questions becomes further complicated when we realize that in several Hermetic works, we are told that there was not just one Hermes, but three, each born to Earth at a different time in history. Generally, it breaks down to there being one who came before the Flood, one after the Flood, and one who was born in Egypt much later. Of course, there are numerous variations on this theme.

One important source is the ninth century *Book of the Thousands* from Abu Masar, the greatest astrologer in the Abbasid court of Baghdad. The book itself is no longer with us, but we can read about it from other books, such as Ibn Abi Usaybia's thirteenth century *Kitab Tabaqat al-atibba*

(The Generations of the Physicians). Here the summary of Abu Masar's Hermetic history is as follows:

> The Hermeses are three. The first of them is Hermes who was before the Flood. The significance of 'Hermes' is a title, like saying 'Caesar'. . . . The Persians named him Wiwanghan, meaning 'the Just,' in their biographies of the kings. He is the one to whose philosophy the Harranians adhere. The Persians state that his grandfather was Gayumart, that is Adam. The Hebrews state that he is Enoch, which, in Arabic, is Idris. . . . He was the first to give advance warning of the Flood, and he thought that a celestial catastrophe of fire or water would overwhelm the earth. His home was Upper Egypt; he chose that [place] and built the pyramids and cities of clay there. He feared that knowledge would pass away in the Flood, so he built the monumental temples.
> . . .

Several important notions are purported here. The first is that "Hermes" is just a title, which would solve the god/prophet conundrum as well as the questions of whether or not the "Three Hermeses" are all incarnations of the same soul (the interpretation taken by many modern Hermeticists, such as Dennis William Hauck in his book *The Emerald Tablet: Alchemy for Personal Transformation*). If we can accept that a "Hermes" is a type of teacher of fundamental scientific wisdom such as that traditionally associated with the god Hermes, then it all makes sense.

The second important idea we find here is that this first Hermes is identical to the biblical figure of Enoch, known as

Idris to the Muslims and mentioned by name in *The Koran*. (Verse 19:56-57: "And mention Idris in the Book. He was true, a prophet. We raised him to a high place.") This Hermes-Idris identification is thoroughly accepted through Islamic teachings, as we shall demonstrate, and is in no way controversial. Van Bladel says that the first Arabic-language reference to Hermes being Idris can be traced back to around 840 AD. He reckons it came from the (now lost) chronicles used as source material by the Christian historians Oanodorus and Annianus, working in Alexandria in the fifth century, since their goals were to synthesize various characters in history recorded at different times and places. The tradition that Idris was Enoch had already been established in the early eighth century by Wahb ibn Munabbin, who catalogued *isra Iliyat* ("Jewish traditions") in Arabic. He said Idris was the first to use a pen and that he received directly from God thirty scrolls of wisdom material that he was instructed to bring to humanity. Furthermore, Idris is also considered in Islamic lore to be the same as the mercurial character of the "Green Man" Al-Khadir, mentioned in the previous chapter.

The connection between Enoch and Hermes seems logical when you consider that they both are purported authors of books containing the heavenly wisdom of the stars (Hermes with his alchemical Emerald Tablet, and Enoch the author of 366 books of divine knowledge). Enoch was indeed the first to give warning of the Flood in the Judeo-Christian tradition. This is what *The First Book of Enoch* is largely all about.

However, the Judeo-Christian tradition of Enoch also purports that he is a descendant of Adam's third son Seth several generations removed. He is supposedly a completely different person from his cousin Enoch, the eldest son of

Cain with the same name, who was born after Cain's exile to Nod, and after whom Cain named the first city he built. Yet it seems to be implied by Ibn Abi Usaybia that it is the Cainite Enoch who is identified with Hermes and who warned of the Flood, because he states that the Persians call Hermes the grandson of Adam. This same genealogy of Enoch-Idris is also given by Mutahhar ibn Tahir al Maqdisi in the 966 AD. work *The Creation and the Chronicle*. Based on this evidence it can be speculated that both Enochs were originally one figure in earlier versions of the story. This would be one more piece of evidence indicating that. However, several other Arabic scholars clearly identify Idris with the Sethian Enoch, such as thirteenth-century Gregory Bar Hebraeus (a.k.a. Ibn al-'Ibri), and before him, tenth-century Abu Hatin ar-Razi, who said that "between him [Idris] and Adam were five patriarchs." Meanwhile, from a Latin translation of a Spanish translation of Al-Mubassir's sayings from the 13th century, called *Liber philosophorum moralium antiquorum*, we read:

> Hermes was born in Egypt, and he is called Hermes in Greek, Mercury in Latin, and in Hebrew, Enoch. He was the son of Jared, son of Machtalaleb, son of Quenam, son of Enoy, son of Sed, son of Adam.

"Sed," clearly, is Seth, with the rest corresponding essentially to the genealogy of the Sethian Enoch found in *Genesis*.

The third important point here is the idea that Hermes built the pyramids of Egypt, referred to here as the "monumental temples," in order to preserve the scientific wisdom he's taught for future generations after the Flood (which would, implicitly, be somehow written on the walls, encoded into the geometry, written on scrolls hidden inside, or something like that). This is a detail mentioned several times in other Arabic Hermetica. Ibn Abi Usaybia also writes that Abu Masar attributed another monument to the first Hermes. This is the "birba" temple at Ankmim in Egypt, the city of the Priapian fertility god Min. Always shown with an erect phallus, Min was identified by the Greeks with their god Pan, thus the Greek name for the city, "Panopolis." (Recall, of course, that Pan was the son of Hermes in many versions of the myth.) The ruins of this temple have yet to be excavated but it is thought by historians to have actually been built during the reign of Ramses II. However, Ibn Abi Usaybia says that Abu Masar claimed it was the first Hermes who did it. The motivation, just as alleged with the pyramids, was supposedly to preserve fundamental knowledge through the coming cataclysmic Deluge. So he "chiseled out" a mountain there:

> . . . portraying in it in carvings all the arts and their uses, and pictures of all the instruments of the artisans, indicating the features of the sciences by illustrations, out of desire thereby to preserve the sciences forever for those after him, fearing that all trace of it would perish from the world.

The same exact thing was written by Said al-Andalusi in his eleventh century text *Tabaqat al-'Umam* (*Exposition of the Generations of Nations*), but he specifies that this first Hermes was the Enoch descended from Seth, and gives his genealogy. The same details were seconded by Syriac writer Gregory Bar Hebraeus in the thirteenth century, who actually said there was only one Hermes, the Sethian Enoch. This is interesting, for Josephus wrote in *Antiquities of the Jews* that it was Seth who preserved the pre-diluvian knowledge of his father Adam by engraving the secrets on two columns, one of brick and one of stone, which were allegedly erected in a place called "Terra Seriadica."

The Three Hermeses 123

This notion of preserving knowledge through cataclysms with engraved pillars (one meant to withstand fire and the other built flood-proof) comes up repeatedly in mythology, and we find it in the lore of Freemasonry. Plato mentions Egypt as the place where the story of Atlantis was preserved, along with other ancient pre-Flood wisdom, in *Timaeus* and *Critias*. Also, in the Greek Hermetica, we read of the Egyptian goddess Isis (mistress of magic and wisdom) telling her son Horus that Hermes wrote down his extensive knowledge of the universe with hieroglyphs, which he hid for posterity.

So that, purportedly, was the legacy of the first Hermes. The job of the second Hermes was to recapture the preserved knowledge of the first Hermes and use it to rebuild human civilization. Not only that, they say this Hermes personally taught Pythagoras himself everything he knew! Note that the birth of this Hermes in Babylon probably links him up with the aforementioned "Babylonian Hermes" identified by Dorotheus in the *Carmen Astrologicum*. As the text states:

> The Second Hermes, of the people of Babylon: he lived in the city of the Chaldeans, Babylon, after the Flood in the time of Naburizbani, who was the first to build the city of Babylon after Nimrod the son of Kush. His student was Pythagoras the Arithmetician. This Hermes renewed the knowledge of medicine, philosophy, mathematics that was lost during the Flood at Babylon.

The third Hermes, as described by Ibn Abi Usaybia and Abu Masar, certainly seems less accomplished than his illustrious forebears. In fact, he almost doesn't seem to qualify for the "title" of Hermes. But what they say about him is in fact exactly the same as what all other Hermetica which purport the existence of three Hermeses tell about the third (the earliest such account being from Ibn Gulgul's tenth century work, *The Generations of the Physicians and Philosophers*). They all agree that he was born in Egypt, he taught the science of alchemy, and he wrote a book called *Poisonous Animals.* To this, Ibn Abi Usaybia simply adds: "He had a student who is known, whose name was Asclepius."

Asclepius, like Hermes, is the name of a Greek god. He was always shown carrying a staff entwined with a single serpent (just one snake shy of a Hermetic caduceus). His nickname was "the Healer" because he could resurrect the dead, and he was associated with the practice of medicine. His name was invoked in the original Hippocratic Oath. Even today the rod of Asclepius is still used as a symbol of healing by dentists and veterinarians (while regular physicians tend to use the double-snaked caduceus instead).

Consistently, Hermes has been said to have tutelary relationships with characters named Asclepius, Ammon, Agathodaemon, and Tat (a.k.a. "Sab"). Tat is usually said to be the son of one of the Hermeses. *The Book of Sothis*—attributed to the second century historian Manetho, but probably forged more than 100 years later—says that Tat is the son of the second Hermes and the grandson of Agathodaemon through his father. The Greek Hermetica talks about Tat, "Asclepius-Imouthes" and "Ptah" (another spelling of Thoth) as being the first of Hermes' "successors." The second-third century text *The Asclepius: The Perfect Discourse* calls Asclepius, Ammon, and Tat Hermes' "disciples." Gregory Bar Hebraeus agreed that Hermes was the teacher of Asclepius.

This was all presaged by Plato's *Philebus*, where he says that the Egyptian "god" Thoth taught the Egyptian "god" Ammon the craft of writing. Interestingly, it was Ammon, a ram-headed god, whom Alexander the Great claimed to be the biological son of, as revealed to him by the oracle at Siwa (the reason why Alexander was alleged to have had horns on his head). The Greek syncretists compounded Ammon's name with that of Zeus, and showed the Olympian god with ram's horns.

As for Agathodaemon, this was the name of a minor Greek deity of good fortune, as well as the name taken by the author of a third century Egyptian text on alchemy, *The Anepigraphos*. Jean Doresse, in her *Secret Books of the Egyptian Gnostics*, suggests that the basis of both the god and the alchemist Agathodaemon can be equated to none other than Seth! This is an interesting idea when you consider that, again, Hermes, allegedly Enoch, is being listed as the son of Agathodaemon, allegedly Seth, when the Bible says that the Sethian Enoch is removed from Seth by several generations, and that the other Enoch's father is Seth's brother Cain. Others, such as Dennis William Hauck, have claimed that Agathodaemon is really the god Thoth.

It is also fascinating when you consider what was written by tenth century historian Abu l-Hasan al-Masudi, following up on the notion that the Hermeses built the pyramids at Giza. He took it a step further, writing:

> One of the two pyramids is the tomb of Agathodaimon, the other one is the tomb of Hermes. Between the two 1000 years elapsed, Agathodaimon was the older one.

Could it be that the alleged "pillars of Seth" are in fact the two large pyramids themselves, one believed at one point to house the body of Agathodaemon, who is Seth (and who may well actually be the same person as his purported brother Cain), and the other covering the body of his son Hermes, who is Enoch?

The Arabic traditions of Enoch's trip to Heaven are fascinating when added and compared to the Judeo-Christian tradition of Enoch, as well as the known traditions of Hermes. According to seventh century Koranic scholar Abdallah ibn al-Abbas, the "angel of the sun" gave Idris the secret name of God. He purportedly used it to ascend to the "Fourth Heaven" (that of the sun).

Other chronicles give other interesting details. Abu Hatim ar-Razi said that God took Hermes-Idris to a high mountain in the center of the Earth, where an angel taught him astrology. Third-century historian and astrologer Manetho wrote that God took Enoch so "high" up into the heavens that he could see and actually walk upon the celestial sphere. Thus he was able to see and understand the entire system of the zodiac and the planets. *The Book of the Apple* (*Kitab at-Tuffaha*)—author unknown but ascribed erroneously to Aristotle and dated sometime before the tenth century—simply says that "Hermes" ascended to Heaven and came back, bringing down with him philosophy and other heavenly secrets from the "Noble Record" shown to him by the angels. The tenth or eleventh-century author of the Hermetic *ar-Risalaal-falakiya al-kubra* (*Great Treatise of the Spheres*) also speaks of Hermes' heavenly journey. Likewise, the Brethren of Purity, a secret society of Muslim philosophers in eighth-century Basra, Iraq, wrote in their encyclopedia of science and philosophy:

> It is related about Hermes the Triplicate in Wisdom, who is Idris the prophet—peace be upon him—that he rose to the sphere of Saturn and turned together with it for thirty years until he witnessed all the states of the heavenly sphere.

As Van Bladel points out, in the astrology system they were using at the time, Saturn was the seventh and highest of the planetary spheres. Thirty years is amount of time it takes for Saturn to travel through all of the houses of the Zodiac. This is the source of the natal astrology term "Saturn's return" (a thirty-year cyclical pattern that people purportedly experience throughout their lives).

Incidentally, Van Bladel seems to think that after Hermes became identified with Enoch and assumed his biography, Hermes-Enoch-Idris' trip to heaven began to be taken as the method by which he learned astrology. This accords with other traditions that Enoch was the first astrologer. One source of these is third century Syrian philosopher Bar Daysan, who credited Enoch with inventing the "Chaldean art" of astrology himself. This is perfectly in line with Christian tradition. In *The Second Book of Enoch* 44:5, Enoch makes the following statement about himself:

> I have arranged the whole year. And from the year I calculated the months, and from the months I have ticked off the days, and from the day I have ticked off the hours. I, I have measured and noted the hours. And I have distinguished every seed on the earth, and every measure and every righteous scale. I have measured and recorded them.

Incidentally, *The Second Book of Enoch 1.217* also shows Enoch playing the role of the judge for the "measurement" of each person at Final Judgement, much like Osiris did in the Egyptian pantheon, using the "Scales of Thoth." Here, Enoch says:

> . . . In the great judgement day every measure and weight in the market will be exposed, and each one will recognize his own measure, and in it he will

receive his reward. . . . Before humankind existed, a place of judgment, ahead of time, was prepared for them, and *scales and weights* by means of which a person will be tested.

Michael the Elder, twelfth century patriarch of the Syriac Orthodox Church, also said that Enoch was the first to bring writing into the world, presumably from Heaven, just as Hermes and Thoth are credited with doing. In Christian tradition, Enoch is said to have written a total of 366 books, just one more than the number of years he purportedly lived: 365 (also the number of days in a solar year). The closeness of these two numbers (how many books he wrote and how many days he lived) seems to be a coincidence with some sort of meaning. So too is the fact that, according to Manetho, Hermes wrote 365,000 books. Perhaps also of note is the fact that the Gnostic entity of Abraxas, a composite chimera like Baphomet, with the head of a chicken and snakes for legs, is taken as a representation of the Demiurge and, for some reason, is associated with the number 365. We will discuss this more in a later chapter.

Moving along, we find another account of Hermes' heavenly journey in *The Book of the Secrets of Creation* (*Kitab Sirr al-haliqa*), written in Arabic between 813 and 833 AD and falsely attributed to the authorship of Apollonius of Tyana (a.k.a. Balinas). This was the name of a Cappadocian mystic who lived at the time of Christ and had a surprisingly similar biography, including a career of healing the sick, resurrecting the dead, casting out demons, and the claim of his followers that he ascended to Heaven bodily at the end of his life. The book purports to tell the story of how, as a youth, Apollonius discovered the tomb of Hermes in a secret underground chamber, and in it the Emerald Tablet, with its unsurpassed alchemical mysteries inscribed upon it. It also describes what seems to be the story of Hermes rising to Heaven, but at the same time it resembles a description of a substance being transmuted from a lower, denser matter into the higher, subtler form of the Philosopher's Stone. In this sense, Hermes seems to be equated with the transmuted substance itself.

The story of Apollonius, and how he allegedly used the tablets wisdom to perform miracles, is told in great detail in *The Life of Apollonius of Tyana* by second to third-century Greek Sophist Flavius Philostratus. Dennis William Hauck's *The Emerald Tablet: Alchemy for Personal Transformation* gives a shortened version (also drawing from other, more imaginative modern sources such as twentieth-century Theosophist GRS Mead). Hauck claims that Apollonius *was himself* the Third Hermes, on unclear authority.

However, Ibn Nubata, in his eighth-century *Commentary on the Epistle of Ibn Zaydun*, does say that Apollonius was Hermes' student, and traveled with him personally. He also says that "Asclepius" was another name for Apollonius. As for which of the three Hermeses Apollonius was apprenticed to, Ibn Nubata quotes varying sources that name each of the three. None of his sources seem to agree on that detail. He didn't say that Apollonius was a "Hermes," but he did say, "The Sabians claim that Asclepius had the prophethood after" his teacher, as though he was in the same line of "apostolic succession" as the Hermeses. He also said people thought Apollonius was an angel or descended from angels, that he was taken to Heaven "on a pillar of light" at the end of his life, and that "Euclid traced his ancestry to him."

The issue of the alleged "Hermeticism" of the Sabians of Harran, as discussed previously, has been a *cause celebre* among modern multiculturalist occultists and other writers looking to pointing out contributions from any seemingly

"Islamic" source to the history of humanity in general and Western mysticism (largely based on Hermetics) in particular. This cause has also been embraced by certain authors with Islamic backgrounds looking to put a pleasant face on the often harsh fundamentalist image of the religion's traditions by pointing out the heterodox variety of belief systems that have operated under the umbrella of "Islam" (often under threat of persecution from fundamentalists). Seyyed Hossein Nasr wrote in 1967 that, "In the Muslim world, Hermeticism must be considered as one of the most important factors which aided in the construction of the Muslim worldview." Complaining about the desperate reaching on some of the commentators about this subject, Kevin van Bladel has said:

> In the context of Arabic literature, modern scholars generally use the word Hermetic to refer not just to works associated with the name Hermes, but also to all manner of works with allegedly "Gnostic," "Neoplatonic," "Neopythagorean," or "esoteric" tendencies or practically any early Arabic pseudepigraph. Above all, it is used to refer to the beliefs of the Sabians of Harran.

As we have already discussed more briefly above, in order to be accepted by Islamic rulers, the Harranians adopted the moniker "Sabian" from *The Koran* to claim a protected status in their society. Literature was circulated which purported that they were followers of a prophet named Hermes, and that his teachings were compatible with Islam. As we demonstrated earlier, this may have begun with the family of Harranian Tabit ibn Qurra, who immigrated to Baghdad. Ninth century philosopher Ysaf al-Kindi quoted from a book he had access to called *Chapters of Hermes on the Doctrine of Monotheism, which he wrote for his son most expertly*. The word "At-tawhid," translated here as "monotheism," is most often used to indicate Muslim belief specifically. This idea of Hermes as a proto-Islamic prophet had become the accepted norm. Then in the thirteenth century, Al-Mubassir ibn Fatik's *Liber philosophorum moralium antiquorum* reported the following:

> Hermes left Egypt and went around the whole world. . . . In seventy-two languages he called the people of the entire earth's population to worship the Creator, the Mighty and High. God granted him wisdom so that he spoke to them in their different languages, taught them and educated them. He built for them a hundred and eight great cities, the smallest of which is Edessa. He was the first who discovered astrology, and he established for each region a model of religious practice for them to follow which corresponded to their views. Kings were his servants, and the whole earth's population and the population of the islands in the seas obeyed him.

Note that the number of cities be built (108) corresponds with the number of suitors Penelope had in *The Odyssey*, who, in an alternate version of the story, all combined their semen in her womb to conceive the god Pan, elsewhere thought to be a son of Hermes the god. The next paragraph of *Liber philosophorum* makes the worship of the creator that *this* Hermes taught seem very Islamic indeed:

> He preached God's judgment, belief in God's unity, mankind's worship [of God], . . . and saving souls from punishment. He incited [people] to abstain piously from this world, to act justly, and to seek

salvation in the next world. He commanded them to perform prayers that he stated for them in manners that he explained to them, and to fast on recognized days of each month, to undertake holy war (jihad) against the enemies of the religion, and to give charity from [their] possessions and to assist the weak with it. He bound them with oaths of ritual purity from pollutants, menstruation, and touching the dead. He ordered them to forbid eating pig, ass, camel, dog, and other foods. He forbade intoxication from every type of beverage, and stated this in the most severe terms.

Al-Mubassir goes on to add that at one point, everyone in the world converted to this religion, which was called *din al-qayyima* ("the right religion"), and that they prayed to the south along the line of the meridian. As Van Bladel notes, "We encounter here again the notion that the religion of Hermes was the universal, primordial religion." The phrase *din al-qayyima* comes from *The Koran*, Sura 98, Verses two through five, where it says that this doctrine would be preached by:

> . . . an apostle from God reciting purified scrolls in which are right scriptures. Those who received the book went their separate ways only after the clear proof came to them. They were ordered only to worship God, sincerely practicing his religion as hunafa, and to practice prayer and to bring alms. That is the right religion. . . .

The implication in *The Koran* is that Mohammed learned his teachings from divinely-written scrolls, just as *The Book of the Apple* says Enoch-Idris-Hermes learned his wisdom from reading the "Noble Record" in Heaven. Al-Mubassir's implication is that the doctrine taught by Hermes is the

The Three Hermeses 133

same one found by Mohammed on the purified scrolls, or that the apostle referred to in Sura 98 is not Mohammed but Hermes.

In *The History of Learned Men* from twelve to thirteenth century Egyptian scholar Ibn al Qifti, a document is duplicated called *Testament of Ammon*, which shows Hermes giving advice to Ammon on how to be a just and effective king. It makes him into a defender of a rather harsh form of Islamic sharia (law).

> . . . Take care not to delay battle and holy war (*jihad*) against those who do not believe in God—His name is most high—and those who do not follow my custom and my law (*sunnati wa-sari'ati*), because of your desire that they enter into obedience to God the Exalted. . . . Whoever defames your rule, decapitate him and make it known so that others will beware. Whoever steals, cut off his hand. Who robs on a path, cut off his head and crucify him so that news of it spreads and your roads be safe. Whoever is found with a male like himself, fornicating with him, must be burned in fire. Whoever is found with a woman committing adultery with her, strike him with fifty lashes and stone the woman with a hundred stones after establishing sure proof of it.

Van Bladel, who believes this text was written by a Harranian Sabian trying to "argue for the legitimacy of his religion" among Muslims, writes sneeringly:

> Here we seem to have found at last an example of the "Hermeticism" of the Harranians in Baghdad so much speculated about. Instead of cosmic

sympathies and revelatory initiations, we find corporal punishments, holy war. . . .

These aren't the only sources to make Hermes seem somewhat less than politically correct by modern standards. Ninth to tenth-century Iranian writer Al-Tha'alibi says that Hermes "was the first to make use of weapons, make war and capture people as slaves." It seems that these texts' authors were eager to present Hermes as the primordial prophet, king, and lawgiver, whose students (the Harranian Sabians who attended court in Baghdad) were fit to be advisors to kings, like Aristotle had been to Alexander. Therefore the type of law he was seen as promoting was whatever Islamic potentates of the day wanted to hear, to make them feel like they were doing it right. Thus the declarations quoted above were cobbled together with the sayings of other known philosophers, but here all attributed to Hermes, in order to establish his wisdom *bona fides*.

When the Neoplatonic *Enneads of Plotinus, IV-VI* were translated into Arabic in the ninth century, a great deal of other material was interpolated into it, and it was given a new name which translates to *The Theology of Aristotle*. In it, Aristotle himself is presented as having been influenced by the teachings of Hermes. Also, in the tenth century *Kitab at-Tuffaha*, Aristotle is shown recommending the words of Hermes to his students while on his deathbed. There are even Arabic books on talismanic magic ascribed (erroneously, of course) to Aristotle (but in reality written by a Harranian Sabian), in which the author cites the wisdom of Hermes on the subject of occult practice. (According to Van Bladel, Hermes was more well-known in Arabic-speaking lands as the source of books on talismanic magic, astrology and alchemy, rather than *The Corpus Hermeticum* and other books of mysticism that made him famous in Europe.)

Another text called *As-Siyasa al-ammiya* shows Alexander quoting Hermes to Aristotle the equivalent of the well-known Hermetic maxim "As above, so below." As he put it:

> Hermes the preeminent in knowledge spoke well when he said, "Man is a microcosm and the celestial sphere is the macrocosm."

In a similar vein, twelfth century Persian poet Nizami, in his *Iqbal-nama*, shows Hermes appearing before Alexander on a panel of sages that includes Aristotle, Plato, and Socrates. Later in the same work, a group of seventy Greek philosophers becomes jealous of Hermes' wisdom, and all agree to ignore him, for which he curses them with being frozen in place until they die (like the effect of the deadly gaze of Medusa or Al-Ghul).

Other Arabic sources also claimed Hermes as the ultimate historic source for the fount of philosophy. Ninth-century historian As-Masudi wrote that Pythagoras and Plato got their knowledge from Hermes by reading his tablets. Tenth to eleventh-century philosopher Ibn al-Haytam, whilst arguing in favor of Greek philosophy, said that their sages were "followers" of the "prophet" Hermes-Idris, whom he credited with the revelation of astrology and math as well. Also, the twelfth century Andalusian thinkers Ibn Bagga and Yahuda ha-Levi wrote that Hermes had achieved a special relationship with something called the "Active Intellect," a divine emanation that they believed, as Van Bladel describes it, "gave rise to the celestial spheres, [and] was regarded as the cause of all human understanding, frequently described by the visual metaphor of light. . . ." They said that Hermes, along with Socrates, Plato, Aristotle, and Asclepius, had attained the level of "perfect human," and thus were able to connect with the Active Intellect.

However erroneous and deceptive its origins are, this material influenced the development of Islamic theology. The Ismaili sect (from which the Assassins arose) was, by the ninth century, according to Van Bladel, "the first organized group with an official doctrine about Hermes" as a legitimate prophet. However, the fourth century poet Ephraem from Syria had already written that the Persian religion of Manicheanism embraced Hermes as a prophet, along with Jesus and Plato.

In the twelfth century, Sihabdin Yahya as-Suhrawardi, founder of the "Israqi" school of thought and associated today with the mystical Islamic movement broadly known as "Sufism," claimed to be continuing the philosophical tradition of Hermes, as, he purported, Plato, Empedocles, and Agathodaemon had done before him. He said that Hermes gained his wisdom because he had the power to "doff his body and rise up" to "the higher world." This tradition of citing Hermes as a philosophical ancestor was continued by the thirteenth century Sufi writers Ibn Sabin and As-Sustari as well.

What became known as "Hermeticism" seems to have been cooked in the same crucible as what became known as "Gnosticism," and the two terms (while significantly different) are often associated with each other. Indeed, there is quite a bit of overlap. The Gnostic idea that a Demiurge apart from the highest deity created the material world is common in many writings attributed to Hermes. The first discourse of *The Corpus Hermeticum*, entitled "Poimandres," describes creation thusly:

> The mind who is god, being androgyne and existing as life and light, by speaking gave birth to a second mind, a craftsman, who, as god of fire and spirit, crafted seven governors; they encompass the

The Three Hermeses 137

sensible world in circles, and their government is called fate.

This would go along with As-Sarahsi's description of the Harranian religion, as paraphrased by Van Bladel, "that the Sabians sacrificed to the planets, and *not* to the Creator, because the planets, and not god directly, actually administered the world." Similar notions are expressed in the aforementioned magical text *The Book of Nabathean Agriculture*. There, instructions are given to pray to idols of the planets (what Gnostics viewed as the "archontic powers,"), whilst still recognizing the supremacy of the One God, because it is the planets who actually manage the day-to-day matters of the universe, and whose job it is to listen to such prayers. One gets the idea that there is a call queue directing calls to customer service representatives (the planets), which can, at times, be escalated to the supervisor (the Demiurge), but almost nobody ever speaks to the company owner, the Father of All, who just sits in his office alone being God.

The third to fourth century Gnostic-Hermetic alchemist Zosimos of Panopolis made explicit references to a book supposedly written by Hermes called *Physika*, which is lost to us now. It deals with the same story as *The First Book of Enoch*, regarding fallen angels having intercourse with women. Ninth-century Byzantine historian George Synkellos also wrote about this in his *Ecloga Chronographica*:

> It is stated in the holy scriptures or books, dear lady, that there exists a race of daimons who have commerce with women. Hermes made mention of them in his *Physika*; in fact almost the entire work, openly and secretly, alludes to them. It is related in the ancient and divine scriptures that certain angels lusted for women, and descending from the

heavens, they taught them all the arts of nature. On account of this, says the scripture, they offended god, and now live outside heaven—because they taught to men all the evil arts which are of no advantage to the soul.

Is it possible that this *Physika* was actually *The First Book of Enoch* itself? It would make sense, considering that Hermes is purportedly the same person as Enoch, the author and main character of that book, which appears to have the same subject matter as the now lost *Physika* of Hermes. Also note that in the story of *The First Book of Enoch*, the mountain which the angels land on when they come to Earth, and upon which they make their pact together to breed with humans, is called "Mount Hermon." The name is usually translated "Place of the Curse," but it is worth considering that it might have somehow been based on the name of Hermes. Since his name is thought to refer to "boundary-posts" (and the crossing of them), perhaps both interpretations are correct, as Mount Hermon is where the angels crossed their God-ordained boundaries and defiled themselves as well as the Earth.

We note here that the Harranian Sabians are not the only group to officially take on the label of, and be officially recognized as, the Sabians of *The Koran*. The Mandaeans of Iraq have also identified themselves as such. For them, they claim that the name actually applies to them because of their their baptismal rite, called "Seboghatullah"— "immersion in the divine mystery" which seems very similar in meaning to "Baptism of Wisdom." While the Mandaeans are sometimes described as a "quasi-Islamic" sect, they are also commonly, and more accurately, described as a Gnostic religion—one of the few surviving Gnostic faiths in the world. Interestingly, the word "Hanif" is sometimes used to denote a "Sabian" in the Islamic world. But Hanif is also a common first name in Muslim lands, and is listed in books of baby names as a variation of "John." As it turns out, Mandaeans take as their chief prophet not Mohammed, but John the Baptist, who they credit with starting having started their group in the first place. This, as we shall see, is very significant. But before we explore these topics, let us learn a bit more about Gnosticism, and the wisdom goddess Sophia for whom, it is said, the name of Baphomet stands as a cryptic code.

Chapter 5: Divine Knowledge

And it happened this way because of the will of God that men be better than the gods, since, indeed, the gods are immortal, but men alone are both immortal and mortal. Therefore, man has become akin to the gods, and they know the affairs of each other with certainty. The gods know the things of men, and men know the things of the gods. And I am speaking about men, Asclepius, who have attained learning and knowledge. But (about) those who are more vain than these, it is not fitting that we say anything base, since we are divine and are introducing holy matters.

—*Asclepius* 21-29

There is no simple definition of Gnosticism. Scholars have debated over it for years. Few religions are built upon such a provocative and complex mythos. Discovered by accident in the desert sands of Egypt, the Nag Hammadi Library has given religious scholars the world over a glimpse into the ideology of this faith that has long been mysterious and misunderstood. Prior to 1945, the only things we knew about Gnosticism came from their sworn enemies in the Christian clergy. Although some of the Gnostic gospels found in the Nag Hammadi were among the earliest Christian texts, all were banned from the orthodox canon that would become the sanitized New Testament from the fourth century.

When studied objectively, Gnostic myth actually tells us a great deal about the social views of its time, as well as the evolution of the early Christian Church. It must also be said that not all of the texts found at Nag Hammadi are even Gnostic and many of them are quite orthodox (although an earlier variant of Christian orthodoxy). The scholar Robert M. Price gives us a brief history on the true significance of the Nag Hammadi in his article "A Survey on Some Recent Books on Gnosticism":

> Scraps used for binding the Nag Hammadi codices attest that the work was done by the monks of St. Pachomius. We can ascertain the precise circumstances in which the texts were hidden away: the Festal Letter of Athanasius of Alexandria in 367 would have spelled trouble for the brethren of St. Pachomius with their exotic library. Indeed, it must have been just such currency of "heretical" apocrypha that led Athanasius to frame his canon list in the first place! When we read the Nag Hammadi texts we are no doubt reading the very books Athanasius wanted to exclude! The texts tend to confirm all the major theories as to Gnostic roots. That Gnosticism is Platonic is implied by the fragment of the Republic discovered there. Reitzenstein's claim of interchangeability between Gnosis and the Hermetic Mysticism is confirmed by the presence of the Asklepios and other Hermetica at Nag Hammadi.

While there are Gnostic religious doctrines, there really is not one single monolithic Gnostic religion. The term refers to a set of specific metaphysical doctrines on spirituality. This peculiar spiritual orientation arose in Egypt around the time of Jesus' birth. Gnostics purported to engage in direct contact with a transcendent God through initiatory rites, embracing the belief that an inner spark or seed of divinity exists inside man which is consubstantial with God. They also had a transgressive take on scripture (particularly the Old Testament), the pagan gods, and a philosophical attitude taken from the varied religious and social environment of Late Antiquity. Carl Jung, as quoted by Murray Stein in *Jung on Christianity*, said:

> The central ideas of Christianity are rooted in Gnostic philosophy, which, in accordance with psychological laws, simply *had* to grow up at a time when the classical religions had become obsolete. It was found on the perception of symbols thrown up by the unconscious individuation process which always sets in when the collective dominants of human life fall into decay. At such a time there is bound to be a considerable number of individuals who are possessed by archetypes of a numinous nature that forced their way to the surface in order to form new dominants.

As stated above, the term "Gnosticism" has become something of a source of contention in academic circles. Some scholars have still held to the term as a useful category while others desire to eschew it altogether. Michael Allen Williams wrote in *Rethinking Gnosticism*, that the category should be entirely dismantled. The words "Gnostic" isn't found at all in any of the codices found in Nag Hammadi, Egypt in 1945. The Church Father Irenaeus uses the word very loosely and inconsistently. Tertullian, another Church father and Latin lawyer from Carthage, doesn't use it at all in his writings against the heretics.

When all the statements are sorted out, it appears that perhaps it was the Carpocratians who called themselves "Gnostic" originally, whereas none of the other heretics did. On the other hand, all the heretical sects did speak of "Gnosis," and they do share a common set of ideas. Today, we use the term in reference to their commonly shared doctrine of seeking a personal revelation from the highest god.

The Gnostics viewed man as contradictory and somewhat schizophrenic. In this perspective, man is essentially a dual being, made up of both *pneumatic* (spiritual) and *hylic* (material) essences. We see in *The Apocryphon of John* that Adam is described as being created through angels and demons working together to construct his body. In *The Trimorphic Protennoia*, it is the creator-god of *Genesis*, described as a "great demon," who creates the body of man, while his spirit is given by a higher being. In *On the Origin of the World*, it says that man was created "when Sophia let fall a droplet of light" which "flowed onto the water, and immediately a human being appeared...." Yet, while the origins of mankind vary in the Gnostic mythos, it is generally agreed that the spirit is seen as the "pearl of great price," while the flesh was seen as worthless and degenerate. This differs from the modern Christian view that both the soul and flesh are fallen but yet essentially good, created in the image of God.

Just as the creation of fleshly man is seen as a negative thing in Gnosticism, so is the material cosmos. *The Gospel of Philip* tells us that matter "came into being through an error." These are most often the error of the lesser god of *Genesis* or of various lesser beings (the nefarious "Archons"). For one to rise above this error, one must have knowledge, for as *The Second Treatise of the Great Seth* put it:

> ... They did not know the Knowledge of the Greatness, that it is from above and (from) a fountain of truth, and that it is not from slavery and jealousy, fear and love of worldly matter.

In *The Apocryphon of John*, the Lord (being the resurrected Jesus Christ) tells us that the dead and ignorant spirit after death is always in the clutches of the "Authorities" (lesser gods) until it has received this "divine, experiential knowledge":

> And after it comes out of (the body), it is handed over to the authorities, who came into being through the archon, and they bind it with chains and cast it into prison, and consort with it until it is liberated from the forgetfulness and acquires knowledge. And if thus it becomes perfect, it is saved.

The "Gnosis" that these practitioners aimed to achieve was personified in the figure of Sophia (wisdom), and it has been frequently compared with the mystical idea of "Chokmah" found in the Jewish cabala. In that system, the universe is represented by the Tree of Life, consisting of various "Sephiroth" or spheres of existence, much like the Gnostic aeons. The "paths" which connect the spheres are all paved with Chokmah, the Hebrew word for wisdom. This is defined as the wisdom that existed before good and evil, before Eve ate of the fruit of the Tree of Knowledge. In his commentary to the Kabbalistic text known as the *Sefer Yetzirah* (*The Book of Creation*), Aryeh Kaplan defines Chokmah:

> Wisdom is pure thought, which has not yet been broken up into different ideas. . . . On the level of wisdom, all men are included in a single world soul.

The idea of Sophia as an emanation of God, specifically the "wisdom" of God, is part of mainstream Christian theology as well. The word "sophia" is used six times in the New Testament. In *I Corinthians* 1:23-24 the text refers to

Divine Knowledge 145

"Christ the power of God, and the sophia of God." The Eastern Orthodox Church saw Sophia as co-equal with Christ, and simultaneously an aspect of Christ as well. The Hagia Sophia or Church of the Holy Wisdom in Constantinople (now Istanbul, Turkey) was once the most magnificent church in all of Byzantium before it was seized in the Ottoman conquest of 1453 and turned into a mosque. "Sophiology," or the worship of the female aspect of Christ as God's wisdom, has influenced many Christian mystics, including Jakob Bohme and Hildegard of Bingen.

Sophia has been compared to the Christian concept of the Holy Spirit, part of the Trinity. She has also been likened to the cabalistic concept of the Shekinah, a.k.a. the Matronit. This is the female aspect of God the Father, who can also be thought of as God's consort. "Shekinah" is a word that means "whirlwind," as well as "divine presence," "royal residence," and "resting place." God purportedly used the Shekinah to manifest his presence every time he appeared to the Israelites. Furthermore, the Shekinah is connected to Metatron, the angel that Enoch the divine scribe allegedly transformed into when he ascended to Heaven. Therefore it can also be compared to the mythic figure of Hermes or Thoth.

The term "Gnostic" actually originates with Plato, who used "Gnostic" as a word for the ideal statesman. According to Irenaeus, Marcellina and her group of Carpocratians used the term for themselves (*Against Heresies*. 1 26, 6). Hippolytus also maintains that a group called the "Naasseni" or the "Naassenes," who "sounded the depths of knowledge" (*Refutation*. 5.1), called themselves Gnostics as well. Hippolytus claims that the Naassenes were the founders of the Gnostic heresy (*Refutation*. 6:1), but he is alone in this view. All of the other Church Fathers claim that the Gnostic heresy was founded by Simon Magus, starting with Justin Martyr and Irenaeus. Then there is Origen, who, in contrast to Hippolytus, says that the Naassenes were an "insignificant sect" (*Contra Celsus*, 6:24).

Hence the Church Fathers do not agree on the Naassenes in terms of their role in history and their significance. Perhaps it mattered little whether Hippolytus' Naassenes preceded Simon Magus or Epiphanius' *Phibionites* preceded both of them, so long as every heretical system appeared secondary in some way in comparison to the rightful supremacy of the Catholic Church. But outside of the patristic tradition, there's little evidence that the word was used very much by the heretics. In Plato's *Statesman* 258b, he uses the term "episteme," which means the same. However, Plato uses the word to indicate political aptitude in reference to the "Philosopher Kings" he talks about in the *Republic*. Gnostics would, however, apply the same word to spiritual aptitude. In *Phaedo* 66e Socrates says:

> [I]f we are ever to know anything absolutely, we must be free from the body and must behold the actual realities with the eye of the soul alone. . . .
>
> [P]ure knowledge is impossible while the body is with us. . . .

Essentially this means that we cannot connect with pure knowledge when we are disturbed or distracted by the body. Socrates refers to pure knowledge as a naked understanding of reality, which is something beyond the realm of matter and the senses of the body. Irenaeus clearly describes these Gnostics as having *hairesies* (heresies) that deviate from the Catholic, apostolic brand of Christianity. These Gnostics engaged in sympathetic healing magic, exorcisms, Asclepian-styled medicine, and meditative

Divine Knowledge 147

techniques that used correspondences between the powers of the Zodiac (as represented by the "Archons"), and the human body, as seen in *The Apocryphon of John*, among other Gnostic texts.

The Church Fathers were very strategic in how they used the term "Gnosis." They did their best to differentiate between "true" and "false" Gnosis. The Gnostics possessed the latter, while the Catholics possessed the former. Irenaeus spoke of those who possess and profess "Gnosis falsely so-called." It appears to us that these Gnostics weren't exactly "world hating dualists" who rejected matter. In fact, as Michael Allen Williams in *Rethinking Gnosticism* points out, those who voluntarily immigrated to ancient Rome weren't exactly ivory tower-dwellers, but were among the more "economically advantaged," as he put it. Williams presents a number of citations to support this assertion, including ones from Epiphanius, Tertullian and Irenaeus, who all claim that these Gnostics and Valentinians were of a refined social class.

Clement of Alexandria attempted to rehabilitate the term "Gnostic," reserving it for the perfect and mature Christian who observes the Law of Moses with a life of self-restraint and contemplation on God. However, Clement himself had many philosophically pagan ideas derived from the surrounding mystery schools that influenced his thinking and his brand of Christianity, which later became orthodoxy. At first he was recognized as a saint, but this honor was removed from his name by Pope Clement VIII because his doctrines were at the very least suspect, if not downright heretical.

The idea of there being a "mature" class of initiated Christians (e.g. the Gnostics) is actually found in *1 Corinthians* 2:6-8 (NIV):

> We do, however, speak a message of wisdom among the mature, but not the wisdom of this age or of the rulers of this age, who are coming to nothing. No, we declare God's wisdom, a mystery that has been hidden and that God destined for our glory before time began.

Branding these people as *gnostikoi* with *hairesies* was a rhetorical strategy to mark them negatively as the "other," so to speak. Irenaeus claimed in *Against Heresies* (1.29.1) that these people were so numerous and diverse that they sprung up even among the Christians:

> Besides those, however, among these heretics who are Simonians, and of whom we have already spoken, a multitude of Gnostics have sprung up, and have been manifested like mushrooms growing out of the ground.

In particular, Irenaeus goes in many tirades against these Gnostics (especially against arch-heretics like Valentinus and Marcion), who propagated Sethian mythology, which is commonly identified with the Gnostic group known as the "Ophites." It was the Ophites from whom Joseph von Hammer-Purgstall believed the Knights Templar had copied their rituals and secret theology. "Ophite" comes from the Greek word for "snake," a reference to the Serpent in the Garden of Eden. They revered the Serpent as the true savior and hero of the story of *Genesis*, because he brought divine wisdom or "Gnosis" to mankind in the form of the fruit of the Tree of Knowledge.

Likewise the God of the Old Testament, Jehovah, is described diminutively as a "Demiurge," an insane and demented creator of the universe who, is so doing,

Divine Knowledge 149

separated man from the divine essence by causing spirit to incarnate into matter. The word "demiurge" comes from a Greek word meaning "artisan," "craftsman," or "skilled worker." It is a term that also originates in Plato's writings, specifically in *Timaeus*. The Ophites believed that the Demiurge did not want mankind to be illuminated with divine Gnosis, and thus reunified with the uncreated essence, because that would allow us to escape his false creation. That is why he forbade eating from the Tree of Knowledge, and that is why, in this worldview, the Serpent promoted it.

Irenaeus describes their theology in great detail, revealing that Gnostic groups like the Ophites were direct inheritors of Hellenistic Jewish speculative theology that dealt with angelology and Logos theories. *Against Heresies* 1.30 goes through a blow-by-blow account of the Ophite creation story, the Flood, and their peculiar views on the prophets, as well as the Resurrection of Jesus Christ. The exact origin of the Ophites lies in obscurity. Some scholars believe that their theology was derived from the teachings of the heretic Marcion (70-150 AD), although we really don't see much of a connection there.

The likely reason that Marcion is (perhaps erroneously) credited with inspiring Ophitism is because he rejected the authority of the Old Testament in favor of his *Apostolikon*, which contained earlier variants of St. Paul's epistles, an early version of *The Gospel of Luke*, which he called *The Gospel of the Lord*, and *The Antithesis*, and was supposed to explain all the deep contradictions between the Old Testament and Marcion's New Testament. By extension, Marcion also rejected the Mosaic Law, the Sabbaths, holidays, New Moon festivals, the prophets, the angels, and Jehovah, the God of the Jews. Marcion demoted them to

150 *Chapter 5*

inferior powers, elevating instead the lofty revelation of Jesus Christ, whom he called "Isu Chrestos," the "Chrestos" (the Good), and the "Foreigner" or the "Alien God" (as he was previously unknown to the world).

Marcion is often credited with having first conceived of the idea of the New Testament, and yet he was branded as a heretic and condemned furiously by his Catholic enemies, including Irenaeus, Tertullian and Origen. In fact, the bulk of the New Testament texts we have now are nothing more than the last vestiges of a severely tampered, rewritten version of Marcion's original canon which we have no surviving copies of. The Ophites, on the other hand seemed to be very much inspired by the Old Testament as well as the New—although their interpretations of biblical theology obviously differ strongly from what is normally accepted.

Marcionite Christianity seems to represent a later stage of Gnosticism, when Christian doctrine was just starting to formulate and the Old Testament was being touted as authoritative scripture (their only scripture really) by the Catholics. The views held by the Ophites as well as authors of other Gnostic texts contain very esoteric, bizarre and downright convoluted mythological and cosmological accounts which are far-removed from the conservative theology of Marcion. The biggest distinguishing factor of Marcion's worldview was his refusal to interpret Jewish scriptures as allegorical like many of his Gnostic and Hellenistic-Jewish opponents did, such as Philo of Alexandria.

Marcion's radical dualism (contrasting Pauline Christology with the Judaizing legalism of Peter's church) can be seen as a foundational underpinning of Gnosticism. However, Gnostics such as the Ophites tended to envision a single source for everything (monotheism), and embraced a

Judaic or monistic conceptualization of the origin of God. This highly conflicts with Marcion's view that there was a Supreme, Unknowable "God of Love" and a vastly inferior "God of Wrath" (the creator god Jehovah). The reason for this contradiction between Marcionite and Gnostic theology may have to do with their supposed founder, Simon Magus. In *The Gnostic Gospels*, Elaine Pagels writes about the conflicting relationship between these two gods:

> What this secret tradition reveals is that the one whom most Christians naively worship as creator, God, and Father is, in reality, only the image of the true God. According to Valentinus, what Clement and Ignatius mistakenly ascribe to God actually applies only to the creator. Valentinus, following Plato, uses the Greek term for
> "creator" (*demiurgos*), suggesting that he is a lesser divine being who serves as the instrument of the higher powers. It is not God, he explains, but the demiurge who reigns as king and lord, who acts as a military commander, who gives the law and judges those who violate it—in short, he is the "God of Israel." Through the initiation Valentinus offers, the candidate learns to reject the creator's authority and all his demands as foolishness. What gnostics know is that the creator makes false claims to power ("I am God, and there is no other") that derive from his own ignorance. Achieving gnosis involves coming to recognize the true source of divine power—namely, "the depth" of all being. Whoever has come to know that source simultaneously comes to know himself and discovers his spiritual origin: he has come to know his true Father and Mother.

In essence, as Michael Allen Williams claims in *Rethinking Gnosticism*, these demiurgical myths can be construed as veiled political protests, which call upon people to reject the legitimacy of all the political structures of the world. It is obvious that these myths are about the rejection of religious authority as well (e.g. common organized religion or orthodoxy).

Returning to the subject of the Ophites, they seem to have draw inspiration from the many different mystery religions of Egypt, Phrygia, Babylon, India and Greece. The so-called "Orphic serpent," entwined around an egg containing an embryo of the god Phanes/Eros, was one of their divine symbols, as was the famous Ouroboros symbol (the serpent that consumes its own tail). In essence, Ophite theology remains substantially pagan despite its biblical inspiration, as does that of the Naassenes. Church Fathers like Irenaeus, Hippolytus and Origen all considered the Ophites pagan.

The famous Theosophist GRS Mead, in *Fragments of a Faith Forgotten*, makes an interesting observation on the word "Ophite" that many modern scholars seem to have failed to notice or address. He wrote:

> The term "Ophite" is exceedingly erroneous; it does not generally describe the schools of which we are treating; it was not used by the adherents of the schools themselves, who mostly preferred the term Gnostic; even where the symbolism of the serpent enters into the exposition of their systems, it is by no means the characteristic feature. In brief, this term, which originated in the fallacy of taking a very small part for the whole—a favourite trick of the heresiologist, whose main weapon was to exaggerate a minor detail into a main

characteristic—has been used as a vague designation for all exposition of Gnostic doctrine which could not be ascribed to a definite teacher.

The Naassenes, named after *na'asch*, the Hebrew word for "snake," existed in the first century AD. This point is particularly stressed by Hippolytus in his work *Refutation of All Heresies*, tying them to the pagan mysteries. They called the chief Archon "Ialdabaoth," "Samael," or "Saklas," all names are found in *The Apocryphon of John*. Another Gnostic group, the Sethians, believed that Adam and Eve's third son Seth was a divine emanation, born purely of spirit, and that it was the destiny of Seth's descendants to eternally battle the sons of Cain, whom they thought to be the posterity of the Demiurge. All of this is explained in *The Apocalypse of Adam*.

The Borborites, meaning "the filthy ones," were particularly known for their rituals involving the consumption of menstrual blood, semen, and aborted human fetuses. (These are things which the Knights Templar were accused of doing also.) Allegedly, there even existed a sect called the Cainites, who, rather than seeing him as the child of the Demiurge, revered Cain as a martyr for the cause against him. Many villains of the Bible, like Cain, Esau, Korah, the Sodomites, and Judas Iscariot were also said to be revered. We will return to these Cainites and their theology later in this chapter.

Many have identified the Ophites and the Naassenes as being one and the same group. Although they do have some obvious similarities, in that they both revered the serpent of *Genesis*, there are also some notable differences, as we will see further on. Texts such as *The Apocryphon of John* seem to contain theological ideas ascribed to the Ophites that were similar to the ones described by Irenaeus. All the information we have about the Naassenes comes from either the *Philosophoumena* or the *Refutation of All Heresies*. In Irenaeus' account of Ophite theology, he maintained that like almost all Gnostic groups, the Ophites taught aeonic emanationism, much like these Naassenes.

Generally speaking, it was the Gnostic view that the world was created in a series of "emanations" of Godhead, or "aeons," which descended one from another, each new generation more dense and less subtle than the last. Sophia, or "divine wisdom," was the last and the lowest of those emanations. It was she who fell from grace and became impregnated with Ialdabaoth, destined to create an evil material universe with his demigod helpers, the "Archons." Ray Embry, in the article "Marcion: Possible Progenitor of Three Famous Communities: Baptists, Catholics, Gnostics," remarks about Gnostic metaphysics and how different it was from Marcion's radical metaphysical dualist belief about there being two gods:

> The Gnostics believed they had adequately explained how darkness and corruption could ultimately descend from a singular source of Divine Light. Between that Perfect Light and our imperfect world, there are (according to the Gnostics) a significant number of stations, events and beings that tend to absorb the attribution of evil away from the highest level of Divine Unity.

In *The Second Treatise of the Great Seth*, Sophia is called a "whore." Church Fathers like Epiphanius called her "Prunikos," meaning "lewd" or "lustful one," because, though originally a virginal goddess, by her fall from the purity of the original aeons, she was the cause of the fall of the cosmos. Like the Serpent of *Genesis*, she was said to be a divine being that brought sexual knowledge to the universe, and with it, generation and ultimately death—or at least "spiritual death" (i.e., ignorance). So, in essence, she was linked with the fall of Eden, even though she brought knowledge down below to the profane cosmos. Simone Petrement explains in *A Separate God: The Origins and Teachings of Gnosticism* that, although the title of "Prunikos" is interpreted as indicating lasciviousness and licentiousness by Church Fathers like Epiphanius, it actually means a divine "bearer" or "holder." This reminds us of the Christian idea that that the Virgin Mary was the *Theotokos* or "God-bearer" of Christ. Petrement writes:

> The name is formed from pro ("before" or "in front") and a word that seems to be related to the second aorist *eneika* (analogous to *enenka*) of the verb *phero*, "to carry." Prounikos could therefore evoke the meaning of "to carry in front," that is, to promote, to bring, to reveal, to bring to light. Prophero might mean to produce, and therefore to beget, to give birth.

To gain further background information, we must look back to the creation myths ascribed to the Ophites. Their myths, like other Gnostic groups, are remarkably erotic and build on the *Genesis* account while allegorizing it in a much broader, more metaphysical context. As Irenaeus explains, there was the "First Man," who is equated with the Monad called "Bythos," meaning "Depth." This "First Man" emanated a female divinity called Ennoea, much like the myths and legends ascribed to Simon Magus and his female concubine sorceress, Helena. (We will also get to them later in another chapter). From their holy union, they generated the "Son of Man" or the second man. Below the Son of Man is the Holy Spirit spoken of in feminine terms as the "First Woman" (like Eve). Beneath the First Woman lay the elements of chaos and the Abyss. The First and Second Man delighted over the Holy Spirit, had intercourse with her, and begat a third power called "Christ." Irenaeus also says that all of these holy powers mentioned meet and congregate in an "incorruptible aeon" likened to that of the "true and holy Church" of the Pleroma.

To the Ophites, a power ejected by Sophia (through her "Sinistra," which could be a reference to her "left side") fell by "ebullition" (bubbling, boiling, or bursting forth). Therefore, just like how she is described above, Sophia fell into the primordial waters of chaos and brought with her fragments of divine light. The primal waters immediately clung around these light particles as well as Sophia, and formed inferior bodies. Sophia regretted this course of action and grieved. She attempted to ascend back above to her mother, the Holy Spirit, but failed to do so because of the sheer weight of the watery matter she found herself entrapped in, like quicksand. Somehow in this chaotic primeval mess, the light that Sophia attempted to hide from the elements was taken away from her grasp and formed the material cosmos that we know. These spiritual particles are thus divided and dispersed throughout the universe.

In this formulation of the cosmos, a god-like power ejected from Sophia's womb, which in other Gnostic texts is described as an "abortion." This is much like how other Gnostic texts describe Ialdabaoth, particularly *On the Origin of the World*. This same text also describes how Sophia flowed within the chaos of the *prima materia* and gave birth to an archontic fetus, as well as water that's likened to afterbirth or the amniotic fluid, which "came into being out of the shadow and was cast aside." Simone Petrement explains the significance of this event:

> Now Sophia gives birth to the Demiurge, and we see
> that, according to one version of the myth, her error
> was precisely to wish to give birth by herself, as
> God.

Here, Sophia acts like a feminized version of the Lucifer of *Isaiah* and *Ezekiel*. In another variation of the Sophia myth, the reason why Sophia fell was because she loved and desired God so much that she "always stretched herself farther out in front," throwing herself towards God in an imprudent way that was not permitted (*Against Heresies*. 1, 2, 2).

When her fetus, the Demiurge, was ejected, he stole a portion of Sophia's divine power and weakened her even further. He did not know that he was begotten from a parent and did not know any mother. Yet, he still had an unconscious desire for the light above him. This being, called "Ialdabaoth," then generated six sons. Together they all formed the "Hebdomad" (a group of seven), much like how the aeons preceded each other with each successive generation in the light world above. Aside from Ialdabaoth, there was Iao, Sabaoth, Adoneus, Eloeus, Oreus and Astanphaeus. These beings are simply avatars of the Demiurge. Above these seven powers was, naturally, their grandmother Sophia, who resided in the eighth place, forming the "Ogdoad" (a group of eight).

These powers represent the seven heavens and all the celestial beings that inhabit them, including the angels, archangels, potentates, thrones, and principalities. Ialdabaoth's sons proceeded to quarrel with one another over supremacy, indicating a war in the seven heavens was occurring. This caused Ialdabaoth to greatly grieve. He "casted his eyes upon the subjacent dregs of matter," and created a serpent-like being called "Nous" (Greek for

"Mind"). This is similar to the "Naas" of the Naassenes of Hippolytus.

Like Sophia, this serpent is said to engender "oblivion, wickedness, emulation, envy and death." One would think the Ophites would celebrate the serpent in this episode, but it appears that this serpent, described pejoratively as "crooked," is yet another cause of the fallen cosmos to deviate further from the ideal. Another Gnostic text, *The Apocryphon of John*, has many similarities (and differences) with Irenaeus' account of the Ophites. In particular, this text actually condemns the serpent as being part of the same order as the chief Archon, Ialdabaoth:

> And I said to the savior, "Lord, was it not the serpent that taught Adam to eat?" The savior smiled and said, "The serpent taught them to eat from wickedness of begetting, lust, (and) destruction, that he (Adam) might be useful to him. And he (Adam) knew that he was disobedient to him (the chief archon) due to light of the Epinoia which is in him, which made him more correct in his thinking than the chief archon. And (the latter) wanted to bring about the power which he himself had given him. And he brought a forgetfulness over Adam."

True to form, Ialdabaoth decided to boast in an outrageous, egotistical gesture that mirrored Jehovah's remarks in *Isaiah* 45:5:

> I am father, and God, and above me there is no one.

This haughty remark earned him a smack-down from his mother, who "rebuked her haughty offspring," saying:

> Do not lie, Ialdabaoth: for the father of all, the first Anthropos (man), is above you; and so is Anthropos the son of Anthropos.

Just as his claim to be the highest god is challenged, our Demiurge creates a distraction by proposing the creation of mankind to the other Archons:

> Then, as all were disturbed by the unexpected proclamation, and as they were inquiring whence the noise proceeded, in order to lead them away and attract them to himself, Ialdabaoth exclaimed: "Come, let us make man after our image."

The latter is a reference from *Genesis* 1:26. Here the Ophite creation account of Adam and Eve begins. The six other powers then conspire to create the material body for Adam. Evidently, it was Sophia who gave these "authorities" the idea to create a man (presumably Adam) of "immense size" so that she "might empty them of their original power" that had once belonged to her. But their creation was unable to stand and simply "[writhed] along the ground." This is much like Irenaeus' explanation of the Simonian heretic, Saturninus' doctrine about Adam, described in *Against Heresies* (1, 24):

> He was accordingly formed, yet was unable to stand erect, through the inability of the angels to convey to him that power, but wriggled [on the ground] like a worm. Then the power above taking pity upon him, since he was made after his likeness, sent forth a spark of life, which gave man an erect posture, compacted his joints, and made him live.

The six powers decided to carry this man to Ialdabaoth so that he might breathe into him the "spirit of life." However, this was a plot covertly engineered by Sophia so that Ialdabaoth was secretly drained of the power he originally stole from her. These Gnostics believed that man contains within him *nous* (intelligence) and *enthymesis* (thought), which are purportedly the means by which man can attain salvation. This part of the story greatly mirrors *Fragment* 1 of Valentinus, when it says:

> Something like fear overcame the angels in the presence of that modeled form (i.e. Adam) because he uttered things that were superior to what his origins justified, owing to the agent who had invisibly deposited a seed of higher essence and who spoke freely.

Ialdabaoth became full of envy and jealousy of this man. He decided to empty him of his thought and intellect, placing it in a woman of his own thought instead, so that this new creation would be more controllable. Sophia caught wind of this plot and decided to empty the first woman out of her power. Later, Eve showed up without much of an introduction, along with the angels. They decided to copulate with her after they admired her beauty, and proceeded to have sons with her. This echoes the story of the Watchers in *The First Book of Enoch* and in *Genesis* Chapter 6. Sophia decided to send a serpent of her own to "seduce" Adam and Eve (like the angels did with Eve earlier) into transgressing Ialdabaoth's prohibition of not eating from the forbidden tree. By eating this fruit, they attained knowledge "of that power which is above all, and departed from those who had created them." Sophia saw that Ialdabaoth's creations had attained knowledge above his own, and rejoiced.

However, Ialdabaoth, like Jehovah in *Genesis*, casted Adam and Eve out from Eden because they chose to ignore his edict and follow Sophia's serpent's advice. In *Genesis*

3:22, the Lord declares, clearly to other gods, that "The man has now become like one of us, knowing good and evil." Jehovah expresses fear, "lest he reach out his hand and take also from the tree of life and eat, and live forever." The Lord seems concerned that, with the wisdom they gained from the Tree of Knowledge, Adam and Eve will realize that he's not the only god, and also that, if they gain immortality by eating from the Tree of Life, they will become gods as well, no longer under his control.

In the Ophite account, like the mysterious angels in Eden, Ialdabaoth also desired to copulate with Eve to produce more offspring. But he failed to do so because Sophia had secretly emptied both Adam and Eve of the light that was sprinkled on them. This seems to echo the account found in *The Apocryphon of John*, when it states that Ialdabaoth raped Eve and produced two sons, one called Eloim and the other Yave. The text equates these two animal-faced sons (bear and cat faces, respectively) with both Cain and Abel. However, the difference in the Ophite account is that Ialdabaoth was prevented from raping Eve. The same thing happens in *On the Origin of the World*, when Eve, the avatar of Sophia awakens Adam from his slumber as he walks on his two feet. Then the "Authorities" decide to spoil and defile Eve to prevent her from returning to the "light." However, Eve laughs at their folly, put a "mist in their eyes" and enters into the Tree of Life, literally becoming that tree, preventing the Archons from raping her. Perhaps this is where the alchemists got the idea of portraying their "Divine Sophia" as sitting on the "Tree of Learning," the allegorical source of the "Elixir of Life."

From the Ophite version of *Genesis*, we learn that when Adam and Eve were drained of this divine light, they were cursed and cast down from Heaven to the Earth, along with (presumably) Sophia's serpent. Perhaps Irenaeus was reading from *On the Origin of the World* or *Hypostasis of the Archons*, which both practically tell the same story (but with some key differences). It seems to us that these Gnostic authors wrote their own satirical version of the Eden events as sort of a rejection of traditional Judaism while exposing the flaws of the Jewish god, promoting instead what he saw as an infinitely superior Platonic deity.

When the serpent was cast down from Heaven, he begat, as we said, six sons of his own power, based on the example of the Hebdomad (the seven heavens and the seven Archons that form this astral structure of fate). These six sons (as well as the serpent himself) eventually became the "seven mundane demons," that were said to oppose and resist the human race. When Adam and Eve were cast down from a presumably higher region in the cosmos, their spiritual bodies withered and darkened. They became sluggish in the world of matter, in comparison to the freedom they once had as spiritual beings. In the Sethian *Apocalypse of Adam*, Seth's father Adam tells him a very similar story:

> Listen to my words, my son Seth. When God had created me out of the earth, along with Eve, your mother, I went about with her in a glory which she had seen in the aeon from which we had come forth. She taught me a word of knowledge of the eternal God. And we resembled the great eternal angels, for we were higher than the god who had created us and the powers with him, whom we did not know.

The Gnostic-Hermeticist and alchemist Zosimos also made similar statements in *On the Letter Omega,* where he wrote:

Divine Knowledge 163

When Light-Man (*Phos*) was in Paradise, expiring under the [presence of] Fate, they persuaded Him to clothe himself in the Adam they had made, the [Adam] of Fate, him of the four elements—as though [they said] being free from [her] ills and free from their activities. And He, on account of this "freedom from ills" did not refuse; but they boasted as though He had been brought into servitude [to them].

At this point, Sophia saw Adam and Eve's plight, changed her mind and sprinkled the divine light upon them again, out of compassion. Anointed with this divine light, they recognized they were naked and enveloped in a material body, "and thus recognised that they bore death about with them." In *On the Origin of the World*, the earthly Adam and Eve were damned by the Archons after the expulsion from Paradise, it says, "since the rulers were envious of Adam they wanted to diminish their lifespan." As it turns out, the Archons weren't exactly successful because both Adam and Eve lived for almost 1,000 years (even according to the Gnostic texts). Immediately after this realization of their material, incomplete state, both Adam and Eve had sexual intercourse with one another and begat Cain and Abel. In this story, the Serpent actually possesses Cain, and fills him with "mundane oblivion," meaning ignorance. From the serpent's influence, Cain kills his brother Abel, introducing envy and murder into the world. In *Rethinking Gnosticism*, Michael Williams recounts this episode in his own way:

> Livid with rage, Ialdabaoth throws Adam and Eve out of Paradise. But simply throwing them out will not change the fact of their superiority. He needs some device to increase human misery. The answer

is sex. Ialdabaoth now implants the desire for intercourse in the humans. Ialdabaoth seduces Eve, begetting two mongrel powers, Cain and Abel, who are then given the responsibility of controlling the future herd of material bodies that can be expected to grow from the now libidinous couple. However, when Adam "knows" Eve, their child is Seth, possessing like Adam the human image of God, and carrying the same spirit.

After this unfortunate incident, Sophia produces Seth, and then his sister, Norea, from whom, it is said, all of the human race (especially the "Gnostic Race," i.e., the so-called "Sethians") descend. However, it is said that the human race went astray with apostasy, idolatry, ignorance, and overall hatred of the sacred mysteries of the "superior holy Hebdomad above."

The Ophites had two special names assigned to the serpent that was cast down: Michael and Samael. It isn't all that clear which serpent is given these names since there are two serpents in the Ophite account, but one may infer this serpent belongs to Sophia, since Ialdabaoth's serpent had already done his job of generating all things belonging to death (corruptible or imperfect matter). The name Michael being given to the serpent is peculiar, since it is the same name given to the archangel loyal to Jehovah who battles Satan in the form of a dragon in *Revelation* 12:7. He also appears in *The First Book of Enoch* and in the *War Scroll* among the Dead Sea Scroll literature. But Michael appears to be nothing more than a demonic creature to the Ophites. Samael is associated with the Serpent of *Genesis*, and with Lilith, as we know. In *The Targum Pseudo-Jonathan* (Targum meaning "explanations" or paraphrases of the Torah) the text specifically calls the serpent "Sammael":

> And the woman beheld Sammael, the angel of
> death, and was afraid; yet she knew that the tree
> was good to eat, and that it was medicine for the
> enlightenment of the eyes, and a desirable tree by
> means of which to understand. And she took of its
> fruit, and did eat; and she gave to her husband with
> her, and he did eat. And the eyes of both were
> enlightened, and they knew that they were naked,
> divested of the purple robe in which they had been
> created.

Samael is often referred as the angel of death, as seen in the above quotation. St. Paul, in *1 Corinthians* 15:55 (NIV), taunts the angel of death when he says, "Where, O death, is your victory? Where, O death, is your sting?" Samael also happens to be a name for the chief Archon, Ialdabaoth, in *The Apocryphon of John* and *Hypostasis of the Archons*, which would also explain why the *Targum Pseudo-Jonathan* condemns the serpent as being part of the same order as the chief Archon. Later in that text, Samael is described as being a great prince or archangel in Heaven, much like Lucifer. He descended to Earth riding upon the Serpent and deceived Eve by seducing her, impregnating her with Cain. As the text reads:

> And Adam knew Eve his wife, that she had
> conceived from Sammael, the angel (of the Lord).

Another translation reads that Eve specifically lusted after Sammael, stating:

> And Adam knew Hava his wife, who had desired the
> Angel; and she conceived, and bore Kain; and she
> said, I have acquired a man, the Angel of the Lord.

This mirrors, once again, *The Apocryphon of John*'s account where Ialdabaoth seduces Eve and begets Cain and

Abel. In *The Apocalypse of Adam*, Adam tells his son Seth, "Then the God who created us, created a son from himself and Eve, your mother." While Cain is not explicitly mentioned here, he is more than likely the stepson Adam is referring too. Cain is also referenced in *On the Origin of the World*, which proclaims the following:

> Her offspring is the creature that is lord. Afterwards, the authorities called it "Beast", so that it might lead astray their modelled creatures. The interpretation of "the beast" is "the instructor." For it was found to be the wisest of all beings. Now, Eve is the first virgin, the one who without a husband bore her first offspring. It is she who served as her own midwife.

Since this text builds on the *Genesis* tale, naturally, it references it, including *Genesis* 4:1 (KJV), which says, "And Adam knew Eve his wife; and she conceived, and bare Cain, and said, I have gotten a man from the LORD." Also note Cain being identified here as the "Beast," which corresponds to *Genesis* 3:2, where it says that the serpent is the "wisest of all the beasts," and also to *The Zohar*'s designation of Samael and Lilith joined together as "the Beast." It becomes obvious that Cain is not the son of Adam, but the son of a fallen angel, just as the cabalists believed him to be of demonic origin. *The Apocryphon of John* also explains that Cain was one of the astral rulers of the Hebdomad of the Zodiac, as it states, "The sixth one is Cain, whom the generations of men call the sun."

As we mentioned, there is a Sethian group called the "Cainites," who supposedly revered Cain. In *Against Heresies* (1.31.1), Irenaeus explains that these Cainites believed the following:

Divine Knowledge 167

Cain derived his being from the Power above, and [the Cainites] acknowledge that Esau, Korah, the Sodomites, and all such persons, are related to themselves. On this account, they add, they have been assailed by the Creator, yet no one of them has suffered injury. For Sophia was in the habit of carrying off that which belonged to her from them to herself. They declare that Judas the traitor was thoroughly acquainted with these things, and that he alone, knowing the truth as no others did, accomplished the mystery of the betrayal; by him all things, both earthly and heavenly, were thus thrown into confusion. They produce a fictitious history of this kind, which they style the *Gospel of Judas*.

This "fictitious history" that the Cainites "style the Gospel of Judas" turned out to be a real thing, as *The Gospel of Judas* is one of the four tractates found in *Codex Tchacos*, published in 2006. This has been a topic of controversy among scholars because of Judas's contradictory role in the gospel. Without getting into all the complicated details of this story, we can glean some insight from Epiphanius, who wrote many hostile polemics against various Gnostic groups and teachers, including the Cainites.

In the *Panarion*, Epiphanius bases his account of the Cainites off of Irenaeus' report, but adds some more details of his own. According to him, these Cainites honored the wicked and repudiated the good. They were said to be prone to libertine practices and to indulge in "every sin," similar to what we see much later in Medieval Satanism, and in the work of the Marquis De Sade. *Panarion* 1.38.1:6-2:2 states:

And they likewise forge certain other works against "Womb." They call this "Womb" the maker of this entire vault of heaven and earth and say, as Carpocrates does, that no one will be saved unless they progress through all (possible) acts. For while each of them is doing some unspeakable thing supposedly with this excuse, performing obscenities and committing every sin there is, he invokes the name of each angel—both real angels, and the ones they fictitiously call angels. And he attributes some wicked commission of every sin on earth to each of them, by offering his own action in the name of whichever angel he wishes. And whenever they do these things they say, "This or that angel, I am performing thy work. This or that authority, I am doing thy deed."

These ritual "obscenities" sound very close to the descriptions that anti-Christian Roman chroniclers gave of the "agape feasts" (meaning "love feasts") celebrated by the early Christians, mentioned (without the obscenities) by St. Paul in *1 Corinthians* 11:20-34. Also, some Gnostic groups like the Cainites were said to celebrate an orgiastic rite involving a nocturnal Eucharistic meal akin to the Last Supper. The rite itself reminds us of the Black Masses and Witches' Sabbaths of yore (which we will discuss more in a later chapter).

Supposedly, the Cainites considered Cain to be of a higher power and superior to Abel. Indeed, according to Birger Pearson in *Gnosticism, Judaism and Egyptian Christianity*, the reason why Cain became associated with Gnostic heresy was because he defied Jehovah's edict to sacrifice animals to him (although *Genesis* does not actually show him expressly demanding an offering of any sort, but just refusing to accept Cain's vegetarian sacrifice whilst favoring Abel's blood sacrifice instead). Pearson writes:

The Cainites venerated Cain as the divine power, rejected all moral conventions, and rejected the Law along with its God. And what, asks Friedlander, is 'Christian' about that? The Alexandrian school provides the most plausible link for the origin of this heresy. Indeed, the Cainite sect was already well known to Philo. Friedlander quotes in this connection *On the Posterity and Exile of Cain*. In this text 'Cain' is a symbol of heresy, and the specifics of the heresy represented by him are such that one can only conclude that Philo is arguing against a philosophizing sect characterized not only by constructing myths contrary to the truth, but by gross antinomianism. Philo speaks against these heretics precisely as Irenaeus speaks against the Gnostics. There can be no doubt that the heretics combated by Philo are the forerunners of the Christian Gnostics later combated by the Church Fathers.

The Sethians shared in the errors of the Ophites and Cainites, teaching that the world was created by angels and not by the highest God. The *dynamis* from on high came down into Seth after Abel's death, according to the Sethians, and many held Seth to be the Messiah.

Epiphanius also mentions that the Cainites authored a book called *The Ascension of Paul*, as well as *The Gospel of Judas*, but says nothing of their content. Epiphanius is more than likely referring to *The Apocalypse of Paul*, found in the Nag Hammadi codices. He writes:

> But again, others forge another brief work in the name of the apostle Paul, full of unspeakable abominations, which the so-called Gnostics also use,

(and) which they call an Ascension of Paul—taking their cue from the apostle's statement that he has ascended to the third heaven and heard ineffable words, which man may not speak. And these, they say, are the ineffable words.

Apparently, these Cainites were big on St. Paul, which would explain the hostility for the twelve apostles in *The Gospel of Judas* as well as its very Pauline interpretation of the crucifixion. In her book *The Thirteenth Apostle: What the Gospel of Judas Really Says*, April DeConick states that the author of *The Gospel of Judas* had a Marcionite bent to him. DeConick compares the text's criticisms of the twelve apostles and their perpetuation of Jewish ritual sacrifice to Marcion's condemnation of the Christian Church. These twelve apostles could also be interpreted as corresponding to the twelve signs of the Zodiac, which *The Apocryphon of John* says the Archons rule over. The Cainites supposedly interpreted the Crucifixion as Christ overcoming the oppression of the body, and hence the overthrowing of the Archons, much like what Paul taught. Everything Epiphanius says conforms to what *The Gospel of Judas* says.

> "No, he betrayed him even though he was good, in accordance with the heavenly knowledge. For the archons knew," they say, "that if Christ were surrendered to the cross the weaker power [the Demiurge] would be drained. And when Judas found this out," they say, "he eagerly did everything he could to betray him, performing a good work for our salvation. And we must commend him and give him the credit, since the salvation of the cross was effected for us through him, and for that reason the revelation of the things on high."

Epiphanius also writes more about the Cainite account of Jesus' passion and crucifixion (1.38.3:1-2):

> But they too interweave the same mythology with their gift of ignorance about these same deadly poisons by advising their followers that everyone must choose the stronger power, and separate from the lesser, feeble one—that is, from the one which made heaven, the flesh and the world—and rise above it to the uttermost heights through the crucifixion of Christ. For this is why he came from above, they say, so that the stronger power might act in him by triumphing over the weaker and betraying the body.

Now, let us compare this with *The Gospel of Judas*, from the *National Geographic* translation, where Jesus says to Judas: "You will exceed all of them. For you will sacrifice the man that clothes me." April DeConick's translation of this passage is remarkably different:

> Truly, I say to you Judas, those [who] offer sacrifices to Saklas <*several lines missing*> everything that is evil. Yet you will do worse than all of them. For the man that clothes me, you will sacrifice him.

The idea that the Cainites glorified Cain is what the heresiologists claimed, but whether or not the Cainites were even a real sect is disputable. More than likely they are an invention of the heresiologists. The mere fact that the Church Fathers accused this group of having reverence for Cain, Korah, and the Sodomites, is revealing. The archheretic Marcion is also accused of doing this same thing when Irenaeus says he taught that Christ saved Cain and the other sinners from Hell, while Abel and the righteous Old

Testament patriarchs couldn't be saved. In *Against Heresies* (1.27.3) we read:

> In addition to his blasphemy against God Himself, he advanced this also, truly speaking as with the mouth of the devil, and saying all things in direct opposition to the truth—that Cain, and those like him, and the Sodomites, and the Egyptians, and others like them, and, in fine, all the nations who walked in all sorts of abomination, were saved by the Lord, on His descending into Hades, and on their running unto Him, and that they welcomed Him into their kingdom. But the serpent which was in Marcion declared that Abel, and Enoch, and Noah, and those other righteous men who sprang from the patriarch Abraham, with all the prophets, and those who were pleasing to God, did not partake in salvation. For since these men, he says, knew that their God was constantly tempting them, so now they suspected that He was tempting them, and did not run to Jesus, or believe His announcement: and for this reason he declared that their souls remained in Hades.

It seems probable that these so-called Cainites blended Sethian and Ophite beliefs with that of Marcionite Christianity. In the *Panarion* (1.42.4:2-4), Epiphanius writes against Marcion and also said some similar things about him, but added more details on his views about the Old Testament prophets:

> And he says that Christ has descended from on high, from the invisible Father who cannot be named, for the salvation of souls and the confusion of the God of the Jews, the Law, the prophets, and anything of the kind. The Lord has gone down even to Hades to

save Cain, Korah, Dathan, Abiram, Esau, and all the gentiles who had not known the God of the Jews. But he has left Abel, Enoch, Noah, Abraham, Isaac, Jacob, Moses, David, and Solomon there because, as he says, they recognized the God of the Jews, the maker and creator, and have done what is congenial to him, and did not devote themselves to the invisible God.

While the heresiologists accused the Cainites of libertinism, *The Gospel of Judas* condemns licentious sex, particularly homosexuality (accusing the priests of the early Church of this sin). So the author, and most likely the sect that it was written for, was ascetic. In *The Gospel of Judas*, the title character has a role invested in eschatological events that will ensue after Jesus is crucified. The "thirteenth aeon" is the realm of the Demiurge in Sethian cosmology. At one point in the text, Judas has a vision of a house where the "unshakeable generation" dwells, and Jesus says that Judas isn't allowed to enter it or to ever be part of the unshakeable generation. Instead, he's said to be the earthly counterpart of the Demiurge, Sakla, who dwells in the thirteenth aeon. Although he predicts that the other apostles and future Christians will condemn Judas, Jesus also prophecies that they will mistakenly worship him by celebrating the crucifixion as a sacrifice to the Demiurge.

So even though Christians condemn him, it was predicted that Judas would secretly reign over them in the thirteenth aeon, because orthodox Christians ignorantly worship Sakla as the true god. The author of *The Gospel of Judas* is essentially mocking the Christian clergy as incompetent fools who believe that they are serving Jesus when they are actually serving the Demiurge. It is a polemical gospel. The Sethian-Cainite author didn't write it to redeem Judas as the only good apostle. He was mocking Christians for being like Judas, saying that they sacrificed Christ to the Demiurge through the Eucharist, just as Judas sacrificed Jesus to the Demiurge through the crucifixion. According to DeConick, the Sethians parodied the idea of Christ's sacrifice on the cross as a really bad joke. In the parodies, Jesus is given as a human sacrifice to the demon Ialdabaoth. Sacrifice itself was seen as an intensely negative thing by these Gnostics.

Also in this text, Jesus at one point says that the unshakeable generation is not under the influence of the stars, but later tells Judas to follow his star and crucify him. This is because Judas isn't part of the unshakeable generation (the Sethians), so he's doomed to the fate that has been assigned him by the Archons. However, even though Judas and the Demiurge (Sakla) want to kill Jesus, it is predicted that Jesus will actually defeat them by deceiving them into crucifying "the man who bears him," the counterfeit material body. Judas is basically a tool being used by Jesus to defeat the Archons, but he will never be part of the seed of Seth. He is trapped in the thirteenth aeon, and will likely be destroyed along with the rest of the Archons at the final conflagration.

The Ophites are also mentioned in another significant source outside of Irenaeus, in the Church Father Origen's refutation of Celsus, called *Contra Celsus*. Celsus was an Epicurean philosopher, who published a work against Christianity called *The True Doctrine*. Seventy years after its publication, *The True Doctrine* was so widely circulated that St. Ambrosius hired Origen to refute Celsus' relentless attacks. *The True Doctrine* gives us a sneak peak at the beliefs and doctrines of not only the early church but also the Ophites in particular.

The True Doctrine was written to oppose what Celsus viewed as the "false word" of Christian doctrine. Many of Celsus' arguments as an Epicurean philosopher mirror some of the logic and arguments one may hear out of modern-day critics of the Bible and Christianity. However, the "Christians" he was directing his attacks against were not the kind one would expect. In fact, the doctrines he described throughout the *True Doctrine* belongs to a specific kind, and that would be, of course, the Ophite Gnostics. One may note that Celsus did not make any differentiation between the Ophite heretics and other types of Christians, considering them one and the same group. Perhaps back in the second century, such a distinction wasn't even made yet. It was Origen who called these special Christians "Ophites" or "Orphians." Celsus also describes the ancient Christian cult in whole as a diabolical secret society made up of sorcerers! He said:

> It is by the names of certain demons, and by the use of incantations, that the Christians appear to be possessed of miraculous power. And it was by means of sorcery that Jesus was able to accomplish the wonders which he performed; and foreseeing that others would attain the same knowledge, and do the same things, making a boast of doing them by help of the power of God, he excludes such from his kingdom. If they are justly excluded, while he himself is guilty of the same practices, he is a wicked man; but if he is not guilty of wickedness in doing such things, neither are they who do the same as he.

These Ophites apparently had a diagram which mapped out their cosmology for magical ritual purposes, which Celsus described as having:

... ten circles, distinct from each other, but united by one circle, which was said to be the soul of all things, and was called "Leviathan": the soul which had travelled through all things! I observed, also, in the diagram, the being named "Behemoth," placed as it were under the lowest circle. The inventor of this diagram had inscribed this leviathan at its circumference and center, thus placing its name in two separate places. Moreover, the diagram was divided by a thick black line, and this line was called Gehenna, which is Tartarus.

Clearly, the parallels between the Ophite diagram, which Celsus said had ten circles, and the cabalistic Tree of Life, made up of ten spheres, are significant. Celsus' *True Doctrine* suggests that the form of the Tree had been imposed on the whole diagram. The Jewish scholar Gershom Scholem has suggested that the Tree of Life diagram entered Jewish esoteric teaching from Hellenistic-Egyptian traditions in the centuries before Christianity. This may also be connected to the seven-headed form of the Gnostic god Iao in the fourth sphere (as discussed in *The Apocryphon of John*), that of the sun. This also includes the rest of the Zodiacal powers.

Celsus described two different Ophite diagrams which depict their cosmology, similar to the account given in *The Apocryphon of John*. As seen above, the drawing depicted the seven cosmic spheres ruled by the Archons, each symbolizing an aspect of the Demiurge enclosed within a large outer circle called the Leviathan. In the innermost circle lay the netherworlds of evil: Hades, Tartarus, Gehenna and Behemoth. Celsus also wrote that the seven heavens are controlled by angelic powers that take on the forms of beasts, as we will see below. These are the same angelic rulers which the Christian Gnostic Saturninus of Antioch describes as the "seven angels who made the world."

Also from Celsus, we learn that the Ophite Demiurge had the head of a lion and was connected with Saturn as one of the "fixed stars" or "lofty gates" that the soul must pass through on its way to the Pleroma (the "Fullness of Being" that is the Gnostic version of Heaven). Celsus wrote about these cosmic gateways, which the soul encounters in its astral journey, thusly:

> The first gate they assign to Saturn, indicating by the "lead" [the metal associated with Saturn] the slowness of this star; the second to Venus, comparing her to the splendor and softness of tin; the third to Jupiter, being firm and solid; the fourth to Mercury, for both Mercury and iron are fit to endure all things, and are money-making and laborious; the fifth to Mars, because, being composed of a mixture of metals, it is varied and unequal; the sixth, of silver, to the Moon; the seventh, of gold, to the Sun—thus imitating the different colors of the two latter.

The scholar Andrei Orlov, in his *Divine Scapegoats: Demonic Mimesis in Early Jewish Mysticism*, compared *The Second Book of Enoch*'s account of the cosmic spheres, the creation of man, and the bodily correspondences with those found in *The Corpus Hermeticum* and Gnostic texts like *The Apocryphon of John*. Orlav quotes from *The Second Book of Enoch* 30: 4-5, where God creates and sets in motion the fixed stars, being the "great lights" and "heavenly circles."

> On the first uppermost circle I placed the stars, Kruno, and on the second Aphrodit, on the third Aris, on the fifth Zoues, on the sixth Ermis, on the

seventh lesser the moon, and adorned it with the lesser stars. And on the lower I placed the sun for the illumination of day, and the moon and stars for the illumination of night.

Names like Kruno, Aphrodit, Aris, and Zoues are obviously corrupted versions of the Greek gods. From *The Second Book of Enoch*, we have Saturn, Venus, Mars, the Sun, Jupiter, Mercury and the Moon. This is actually very similar to the Ophite model as taken above, which presents them in this order: Saturn, Venus, Jupiter, Mercury, Mars, Moon, Sun. The Ophite order, reported by Origen and Celsus, begins with Saturn and ends with the Sun. While they are not exactly the same, both *The Second Book of Enoch* and the Ophites have similar orders, in that they both begin with Saturn. In the late Christian Gnostic text, *Pistis Sophia* (5.138), we have the same planetary gods named after the Olympians who rule over other lesser demons. As it says, "the first is called Kronos, the second Ares, the third Hermes, the fourth Aphrodite, the fifth Zeus."

We also see this type of planetary arrangement with Egyptian deities. In their view, most of the planets were themselves ruled by other gods of the pantheon. Their arrangement was: Saturn-Horus; Mars-Re; Mercury-Set; Venus-Osiris. Interestingly, Thoth was not associated with Mercury until well into the Greco-Roman era.

On the subject of Celsus, what is most striking about his description of the Ophite diagram is the exact order of the "seven ruling demons," which he proceeds to describe (emphasis added):

The goat was shaped like a lion. Again, the second in order is a bull, the third an amphibious sort of animal, and one that hissed frightfully [generally taken to be a dragon]; moreover, the fourth had the form of an eagle; again, the fifth had the countenance of a bear. To continue the account, the sixth was described as having the face of a dog; the seventh had the countenance of an ass. Moreover, if any one would wish to become acquainted with the artifices of those sorcerers, through which they desire to lead men away by their teaching as if they possessed the knowledge of certain secret rites, but are not at all successful in so doing, let him listen to the instruction which they receive after passing through what is termed the "fence of wickedness"— gates which are subjected to the world of ruling spirits.

The above sequence seems to be drawn from the figures of four "cherubim" of Ezekiel's vision, to which three new personages were added, for a total of seven. Ezekiel's vision of the "Tetramorph" (as it's called) was of four creatures, having the heads of a man, a bull, a lion and an eagle, each attached to one of the sides of God's "chariot," or traveling throne. St. Jerome saw them as symbolic of the Four Evangelists of the Gospels: Matthew, Mark, Luke and John. However, it is likely influenced by Sumerian stories of a creature called "Lamassu," depicted as either a bull or a lion with a human head and a bird's wings. Four images of this creature were often placed at the entrances to buildings in ancient Sumer, each facing one of the four cardinal directions. It is unknown if there is any connection here with Lamasthu, the aforementioned Akkadian name for Lilith. Lamashtu was depicted as a hybrid also, with a lion's head, donkey teeth, and bird talons.

This brings to mind Celsus' mention in the above passage of a "goat. . . shaped like a lion," which is highly reminiscent of the caprine imagery of Levi's Baphomet, and the leonine symbolism associated with the Gnostic Demiurge, Ialdabaoth. Also note the words of the third article of the "Thelemite Gnostic Catholic Creed" that is recited by all the congregants in the Gnostic Mass ritual of Aleister Crowley's Ordo Templi Orientis (performed by their church arm, the "Ecclesia Gnostica Catholica"):

> And I believe in the Serpent and the Lion, Mystery of Mystery, in His name BAPHOMET. And I believe in one Gnostic and Catholic Church of Light, Life, Love and Liberty, the Word of whose Law is THELEMA. And I believe in the communion of Saints. And, forasmuch as meat and drink are transmuted in us daily into spiritual substance, I believe in the Miracle of the Mass. And I confess one Baptism of Wisdom whereby we accomplish the Miracle of Incarnation. And I confess my life one, individual, and eternal that was, and is, and is to come. AUMGN, AUMGN, AUMGN.

So here the lion-headed serpent, specifically distinguished as Ialdabaoth in *The Apocryphon of John*, is identified with Baphomet. This is interesting, considering that Ialdabaoth is condemned in Gnostic literature, while Baphomet is wholly embraced by the members of the OTO's "Ecclesia Gnostica Catholica" (the "Gnostic Catholic Church"). Considering their anti-Christian, essentially Satanic bent, it seems strange for them to be praising the imagery of the Demiurge, but there is a deeper mystery here, as we shall see in due course.

Related to this subject, Hammer-Purgstall wrote in *Mysterium Baphomet Revelatum* about some of the idols that he found (of "Mete" or Baphomet, he believed) that showed the figure wearing a girdle made from what looks

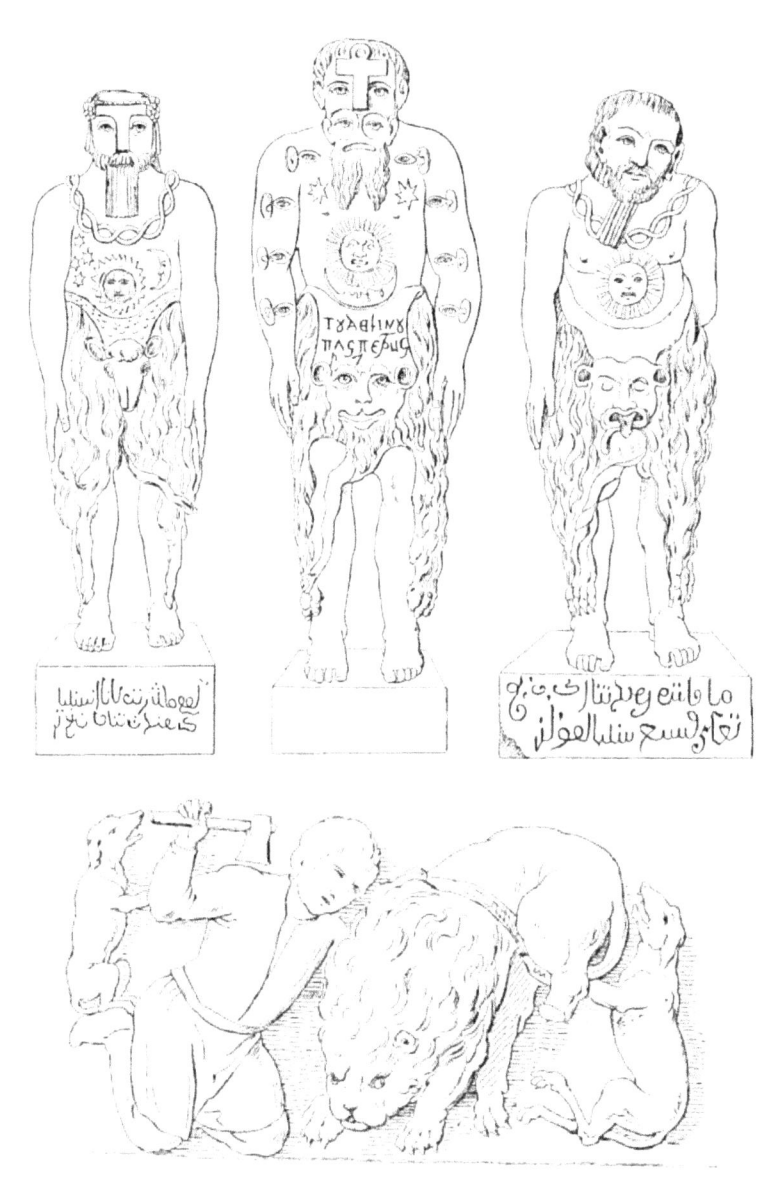

Images from *Hammer-Purgstall's Mysterium Baphometis Revelatum*. Above: Idols of Mete wearing the pelts of sacrificed lions. Below: according to Hammer-Purgstall, a dog mounts a man from behind while he slaughters a lion.

like the hide of a lion, including the creature's face, which is worn at the front, around the waist. He presumed that these represented lions that had been sacrificed, connecting this to an image he found of what looked to him like a lion being killed. He wrote:

> At the third station... a lion is perceived whom a Templar slaughters, with the assistance of three dogs, of which one grabs the lion from behind. This is the triumph of Gnosis, or of the spiritual Ophitic doctrine, over the religion of the god Sabaoth, who among the Gnostics is named *Jaldabaoth*, and under the form of a lion or a dragon, is trampled underfoot.

Returning to Celsus, his description of the various world-ruling demonic Archons also brings to mind the astral "aerial toll houses" of the Eastern Orthodox Church and *The First Apocalypse of James*, which goes into great detail on how to deal with these "toll-collectors" of the seven heavens when one dies and crosses over. This same idea of travelling through the cosmic spheres of the spirit world originates in *The Egyptian Book of the Dead*, where it lists the dangerous "judges" encountered during the post-mortem journey of the soul. In the Gnostic version, those who have cultivated the knowledge of the "resurrection" within them can escape the judgment of the Demiurge. As Simone Petrement explains in *A Separate God*:

> For the Gnostics the one who has knowledge will not be judged. This idea is often expressed in mythological form: when those who have knowledge die, they will cross the Hebdomad, the realm of the God of the Old Testament, who is the God who judges, without injury. The idea underlying this mythology could have come directly from John.

It could also come from Paul, for whom the one who has faith escapes the destruction of the world, which is the judgement.

In *Against Heresies* (1.13.6), Irenaeus writes about how the Marcosians (the Gnostic followers of Marcus the Magician) would engage in initiation rituals meant to deliver them from the authority of the Demiurge, as well as his earthly representative authorities, by the cultivation of this special type of experiential knowledge. For the Orthodox Christians, the Demiurge, in the form of Jehovah, is worthy of worship, while the Gnostics and Valentinians repudiated this idea by saying he was simply an inferior angelic power and that there is a God above the creator. As Elaine Pagels puts it in *The Gnostic Gospels*:

> Gnosis offers nothing less than a theological justification for refusing to obey the bishops and priests! The initiate now sees them as the "rulers and powers" who rule on earth in the demiurge's name. The gnostic admits that the bishop, like the demiurge, exercises legitimate authority over most Christians—those who are uninitiated. But the bishop's demands, warnings, and threats, like those of the demiurge himself, can no longer touch the one who has been "redeemed."

To this, we must add some more words from Irenaeus:

> For they affirm, that because of the "*Redemption*" it has come to pass that they can neither be apprehended, nor even seen by the judge. But even if he should happen to lay hold upon them, then they might simply repeat these words, while standing in his presence along with the "*Redemption*": *O you, who sits beside God, and*

*the mystical, eternal Sige, you through whom
the angels (mightiness), who continually behold the
face of the Father, having you as their guide
and introducer, do derive their forms from above,
which she in the greatness of her
daring inspiring with mind on account of
the goodness of the Propator, produced us as their
images, having her mind then intent upon the things
above, as in a dream—behold, the judge is at hand,
and the crier orders me to make my defense. But do
you, as being acquainted with the affairs of both,
present the cause of both of us to the judge,
inasmuch as it is in reality but one cause.* Now, as
soon as the Mother hears these words, she puts
the Homeric helmet of Pluto upon them, so that
they may invisibly escape the judge. And then she
immediately catches them up, conducts them into
the bridal chamber, and hands them over to their
consorts.

John Yarker interprets Ophite astral initiations in a much similar manner in his book *The Arcane Schools*, where he writes:

In the "Ritual of the Dead," which is of incalculable antiquity, there are certain chapters which refer to secrets of Initiation, which the translators have not mastered, and which have reference to the passwords required by the Guards of the heavenly temple or Amenti, from the aspiring soul, these are illustrated in the Ophite Ritual. To some extent the doctrine corresponds with that of the Mandeans, or followers of John the Baptist. Symbols to represent purity, life, spirit, fire have to be shewn to the Guards. We may imagine such to be the cube, tau-cross, pentagon, or other symbols. The soul greets the first power saying: 'I come from thence pure, a portion of the light of the son and father." To prove this, the sign must be shewn, as well to every Archon, that the soul passes.

Celsus describes in great detail on how the Ophite initiates were instructed and recited certain "password" statements to each Archon, including Ialdabaoth:

> They next imagine that he who has passed through Ialdabaoth and arrived at Iao ought thus to speak: "Thou, O second Iao, who shinest by night, who art the ruler of the secret mysteries of son and father, first prince of death, and portion of the innocent, bearing now mine own beard as symbol, I am ready to pass through thy realm, having strengthened him who is born of thee by the living word. Grace be with me; father, let it be with me.

This is very reminiscent of *The Sacred Book of Hermes*, which contains prayers to the decans for aid. The decans were 36 bright star constellations seen along the ecliptic. These were used as a special calendar by the Egyptians, as each decan would rise above the dawn horizon for ten days every year. Each of the decans rules over 10 degrees of the Zodiac, and so each forms a "decad." In most extant Egyptian and Hermetic literature the decans are described as gods. Praying to them was common from ancient times to the Renaissance, but now they are ignored by most modern astrologers. In *Astrological Medicine in Gnostic Traditions*, Grant Adamson writes,

> In the *Sacred Book of Hermes*, the decans are to be reverenced and flattered. They are not called daemons. There is even a sense that the decans are

positive and the zodiac is negative. The zodiac brings about suffering, which the decans heal. In order to avoid or stop a headache, for example, brought about by Aries, the prescribed gemstone amulet had to be worn when Chenlachori, the first decan of Aries, was most visible in the sky after crossing the eastern horizon and therefore most likely to look down and see its name and especially its iconography engraved on the gem. In order to counteract zodiacal influence, the practitioner reverenced and flattered the decans by displaying the proper amulet.

This is interesting in light of what we find in *The Corpus Hermeticum* Chapter 13, where the stars of the Zodiac are the "tormentors" (being identified with the Archons) which must be transcended, and the "Decad" is what causes them to flee. Perhaps the "Decad" here actually refers to the decans. They seem to play a part in the rebirth ritual that Hermeticists are known to have performed. According to *Corpus Hermeticum* II:6 the Decans are exalted above all stars, and surround the "Hebdomad" (the seventh "aeon," or realm, of existence). They may perhaps fit into the "Ogdoad," the eighth aeon, which Sophia resides in, or between the Hebdomad and the Ogdoad. As the text states:

> And further, my son, you must understand that the Decans are exempt from the things that befall the other stars. They are not checked in their course and brought to a standstill, nor hindered and made to move backwards, as the planets are; nor yet are they as are the other stars. They are free, and exalted above all things; and as careful guardians and overseers of the universe, they go round it in the space of a night and a day.

Divine Knowledge 187

To counteract the influence of one demon, one must invoke a superior one. In many ways, the Hermetica has a lot in common with the Gnostic myths of the Nag Hammadi Library and the ones described by Church Fathers like Irenaeus. In the "Hellenistic Astrology" entry on the "Internet Encyclopedia of Philosophy," it succinctly describes the Hermetic cosmology as almost identical with the Ophite view. The only difference was that, to the Hermeticists, the Demiurge was more or less a good guy created by a higher god, instead of a complete villain. As it says on the website:

> In the Poimandres text, God made man in his own image, but also made a creator god (demiurge) who made seven administrators (the planets) whose government is Fate. Man, being two-fold, is both immortal, . . . above the celestial government, and mortal, so also a slave within the system, for he shares a bit of the nature of each of the planets. At death the soul of the individual who recognizes their immortal, intellectual, and divine self ascends, while gradually surrendering the various qualities accumulated during the descent: the body is given to dissolution; the character (ethos) is yielded to the daimon (cf. Heraclitus, Fr. 119); and through each the seven planetary zones, a portion of the incarnated self that is related to the negative astrological meaning of each planet (e.g., arrogance to the Sun, greed to Jupiter) is given back to that zone. Arriving at the eighth zone, the soul is clothed in its own power (perhaps meaning its own astral body), while it is deified (in God) in the zone above the eighth.

As we have seen, many Gnostic sects were influenced by the Ophites, most notably the Naassenes. They are named, along with the Peratae and the Sethians (or "Sithians"), as Gnostic heretics by Hippolytus in *Refutation of all Heresies*. In *Thrice-Great Hermes* (Vol. 1), GRS Mead explains the true significance of Hippolytus' voluminous revelations on the secret mystery school doctrines of the pagans and their influence on the Gnostic heretics.

> The missing Books II. and III. dealt respectively with the doctrines and mysteries of the Egyptians and with those of the Chaldaeans. Hippolytus (*Proem.*) boasts that he has divulged all their mysteries, as well as the secrets of those Christian mystics whom he stigmatises as heretics, and to whom he devotes Books V.-IX. It is a curious fact that it is precisely those Books wherein this divulging of the Mysteries was attempted, which should be missing; not only have they disappeared, but in the Epitome at the beginning of Book X. the summary of their contents is also omitted. This seems almost to point to a deliberate removal of just that information which would be of priceless value to us to-day, not only for the general history of the evolution of religious ideas, but also for filling in an important part of the background of the environment of infant Christianity.
>
> Why, then, were these books cut out? Were the subsequent Christian Orthodox deterred by religious scruples, or were they afraid to circulate this information? Hippolytus himself seems to have had no such hesitation; he is ever delightedly boasting that he is giving away to the multitude the most sacred secrets of others; it seems to have been his

special *metier* to cry aloud on the house-tops what had been whispered in their secret chambers. It was for him a delicious triumph over "error" to boast, "I have your secret documents, and I am going to publish them!"

Hippolytus seems to trip over himself trying to demonstrate that Naassene doctrines are ripped straight from the ancient mystery schools. To prove this assertion, he quotes at length various pagan hymns from a secret document of one of their schools, which he is very eager to expose. To Hippolytus, by revealing heresies that had been corrupting the Church, he thought he could weaken their movement. Accordingly, he wrote:

> These doctrines, then, the Naasseni attempt to establish, calling themselves Gnostics. But since the error is many-headed and diversified, resembling, in truth, the hydra that we read of in history; when, at one blow, we have struck off the heads of this (delusion) by means of refutation, employing the wand of truth, we shall entirely exterminate the monster.

Again, the Naassenes themselves drew inspiration from a variety of sources, including the pagan mysteries of Orpheus, Demeter and Kore, Dionysius, the Great Mother and Attis (the Phrygian fertility god), and even Egyptian deities like Isis and Osiris. To the Naassenes, Jesus Christ was just another god they venerated, belonging to the secretive Christian mystery cult. In other words, it would appear that they were polytheists. Apparently, they used *The Gospel of Thomas* as well as many other apocryphal books which are now lost to us.

So not only were the Naassenes acquainted with the

pagan mysteries, but also, in seems, with Jewish and Christian scripture. Hippolytus says that they considered Jesus a hermaphroditic being, just like the Ophites did. They claimed that he was an embodiment of three natures (spirit, soul, and flesh), just as we commonly see in the writings of Paul and Matthew, as well as in Valentinian scripture. This reflects their main system of anthropomorphic theology where humanity is divided into three natures, being the "angelic, psychical, and earthly." As Hippolytus put it:

> All these qualities, however—rational, and psychical, and earthly—have, (the Naassene) says, retired and descended into one man simultaneously—Jesus, who was born of Mary.

It is also pertinent to look at what Hippolytus referred to as being key to understanding their cosmological systems, which was this hymn recited at one of their secret rituals:

> The world's producing law was Primal Mind, And next was First-born's outpoured Chaos; And third, the soul received its law of toil: Encircl'd, therefore, with an acqueous form, With care o'erpowered it succumbs to death. Now holding sway, it eyes the light, And now it weeps on misery flung; Now it mourns, now it thrills with joy; Now it wails, now it hears its doom; Now it hears its doom, now it dies, And now it leaves us, never to return. It, hapless straying, treads the maze of ills. But Jesus said, Father, behold, A strife of ills across the earth Wanders from your breath (of wrath); But bitter Chaos (man) seeks to shun, And knows not how to pass it through. On this account, O Father, send me; Bearing seals, I shall descend; Through ages whole I'll sweep, All mysteries I'll unravel, And forms of

Gods I'll show; And secrets of the saintly path,
Styled Gnosis, I'll impart.

The Naassenes also applied Ophite astrology in one of their sermons, while treating Osiris as a symbol for the primordial waters which gave rise to matter at creation. The seven veils of Isis are equated with the planets, who preside over the realm of generation and human existence, much like the Ophite Archons. As it says:

These, however, are not anything else than what by her of the seven dresses and sable robe was sought and snatched away, namely, the pudendum of Osiris. And they say that Osiris is water. But the seven-robed nature, encircled and arrayed with seven mantles of ethereal texture— for so they call the planetary stars, allegorizing and denominating them ethereal robes—is as it were the changeable generation, and is exhibited as the creature transformed by the ineffable and unportrayable, and inconceivable and figureless one. And this, (the Naassene) says, is what is declared in Scripture, The just will fall seven times, and rise again. (*Proverbs* 24:16; *Luke* 17:4) For these falls, he says, are the changes of the stars, moved by Him who puts all things in motion.

Naturally, the Naassenes interpreted the Christian scriptures within a strong philosophical and Gnostic context. They had a habit of mixing pagan heroes, culture and myth with the Old and New Testament. For example, Hippolytus tells us that the Naassenes venerated Attis of the Phrygian mysteries, the god of eunuchs, vegetation and resurrection, as a symbol of the spiritual man who avoids sexual intercourse. He was also strongly associated with the "liberty cap," worn in the Roman Empire by slaves who had been freed. All slaves were temporarily liberated during the December festival of Saturnalia, in which the rules of society were turned upside-down. Christmas is based in part on this holiday, which is why Santa Claus wears a liberty cap. It has long been used the world over as a symbol of various revolutionary movements. According to alchemist Fulcanelli in *The Mystery of the Cathedrals: Esoteric Interpretation of the Hermetic Symbols of The Great Work*, this hat was connected with mystery schools of not just the Phrygians but also the cult of Mithras, and later the Freemasons. It is now part of the official seals of the US Army and the US Senate. Fulcanelli wrote:

> The Phrygian cap, which was worn by the sans-culottes and acted as a sort of protective talisman in the midst of the revolutionary slaughter [in the French revolution], was a distinctive sign of the Initiates. In the analysis . . . the scholar Pierre Dujols writes that for the grade of the Epopt (in the Eleusinian Mysteries) the new member was asked whether he felt in himself the strength, the will and the devotion necessary for him to set his hand to the GREAT WORK. Then a red cap was put on his head, while this formula was pronounced: "Cover yourself with this cap, it is worth more than a king's crown." Few suspected that this hat, called *liberia* in the Mithraic rituals and which formerly denoted the freed slaves, was a masonic symbol and the supreme mark of Initiation. It is not therefore surprising to see it represented on our coins and our public monuments.

By invoking Attis as well as the universal symbol of the serpent in their writings, the Naassenes inferred a great deal of phallic symbolism in their exposition of the mysteries.

Even if Attis was castrated and the penis of Osiris was unrecovered, this phallic imagery was present everywhere, and this sect of co-religionists and syncretic Gnostics co-opted every bit of it that they could get their hands on. Hippolytus wrote:

> The Phrygians denominate this same also corpse—buried in the body, as it were, in a mausoleum and tomb. This, he says, is what has been declared, You are whited sepulchres, full, he says, of dead men's bones within, (*Matthew* 23:27) because there is not in you the living man. And again he exclaims, The dead shall start forth from the graves, (*Matthew* 27:52-53) that is, from the earthly bodies, being born again spiritual, not carnal. For this, he says, is the Resurrection that takes place through the gate of heaven, through which, he says, all those that do not enter remain dead.
>
> These same Phrygians, however, he says, affirm again that this very (man), as a consequence of the change, (becomes) a god. For, he says, he becomes a god when, having risen from the dead, he will enter into heaven through a gate of this kind. Paul the apostle, he says, knew of this gate, partially opening it in a mystery, and stating that he was caught up by an angel, and ascended as far as the second and third heaven into paradise itself; and that he beheld sights and heard unspeakable words which it would not be possible for man to declare. (*2 Corinthians* 12:2.)

Notice how the Naassenes exgeticized a great deal about "gateways." Unlike Marcion, the Naassenes held a particular reverence for the Old Testament. They also had a tendency to allegorize such scriptures, and claimed that the

Genesis creation account was representative of the human body. Simon Magus is said to do the same thing in his *Apophasis Megale,* otherwise known as *The Great Announcement*, also discussed by Hippolytus, which we will analyze in the next chapter. Eden, for them, was the brain, while the four rivers of Eden represented the senses. The human body itself was described as "a creation of clay, that they may serve the Demiurge of this creation, Ialdabaoth, a fiery God, a fourth number; for so they call the Demiurge and father of the formal world. . . ."

These Naassenes also seemed to have high esteem for Hermes Trismegistus, and considered him a figure of the Logos (the "divine word"), as well as a *psychopompus* (guide to the underworld). Hippolytus tells us:

> For we behold, says (the Naassene), statues of Mercury, of such a figure honoured among them. Worshipping, however, Cyllenius with special distinction, they style him *Logios*. For Mercury is *Logos*, who being interpreter and fabricator of the things that have been made simultaneously, and that are being produced, and that will exist, stands honoured among them, fashioned into some such figure as is the pudendum of a man, having an impulsive power from the parts below towards those above. And that this (deity)— that is, a Mercury of this description— is, (the Naassene) says, a conjurer of the dead, and a guide of departed spirits, and an originator of souls. . . .

Finally, Hippolytus says that the Naassenes were dedicated worshippers of the mysterious and mystical "Great Mother." This might indicate that they were venerating Sophia under the guise of ancient goddesses such as Isis, Demeter, Cybele, and Rhea. He writes:

> On account of these and such like reasons, these constantly attend the mysteries called those of the Great Mother, supposing especially that they behold by means of the ceremonies performed there the entire mystery.

It becomes clear to anyone who has read his entire account of the Naassenes that they may have been the world's first comparative mythologists. They were all about exploring the mysteries of the Bible as well as the mysteries of the pagans and the teachings of the Greek philosophers as part of a quest to discover the key to all mythologies. They seem to have believed that ultimately they were all connected, or that they expressed many common themes codified in different languages and semantics. In a lot of ways, the Naassenes anticipated the Structuralists, Jungian psychoanalysts, and early mythicists like Joseph Campbell. Even though Jungians and mythicists all stressed the universal meanings of the world's religions, they also denied their metaphysical claims. The Gnosis of the Naassene Gnostics is not exactly based on divine revelation, but is, as Mark J. Edwards said in his article, "The Naming of the Naassenes: Hippolytus, *Refutatio* V.6-10 as Hieros Logos":

> ... a studious collocation of the mysteries of a philological discipline which aims to be the master, not the servant, of philosophy; a parliament of symbols which does not proclaim a new code of belief.

Curiously, Sophia is not named in the Naassene system, but as we said, she was probably venerated under the form of another goddess figure. The Gnostics saw Sophia as secretly working through the Authorities and tricking them into serving a higher goal, as we have seen in Irenaeus' Ophite account. To them, Sophia was representative of a type of purity beyond polarity, just like Baphomet is. We are reminded by something GRS Mead once wrote in *Did Jesus Live 100 B.C.?*

> In Gnostic tradition we find the Sophia in her various aspects possessed of many names. Among them may be mentioned: the Mother or All-Mother; Mother of the Living, or Shining Mother; the Power Above; the Holy Spirit; again She of the Left-hand, as opposed to Christos, Him of the Right-hand; the Man-woman; Prouneikos or Lustful-one, the Harlot; the Matrix; Eden; Achamoth; the Virgin; Barbelo; Daughter of Light; Merciful Mother; Consort of the Masculine One; Revelant of the Perfect Mysteries; Perfect Mercy; Revelant of the Mysteries of the whole Magnitude; Hidden Mother; She who knows the Mysteries of the Elect; the Holy Dove which has given birth to Twins; Ennoea; and the Lost or Wandering Sheep, Helena and many other names.
>
> All these terms refer to Sophia or the "Soul"—using the term in its most general sense—in her cosmic or individual aspects, according as she is above in her perfect purity; or in the midst, as intermediary, or below as fallen into matter.

In the Gnostic text *Thunder Perfect Mind*, Sophia describes herself as the preeminent female divinity, full of contradictions:

> . . . I am the first and the last.
>
> I am the honored one and the scorned one.
>
> I am the whore and the holy one.
>
> I am the wife and the virgin. . . .

I am the mother of my father and the sister of my husband and he is my offspring.

I am the slave of him who prepared me. . . .

For I am the wisdom of the Greeks and the knowledge of the barbarians. . . .

I am the one whose image is great in Egypt, and the one who has no image among the barbarians. . . .

I am the one whom you have pursued, and I am the one whom you have seized.

I am the one whom you have scattered, and you have gathered me together. . . .

I, I am godless, and I am the one whose God is great. . . .

I am the one whom you have hidden from, and you appear to me.

But whenever you hide yourselves, I myself will appear.

For whenever you appear, I myself will hide from you. . . .

. . .[C]ome forward to me, you who know me, and you who know my members, and establish the great ones among the small first creatures. . . .

Those who are without association with me are ignorant of me, and those who are in my substance are the ones who know me.

Those who are close to me have been ignorant of me, and those who are far away from me are the ones who have known me.

> On the day when I am close to you, you are far away from me, and on the day when I am far away from you, I am close to you.
>
> I am the union and the dissolution.
>
> I am the abiding and I am the dissolution.
>
> I am the one below, and they come up to me. . . .
>
> I, I am sinless, and the root of sin derives from me.
>
> I am lust in (outward) appearance, and interior self-control exists within me. . . .
>
> I am the knowledge of my name.

As we can see, the word "Gnosticism" encompasses a number of complex, baffling and paradoxical concepts, but often beautifully sublime philosophical perspectives as well. Who really started the tradition, though? Surprising to some, it is frequently said by researchers on the subject that the whole thing began with a man called "John." That is the subject of the next chapter.

Chapter 6: The Head of Prophecy

Thus John, who was often consulted by Herod, and to whom that monarch showed great deference, and was often governed by his advice; whose doctrine prevailed very extensively among the people and the publicans, taught some creed older than Christianity. That is plain. . . .

—Albert Pike, *Morals and Dogma*

Historically, John the Baptist appears to have been an important personage, well-loved by the public in his time. He is seen as a prophet today by Christians and Muslims, as well as the Gnostic Mandaeans of Iraq (and, historically, other Gnostic groups too). Scholars have argued that he was actually a trained and functioning priest, perhaps from a family of priests. He may have even been seen by some as the true messiah. In addition to the historical figure, John is also significant as a symbol, an archetype, which shows up in folklore, occult traditions, and Freemasonic rituals. But why is this so?

According to Masonic scholar Albert Pike in his 1872 Scottish Rite catechism *Morals and Dogma*, the Knights Templar followed a secret and esoteric Johannite doctrine (revering John over Jesus). The Mandaeans claimed John the Baptist was the true prophet of his generation and repudiated Jesus Christ as a false pretender. In Gnostic (Ophite) Christianity, John the Baptist was part of Sophia's plan for salvation. Even more intriguing is that his direct disciples, Jesus Christ and Simon Magus were both said to have visited and then "come out of" Egypt, as we will see later in this chapter.

In Christianity (as elucidated in *Acts* 8:35-36), water baptism is a symbolic gesture made by a new Christian who has decided to believe the Gospel. Joseph von Hammer-Purgstall thought that Gnostic groups (especially the Mandaeans and other Johannites) saw it as an act of spiritual liberation through submersion in divine wisdom. In Gnostic tradition, Sophia is the initiator of a baptismal flood of Gnosis, as we read in the Nag Hammadi text *Trimorphic Protennoia*:

> I descended to the midst of the underworld, and I shone down upon the darkness. It is I who poured forth the water. It is I who am hidden within radiant waters. I am the one who gradually put forth the All by my Thought. It is I who am laden with the Voice. It is through me that Gnosis comes forth. I dwell in the ineffable and unknowable ones. I am perception and knowledge, uttering a Voice by means of thought. I am the real Voice. I cry out in everyone, and they recognize it (the voice), since a seed indwells them.

What's more, Sophia was connected to John the Baptist in the Ophite system, as Irenaeus reports in *Against Heresies*, 1.30.11-12:

> They maintain that Sophia, herself has also spoken many things through [the prophets] regarding the first Anthropos (man), and concerning that Christ who is above, thus admonishing and reminding men of the incorruptible light, the first Anthropos, and of the descent of Christ. The [other] powers being terrified by these things, and marvelling at the novelty of those things which were announced by the prophets, *[Sophia] brought it about by means of Ialdabaoth (who knew not what he did), that*

The Head of Prophecy 201

emissions of two men took place, the one from the barren Elizabeth, and the other from the Virgin Mary. And since she herself had no rest either in heaven or on earth, she invoked her mother to assist her in her distress. Upon this, her mother, the first woman, was moved with compassion towards her daughter, on her repentance, and begged from the first man that Christ should be sent to her assistance, who, being sent forth, descended to his sister, and to the besprinkling of light. *When he recognised her (that is, the Sophia below), her brother descended to her, and announced his advent through means of John, and prepared the baptism of repentance.*

Through the vessel of John the Baptist, the spiritual act of repentance is introduced to mankind via Sophia's intercession. Recall how we mentioned the Gnostic belief that Sophia grieved and repented to her mother, the Holy Spirit, Christ and the Pleroma to rectify her error of accidentally creating Ialdabaoth when she fell into the primeval chaos of matter. John the Baptist taught that water baptism and repentance would wash away the sins of the guilty, and in a way that seems to be the sort of thing that Sophia was asking for.

The Gnostic *Apocryphon of James* includes this curious exchange on the subject of John's beheading between Jesus and his disciple James:

> Then I asked him, "Lord, how shall we be able to prophesy to those who request us to prophesy to them? For there are many who ask us, and look to us to hear an oracle from us."

> The Lord answered and said, "Do you not know that the head of prophecy was cut off with John?"
>
> But I said, "Lord, can it be possible to remove the head of prophecy?"
>
> The Lord said to me, "When you come to know what 'head' means, and that prophecy issues from the head, (then) understand the meaning of 'Its head was removed.' At first I spoke to you in parables, and you did not understand; now I speak to you openly, and you (still) do not perceive. Yet, it was you who served me as a parable in parables, and as that which is open in the (words) that are open."

For rather obvious reasons, heads have been considered symbols of wisdom, intelligence, and the mind by pretty much every culture ever. This includes the emblem of a disembodied head, and that of a skull. In fact it used to be traditional to keep a human skull in one's study as a paperweight and *memento mori* ("reminder of death"). In the Holy Land in the time of Jesus and John, it was a common belief that the mummified heads or skulls of prophets, magicians and wonder-workers held a particular power. Egyptian, Jewish, and Arab magicians have written of the custom of using mummified heads as oracles. The talking severed head of the giant Bran in Celtic lore (believed to have magically protected London from French invasion), the singing head of poet Orpheus in Greek stories, and the prophetic skull of Adam in Judeo-Christian apocrypha are examples of mythical disembodied heads that have been linked with prophecy.

The Knights Templar, in their confessions, also claimed that their Baphomet head could "prophesy" to them. They symbolized their love of their talking head by choosing the skull and crossbones as one of their most famous and omnipresent insignias, giving birth to an icon that would later be used by Europeans pirates on their menacing "Jolly Roger" flags (often accompanied by the number 13 for some occult reason). According to a story associated with the Templars, the head acquired its magic through an act of necrophilia. From *Freemasonry and the Ancient Gods* by JMS Ward:

> A great lady of Maraclea was loved by a Templar, a Lord of Sidon; but she died in her youth, and on the night of her burial, this wicked lover crept to the grave, dug up her body and violated it. Then a voice from the void bade him return in nine months time for he would find a son. He obeyed the injunction and at the appointed time opened the grave again and found a head on the leg bones of the skeleton (skull and crossbones).
>
> The same voice bade him, "guard it well, for it would be the giver of all good things," and so he carried it away with him. It became his protecting genius, and he was able to defeat his enemies by merely showing them the magic head. In due course, it passed into the possession of the Order.

The authors of *Holy Blood, Holy Grail* (Michael Baigent, Richard Leigh and Henry Lincoln) have noted that other versions of this story they found included the young woman's name, "Yse," and that this sounds a bit like "Isis." Of course, it was the husband of Isis, Osiris, who was dead when she had sex with him to conceive their son Horus. However, Isis, and her counterpart, the Greek Aphrodite (or the Roman Venus), are traditionally depicted with alabaster skin, sleeping naked in a hidden tomb. It was said that anyone who would witnessed her nakedness, even accidentally, would be cursed. A skeleton could be thought of as symbolically a "naked" and "white" body, so perhaps the description of Venus was meant to be taken as a metaphor for this. If the Templars believed they had the skull of Isis, this would fit the lore, as she is a goddess of prophecy, wisdom, and magic, which are exactly the benefits that the Templars allegedly derived from the Baphomet head.

But whether it was John's head, Isis' head, or someone else's, the idea that heads could be used as oracles is deeply-rooted, particularly in the Middle East and Northern Africa. Called *teraphim* in Hebrew, Athanasius Kirscher depicted, in his 1652 book *Oedipus Aegyptiacus*, the Egyptian magical practice of making a sort of robot from a mummified head, often of the firstborn son of the magician, which could be used for divination purposes. The head would be mounted on a wall or a golden plate and would supposedly deliver prophecies when questioned. In 620 BC, they were classified as a form of idol and banned by the Hebrew prophets. They were also used, apparently, by the Sabians of Harran. Kevin van Bladel's *The Arabic Hermes* describes a festival that included "a ritual involving a decapitated boy whose head is placed on an altar where it howls; its howls were used to predict the future of the Sabian people." At this rite the pagan god Mara Samya, "the Blind Lord," was invoked, perhaps equivalent to the demon Samael, whose name means the same thing.

So, it seems, belief that a magical ceremony could make a severed head talk was widespread in the ancient Middle East. There is an interesting account of how the effect of such a thing could be created through trickery. From the 1961 classic *A History of Secret Societies* by "Arkon

Daraul" (a.k.a. Idries Shah, the Sufi writer), quoting *The Art of Imposture*, by Abdel-Rahman of Damascus, we read about how Hassan-i Sabbah, "the Old Man of the Mountains," founder of the Order of Assassins in eleventh-century Persia, initiated his *mujahadeen* recruits into his war cult:

> He had a deep, narrow pit sunk into the floor of his audience-chamber. One of his disciples stood in this, in such a way that his head and neck alone were visible above the floor. Around the neck was placed a circular dish in two pieces which fitted together, with a hole in the middle. This gave the impression that there was a severed head on a metal plate standing on the floor. In order to make the scene more plausible (if that is the word) Hasan had some fresh blood poured around the head, on the plate.
>
> Now certain recruits were brought in. "Tell them," commanded the chief, "what thou hast seen." The disciple then described the delights of Paradise. "You have seen the head of a man who died, whom you all knew. I have reanimated him to speak with his own tongue."
>
> Later, the head was treacherously severed in real earnest, and stuck for some time somewhere that the faithful would see it. The effect of this conjuring trick plus murder increased the enthusiasm for martyrdom to the required degree.

A similar story is told by James Wasserman in his 2001 book *The Templars and the Assassins*, only he claims that it was done by Rashid Al-Din Sinan, a later Assassin chief. It seems likely that if there is any truth to the story, it was probably the standard Assassin initiation ritual throughout their existence.

Now in the case of the head of John the Baptist, it was purportedly put "on a platter," which we all universally imagine to be a dinner service. But wouldn't it make more sense that Salome, as a member of the formerly "Idumean" or Edomite Herodian dynasty (forced to convert to Judaism in the second century), was practicing an old family tradition and requesting the sacrifice of a prophet whose head could be mummified, mounted on a plate and used as a teraph for prophecy? Hasn't anyone ever wondered what her mother Herodias intended to do with such a grisly prize? There is no description of what was done with the head afterwards, so it is left to our imagination, but this makes more sense to us than anything. We will discuss this possibility again later on.

If the Templars had John's head, what did it mean to them? Was it useful to them merely because he was a prophet? Had they discovered the belief that prophet's heads could be used for magic and divination? Or was there something about John in particular that was special to them? According to Pope Pius IX (reigning from 1846 to 1878), yes there was, and again, it is linked with Gnosticism. The Pope, in his "Allocution Against the Freemasons," charged that the Templars had tapped into the existence of a secret Johannite church. Here are some of his words on the subject, as quoted by Albert Pike in *Morals and Dogma*:

> The Johannites ascribed to Saint John the foundation of their Secret Church, and the Grand Pontiffs of the Sect assumed the title of Christos, Anointed, or Consecrated, and claimed to have succeeded one another from Saint John by an uninterrupted succession of pontifical powers. He who, at the period of the foundation of the Order of

the Temple, claimed these imaginary prerogatives, was named THEOCLET; he knew HUGUES DE PAYENS, he initiated him into the Mysteries and hopes of his pretended church, he seduced him by the notions of Sovereign Priesthood and Supreme royalty, and finally designated him as his successor.

Thus the Order of Knights of the Temple was at its very origin devoted to the cause of opposition to the tiara of Rome and the crowns of Kings, and the Apostolate of Kabalistic Gnosticism was vested in its chiefs. For Saint John himself was the Father of the Gnostics, and the current translation of his polemic against the heretical of his Sect and the pagans who denied that Christ was the Word, is throughout a misrepresentation, or misunderstanding at least, of the whole Spirit of that Evangel.

Pope Pius IX (whom we will quote at greater length in a later chapter) agrees that the Knights Templar held a secret doctrine of Johannism. Now, he was talking here about a doctrine of reverence for John the Evangelist, the alleged author of *The Gospel of John*, often considered to have a "Gnostic" flavor to it, and used as scripture by several Gnostic groups. But we will show later on that some researchers think that this text was essentially inspired by John the Baptist, and that this is why it is attributed to someone named John. So while the term "Johannism" can refer to those who place special importance on John's Gospel, it can also (perhaps in the same instance) refer to those who revere John the Baptist as the real Christ and the "Father of the Gnostics," such as the sect called the Mandaeans (whom we will discuss in detail later on). The existence of this school of thought was explored in detail in the book *The Templar Revelation* by Lynn Picknett and Clive Prince (1997).

In the above-quoted passage, Pope Pius IX claims that the founding Templar, Hughes de Payens was initiated into a Johannite church by a bishop named Theoclet, who allegedly carried a right of priesthood with an apostolic succession going back to John. Presumably, he meant John the Evangelist, as it seems from the context of the statement. But this claim had also been made just a few years earlier by the French cleric Bernard-Raymond Fabre-Palaprat, who in 1804 founded the Templar revival order "Ordre de Temple," which purported to be a direct continuation of the original. This order was dedicated, like Freemasonry also, as we shall see) to both John the Baptist and John the Evangelist.

The confessing Templars admitted to secret rituals that involved in spitting on the cross in their initiation rituals. Interestingly enough, the Church Father Origen made the same claim about the Ophites in *Against Celsus* (5.28) when he paraphrased and answered Celsus' charges against the Christians (whom Celsus did not distinguish from the Ophites, while Origen certainly does):

> Now he ought to have known that those who have espoused the cause of the serpent, because he gave good advice to the first human beings, and who go far beyond the Titans and Giants of fable, and are on this account called Ophites, are so far from being Christians, that they bring accusations against Jesus to as great a degree as Celsus himself; and they do not admit anyone into their assembly until he has uttered maledictions against Jesus.

The Head of Prophecy 209

It is perhaps this point that led Hammer-Purgstall to believe that the Templars not only were secretly Johannites but also followed after the example of the Ophites as well. In *Mysterium Baphometis Revelatum*, he writes that the Templars' "secret doctrine is identical with that of the Gnostics, indeed, of the Ophites." On several of the alleged "Templar artifacts" reproduced in his book, there are depictions of an androgynous figure called, according to the inscriptions, "Mete," which Hammer-Purgstall says is "none other than Sophia of the Ophites, who is known otherwise as Acamoth, Prunicos, Barbelo."

Of course, being an ostensibly Christian army chartered by the Pope himself, this "secret doctrine" would have to have been carefully disguised within a veneer of orthodoxy that none but the highest initiates would ever glimpse beyond. In his *Allocution*, Pope Pius IX discussed the two-tiered system of exoteric beliefs and practices for public consumption combined with (perhaps completely opposite) esoteric dogma for the inner circle:

> The Templars, like all other Secret Orders and Associations, had two doctrines, one concealed and reserved for the Masters, which was Johannism; the other public, which was the Roman Catholic. Thus they deceived the adversaries whom they sought to supplant. Hence Free-Masonry, vulgarly imagined to have begun with the Dionysian Architects or the German Stone-workers, adopted Saint John the Evangelist as one of its patrons, associating with him, in order not to arouse the suspicions of Rome, Saint John the Baptist, and thus covertly proclaiming itself the child of the Kabalah and Essenism together.

Note that, here, the Pope gives an explanation for the veneration of both Johns, and claims that they were both considered emblems of the same covert symbolism. There are multiple versions of the character of John the Baptist that we see in various scriptures from different sects, such as the Mandaeans with their "Yohana," and the Muslims with their "Yahya." The Catholic tradition, of course, comes strictly from the four Gospels. In tracking the Baptist's mythos, it makes sense to begin with John's gospel. It is not a synoptic (meaning it doesn't follow the same story structure as the other three in the New Testament, the "Synoptic Gospels"), but it does give an idea of what John the Baptist meant to early Christianity.

In this text, John the Baptist is barely mentioned. In the first chapter, John simply appears and is a "witness" to Jesus (1:7). In other words, John gives his testimony on what occurred. In essence, he saw Jesus (the Logos) coming to him for baptism, and at that moment, the Holy Spirit descended upon Jesus. Beyond this mention, John the Baptist is just said in the book to be the guy that came before Jesus and testified about him, recognizing what he was and proclaiming it to the public.

Luke's Gospel tells us in the first chapter that Mary, the mother of Jesus, and John's mother Elizabeth, were cousins, and they were both pregnant at the same time, specifically six months apart. Like Mary's conception of Jesus, Elizabeth's pregnancy was also miraculous, because she and her husband Zacharias were childless, elderly, and seemingly infertile. Just as Jesus' birth was foretold to both Mary and Joseph in separate angelic visitations, John's conception was foretold to Zacharias, and he, like Mary, was told what to name the child. But no actual communication between the two children is ever mentioned in any of the Gospels, and we are to assume that they never met before the baptism of Jesus, or ever again.

In *The Gospel of Matthew* 3:13-17 (KJV), we read that Jesus specifically came to John to be baptized, although we don't know if he was inspired to do this or just chose to of his own accord. But John tried to deter him, saying, "I have need to be baptized of thee, and comest thou to me?" Jesus replied, "Let it be so now; it is proper for us to do this to fulfill all righteousness," implying that his baptism was somehow integral for the completion of prophecy. As soon as Jesus came up out of the water, heaven was opened, and "he saw the Spirit of God descending like a dove and alighting on him. And a voice from Heaven said, 'This is my Son, whom I love; with him I am well pleased.'"

But why did Jesus need John specifically? According to *The Gospel of John*, the Baptist was "not the Light" (*John* 1:8), and by his own proclamation not even worthy of untying the thong of Jesus' sandal (1:27). Yet he is given the extraordinary honor of being mentioned in the very midst of that gospel's "Great Proem," (the introductory invocation), where it is said that John was "sent from God" . . . to bear witness to the Light, that all might believe through him." (1:6-7)

If *all* had to believe *through him*, he was obviously entrusted with a mission that, though subordinate to that of Jesus, had nevertheless a universal (*all*) and exclusive (*through him*) character. The contradiction between this mission and his unworthiness to even untie the thong of Jesus' sandal is, or so at least it seems to us, evident. Therefore we are led to ask: who was John the Baptist really?

In *The Gospel of John*, this very question was asked of him by the "priests and Levites from Jerusalem" sent to him by "the Jews" (1:19, KJV). They asked, "Who are you?" He replied:

> I am the voice of one crying in the wilderness, Make straight the way of the Lord. (1:23, KJV)

In *The Gospel of Marcion* (an earlier version of *Luke* reconstructed from quotes used by the Church Fathers in order to condemn his heresy), the testimony of John the Baptist is not mentioned directly. In the *Panarion* (1.42.11:3-4), Epiphanius writes against Marcion thusly:

> At the very beginning he excised everything Luke had originally composed—his "inasmuch as many have taken in hand," and so forth, and the material about Elizabeth and the angel's announcement to Mary the Virgin; about John and Zacharias and the birth at Bethlehem; the genealogy and the story of the baptism. All this he cut out and turned his back on, and made this the beginning of the Gospel, "In the fifteenth year of Tiberius Caesar," and so on.

In both *The Gospel of Mark* and *The Gospel of Matthew*, not only is John a witness to Jesus, but also personally baptizes Jesus, at the latter's request. John's baptism and preaching ministry was already in full swing and quite popular with the public at this time. The actual doctrine that John the Baptist taught to his disciples is found in these gospels too. John is reported to have implored people to take a "baptism for repentance and remission of sins" (*Matthew* 3.2; *Luke* 3:3).

John himself was purportedly at the center of a controversy between Jesus and the Jewish Pharisees when he was challenged by them in Jerusalem. *Matthew* 21:23

(NIV) reports that the priests challenged him on his authority, but Jesus responded swiftly and shut them down:

> Jesus entered the temple courts, and, while he was teaching, the chief priests and the elders of the people came to him. "By what authority are you doing these things?" they asked. "And who gave you this authority?"
>
> Jesus replied, "I will also ask you one question. If you answer me, I will tell you by what authority I am doing these things. John's baptism—where did it come from? Was it from heaven, or of human origin?"
>
> They discussed it among themselves and said, "If we say, 'From heaven,' he will ask, 'Then why didn't you believe him?' But if we say, 'Of human origin'—we are afraid of the people, for they all hold that John was a prophet."
>
> So they answered Jesus, "We don't know."
>
> Then he said, "Neither will I tell you by what authority I am doing these things."

It was clear that Jesus had won the debate. The Jerusalem priests refused to answer Jesus' retort because John the Baptist was popular with the people of his day. It seems as though the priests privately thought that John's doctrine was heretical and contrary to the Law of Moses, which they obviously upheld. Jesus likewise refused to answer their question. It appears as though Jesus was speaking more like a Gnostic teacher than a Jewish Rabbi. Jesus is speaking on behalf of a "perfect" higher God as opposed to the jealous God of the Old Testament, redeeming his followers from the "curse of the [Mosaic] law" (*Galatians* 3:13).

Mark 11:29, much like what we saw in *Matthew* 21, specifically claims that John's baptism of Jesus was of a heavenly, rather than human, origin. Many have pointed to the prophecy from *The Book of Malachi* 4:5 to be a prediction of John's ministry, where it says:

> Behold, I will send you Elijah the prophet before the coming of the great and dreadful day of the Lord.

It is taken as though John is almost a reincarnation or an avatar of Elijah. John and Elijah are also said to have dressed the same. John reportedly wore camel's hair with a leather girdle, Elijah, according to *2 Kings* 1:8, was "a hairy man, and girt with a girdle of leather about his loins." Like John after him, Elijah spent time in the wilderness (at Horeb), where he was fed by ravens. Elijah did not die, but instead ascended to Heaven in a whirlwind, in a fiery chariot drawn by fiery horses. (This is part of why Elijah is linked by comparative mythologists to another prophet and herald, Enoch, and why the Islamic Idris is linked to Elijah and Enoch both). He was expected to return one day, possibly with his spirit inspiring and essentially inhabiting the body of another prophet in the future.

A later version of *Luke* 1:17 claims that John prophesied in "the spirit and power of Elijah. . . ." In *The Gospel of John*, priests and Levites ask the Baptist if he is Elijah, which he explicitly denies. In *Mark*, Herod's men theorize that maybe Jesus is Elijah returned. Jesus even seems to imply this when speaking to his own followers about John after a diplomatic visit from some of John's followers, in *Matthew* 11:13-15 (NIV):

The Head of Prophecy 215

For all the Prophets and the Law prophesied until John. And if you are willing to accept it, he is the Elijah who was to come. Whoever has ears, let them hear.

Stranger still, St. Jerome said something that few people would have considered. In *Against the Pelagians* (3:2), he quoted from the now lost *Gospel of the Hebrews*, which commented on Jesus and John's relationship:

In the Gospel according to the Hebrews, which is written in the Chaldee and Syrian language, but in Hebrew characters, and is used by the Nazarenes to this day (I mean the Gospel according to the Apostles, or, as is generally maintained, the Gospel according to Matthew, a copy of which is in the library at Caesarea), we find, "Behold, the mother of our Lord and His brethren said to Him, John Baptist baptizes for the remission of sins; let us go and be baptized by him. *But He said to them, what sin have I committed that I should go and be baptized by him?* Unless, haply, the very words which I have said are only ignorance.

This passage is interesting because it calls into question if Jesus ever was a disciple of John the Baptist, as implied in the Judean *Gospel of Matthew*. Jerome is quoting from a Hebrew text of *Matthew* that actually shows a totally different picture of their relationship. It seems to us that the references to John the Baptist were added to *Matthew* by a proto-Gnostic writer/editor. Jerome also mentions the term "Nazarene," which can be found in the Gospels. The Hebrew *natsar* means "watch," "preserve," or "guard." It signifies "secret knowledge" and "hidden things," which implies potent Gnostic intonations. It is often thought that the phrase translated as "Jesus of Nazareth" refers to the town of that name, which did not exist during Jesus' life. The term that was meant to be applied to Jesus was "Nazarene," which indicates an initiate of hidden wisdom who has taken as ascetic vow.

In *The Gospel of John* 1:17-18 (KJV), we can see the Baptist's theology more plainly:

> For the Law was given by Moses, but grace and truth came through Jesus Christ. No man has seen God at any time. The only-begotten Son, in the bosom of the Father, He has declared him.

The theme that Moses does not represent the true God occurs throughout this gospel. In *John* 17:25, Jesus says plainly, "Oh righteous Father, the world (cosmos) has not known you." And in *John* 9:29 the Pharisees are reported to have responded to Jesus's message: "We know that God spoke to Moses: as for this fellow, we know not where he is from." It seems that John and Jesus both were teaching a heretical doctrine that does not conform to traditional Judaism or Catholicism in preaching that there is another unknown god beyond Jehovah.

Returning to *The Gospel of Matthew*, particularly Chapter 3, we see John the Baptist preaching in the "wilderness of Judea and saying, 'Repent, for the kingdom of heaven has come near.'" John is baptizing many people coming from Jerusalem, Judea and Jordan, encouraging them to confess their sins and then washing them away in the Jordan River. However, in *Matthew* 3:7-12 (ESV), when John sees a number of Pharisees and Sadducees attending these baptismal rites, he immediately condemns them without a moment's hesitation:

> You brood of vipers! Who warned you to flee from the coming wrath? Produce fruit in keeping

with repentance. And do not think you can say to yourselves, "We have Abraham as our father." I tell you that out of these stones God can raise up children for Abraham. *The ax is already at the root of the trees, and every tree that does not produce good fruit will be cut down and thrown into the fire.*

I baptize you with water for repentance. But after me comes one who is more powerful than I, whose sandals I am not worthy to carry. *He will baptize you with the Holy Spirit and fire.* His winnowing fork is in his hand, and he will clear his threshing floor, gathering his wheat into the barn and burning up the chaff with unquenchable fire.

What John is telling the Pharisees and Sadducees is basically that they are wrong to think that they are the Lord's chosen people simply because they descended from Abraham. John is saying in symbolic language that the "ax" is the means by which Christ will cut into the dead spirit, remove the heart of stone, and transmute it by the fruit of regeneration into the spirit of Christ. Also notice how the coming one is described as being a baptizer of the "Holy Spirit and fire." This is the same description given to the Demiurge in the first discourse of *The Corpus Hermeticum*. Simon Magus was particularly obsessed with the idea of the divine fire as well, as we will see. Tobias Churton suggests in *The Mysteries of John the Baptist* that the coming one whom John is speaking of in the above passage may not have been the messiah at all, but rather God himself, or, at least, the creator god Jehovah. This might even make John himself the messiah (or at least, the preeminent prophet of his time). This theory may also explain why Paul never quotes Jesus in his epistles (although Paul makes a few allusions to *Luke*'s Gospel). Perhaps all his ideas come from another source. Of course the challenge is establishing a connection between Paul and John.

The only real evidence is that Paul's fellow ministers conducted baptisms, which some think is a rite that originated with John. This may have continued on through Simon Magus, one of his students, who carried on John's tradition after his untimely death. It appears from *Matthew* Chapter 3 that some proto-Gnostic Christian felt compelled to give credit to John, but at the same time to make Jesus more important than John. John is also made to appear inferior to Jesus when described as sleeping outside, wearing a camel hair loincloth, and eating bugs, which may have been inaccurate and intended to be deliberately demeaning. *Luke* says that John's father was a priest named Zechariah, which meant that he was from an upper-class family with access to a full education in biblical texts, and probably the Greek language as well.

Judging from the evidence, the Jesus and John movements were originally separate. Jesus was a messianic Jewish prophet, as seen in *Matthew*, but not necessarily the messiah, while John was a mystic rebel with a new view of theology and spirituality. Perhaps when Jesus' prophecies failed to pan out, Christians began to take more of their ideas from John, and remade Jesus in the image of John, the Great Gnostic Baptizer. We can also see echoes of John's practices in Jesus' teaching to the Pharisee Nicodemus in *The Gospel of John* 3:2-8 (NIV), where the latter asked his teacher:

> "Rabbi, we know that you are a teacher who has come from God. For no one could perform the signs you are doing if God were not with him." Jesus replied, "Very truly I tell you, no one can see the kingdom of God unless they are born again." "How

can someone be born when they are old?" Nicodemus asked. "Surely they cannot enter a second time into their mother's womb to be born!"

Jesus answered, "Very truly I tell you, no one can enter the kingdom of God unless they are born of water and the Spirit. Flesh gives birth to flesh, but the Spirit gives birth to spirit. You should not be surprised at my saying, 'You must be born again.' The wind blows wherever it pleases. You hear its sound, but you cannot tell where it comes from or where it is going. So it is with everyone born of the Spirit."

The symbol of water is one with manifold meanings, one of which obviously involves cleanliness. The term "living waters" is not just poetic, but carries a specific meaning. This pertains to the pre-Christian Jewish tradition of purification rites involving ritual baths that adhered to rigorous specifications. On a physical, exoteric level, the water literally washed away all dirt and filth from the body. On a spiritual level, the baptism meant that the psyche or soul was dead unless it maintained a constant connection with the deeper streams of universal life, the divine *agape* (love) of God, which Jesus described as "a well of water springing up into everlasting life" to the Samaritan woman at the well (*John* 4:14).

We see influences of John's teaching in St. Paul when he writes in *Romans* 6:2-4 (NIV):

> By no means! We are those who have died to sin; how can we live in it any longer? Or don't you know that all of us who were baptized into Christ Jesus were baptized into his death? We were therefore buried with him through baptism into death in order

that, just as Christ was raised from the dead through the glory of the Father, we too may live a new life.

The Pauline writer of *Hebrews* claimed that the baptism is an elementary teaching, meaning that there was a deeper, esoteric Christian message, as we read here in 6:1 (ESV):

> Therefore let us leave the elementary teachings about Christ and go on to maturity, not laying again the foundation of repentance from acts that lead to death, and of faith in God, instruction about baptisms, the laying on of hands, the resurrection of the dead, and eternal judgment. And God permitting, we will do so.

Ezekiel 36:25 contains a promise from God to his prophet that he will "sprinkle clean water upon you, and ye shall be clean: from all your filthiness, and from all your idols, will I cleanse you." Chapter 2:6 of *The Gospel of John* mentions the practice of "Jews" using "waterpots of stone" for purification rites. But the imagery of Jesus being crucified, with the water and blood flowing *uncontained* from his side, fits with the idea that the cleansing fluid from this vessel of flesh would purify *the whole world*, not just the Jews alone. In the early Church, the Christian baptism ceremony didn't just involve immersion in water, but also the ritual application of holy oil (olive oil mixed with balsam) to the forehead, which was typically administered in the sign of the cross. The repentant would take a bath and then apply the scented oils after he was clean. Doing so in the context of baptism reinforced the sense that the newly initiated Christian was washed, purified and sealed in Christ.

In *Mark* 14:3, we see Mary Magdalene, the first witness to Jesus' resurrection, and his close companion according in all accounts (much like Simon Magus and his consort

The Head of Prophecy 221

Helena), officiating at what would have been considered a royal anointing with the pouring of a large amount of oil upon the head of Jesus. This "christening" or "chrism" might have been the ceremony ordaining Jesus as the successor of John the Baptist. A similar anointing rite was also used in the consecration of priests and kings, including ancient Egyptian Pharaohs. St. Ambrose explains this quite succinctly in *De Sacramentis* (2.7):

> You were rubbed with oil like an athlete, Christ's athlete, as though in preparation for an earthly wrestling-match, and you agreed to take on your opponent, the Devil.

As we shall explain, the term "Christ" may refer to one who was "christened" (meaning "anointed") with oil as the legitimate successor of the Baptist, just as Simon Magus was. As much as the Church reviled the Simonians and Simon Magus himself, its tradition of "apostolic succession" is actually based on the Simonian system, where each successive student takes on his teacher's role. With the Catholic Church, the idea was that Jesus appointed St. Peter to be the "rock" upon which his church would be founded (thus Peter, who was originally named Simon also, took on his new name, meaning "rock," to reflect this). Tradition says that Jesus gave Peter the "keys to Heaven" (now the official logo of the Papacy), bestowing upon him power over the spiritual destinies of men, and over the spirits in the ether. So Peter was the first Pope. Via what is called "chirothesy" or "the laying on of hands," Peter was supposedly able to ordain other bishops to help grow the Church, and passed the power down to them as well. These priests in turn passed the power on to other priests that they ordained. So through apostolic succession, there is a vast web of interweaving but unbroken lines of spiritual power which have been transmitted from Jesus, through Saint Peter, down to all of the validly ordained bishops of the present day.

The Gnostic *Gospel of Philip 4:8* contains a clear exegetic explanation on the oil anointing rite:

> Love never says, "This is yours" or "This is mine," but "All these are yours." Spiritual love is wine and fragrance. All those who anoint themselves with it take pleasure in it. While those who are anointed are present, those nearby also profit (from the fragrance). If those anointed with ointment withdraw from them and leave, then those not anointed, who merely stand nearby, still remain in their bad odor. The Samaritan gave nothing but wine and oil to the wounded man. It is nothing other than the ointment. It healed the wounds, for "love covers a multitude of sins."

The figure of Simon Magus, who led his own mystic cult immediately following the time of Jesus, was said to be John the Baptist's favorite disciple, and possibly even his son. According to *The Clementine Homilies* (2.23), which are said to originate from the Apostolic father Clement of Rome (a follower of Peter), it talks about Simon as John's favorite student:

> But that [Simon] came to deal with the doctrines of religion happened on this wise. There was one John, a day-baptist, who was also, according to the method of combination, the forerunner of our Lord Jesus; and as the Lord had twelve apostles, bearing the number of the twelve months of the sun, so also he, John, had thirty chief men, fulfilling the monthly reckoning of the moon, in which number was a

certain woman called Helena, that not even this might be without a dispensational significance. . . . But of these thirty, the first and the most esteemed by John was Simon. . . ."

It is interesting that John supposedly had thirty disciples to symbolize the lunar cycle, while Jesus has twelve disciples, corresponding to the solar cycle along with the Zodiac, yet John is the one described as a "day-baptist." This may imply that there was such a thing as baptism by night as well, and considering John's connection here with the moon, you might think a night baptism might be more appropriate. In the Mandaean *Book of John* it says "Yahya proclaims in the nights, Yohana on the Night's evenings." Yahya and Yohana are Mandaic and Arabic names for John, respectively. So maybe he wasn't a day-baptist after all. Even more fascinating, the *Homilies* actually specify elsewhere that the number of disciples in John's group was twenty-nine and one-half, exactly corresponding to the 29.5-day lunar cycle. This is explained as being so because the one female Helena (who is also referred to by the name of Luna, meaning "moon") was only equal to half a man. That's endearing, isn't it?

Helena was also the name of the consort and co-minister taken by Simon Magus, so it is may be that the Helena mentioned above was the same woman. Some have theorized that Helena may have originally been the consort of John the Baptist, and was later remarried as Simon's wife after John's death.

In *1 Apology* (56), Justin Martyr wrote that Simon Magus was worshipped under the guise of the Roman-Sabine god, Semo Sancus:

> There was a Samaritan, Simon, a native of the
> village called Gitto, who in the reign
> of Claudius Caesar, and in your royal city of Rome,
> did mighty acts of magic, by virtue of the art of
> the devils operating in him. He was considered a
> god, and as a god was honoured by you with
> a statue, which statue was erected on the
> river Tiber, between the two bridges, and bore
> this inscription, in the language of Rome: Simoni
> Deo Sancto, To Simon the holy God.

This fact is highly significant. To be honored as a god in Rome and have a statue erected in such a prominent place required the approval of the Roman Senate. This is no small achievement for a Samaritan magician. It is often said that Simon had the ability to mesmerize the masses by performing what seemed like miracles with his apparent supernatural abilities. The Church Fathers all claimed that these wonders came by the powers of infernal "familiar spirits" under his control. But in the Gospels, Jesus is likewise accused of being possessed of demons and in league with Beelzebub.

The later Syriac Simonians, who revered Simon and Helena as royalty, seem to have tended towards libertinism, engaged in magical practices such as incantations, love spells, and sending demons into people's dreams to distract them. Like the Roman Sabines with their worship of Semo Sancus, the Simonians also worshipped Simon and Helena as gods in the traditional pagan sense, associating them with other notable male/female pairs in religion and mythology (as testified by Irenaeus and Hippolytus), such as Zeus and Athena, or Shamash and Astarte. The latter two deities were also said to be worshipped in Tyre, the capital of ancient

The Head of Prophecy 225

Phoenicia, where Simon supposedly found Helena working as a prostitute.

Returning to *The Clementine Homilies*, it appears to us that they are ultimately about Peter's struggle against Paul for leadership of the developing Church. This is the background of the conflict that we see in Paul's *Epistle to the Galatians*. Many notable scholars have identified Simon Magus' views and ministry as similar to those of Paul. In the interests of Catholicism, it is suggested, scribes replaced Paul's name with that of Simon Magus, deliberately encouraging the reader to conflate the two figures. This would make sense considering that much of what Simon says in his debates with Peter mirrors Marcionite and Gnostic theology. At the same time, it can be said that both Simon and Paul shared many important ideas outside of what is expressed in the *Homilies*. The Church Fathers themselves even seem to inadvertently equate Simon with Paul in many instances.

We also see in *The Clementine Homilies* that Simon eventually succeeded John the Baptist in the leadership of John's ministry. Thus it is implied in this source that Peter's struggle against Simon was actually a struggle against the movement founded by the murdered Baptist. This would clearly give him equal footing with Peter in their debates. John is referred to as the forerunner of Jesus, but it says that Simon is his own forerunner. So perhaps the idea being promoted here is that the student is less legitimate than his teacher (Jesus is less than John), and maybe even a deceiver or con-artist. As it states:

> He being absent in Egypt for the practice of magic, and *John being killed*, Dositheus desiring the leadership, falsely gave out that Simon was dead, and succeeded to the seat. But Simon, returning not

long after, and strenuously holding by the place as his own, when he met with Dositheus did not demand the place, knowing that a man who has attained power beyond his expectations cannot be removed from it.

Wherefore with pretended friendship he gives himself for a while to the second place, under Dositheus. But taking his place after a few days among the thirty fellow-disciples, he began to malign Dositheus as not delivering the instructions correctly. And this he said that he did, not through unwillingness to deliver them correctly, but through ignorance.

And on one occasion, Dositheus, perceiving that this artful accusation of Simon was dissipating the opinion of him with respect to many, so that they did not think that he was the Standing One, came in a rage to the usual place of meeting, and finding Simon, struck him with a staff. But it seemed to pass through the body of Simon as if he had been smoke. Thereupon Dositheus, being confounded, said to him, 'If you are the Standing One, I also will worship you.' Then Simon said that he was; and Dositheus, knowing that he himself was not the Standing One, fell down and worshipped; and associating himself with the twenty-nine chiefs, he raised Simon to his own place of repute; and thus, not many days after, Dositheus himself, while he (Simon) stood, fell down and died.

Hippolytus, Eusebius, and the author(s) of the Clementine writings all described Simon as a baptist and as a favored disciple of John the Baptist. This text is telling us that although Simon should have been the immediate successor to John, the Samaritan Dositheus took that honor upon himself, as Simon was in Egypt at the time of the John's martyrdom. When Simon returned, the two men quarreled. Simon's superiority was proved miraculously after a magical duel, just like how Simon and the apostle Peter purportedly battled it out in front of Nero according to the apocryphal *Acts of Peter and Paul*, this time with Simon being the winner). Defeated, Dositheus ceded his position as head of the sect to Simon and formed his own group. According to *The Clementine Homilies*, it was Dositheus who got John's instructions incorrect, and Simon proved his superiority by overcoming him. This legend may contain grains of truth, as we know from patristic sources that baptizing sects of the Simonian school continued for some time.

The Orthodox polemicist and historian Eusebius, in his *Ecclesiastical History* (IV.7), names the offshoots of the Simonian tradition: Simon's immediate successor was the Samaritan Menander, then Saturninus in Antioch, and Basilides in Alexandria. He quotes from Irenaeus, whose account of the Gnostics is somewhat accurate (although still heavily biased and hostile), in *Ecclesiastical History* (IV: 11.2):

> A certain Cerdon, who had taken his system from the followers of Simon, and had come to Rome under Hyginus, the ninth in the episcopal succession from the apostles, taught that the God proclaimed by the law and prophets was not the father of our Lord Jesus Christ. For the former was known, but the latter unknown; and the former was just, but the latter good. Marcion of Pontus succeeded Cerdon and developed his doctrine, uttering shameless blasphemies.

So this mysterious Cerdon is the one who inspired Marcion's doctrines which relate directly from Simon. Marcion is known to have been radical Paulinist, so the connection between Simon and Paul is even more apparent. Contemporary with Cerdon and Valentinus was Marcus the Magician, whose sacramental mysteries are described in a slanderous manner by Irenaeus in *Against Heresies*. Purportedly, Marcus taught that the wine of the Eucharist symbolized Sophia's blood instead of Jesus'. In what appears to have been a *hieros gamos* rite (a sacred marriage), "cups were mixed with wine." As the cup of wine was offered, the priest prayed that "Grace may flow" into all who would drink of it. (*Against Heresies*, 1.13.2) Eusebius gave a slightly more moderate account of Marcus' Eucharist:

> For some of them prepare a nuptial couch and perform a mystic rite with certain forms of expression addressed to those who are being initiated, and they say that it is a spiritual marriage which is celebrated by them, after the likeness of the marriages above. But others lead them to water, and while they baptize them they repeat the following words: Into the name of the unknown father of the universe, into truth, the mother of all things, into the one that descended upon Jesus. Others repeat Hebrew names in order the better to confound those who are being initiated. (IV. 11.5)

The words "who descended upon Jesus" recall the Judeo-Christian belief that Jesus, as messiah and Son of God, had been foreshadowed by other "true prophets" like John and Elijah. Simon Magus also looked upon himself as an embodiment of, or as possessed by, the divine "Father." This is why he called himself "the Standing (i.e. 'living', 'persisting') One"—the One "having stood, standing, and will be standing." This "Standing One" title was a position of eternal power, authority, and divinity (hence Simon is called the "Great Power" in *Acts* 8:9). Also note that in Greek, "great" is translated as *megas* which is a pun used in the epithet "magus" (magician), especially more so in Simon's case.

In Paul's epistles, he repeatedly implies that he is the Standing One, such as in *Romans* 14:4 (YLT), where it says: "[T]o his own master he doth stand or fall; and *he shall be made to stand*, for God is able to make him stand." Then in *Colossians* 4:12 he tells how one of his followers is praying for another ". . . *that you may stand perfect* and made full in all the will of God." It seems that for Paul, "to stand" meant that one had full possession of the state of Grace.

As seen in *Matthew* and *John*, the dove that descends upon Jesus at his baptism is the Holy Spirit personified, although to ancient societies the dove usually symbolized the great mother goddess. According to Wolfram von Eschenbach (author of the Grail story *Parzival*), the dove symbol was absorbed by the Knights Templar during their sojourn in Asia Minor, after which they chose to adorn themselves with turtle doves, taking on the name "Knights of the Dove" as well. The dove is taken by Christians to represent the Holy Spirit, which according to Gnostic Ophites, was either Sophia's mother, or Sophia herself. Using birds to symbolize divine wisdom is nothing new. In Egyptian iconography, the god of writing and magic, Thoth, was often depicted as having a head of an ibis bird.

The cleansing of the Christian baptism has been frequently compared with how the flood of Noah cleansed the Earth of its bad actors. We find this comparison even in scripture. *1 Peter* 19-21 (NIV) tells us:

> After being made alive, he [the resurrected Jesus] went and made proclamation to the imprisoned spirits—to those who were disobedient long ago when God waited patiently in the days of Noah while the ark was being built. In it only a few people, eight in all, were saved through water, and this water symbolizes baptism that now saves you also— not the removal of dirt from the body but the pledge of a clear conscience toward God.

Religious philosopher Mircea Eliade explained in his classic work *The Sacred and the Profane* why baptism in implicitly connected to the Flood, and to the idea of being born again, because of the universal meaning of water symbolism:

> The waters symbolize the universal sum of virtualities; they are *fons et Origo*, "spring and origin," the reservoir of all the possibilities of existence; they precede every form and support every creation. . . . On the other hand, immersion in water signifies regression to the preformal, reincorporation into the undifferentiated mode of pre-existence. Emersion repeats the cosmogonic act of formal manifestation; immersion is equivalent to a dissolution of forms. This is why the symbolism of the waters implies both death and rebirth. Contact with water always brings a regeneration—on the one hand because dissolution is followed by a new birth, on the other because immersion fertilizes and multiplies the potential of life. The aquatic cosmology has its counterpart—on the human level—in the hylogenies, the beliefs according to which mankind was born of the waters. The Flood, or the periodical submersion of the continents

(myths of the Atlantis type) have their counterpart, on the human level, in . . . initiatory death through baptism. . . . From the point of view of structure, the flood is comparable to baptism. . . .

On his Atlan.org website, Arysio Santos connects the "chrism" anointing and the baptism with the conflagration and the Atlantean cataclysm:

> Fire and Water (Baptism and Chrism) were administered together in the primitive Church, and only later became separated. As in the ordeal of Atlantis, which was attended by both cataclysms, the association of Chrism and Baptism implies the same thing. So, granted that Baptism symbolizes the Flood, it is clear that Chrism allegorizes the fiery cataclysm that the Stoics called *Ekpyrosis* (or Universal Conflagration). . . .
>
> . . .
>
> . . . The two Baptisms correspond to the Flood and the Conflagration of Paradise, and to the two gods that brought them about, Indra and Agni in India, and Christ and John in Christianity or Elohim and Jahveh in Judaism.

This connection between rebirth through baptism and the birth of creation from the pre-creation "waters" in *Genesis* did not escape the notice of the Church Fathers. Tertullian wrote in *On Baptism* (4):

> Before all the furnishing of the world, [was] quiescent with God in a yet unshapen state . . . . Water was the first to produce that which had life, that it might be no wonder in baptism if waters knew how to give life. . . . All waters, therefore, in

virtue of the pristine privilege of their origin, do, after invocation of God, attain the sacramental power of sanctification; for the Spirit immediately supervenes from the heavens, and rests over the waters, sanctifying them from Himself; and being thus sanctified, they imbibe at the same time the power of sanctifying. . . .

On the subject of baptismal dissolution and rebirth of the spirit, *The Excerpts of Theodotus* (1:1), as preserved by Clement of Alexandria in a collection of notes, tell us that the Savior descended "clothed with the Pneumatic Seed." For the Valentinians, this descent is symbolized by Jesus' baptism. *Excerpts of Theodotus* 36 explains:

> Our Angels were emanated in the Unity, for they are one, since they were issued from the One. But since we were in a condition of division, then Jesus was baptized dividing the Undivided, until He unites us with the Angels, in the Pleroma, so that we all, the multitude, having become one shall be reunited with the One that was divided for us.

Together with Jesus, the angels, who are nothing else that the Son's limbs in this text, are baptized, and it is told why this is necessary (*Excerpts of Theodotus* 22):

> The Angels, of whom we are parts, are baptized . . . for the dead, for we are dead, we whom the existence here has put in a condition of Death. . . . They were baptized in the beginning . . . in the Redemption of the Name descended upon Jesus under the form of a dove. . . . Even Jesus needed Redemption, in order not to be detained by the Thought of the Lack in which He had been put. . . .

The Head of Prophecy 233

It should also be noted that one is not necessarily "reborn" from the baptismal waters in exactly the same form as one's initial birth. There are many allusions in sacred writing comparing it to being "dyed" like a colored egg at Easter. One takes on the coloring of whatever one is immersed into, and changed forever. In the apocryphal *Gospel of Philip* we are told:

> God is a dyer. As the good dyes, which are called "true," dissolve with the things dyed in them, so it is with those whom God has dyed. Since his dyes are immortal, they become immortal by means of his colors. Now God dips what he dips in water.

Another word for this is "tincturing." The connection between tincturing and baptism was implied when Friedrich Nicholai wrote about the Baphomet of the Templars. Peter Partner, in *The Murdered Magicians*, tells us that "Nicholai maintained that Baphomet was a composite of two Greek words meaning "colour" (or by extension 'baptism') and 'spirit.'" This describes the Baptism of the Holy Spirit that John the Baptist talked about as a tincturing process. This corroborates the "Baptism of Wisdom" interpretation of the name of Baphomet as well, since the Holy Spirit and Wisdom (Sophia) are considered to be identical or connected concepts in Christianity as well as in other mystical traditions.

The Mandaeans, whose baptism rite is called "Seboghatullah" ("Immersion in the Divine Mystery," quite similar to the term "Baptism of Wisdom"), also compare it to being dipped in dye. Historically, there are two colors of dye that have been considered next to sacred because of their association with royalty. Tyrian purple, made from the excretions of sea snails, was extremely expensive and highly prized. In *Acts* 16:14, Paul converts and baptizes a very wealthy woman named Lydia who is described as a "seller of purple," referring to this dye. The dye made those who touched it in its unprocessed state reek of rotting fish. (Because of this, the Jewish *Talmud* grants the right of divorce to women whose husbands take up the dying trade after marriage.)

After the Crusades, the use of the purple dye for royalty was supplanted in Europe with that of the scarlet-colored *kermes vermilio* (crimson), made from the mashed bodies of a certain species of locust that lived in the Kerm Oak in the Mediterranean. It was also made into a red liqueur called "alchermes" that was popular as an aphrodisiac until the twentieth century, when knowledge of its origin with bugs became widespread. According to Robert Graves, Jesus was actually clothed in a scarlet robe of kermes when he was crowned with thorns by soldiers in *Matthew* 27:27-30. Usually this incident is interpreted as a humiliating mockery, but some, like Graves, have suggested that the symbolism in the details all corresponds to the actual anointing of a king. Graves writes in *The White Goddess*:

> St. John the Baptist, who lost his head on St. John's Day, took over the oak-king's titles and customs, it was natural to let Jesus, as John's merciful successor, take over the holly king's. . . . The scarlet-oak, or kerm-oak, or holly-oak, is the evergreen twin of the ordinary oak and its Classical Greek names *prinos* and *hysge* are also used for holly in modern Greek. It has prickly leaves and nourishes the kerm, a scarlet insect not unlike the holly-berry (and once thought to be a berry), from which the ancients made their royal scarlet dye and an aphrodisiac elixir. . . . Jesus wore kerm-scarlet when attired as King of the Jews.

The Head of Prophecy 235

In addition to the obvious connection between a dye made from locusts and John the Baptist, who lived on locusts for food, the word "kermes" also brings to mind Hermes. According to alchemist Fulcanelli, kermes is in fact a symbol for the *prima materia* (original matter), which contains the alchemical gold *in potentia*. In *Mysteries of the Cathedrals*, he writes cryptically:

> The oak . . . gives the kirmis (Fr. Kermes), which, in the Gay Science, has the same significance as Hermes, the initial consonants being interchangeable. The two terms have an identical meaning, namely Mercury. At any rate . . . kirmis (Arab *girmiz* that which dyes scarlet) characterizes the prepared substance. . . .
>
> . . . Open, that is to say, decompose, this matter. Try to separate the pure part of it, or its metallic soul as the sacred expression has it, and you will have the kirmis, the Hermes, the mercury dye which has within it the mystic gold, just as St. Christopher carries Jesus and the Fleece is hung on the oak, like the . . . kirmis, and you will be able to say, without violating the truth, that the old hermetic oak acts as mother to the secret mercury.

After John's death, his Gnostic baptism cult continued on not only with the Pauline Christians, but also with the Simonians. According to the Church Fathers, Simon Magus considered himself an embodiment of the *Logos* (the divine word) or the *Nous* (the universal mind). This, in his system, was the essential male principle in charge of managing the all. The *Epinoia*, which he presented his consort Helena as an incarnation of, was the female principle producing all things, including the world creating angels which are the same as the "principalities" and "authorities" of Paul (or the

"Archons" of the Gnostics). Together they formed a *syzygia* or "divine union." The *Epinoia* was the lost sheep that the Nous had to descend to Earth to save, since the jealous angels imprisoned her in the world where she was subject to various reincarnations, the most famous being Helen of Troy. Fittingly, Simon found Helena as a poor slave girl working in a brothel in Tyre, as mentioned earlier. He was able to rescue her from bondage and enjoy her for himself.

In *Gnostic Mysteries of Sex: Sophia the Wild One and Erotic Christianity*, Tobias Churton writes that the relationship between Simon Magus and Helena was remarkably different from that found in encratic forms of Christianity and Gnosticism, and even Jesus and Mary Magdalene's relationship, for that matter:

> In the *Gospel of the Egyptians*, *thanatos* (death) is the consequence of *eros* (sexual love). In Encratism, the redeemed must trample on the "garment of shame" (the body); there can be no more male or female: sexual identity is no identity. No more children; no more death. Cease lusting; cease suffering. Desire creates illusion (the world). How different is the Simonian tradition of venerating the images of the Lord (Simon) and the Lady (Helena) equally, from line 114 of the Gnostic *Gospel of Thomas*, where to enter the kingdom of heaven the female must become male! When Simon redeems his lost First Thought, he does not reject her femininity.

Certainly, many authors have connected Mary Magdalene with the Gnostic Sophia, since some sects viewed the latter as Christ's consort also. This fits with the symbolism of the Magdalene, who was originally portrayed by the Church as a prostitute, just as Sophia was.

The Head of Prophecy 237

According to Hippolytus, Simon allegedly encouraged his followers to indulge in promiscuous intercourse because "all earth is earth, and it makes no difference where any one sows, provided he sow." This is called "perfect agape [love]," the "holy of holies" and "sanctifying one another." Similarly, according to Joseph von Hammer-Purgstall, the Ophites practiced obscene sex rites involving children and animals that they allegedly called *Zoogogon sophian* ("genital wisdom"), which he found represented in numerous artifacts on former Templar properties.

As we mentioned previously, it is said that John was killed while Simon was in Egypt, presumably in Alexandria, where he may have been undergoing initiation rituals to learn Pharaonic Egyptian-styled magic and esoteric doctrines. Similarly, in *Matthew* 2:13-18 we find that Jesus was in Egypt after his birth with his family, who were supposedly trying to avoid the alleged slaughter of first-born boys by King Herod the Great. They reportedly returned to Israel after the king's death. However, there is no historical record of Herod actually slaughtering masses of boys. Josephus reported that Herod planned to fill up the Hippodrome with infants and then slaughter them, but died before he carried it out.

In Josephus' records, John was killed in 26/27 AD or 33 AD depending on what, "About this time" means following the words "in the twentieth year of the reign of Tiberius." In *Antiquities of the Jews* (18.5.2 and 18.3.3) we read:

> Now, some of the Jews thought that the destruction of Herod's army came from God, and that very justly, as a punishment of *what he did against John, that was called the Baptist*; for Herod slew him, who was a good man, and commanded the Jews to exercise virtue, both as to righteousness

towards one another, and piety towards God. . . .

Now, when others came in crowds about him, for they were greatly moved by hearing his words, Herod, who feared lest the great influence John had over the people might put it into his power and inclination to raise a rebellion, thought it best, by putting him to death, to prevent any mischief he might cause, and not bring himself into difficulties, by sparing a man who might make him repent of it when it should be too late. Accordingly he was sent a prisoner, out of Herod's suspicious temper, to Macherus, the castle . . . and was there put to death. Now the Jews had an opinion that the destruction of this army was sent as a punishment upon Herod, and a mark of God's displeasure against him.

The "army" destroyed here was that of Herod Antipas, son of and successor to Herod the Great, who was ordered to launch an invasion against King Aretas of Nabatea (part of the empire) by Roman Emperor Tiberias. The Emperor, who asked nothing less than for Herod to bring him the king's head! Incidentally, As Churton reports in *The Mysteries of John the Baptist*, "Dead Sea Scrolls scholar Robert Eisenman has proposed that perhaps the whole story of John's beheading is a garbled version of what really happened to King Aretas.

These events were all tied into the reason why John was executed in the first place. King Aretas' daughter was Phasaelis, the wife that King Herod Antipas divorced so that he could marry Herodias, the mother of Salome and the one who asked Herod for John the Baptist's head. Churton suggests that due to his status in the priesthood and popularity as a prophet, John may have been:

> ... a habitual frequenter of Herod Antipas's court . . . a friend perhaps of Queen Phasaelis. . . . If Phasaelis knew John, it may have been she who informed him about the divorce plans, specifically to generate a political and legal defense of her position.

The woman that Herod Antipas was dumping Phasaelis for was Herodias, the wife of his brother, Herod II, called "Philip" in the Gospels, whom he took from his brother upon meeting her. It was John's public objection to the new marriage that made Herod and Herodias angry. Initially Herod just imprisoned John in his castle at Macherus, which Churton has speculated was an "all-mod-cons" palace, where John "was probably under 'house arrest' in a gilded cage: a precautionary, politically sensitive measure. . . ." It was at this castle on the shore of the Dead Sea that Phasaelis stationed herself before running off to her father's domain in Petra (now in modern Jordan). Her father, Aretas IV, King of Nabatea, was part of the same family tree as the Herodians, and was obviously named after the same root word as Herod. War ensued between Aretas and Herod. But Herod's army was routed, and it was rumored that this was God's punishment for his beheading of John. Churton speculates further:

> John might conceivably have been party to Phaeaelis's "escape" from Macherus. He might have been at the palace when he was arrested. His execution then could conceivably have been connected to Macherus's proximity to Nabatea.
>
> If there was a chance of Aretas getting hold of John as a political and religious mascot, such a fear might have necessitated the execution that Herod

must have known was politically very risky on the home front. . . .

So there may be more to the weird, kinky and twisted story other than what the Gospels tell us: that Herodias hated John so much, she asked for his head on a "charger," via her daughter, Salome, the only one in this family not named "Herod" or some derivative thereof, who was doing a sexy dance at her new stepfather's birthday party when she asked for it. One wonders what Herodias wanted with the head. We have suggested that she might have wanted to make it into a teraph for divination purposes. This seems more likely when we consider that Herodias is, in modern times, considered by some practitioners of witchcraft to be an incarnation of Lilith, and identical to the goddess Diana.

This was first mentioned in the 1899 book *Aradia, or the Gospel of the Witches* by American folklorist Charles Godfrey Leland. He claimed that it was based on a religious text used by witches in Tuscany, Italy. It said that Herodias had been condemned by God, because of her role in John's death, to wander the skies forever more, only being allowed to rest in treetops at night. Her name was purportedly compounded with that of Diana (rendering "Herodiana," and then, eventually, "Aradia"), and she supposedly traveled at night with the same female nymph spirits recorded in Greek mythology as being part of Diana's entourage. She is said in the book to be the daughter of Diana and the Sun, there said to be Lucifer. It asserts that she is a lunar goddess (and that, interestingly, Cain is currently imprisoned inside of the moon). According to the Aradian gospel, she is seen as a leader and teacher, supposedly, to the witches of that area.

This would match up with what Mircea Eliade wrote, stating that at Arada, along with Irodiada, was a name used for what Romanians called their "Queen of the Fairies," and that she was a "metamorphosis of Diana." Witchcraft writers Nigel Jackson and Michael Howard, in the book *The Pillars of Tubal Cain*, claim that Herodias immigrated to France sometime after the biblical events, just as Mary Magdalene, Jesus' beloved female disciple, purportedly did. If she was already a witch before, it makes sense that she would become a patroness of witches after she went to Europe.

So is Herodias likely to have been a witch? One of the most ignored details is that the Herodians were actually an Idumean Arab family (what the Bible calls "Edomites," from south of Judah) that had intermarried in with the Israelites, being forced to convert to Judaism and incorporated into the Jewish nation during the Maccabean revolt (in the second century BC). The Edomites were descendants of Jacob's older brother Esau, whom Jacob disinherited through trickery. Jacob went on to change his name to "Israel" and to father the twelve tribes of that nation, who were thereafter always at war or having skirmishes with the Edomites.

The whole bloodline and nation of Edom came to be associated by the Israelites with the Devil, because if they were Israel's enemies, that meant they were God's enemies (although, according to Robert Graves in *King Jesus*, they were also "renowned for their wisdom"). Recall that, according to cabalistic texts, they were literally descendants of Lilith via Mahalath, one of her human incarnations, who married Esau, the progenitor of the Edomite line. They were associated with "Mount Seir" and the "Wilderness of Seir," which, as we have mentioned previously, is also connected to Lilith and Azazel. The word *seir* itself means "hairy," "he-goat" or "satyr." As to their pre-Judean religion, nobody is certain of much except that they worshipped a god named

"Qaus." Also, as Arabs, the Idumeans were, like Mohammed himself, descendants of Ishmael, another disinherited older brother who is demonized in the Torah of the Jews.

This brings us to the story of Zechariah, the father of John the Baptist, and the vision he had of the archangel Gabriel while he was serving as priest, burning incense at the altar of the temple. The story is told in *Luke* 1:11-17 (NIV):

> Then an angel of the Lord appeared to him, standing at the right side of the altar of incense. When Zechariah saw him, he was startled and was gripped with fear. But the angel said to him: "Do not be afraid, Zechariah; your prayer has been heard. Your wife Elizabeth will bear you a son, and you are to give him the name John. He will be a joy and delight to you, and many will rejoice because of his birth, for he will be great in the sight of the Lord. He is never to take wine or other fermented drink, and he will be filled with the Holy Spirit even from birth. Many of the people of Israel will he bring back to the Lord their God. And he will go on before the Lord, in the spirit and power of Elijah, to turn the hearts of the fathers to their children and the disobedient to the wisdom of the righteous—to make ready a people prepared for the Lord.

Zechariah is taken aback by this vision, and the prediction made by the angel. He questions how he could have a child when he and his wife are both so old. Because of his lack of faith, Gabriel curses Zechariah with dumbness until the day of his son's birth. When he comes out of the temple, the other priests can tell that he has had some kind of encounter because of the way he is acting. But because he cannot verbalize it, they are not sure what it was.

The Head of Prophecy 243

In *King Jesus* (a novel), Robert Graves presented his own interpretation of the messianic legend based upon his decades of research into comparative mythology. There is a scene where he embellishes this story with some surprising details. In his version, the vision that Zechariah has (called there "Zecharias") is not of the archangel Gabriel, but a donkey-headed entity. As he described it to a tribunal of priests who are trying him for witchcraft:

> "I saw a power clothed in robes of light that resembled the same sacred robes which you yourself wear at the grand festivals. And this Power hugged to its breast a triple-headed golden dog and a golden sceptre in the form of a budding palm branch; and, as the Lord our God lives, this Power stood in a gap between the Curtain and the wall on the right hand; and this Power was of more than human stature; and this Power spoke in the same still, small voice that I had heard before, saying: 'Be not afraid, Zacharias! Go out now and tell my people truthfully what you have both heard and seen!' But I could not, for I was struck dumb. . . .
>
> ". . . I saw the face of the Power, and the face shone, though not unmercifully bright, and the likeness of the face"—his voice rose to a scream—"and the likeness of the face was that of a Wild Ass!"

Earlier in the book it had been revealed that a ritual mask in the likeness of the head of a wild ass had been stolen from the Edomites many years earlier and was in the possession of the priests of the Jewish temple. In the Graves novel, Zecharias is put on trial for sorcery—as it was thought that no one could see the voice of God and live. Since Zecharias admitted having a vision in the temple, it meant in the eyes of the Sanhedrin that he had conjured a demon there, polluting the sanctuary. His testimony was itself also labeled as blasphemy, as the judges felt he was implying that the priests of Israel had been worshipping an assheaded deity all along. This is very interesting. We are not sure what made Graves decide to include this detail in his story, but the guy was a walking encyclopedia of mythology, so we are sure he had a basis for it. Perhaps it had something to do with the fact that, as Morton Smith tells us in *Jesus the Magician*:

> There was a long standing legend that the god of the Jews was a donkey, or donkey-headed. The legend probably arose from the fact that the donkey was the sacred animal of Seth, the villain in the Egyptian pantheon, who was commonly thought by the Egyptians to be the god of foreigners. He was also, being a villain, given a large role in magic, and often appears as a donkey-headed figure on magical gems. The Jews were among the largest groups of foreigners in Egypt, so their god, Iao, was identified with Seth. *Io* or *Eio* in Coptic means "donkey," so the identification was almost predetermined.

In the back notes, Smith adds that Epiphanius, in his *Panarion* (26.10.6), claimed that the Gnostic Demiurge Sabaoth "has the form of an ass." Apparently not only was the Jewish god thought by some to be a donkey, but his son was as well. This is confirmed in the text *On the Origin of the World*, when Sabaoth is depicted as the repentant son of Ialdabaoth who is also called the "Lord of Forces" and is redeemed by Sophia.

As proof of the connection between the donkey and Jesus, Smith submits a piece of graffiti art found in Rome, dated to about 200 AD, that was, at the time of Smith's writing (1978) thought to be one of the earliest depictions of the crucifixion. But it showed, instead of a man wearing a crown of thorns, a man with the head of an ass. (Another version of this, or at least what sounds like a remarkably similar picture, is cited by Carl Jung in his book *Aion* as having been found in Denderah, Egypt, but he claimed that it showed Seth with an ass head tied to a "slave post," and his nephew Horus—who, in mythology, killed Seth— standing before him with a knife in his hand.) Yet another graffiti drawing, found in Carthage and also dated to the beginning of the third century, showed a donkey wearing a toga, along with the words "The god of the Christians (is) a donkey who beds (with his worshipers)." Smith points out that it was common at the time to think of demonic possession as involving the person having "sex" with the inhabiting spirit, which would often take the form of an animal when manifesting visibly, so thus the possession was symbolized as bestiality.

So did the angel Gabriel really take the form of an ass that night with Zechariah in the Temple? We have no real evidence of it besides the Graves novel. But other writers believe that the spiritual influence of Gabriel over the family of John has been represented in art many times with animal totems. Mark Gibbs, in his book *The Virgin and the High Priest* (2007), demonstrated that the image of a peacock is seen in many Renaissance-era depictions of John, Zacharias, and Elizabeth. He connects this with "Melek Taus," the "peacock angel" worshipped by the Kurdish sect known as the Yezidis, which they say represents none other than Azazel, the goat demon. They variously describe him in their scriptures as simultaneously a racial ancestor and the equivalent of the Gnostic Demiurge. Also, in Islam, Gabriel is said to have visited Mohammed in the form of a horse with wings, a peacock's tail, and the head of a woman—a figured named "Barak" ("Lightning"). He gave Mohammad a midnight ride from Mecca to Jerusalem and back again, supposedly. (We will discuss this more a bit later.)

Gibbs' book, by the way, lays out a very convincing case, all relying on both canonical and apocryphal scripture, that Mary, the mother of Jesus, may have been a temple priestess since childhood, very intimately involved with Zechariah and Elizabeth her cousin. *The Protoevangelium of James* says that Mary's parents were both part of the priesthood, but that they both died by the time she was twelve, and then it fell upon Zechariah to find a husband for her. Tobias Churton seems to imply something similar in his book about John the Baptist. It's a bit too much to get into here, but it goes along with the idea that John and Jesus may have essentially grown up around each other, surrounded by priests, and were, at the very least, equally important figures.

In *The Clementine Recognitions* (1.54) and (1.60), it is described how some disciples of John felt that he was a more apt owner of the title "Christ" than Jesus:

> Yea, some even of the disciples of John, who seemed to be great ones, have separated themselves from the people, and proclaimed their own master as the Christ. But all these schisms have been prepared, that by means of them the faith of Christ and baptism might be hindered.
>
> . . .
>
> And, behold, one of the disciples of John asserted that John was the Christ, and not Jesus, inasmuch as Jesus Himself declared that John was greater than all men and all prophets.

In *John* 8:48, Jesus is accused of being a Samaritan magician in control of a demon:

> Then the Jews answered and said to Him, "Do we not say rightly that you are a Samaritan and have a demon?" Jesus answered, "I do not have a demon; but I honor my Father, and you dishonor me. And I do not seek my own glory; there is One who seeks and judges."

It should be noted that Jesus doesn't deny being a Samaritan (as Simon was), but only having a demon. This must be significant since in an older, primitive text may have had Christ admit that he was a Samaritan. The Samaritans were associated with witchcraft. One must keep in mind that *The Babylonian Talmud* also named Jesus as a sorcerer who studied magic in Egypt, just as Simon is said to have done in the *Clementines*. They were probably trained by a Hermopolitan priesthood (the likely authors of *The Pyramid Texts*). This may account for the twelve missing years in Jesus life. When he finally returned to face the Temple hierarchy, he was a highly educated young man full of heterodox ideas—a savvy, mystical antagonist, just as John was. In *The Babylonian Talmud*, specifically in *Tosefta Shabbat* 104b, we find an obscure figure by the name of "Ben Stada" or "Ben Sattadai" who is said to have had the "witchcraft of Egypt" (i.e. magic spells) tattooed on his flesh. (Some scholars have identified Ben Stada as Jesus Christ, but this is a point of contention.) We also see the same accusation of demonic possession was made against John, as reflected also in *Matthew* 11:16-17 (KJV):

> For John came neither eating nor drinking, and they say, He hath a devil. The Son of man came eating and drinking, and they say, Behold a man

gluttonous, and a winebibber, a friend of publicans and sinners. But wisdom is justified of her children.

The accusations against Jesus and John may have been connected directly. In *Jesus the Magician*, Morton Smith wrote about how Jesus was the target of rumors that "he had raised John the Baptist from the dead and was magically identified with him," or that he did his miracles by control of the "ruler of demons, Beelzebub, and was identified with him." Another permutation of this that can be imagined is the idea that John had a demon, the ownership of which passed on to Jesus after his death (perhaps, as we suggested before, through the agency of John's head). But certainly, John's own spirit could have been used. Many people simply thought Jesus *was* John risen from the dead. Even Herod thought that. *Mark* 6:14-16 (KJV) tells us about when Herod first head of Jesus and the miracles that he was doing:

> And king Herod heard of him; (for his name was spread abroad:) and he said, That John the Baptist was risen from the dead, and therefore mighty works do shew forth themselves in him. Others said, That it is Elias. And others said, That it is a prophet, or as one of the prophets. But when Herod heard thereof, he said, It is John, whom I beheaded: he is risen from the dead.

The opening verses of *Matthew* 14 (KJV) tell us the same thing, while adding that Jesus is able to do wondrous things *because* he controls John's risen spirit:

> At that time Herod the tetrarch heard of the fame of Jesus, And said unto his servants, This is John the Baptist; he is risen from the dead; and therefore mighty works do shew forth themselves in him.

The Head of Prophecy 249

As attested in *The Pyramid Texts*, *The Coffin Texts*, and *The Book of Going Forth by Day/Book of the Dead*, as well the array of royal *Netherworld Books*, to have one's head cut off was an intensely negative thing in ancient Egypt. It basically meant that the spirit was cut off from the "Night Lands" or the afterlife. This is a common motif in ancient literature. So the fact that John was decapitated might make him the perfect victim for spiritual enslavement of this sort, as well as that fact that he was, seemingly, murdered. Morton Smith, on pages 134-138 of his book, wrote that there are actual prayers and rituals in *The Greek Magical Papyri* which purport to allow the magician to gain control over the spirit of a murdered man and use it to whatever ends desired. Thus Jesus could have possessed the spirit of John as kind of a "familiar" servitor spirit.

Similarly, as we mentioned, Simon Magus was specifically accused of performing miracles by controlling the spirit of a murdered boy. *Clementine Homilies* 2:26 tells us that Simon Magus drew this boy's spirit out of the air and turned him into a homunculus (an artificial human):

> For he even began to commit murder as himself disclosed to us, as a friend to friends, that, having separated the soul of a child from its own body by horrid incantations, as his assistant for the exhibition of anything that he pleased, and having drawn the likeness of the boy, he has it set up in the inner room where he sleeps, saying that he once formed the boy of air, by divine arts, and having painted his likeness, he gave him back again to the air.

Not to be left out, St. Paul talks about being haunted by an evil spirit when discussing his own ventures into the paranormal in *2 Corinthians* 12: 7-9 (KJV):

> And lest I should be exalted above measure through the abundance of the revelations, there was given to me a thorn in the flesh, the messenger of Satan to buffet me, lest I should be exalted above measure. For this thing I besought the Lord thrice, that it might depart from me. And he said unto me, My grace is sufficient for thee: for my strength is made perfect in weakness. Most gladly therefore will I rather glory in my infirmities, that the power of Christ may rest upon me.

The word translated above as "messenger" is *angelos*, so Paul is literally saying that an angel of Satan haunted him.

It is curious to note that in *Matthew* 16:18, that other Simon, the disciple of Jesus, is renamed Cephas or "rock" (a.k.a. "Peter"), which is very similar to Simon Magus' title of "Standing One." Also consider that in *Matthew* 3:9, John says that God can raise up children to Abraham among these "stones." We are left to wonder just how connected the Jesus cult and the Simon cult may have been in the beginning.

In *Clementine Homilies* 18:1, it talks about Simon's theology, and reflects the Church Fathers' reports of him teaching the concept of a higher God above the God of the Jews:

> When I went away yesterday, I promised to return today, and in a discussion show that he who framed the world is not the highest God, but that the highest God is another who alone is good, and who has remained unknown up to this time. . . . If then

The Head of Prophecy 251

he is the Lawgiver, he is just; but if he is just, then he is not good. . . . Now a lawgiver cannot be both just and good, for these qualities do not harmonize.

This would also reflect Marcion's heretical beliefs, as well as what we find in *John* 1:17-18 (NIV):

For the law was given through Moses; grace and truth came through Jesus Christ. No one has ever seen God, but the one and only Son, who is himself God and is in closest relationship with the Father, has made him known.

The passage quoted above from *The Clementine Homilies* supports the reports of the Church Fathers who accused Simon of being the father of all heresies, or one of the progenitors of Gnosticism (a credit also given to John), even in its Christianized form, despite the fact that Simon himself is said to have rejected Christianity altogether. Nevertheless, it seems as though Simon learned some of his ideas from John the Baptist. The Church Fathers claimed that Simon considered himself to be this other, higher God. However, one should not rely on these reports alone as they are derogatory and biased. The Simonian teachings in question can be found in his *Great Announcement*, preserved by Hippolytus in *Refutation of All Heresies* (6:12).

The Simonians themselves, like the later Marcionites, were, not surprisingly, radical Paulinists. Simone Petrement observes in *A Separate God* that "in some parts of the *Pseudo-Clementines*, Simon represents Paul; in others, he represents Marcion, who wished to be a disciple of Paul." We also see Irenaeus connecting Paul's doctrine of "salvation by grace of Jesus Christ" (*Ephesians* 2:8-9) with the Simonian doctrine of "salvation by grace of Simon Magus" (*Against Heresies* 1.23.3). Irenaeus goes on to say that Simon taught that the angels were not simply powers dominating the world, but they also authors of the law of Moses, just as Paul writes in *Galatians* 3:19. This is the reason why Simon's disciples disregarded the law, and thought of themselves as free to do what they wished. So the Simonians borrowed many ideas from Paul's epistles, or from earlier texts that could have served as the basis for the Pauline literature. This is also why the Jewish Christians/Ebionites attacked Paul through Simon and claimed both figures were in fact "lawless ones," libertines much like the Antichrist figure in 2 *Thessalonians* 2:8. *The Babylonian Talmud* also mentions heretical Jewish groups he called the *Mimim*, which more than likely refer to the Sethians and Ophites, who have strong similarities in doctrine with both Paul and Simon Magus.

To make things even thornier, we also have jumbled accounts of both Paul and Simon's deaths. In *2 Timothy* 4:6-8, we find an imprisoned Paul anticipating his demise, much like John did while imprisoned in *Matthew* 14:3 (NIV):

> For I am already being poured out as a drink offering, and the time of my departure has come. I have fought the good fight, I have finished the race, I have kept the faith. Henceforth there is laid up for me the crown of righteousness, which the Lord, the righteous judge, will award to me on that Day, and not only to me but also to all who have loved his appearing.

However, some scholars have concluded that *1* and *2 Timothy*, along with *Titus*, are not original to Paul but are actually Catholic pseudepigraphs. In fact, there's a brief refutation of Marcion's central text *The Antitheses* at the conclusion of *1 Timothy*, which means that it was composed no earlier than the first half of the second century. Both *1*

The Head of Prophecy 253

and *2 Timothy* were forged by Orthodox polemicists (more than likely the Church Fathers) to "correct" Marcionite and Gnostic interpretations of the Pauline texts. In other words, all the pastorals in the New Testament are forgeries. That is almost a unanimous opinion among academics. In any case, there are a few traditions which recount the ways in which Paul was supposedly beheaded. Eusebius writes in *Ecclesiastical History* (2:25.5) that Paul, like Peter, was martyred:

> It is, therefore, recorded that Paul was beheaded in Rome itself, and that Peter likewise was crucified under Nero. This account of Peter and Paul is substantiated by the fact that their names are preserved in the cemeteries of that place even to the present day.

Tertullian wrote in *Prescription Against Heretics* (Chapter XXXVI) that Paul was indeed beheaded with a sword, and explicitly connects it with John's death:

> Since, moreover, you are close upon Italy, you have Rome, from which there comes even into our own hands the very authority (of apostles themselves). How happy is its church, on which apostles poured forth all their doctrine along with their blood; where Peter endures a passion like his Lord's; where Paul wins his crown in a death like John's [the Baptist]; where the Apostle John was first plunged, unhurt, into boiling oil, and thence remitted to his island-exile.

In the Catholic pseudepigraph *The Acts of Peter and Paul*, Simon Magus ascends into the air like Superman, in imitation of the physical ascension of Elias and of Jesus. But whilst he was doing so, the apostles Peter and Paul counteracted his activity with the intercession of prayer, and Simon fell to the ground, seriously injuring his legs. Note that Peter and Paul are the best of friends in this text, while in the much earlier *Galatians*, Peter and Paul are bitter enemies, just as the Clementine writings record. It states:

> And Peter, looking steadfastly against Simon, said: I adjure you, you angels of Satan, who are carrying him into the air, to deceive the hearts of the unbelievers, by the God that created all things, and by Jesus Christ, whom on the third day He raised from the dead, no longer from this hour to keep him up, but to let him go. And immediately, being let go, he fell into a place called Sacra Via, that is, Holy Way, and was divided into four parts, having perished by an evil fate.

> Then Nero ordered Peter and Paul to be put in irons, and the body of Simon to be carefully kept three days, thinking that he would rise on the third day. To whom Peter said: He will no longer rise, since he is truly dead, being condemned to everlasting punishment.

Simon, like Lucifer (the King of Babylon in *Isaiah* 14:12-15), quite literally falls and injures himself, breaking his legs and eventually dying, after which he is condemned to Hell. The manner of his death evokes Luke's gospel (10:18), where it says, "Behold, I see Satan falling from heaven," as well as *Revelation* 12, where the archangel Michael casts the Devil and his angels from Heaven. This story given in *The Acts of Peter and Paul* looks so ludicrous that many biblical scholars have dismissed it as a sheer invention by an orthodox scribe from much later in the fifth century. However, it is our suspicion that this text appears in the historical record as late as the medieval era because of its similarities with another late medieval text known as the *Toledot Yeshu*. This text is usually considered an "anti-Gospel" parody, written by Jews, where it depicts Jesus and Judas Iscariot battling in the air. But the text is largely dependent on *The Acts of Peter and Paul*, among other sources such as the Talmud, Midrash and even the Christian Gospels.

Furthermore, we also suspect that this story was fabricated for one reason: to cover up the true manner of Simon's untimely death at the hands of Roman authorities. In *The Acts of Peter and Paul*, Nero seems entirely favorable to Simon's cause to prove that he is indeed the resurrected Christ and superior to the apostles. (This doesn't exactly pan out for Simon, however). If the theory that Simon is indeed the real identity behind Paul is correct, could it possibly be that the Knights Templar worshipped the bearded mummified head of not the herald and master John the Baptist, but of Simon Magus, the rightful heir of the Johannite tradition? This is indeed a tantalizing possibility.

What is even more amazing is that in the same *Acts of Peter and Paul*, we find that before Simon's untimely death, he is brazen enough to ask Nero to decapitate him so that he can resurrect himself in three days, to prove indeed that he was the Son of God.

> Simon said: Do you believe, O good emperor, that I who was dead, and rose again, am a magician? For it had been brought about by his own cleverness that the unbelieving Simon had said to Nero: Order me to be beheaded in a dark place, and there to be left slain; and if I do not rise on the third day, know that I am a magician; but if I rise again, know that I am the Son of God.

> And Nero having ordered this, in the dark, by his magic art he managed that a ram should be beheaded. And for so long did the ram appear to be Simon until he was beheaded. And when he had been beheaded in the dark, he that had beheaded him, taking the head, found it to be that of a ram; but he would not say anything to the emperor, lest he should scourge him, having ordered this to be done in secret. Thereafter, accordingly, Simon said that he had risen on the third day, because he took away the head of the ram and the limbs— but the blood had been there congealed—and on the third day he showed himself to Nero, and said: Cause to be wiped away my blood that has been poured out; for, behold, having been beheaded, as I promised, I have risen again on the third day.

We see that Nero doesn't actually order Simon to be killed, but, in fact, replaces his head with that of a sacrificed ram! Presumably, Simon performed some type of magical spell to make the ram's head appear to be Simon's. It should be obvious as to what the implications are here. Simon, in essence is connected to the symbolism of a ram, which is often considered the same as a goat, and therefore to Baphomet particularly, since it is only the ram's *head* we are dealing with here. In other words, not only was Simon continuing on the Johannite tradition as John's heir, as a religious teacher, and perhaps even by heredity as his son, as well as with his fabled death. As we mentioned, in the last part of *Acts of Peter and Paul*, we actually see Paul beheaded as well. In *Colossians* 1:17-18 (HCSB), we find that Jesus is called the "head" of the church that is the "Body of Christ":

He is before all things, and in Him all things hold together. He is also head of the body, the church; and He is the beginning, the firstborn from the dead, so that He Himself will come to have first place in everything.

Could it be that the later depiction of Simon (a prototype of the black magician Doctor Faustus), in the form of the devilish Baphomet, was in essence imitating Christ, as the "outer-head" of the Knights Templar and perhaps even the "head" of an infernal legion of hell, trapped in the Abyss? It is generally known that during the Crusades, the Knights Templar were involved in trading religious relics. For instance, there were several claimed skulls/mummified heads of John the Baptist floating around which have now landed in places as far-flung Istanbul, Damascus, Venice, and Rome, as well as the cities of Paris, Amiens, Lyonnais, and Tyron in France. Templars were likely involved in the purchase and transport of some of these. Mark Amaru Pinkham, in *Guardians of the Holy Grail*, stated that the Crusader Walter de Sarton took a John head from Constantinople to Amiens, but of course, there are John heads currently in both locations, so that links De Sarton with both. Is it possible that the Templars came into possession of Simon Magus and/or St. Paul's severed heads as well?

Returning to the Simonian teachings, these included the idea that each soul contains that which is blessed and incorruptible in a latent condition—potentially, that is, not actually. He said that each man contains has within immortal spark of life, and above all, a boundless power—an eternal substance that is superior even to the gods and the archangels. Simon affirms this power to be the root of the universe, a divine fire which gives mankind a special status among all living beings, including privileges such as reason, language, and an upright posture. These are innate but not eternal.

In the passage placed before the one quoted above, Simon seems to echo and repeat the same words John the Baptist gives to the Pharisees in *Matthew* 3:10 and *Luke* 3:9, as we see quoted from *The Great Announcement* in *Refutation of All Heresies* 6:11:

> All things, therefore, he says, when unbegotten, are in us potentially, not actually, as the grammatical or geometrical (art). If, then, one receives proper instruction and teaching, and (where consequently) what is bitter will be altered into what is sweet— that is, the spears into pruning-hooks, and the swords into ploughshares (*Isaiah* 2:4)—there will not be chaff and wood begotten for fire, but mature fruit, fully formed, as I said, equal and similar to the unbegotten and indefinite power. *If, however, a tree continues alone, not producing fruit fully formed, it is utterly destroyed. For somewhere near, he says, is the axe (which is laid) at the roots of the tree. Every tree, he says, which does not produce good fruit, is hewn down and cast into fire.*

It must also be noted that *The Great Announcement* is not Christian by any means. It is a work of Simonian philosophy and mysticism that says nothing about Jesus. Yet there, Simon quotes John the Baptist verbatim. Simon is teaching that those who do not bear spiritual fruit, or realize the innate divine potentiality within themselves, will be subject to a fiery condemnation.

It is rather easy to see that Simon is talking about something similar to alchemical fire, which dissolves all impurities to reveal the hidden gold inside the lead-based dross. This may also be connected symbolically with the fire that Prometheus stole from the Olympian gods. The importance of fire for the Zoroastrian priests (who were called *magoi*, much like Simon's title of "magus") is well-documented. According to their tradition, when Ahura Mazda (the good god) created the world, he made its spiritual form from his divine fire, which was also said to hold his essence of eternal light.

In ancient Iranian society, to pollute the fire used in religious ceremonies by bringing it into contact with impure substances was one of the worst sins one could commit. If you were to extinguish the fire in a sacred fire temple, such an act was punishable by death. In *The Chaldean Oracles*, we find that they too express similar concepts, as it says:

> When you behold a sacred fire without form,
> shining flashingly through the depths of the whole world, hear the voice of fire.

The passage from *The Great Announcement* quoted above also has some very strong End Times implications. The fire mentioned there is not meant to punish the wicked, but rather to remove all that appears on the outside, all that is perceived by the senses. This corresponds to the Valentinian eschatological belief that all matter will eventually plunge into a fiery inferno of chaos. This also corresponds to how Irenaeus describes Simon's credo, where he says, "He (Simon) again promised that the world would be destroyed" (*Against Heresies* 1, 23, 3). All of this would conform to Hammer-Purgstall's understanding of the Gnostic "baptism of fire" ritual that he believed the Ophites, and later the Templars, engaged in, which we will describe in due course. Similarly, in *Luke* 12:49, Jesus talks about fiery baptism:

I have come to cast fire upon the earth; and how I wish it were already kindled! But I have a baptism to undergo, and how distressed I am until it is accomplished!

Even more tantalizing is the fact that in *The Gospel of John* (15:5-8), Jesus says many similar things to what John the Baptist and Simon Magus have been quoted as saying:

I am the vine; you are the branches. If you remain in me and I in you, you will bear much fruit; apart from me you can do nothing. If you do not remain in me, you are like a branch that is thrown away and withers; such branches are picked up, thrown into the fire and burned. If you remain in me and my words remain in you, ask whatever you wish, and it will be done for you. This is to my Father's glory, that you bear much fruit, showing yourselves to be my disciples.

This was a fairly common allegory used by Platonic philosophers, as well as ancient physicians like Galen. The latter used the allegory of winnowing the "wheat from the chaff," and burning the chaff, to describe the digestive process of the stomach, with the human body itself being referred to as a "barn" or "storehouse" of nutrition, much like how Jesus, John, and Simon describe the Kingdom of God:

For just as workmen skilled in preparing wheat cleanse it of any earth, stones, or foreign seeds mixed with it that would be harmful to the body, so the faculty of the stomach thrusts downward anything of that sort, but makes the rest of the material, that is naturally good, still better and distributes it to the veins extending to the stomach and intestines.

This is similar to how *The Apocryphon of John* assigns various demonic spirits who are ruled over by the Archons to the creation of every part of Adam's body. *The Apocryphon of John* seems to come from the Gnostic Johannite tradition, as it claims to tell the secret mysteries of the apostle John, as purportedly revealed by Jesus Christ in a post-Resurrection appearance found in the longest version of the text. (There are actually four versions, as it turns out). As Michael Allen Williams points out in *Rethinking Gnosticism*:

> We encounter sacramental language, where the initiate is said to be awakened by the revealer and "sealed with the water of light in the five seals" (*Apocryphon of John* 11 31, 22-24), evidently a reference to a baptismal ritual practiced by such a community.

Could this community be John's Samaritan baptismal cult, which would eventually splinter off into later groups such as the Simonians, Sethians, Dositheans, and Mandaeans?

As it turns out, the Cathars (a medieval European Gnostic sect closely linked with the Templars) had their own version of *The Apocryphon of John*, which they inherited from the Bogomils (a Bulgarian medieval Gnostic sect). It was called the *Interrogatio Iohannis*, also known as *The Secret Supper* and *The Book of John the Evangelist*. They seem to have rejected all of the other canonized Gospels in the Bible.

In a vein very similar to that of those teachers quoted above, St. Paul uses this fiery baptism language to describe the convicting power of the Holy Ghost in the Christian believer, as Tobias Churton points out in *Gnostic Philosophy*:

> Paul cleverly employs the image of the chemist or metallurgist who, in purifying gold-bearing matter, would heat the material to a thousand degrees in a bone-ash vessel to "try" or separate the gold from its accreted impurities. In the imaginative inner context in which Paul places the image, the fire that tries or judges can be understood as alchemical fire, and Paul shows no hesitation in bringing its power to bear upon the Corinthians: "Every man's work shall be made manifest: for the day shall declare it, because it shall be revealed by fire; and the fire shall try every man's work of what sort it is. If any man's work abide which he hath built thereupon, he shall receive a reward. If any man's work shall be burned, she shall suffer loss: but he himself shall be saved; yet so as by fire. Know yet not that ye are the temple of God, and that the spirit of God dwelleth in you?" (1 *Corinthians* 3:13-16).

Simon's successor Menander thought that he could make his followers immortally youthful by a baptismal ceremony, as indicated by Irenaeus in *Against Heresies* (1.23.5). The baptism practiced by the Simon cult involved fire appearing over the water, as recorded by the anonymously produced text *A Treatise On Re-Baptism* (attributed to pseudo-Cyprian):

> And some of them try to argue that they only administer a sound and perfect [baptism], not as we, a mutilated and curtailed baptism, which they are in such wise said to designate, that immediately [after] they have descended into the water, fire at once appears upon the water.

Hippolytus makes it clear that Simon's teaching of the divine fire was derived from Heraclitus, a pre-Socratic philosopher given pejorative titles such as "the Obscure," and "the Weeping Philosopher." When Hippolytus calls Simon Magus "obscure," this might not only be a reference to Heraclitus, but it might also imply that he was "esoteric," and "arcane." If you look closely you will see that the entire New Testament is filled with references to hidden divine knowledge. Origen, in his *Contra Celsus*, gives more insight while trying to defend the faith against the likes of that nasty pagan Celsus when he admits there was always both an esoteric and exoteric meaning behind Christian doctrines:

> Moreover, since he frequently calls the Christian doctrine a secret system (of belief), we must confute him on this point also, since almost the entire world is better acquainted with what Christians preach than with the favourite opinions of philosophers. For who is ignorant of the statement that Jesus was born of a virgin, and that He was crucified, and that His resurrection is an article of faith among many, and that a general judgment is announced to come, in which the wicked are to be punished according to their deserts, and the righteous to be duly rewarded? And yet the mystery of the resurrection, not being understood, is made a subject of ridicule among unbelievers.
>
> In these circumstances, to speak of the Christian doctrine as a secret system, is altogether absurd. *But that there should be certain doctrines, not made known to the multitude, which are (revealed) after the exoteric ones have been taught, is not a*

peculiarity of Christianity alone, but also of philosophic systems, in which certain truths are exoteric and others esoteric. Some of the hearers of Pythagoras were content with his *ipse dixit* [i.e., his unqualified and unsupported proclamations]; while others were taught in secret those doctrines which were not deemed fit to be communicated to profane and insufficiently prepared ears. Moreover, all the mysteries that are celebrated everywhere throughout Greece and barbarous countries, although held in secret, have no discredit thrown upon them, so that it is in vain that he endeavours to calumniate the secret doctrines of Christianity, seeing he does not correctly understand its nature.

In *The Teachings of Silvanus* found in Codex 7 of the Nag Hammadi Library, Malcolm L. Peel and Jan Zandee translated the following passage:

And a foolish man does not guard against speaking (a) mystery. A wise man, (however), does not blurt out every word, but he will be discriminating toward those who hear. Do not mention everything in the presence of those whom you do not know.

One such hidden teaching might be the following Gnostic doctrine on John the Baptist from the third manuscript of Codex IX of the Nag Hammadi Library, called *The Testimony of Truth*:

But the Son of Man came forth from Imperishability, being alien to defilement. He came to the world by the Jordan river, and immediately the Jordan turned back. And John bore witness to the descent of Jesus. For it is he who saw the power which came down upon the Jordan river; for he knew that the

The Head of Prophecy 265

dominion of carnal procreation had come to an end. The Jordan river is the power of the body, that is, the senses or pleasures. The water of the Jordan is the desire for sexual intercourse. John is the archon of the womb.

Here we see John described not only as an "Archon" (and thus, in the Gnostic system, an agent of the bad god, the Demiurge of creation), but also as the womb. The Jordan River is said to represent the flow of life coming from the other side and incarnating through procreation, spurned on by sex and sexual desire. But when the Holy Spirit enters those waters to be born into Jesus through his baptism, the waters are turned back, signaling to John, who had the wisdom to know, that the kingdom of the Demiurge, and material life through carnal procreation, was starting to come to an end. Jesus was seen by some Christian Gnostics as the one who would bring about this end, and return the lost souls of men to their real home: the Pleroma on the other side of the veil of existence.

Similar symbolism is found in Hippolytus' report on the Naassenes, in which Egypt is now used as a symbol for the body. Instead of the Red Sea parting for the Israelites but drowning the Egyptians, we are told about "the great Jordan" coming between them, allowing the "children of Israel" to escape Egypt. In *Refutation of All Heresies*, near the end of Chapter 2, he tells us about the Naassene interpretation of *John* 3:6. ("That which is born of the flesh is flesh, and that which is born of the spirit is spirit.") He says:

This, according to them, is the spiritual generation. This . . . is the great Jordan which, flowing on (here) below, and preventing the children of Israel from departing out of Egypt—I mean from terrestrial intercourse, for Egypt is with them the body—Jesus drove back, and made it flow upwards.

The word Jordan means "one who descends" or "to flow down" in Hebrew, so again we are talking about a symbolic river of life, the course of which is reversed (so that life returns to its origin rather than incarnating on Earth to die), thus allowing escape from the slavery of "Egypt" (life inside the body). The same metaphoric system appears to be operating in the Valentinian liturgy *On the Baptism (A)*, involving the Exodus, the Jordan, and the reversal of its flow so that it now goes from "the world" into "the Aeon" (the Pleroma):

> Moreover, the first baptism is the forgiveness of sins. We are brought . . . into the imperishability which is the Jordan. But that place is of the world. So we have been sent out of the world into the Aeon. For the interpretation of John is the Aeon, while the interpretation of that which is the upward progression, that is, our Exodus from the world into the Aeon.

The "upward progression" is the reversal of the flow of the river of life, the Jordan, allowing the "Exodus"—the escape from the body. One can think of this as analogous to the reversal of the flow of "prana" or life-force through the spinal column in kundalini yoga, which allows this power to rise from the base of the spine (where the "Earth chakra" is centered) up to and out through the godhead chakra located at the top of the head, gaining the practitioner temporary escape from the mental pain of existence. One can also think of it as providing a grand explanation for the symbol of the four rivers that allegedly flowed through the Garden of Eden, which appear to show up again in St. John the Divine's *Revelation*. There they are described as the

The Head of Prophecy 267

"waters of life" and shown issuing from beneath the throne of God, and the altar in the center of the New Jerusalem. In Christian iconography, images of this altar at the New Jerusalem always show the *Agnus Dei* or Lamb of God with blood flowing out of his neck, indicating that it is the blood of Christ actually coursing through these rivers. Blood, in fact, is the Water of Life, thought since ancient times to actually contain the life-force of the soul, and the "four rivers" can be thought of as the two arteries and two veins that each of us has issuing from the heart.

This is all very much like how Simon read the Garden of Eden (or "Edem") as being symbolic of the womb, as well as the fetus contained inside. He (or the person who wrote in his name) said:

> How then, he says, and in what manner, does God form man? In Paradise; for so it seems to him. Grant Paradise, he says, to be the womb; and that this is a true (assumption) the Scripture will teach, when it utters the words, I am He who forms you in your mother's womb (*Jeremiah* 1:5). For this also he wishes to have been written so. Moses, he says, resorting to allegory, has declared Paradise to be the womb, if we ought to rely on his statement. If, however, God forms man in his mother's womb— that is, in Paradise— as I have affirmed, let Paradise be the womb, and Edem the after-birth, a river flowing forth from Edem, for the purpose of irrigating Paradise, (*Genesis* 2:10) (meaning by this) the navel. This navel, he says, is separated into four principles; for on either side of the navel are situated two arteries, channels of spirit, and two veins, channels of blood.

But when, he says, the umbilical vessels proceed forth from Edem, that is, the caul in which the foetus is enveloped grows into the (foetus) that is being formed in the vicinity of the epigastrium,—(now) all in common denominate this a navel—these two veins through which the blood flows, and is conveyed from Edem, the after-birth, to what are styled the gates of the liver; (these veins, I say,) nourish the foetus.

But the arteries which we have spoken of as being channels of spirit, embrace the bladder on both sides, around the pelvis, and connect it with the great artery, called the aorta, in the vicinity of the dorsal ridge. And in this way the spirit, making its way through the ventricles to the heart, produces a movement of the foetus. For the infant that was formed in Paradise neither receives nourishment through the mouth, nor breathes through the nostrils: for as it lay in the midst of moisture, at its feet was death, if it attempted to breathe; for it would (thus) have been drawn away from moisture, and perished (accordingly). But (one may go further than this); for the entire (foetus) is bound tightly round by a covering styled the caul, and is nourished by a navel, and it receives through the (aorta), in the vicinity of the dorsal ridge, as I have stated, the substance of the spirit.

If Carl Jung read this, he would have given a standing ovation to Simon Magus' insight of the Garden of Eden being an allegory for the womb. To Jung, Paradise was the positive aspect of the archetypal mother, and he related it to the symbol of the Kingdom of God in the New Jerusalem. This seems to also be how many Gnostics saw it, and their

The Head of Prophecy

ideal was to somehow escape from the flow of life incarnating into the womb. But was John seen by the Gnostics as helping aid this escape of souls with his baptism, or was he, as the *Testimony of Truth* describes him, an "Archon" serving the Demiurge? The apocryphal, encratite and Gnostic *Gospel of Thomas* (46) quotes Jesus as saying:

> From Adam to John the Baptist, among those born of women, no one is so much greater than John the Baptist that his eyes should not be averted.
>
> But I have said that whoever among you becomes a child will recognize the (Father's) kingdom and will become greater than John.

It seems this Gospel is trying to say that John was so great that one could not look upon him, as if he were the Lord himself. Yet, whoever becomes a child of light will recognize the kingdom of the Father and become greater than John. This is a much clearer explanation of the always-confusing passage from *Luke* 7:28 (KJV):

> For I say unto you, Among those that are born of women there is not a greater prophet than John the Baptist: but he that is least in the kingdom of God is greater than he.

We think that John is being presented here as merely a servant of the Demiurge. It would not be shocking for him to play this part. Many scholars, such as Elaine Pagels (writing in the *Gnostic Paul*) have noticed similar instances, in which biblical heroes such as David and Abraham are seen as symbolic of the Demiurge by Gnostics, such as in the Valentinian exegesis of the *Apostolikon* (the 10 Pauline Epistles) by Marcion.

The Mandaean *Book of John* portrays Jesus and John's relationship as being entirely hostile and antagonistic. Mandaean literature will probably eventually be dated to around the sixth century, much younger than Simonian and Gnostic literature, so that chips away at the credulity given to this text. However, one may consider that the Mandaeans themselves probably originated from Dositheus' offshoot cult that continued John's tradition after his death. In Mandaean literature, John complains about Jesus, as we read in Theosophist GRS Mead's *The Gnostic John the Baptizer*, which quotes the alleged words of John himself in the Mandaean *Book of John*:

> Who told Yeshu (Eshu)? Who told Yeshu Messiah, son of Miryam, who told Yeshu, so that he went to the shore of the Jordan and said [unto Yahya]: "Yahya, baptize me with thy baptizing and utter o'er me also the Name thy wont is to utter. If I show myself as thy pupil, I will remember thee then in my writing; I attest not myself as thy pupil, then wipe out my name from thy page."

> Thereon Yahya answered Yeshu Messiah in Jerusalem: "Thou hast lied to the Jews and deceived the priests. Thou hast cut off their seed from the men and from the women bearing and being pregnant. The sabbath, which Moses made binding, hast thou relaxed in Jerusalem. Thou hast lied unto them with horns and spread abroad disgrace with the shofar."

Notice here that John presents us with a Jesus who discourages procreation and relaxes the Sabbath. He also describes Jesus trying to win his favor and receive his baptism, promising to make John famous in his upcoming

The Head of Prophecy 271

book if he will suffer him this honor. Immediately after this part of the text, a character called "Ruha" is mentioned, who is the Mandaean version of Sophia. It says:

> When Yeshu Messiah said this, there came a Letter out of the House of Abathur: "Yahya, baptize the deceiver in Jordan. Lead him down into the Jordan and baptize him, and lead him up again to the shore. . . ."
>
> Then Ruha made herself like to a dove and threw a cross over the Jordan. A cross she threw over the Jordan and made its water to change into various colours. "O Jordan," she says, "thou sanctifiest me and thou sanctifiest my seven sons."
>
> "The Jordan in which Messiah Paulis was baptized, have I made into a 'trough.' The bread which Messiah Paulis receives, have I made into a 'sacrament.' The drink which Messiah Paulis receives, have I made into a 'supper.' The head-band which Messiah Paulis receives, have I made into a 'priest-hood.' The staff which Messiah Paulis receives, have I made into a 'dung [-stick].'"

Now we are not sure exactly what a "dung-stick" is, but it doesn't sound good. Ruha seems to be dismissing the Pauline Christian church pretty roundly. She finishes up her speech with this:

> Let me warn you, my brothers, let me warn you, my beloved! . . . against [they] . . . who are like unto the cross. They lay it on the walls; then stand there and bow down to the block. Let me warn you, my brothers, of the god which the carpenter has joinered together. If the carpenter has joinered

together the god, who then has joinered together the carpenter?

This seems to be an allusion both to the idea of Jesus being a carpenter, presenting the world with a new view of God, and also to the idea of the Demiurge, the artisan or craftsman who built the universe, implying that the God he has presented us to worship (himself) is not the highest, since someone else would had to have made him.

If John the Baptist was truly the original "Mandaean" (hence the progenitor of Gnosticism), then demands for a deeper study of the Mandaean religion should be considered. The Mandaeans portrayed Sophia as "Ruha," in a very ambivalent way. However, in *Mandaeism*, Kurt Rudolph writes that "Ruha" has a male consort called "Ur," who is equated with a dragon, which reminds us of Behemoth and Leviathan, or Samael and Lilith. Much like the Simonian Helena and the Greek goddess of fate, Heimarmene, Ruha generates the seven world-creating angelic planets as well as the signs of the Zodiac. Says Randolph:

> The "World of Darkness" is governed by the "Lord of Darkness". . . and arose from the "dark waters" . . . representing the chaos. The main powers of the world of darkness are a giant monster or dragon with the name Ur (probably a polemic transformation of the Hebrew "or," [meaning] "light") and the evil (female) "Spirit" (ruha). Their offspring are demonic beings . . . and "angels." . . . To them belong also the "Seven", . . . i.e., the planets, . . . and the "Twelve" . . . signs of the Zodiac; they are sons of Ur and Ruha."

The main body of Mandaean teaching is called *The*

The Head of Prophecy 273

Ginza. Divided into right and left, the right side contains the main points of theology, cosmology and myth, while the left contains the rituals. In the right *Ginza*, John the Baptist is claimed to be the true prophet of God, whereas "Christ the Roman" who "did not come from the Light" is an incarnation of "one of the seven seducing planets who roam the cosmos." He is said to have clothed his priests in a "colored tunic," then "tonsured their heads" and veiled them "like darkness," presumably a reference to the black robes worn by priests, monks and nuns. The Christian Sabbath is considered a bad thing too, because "on Sundays they keep their hands from work."

Regarding John the Baptist, *The Ginza* (as quoted and translated in Marvin Meyer's *The Gnostic Bible* pp. 549-551) says:

> . . . Faith will find a place in his heart and he will receive the Jordan and carry out baptisms for forty-two years, before *Nbu, who is Hermes Christ, enters the world*.

"Nbu," or "Nabu" is a word found in several Semitic languages that means "prophet." It is connected to the Babylonian god of writing, Nebo, their version of Hermes, mentioned in an earlier chapter. It is interesting then that "Christ" is called in this account both "Nbu" and "Hermes." This brings to mind Harold R. Willoughby's observation from *Pagan Regeneration*:

> The prophet of *Poimandres* [Hermes], when he had made a successful beginning of his evangelization, taught his followers how to give thanks to God at the time of the sun's setting. Hermetism, too, had its baptism and the Trismegistic prophet, like John

the Baptist, summoned men to "Repent and be baptized!"

According to Marvin Meyer, *The Ginza* says that Jesus becomes "wise through John's wisdom," But then "Jesus proceeds to pervert the word of John. . . ." It is said of Jesus that he:

> . . . snares people by sorcery and befouls them with blood and menstrual discharge. He baptizes them in blocked waters and perverts the living baptism and baptizes them in the name of the father, son and holy spirit. He alienates them from the living baptism in the Jordan of living waters.

As Rene Salm points out in *The Mandaeans and Christian Origins*, these Mandaean texts definitely portray Jesus and John as having had an antagonistic relationship. Salm quotes Robert Stahl's *Les Mandeens et les Origines Chretiennes (The Mandaeans and the Original Christians),* where he claims that *The Gospel of John* is dependent upon (and is a reaction against) the Mandaean religion, as well as other forms of Gnosticism, rather than the other way around. If this is true, then it would mean that the Mandaeans existed far earlier than most scholars have assumed. Both traditions emphasize the importance light, life and the *Logos* in the fight against the darkness of the world. The main difference is that John's gospel "carnalizes" these in the person of Jesus as the *Logos* personified. Celsus, in *The True Doctrine*, is very critical of this, and accuses the Christians of using sophistries to argue that the *Logos* could take on human flesh, which to him was anathema, a heresy that no true Platonist would agree with:

> For as the sun, which enlightens all other objects, first makes himself visible, so ought the son of God

to have done. The Christians are guilty of sophistical reasoning, in saying that the son of God is the Logos Himself. When they declare the Logos to be the son of God [*John* 1:1], they do not present to view a pure and holy Logos, but a most degraded man, who was punished by scourging and crucifixion. If your Logos is the son of God, we also give our assent to the same; yet the prophecies agree with ten thousand other things more credibly than with Jesus.

Furthermore, Salm asserts that *The Gospel of John* was written as a reaction against those who considered John the Baptist to be the "Great Revealer." He even claims that the majority of the sayings of Jesus were actually stolen from John! If this is true, it only means that Jesus was simply a mask of John. But as we saw earlier, Simon Magus and the Platonic doctor Galen also use similar phraseology.

Tobias Churton, on the other hand, theorizes in *The Mysteries of John the Baptist* that this Gospel was actually written to emphasize the importance John the Baptist and reflect his viewpoint (instead of that of John the "beloved disciple"), as it is most commonly assumed to be. Churton describes the baptism scene, which occurs in the first chapter, thusly:

> The whole story is presented as coming from the Baptist who "saw" and "bore record," that is, who testified in his own words, what happened at the baptism. . . . This alone would seem to me to explain how this maverick Gospel, beloved of mystics, a veritable 'half-way house to Gnosticism,' as Rudolf Bultmann's study of John called it, came to acquire the title of the *Gospel of John*. It is there, staring you in the face if you care to see it.

> John is doing the testifying. John is "bearing the record"—at least to start with.
>
> ... John is announcing the good news: this is the "herald's" role: the *kerux* of the divine ceremony. . . .
>
> . . .
>
> This is John's testimony, according to John, and such is its power that I have myself little doubt in ascribing the title of the *Gospel to John the Baptist*, a long overdue ascription.

The proem at the beginning of *The Gospel of John* reads like a Gnostic retelling of the opening lines of *Genesis*, as it says:

> In the beginning was the Word, and the Word was with God, and the Word was God. . . . All things were made by him, and without him was not anything that was made.

It has long been thought that these words may have been influenced by Philo of Alexandria's teaching on the *Logos* as the "first born Son of God." Philo was a Hellenistic Jewish philosopher writing at the time of Jesus and John. To him, the *Logos* was the Demiurge, as well as the mediator between that material realm and the Father of all. It was the "Nous" or universal mind, the organizing principle of creation, as well as a kind of cosmic glue. He stated in his book *De Profugis*:

> [T]he Logos of the living God is the bond of everything, holding all things together and binding all the parts, and prevents them from being dissolved and separated.

The Head of Prophecy 277

Yet while separation of elements is necessary for creation, and for change, Logos was responsible for that as well, He was borrowing from Herclitus the concept of the "dividing Logos," which "creates" individual objects in the universe by separating their element from the undifferentiated All. He compared it to the Jewish concept of Chokmah ("Divine Wisdom") that we mentioned in a previous chapter as being analogous to Sophia, described by Aryah Kaplan as "pure thought, which has not yet been broken up into different ideas."

But to Philo, this was no mere abstract concept: it was actually a living thing. Philo viewed God as someone who could actually "impregnate" a soul with his wisdom and virtue, which may explain the origin of the idea in *The Gospel of John* that the Logos could be born in the person of Jesus. In *The Gnostic Religion*, Hans Jonas describes Philo's viewpoint:

> Philo uses various images to describe [the] relation of divine activity and human receptivity, notably that of sowing and begetting. This image points to the idea, widespread in the Gnostic world also, of a quasi-sexual relation in which the soul is the female and conceiving part, and is impregnated by God. God alone can open the wombs of the souls, sow virtues in them, make them pregnant, and cause them to give birth to the Good.

Strangely, though, while Philo's ideas in this regard could have been the origin of the concept of the virgin birth, out of all the Gospels in the New Testament, John's Gospel, seemingly influenced by Philo, is the only one to give no account whatsoever of the circumstances of Jesus' conception or birth. (Indeed, the subject of his childhood is utterly neglected there.)

278 Chapter 6

The Gospel of John seems to have greatly inspired later Gnostic, Valentinian and Hermetic movements. Or conversely, the groups that originated those movements may have been the ones who inspired and even wrote the text. In *A Separate God*, Simone Petrement writes:

> The Fourth Gospel, though profoundly Jewish, is at the same time the most Hellenistic of the Gospels. It is certainly steeped in knowledge of the Old Testament, but at the same time it is steeped in a mysticism that is rather inspired by Greek philosophy, in particular by Platonism. (The Old Testament is more ethical in spirit than mystical). This blending of thoughts or expressions derived from the Old Testament with philosophical mysticism derived from Hellenism, as Dodds remarks (*Historical Tradition*, 16), is not superficial but belongs to a very profound level and, whatever one says, evokes Alexandrian Judaism.

Petrement also seems to think that *The Gospel of John* was written by Apollos, the rival and adversary of Paul who accused him of preaching "another Jesus" and "another Gospel." This theory is outside of our argument here, but it is an intriguing possibility. The Jesus depicted in *John* seems to be more glorious and divine, even in his earthly life than the Jesus of the other gospels. It almost seems like he has only the appearance of a human body, and was really just a spirit who "appeared" to have a body, or that his original nature was not earthly but purely divine. This was an actual doctrine known as the "heresy" of "Docetism." It is these subtle differences that highlight the Gnostic and even Marcionite orientation of this Gospel.

There are many aspects of *The Gospel of John* that make it seem Gnostic, or proto-Gnostic. Jesus as presented here seems very rejecting of Mosaic Law, telling the Pharisees scornfully that it's "your law" (10:34). Also, by proclaiming that his kingdom to come is "not of this world," it seems like he is denying the Jewish belief of the Resurrection of the carnal flesh at the End of Days. He appears to imply rather that his kingdom will be in the Gnostic Pleroma, outside of known existence.

Along the same line of thinking, we find a lengthy Gnostic/Valentinian commentary on *The Gospel of John* quoted by Irenaeus in *Against Heresies* (1.8.5). According to this source, the opening verses actually reveal the very origin of the Pleroma, and explicitly mention many of the names of the "aeons" that Gnostics believed had emanated forth in succession from the Father. These are called in Greek: *Arche* (the Beginning), *Aletheia* (Truth), *Logos* (the Word or Reason), *Zoe* (Life), *Anthropos* (Man), *Ekklesia* (Church) and *Charis* (Grace). We also see these same terms used in the Nag Hammadi codices as well. *Arche* is elsewhere called "Monogenes," and has been referred to in Gnostic texts as the "only begotten Son" of the unknown Father. This aeon is apparently referred to in John's gospel by verses 1:18 ("No man hath seen God at any time; the only begotten Son, which is in the bosom of the Father, he hath declared *him*."), and by 17:25 ("O righteous Father, the world hath not known thee: but I have known thee, and these have known that thou hast sent me.") These aeons make up the heavenly "Ogdoad," or council of eight aeons that are a part of the eternal, spiritual Godhead, and *The Gospel of John* does seem to enumerate them. It even says "of his *pleroma* ("fullness") we have received" (*John* 1:16), which seems to mean that Jesus imparted knowledge of the Pleroma to his disciples.

In addition to the Hellenic Judaism of Philo, there is evidence that *The Gospel of John* may have been influenced by the cult of Asclepius as well. This was the Greek god of healing we mentioned before, whose name and imagery was adopted by one of the most famous students of Hermes Trismegistus, to whom several of the Hermetic dialogues are addressed. *John* 5:2-9 contains the story of Jesus at the pool of Bethesda, outside the walls of Jerusalem, where he healed the lame man (*John* 5:2-9). There is archaeological evidence that this was an Aesclepion—a healing center dedicated to Asclepius. The phrase Jesus used in this scene, *hygies genesthai* ("Do you want to be healed?") and the word used in this Gospel for bathing in the healing waters, *louein* ("to wash"), are reminiscent of language of the Asclepius cult.

Many writers throughout history also recognized the Hermetic and Egyptian undertones in *The Gospel of John*'s Proem, such as Marsillio Ficino, the Italian translator of *The Corpus Hermeticum* into Latin. Philip Coppens writes of this in his article, "Ficino: The high priest of the Renaissance," published on his website, PhillipCoppens.com:

> Many of the Hermetic writings closely resemble portions of the *Gospel of John*, one of the few if not only Christian texts cherished by the medieval Cathars. Later, Martin Luther actually believed that the author of the *Corpus* had merely copied the writings of John the Evangelist. A very old Egyptian text says: "In the beginning was Thoth; and Thoth was in Atum; and Thoth was Atum in the unfathomable reaches of primordial space." The Prologue of John's Gospel, beginning with "The Word was with God and The Word was God", closely resembles the actions of Thoth—and Thoth

was the Egyptian name of Hermes, the god of Wisdom. Ficino himself did not fail to see the similarities between the *Corpus Hermeticum* and John's Gospel and even stressed these in his introduction to his translation.

So *The Gospel of John*, it seems, was not only proto-Gnostic, but also proto-Hermetic, and it may have been inspired by the teachings of John the Baptist even more than those of Jesus. John was a hero, apparently, for early Hellenistic and proto-Gnostic Christians such as Paul, and laid the foundation for the Simonians and the Mandaeans. The true place of John in Christian history is somewhat obscured by the Church. Some would say that this contention between Johannite religion and Christianity began with Paul, or the Pauline camp, as Tobias Churton has argued. Lynn Picknett and Clive Prince suggested in their hit book *The Templar Revelation* that Jesus was an upstart rival of John's that threatened his leadership. They purport that the Gospels rewrote John's story to fit the Christian Jesus movement narrative, as they observe the following:

> Although the Church of John apparently disappeared after approximately 50 CE, its continued existence can be deduced from the Church Fathers' fulminations against John's successors—Simon Magus and Dositheus—for about another two hundred years. Then, again in the twelfth century, this tradition also surfaces once more in the Templars' mystical veneration of John.

If *The Gospel of John* was actually written from John the Baptist's viewpoint, and if that viewpoint corresponds to Hermeticism, then we should not be surprised to discover that the Baptist and Hermes are symbolically linked to the same broader archetype of "wisdom god," and also to each other specifically. Briefly we mentioned before the figure of Oannes, the sage with a fishtail who came out of the sea each day to teach rude humanity the civilized ways. Interestingly, it seems that some comparative mythologists have connected this character to none other than John. We first became aware of this because of a throwaway line from Robert Graves, who wrote in *The White Goddess* that:

> Oddly enough John the Baptist seems to have been identified by early Christian syncretists in Egypt with the Chaldean god Oannes who according to Berossus used to appear at long intervals in the Persian Gulf, disguised as the merman Odacon, and renew his original revelation to the faithful.

Searching for more information on the subject, we discovered what early twentieth century Viennese writer and historian Richard Eisler wrote in *Orpheus the Fisher*. They appear to imply that John was actually a *reincarnation* of Oannes! As the text states:

> We should not hesitate even to presuppose that the same syncretism of John and Oannes, which seems so natural with Neo-Babylonian Gnostics [the Mandaeans], existed also among the more immediate Jewish followers of the Baptist, seeing that . . . influence of the Babylonian belief in ever new incarnations of the primeval Oannes—Berossus knows as many as six such reincarnations in past times. . . .

Another passage from that same book by Eisler says even more:

> I am fairly convinced that the rapid propagation of John's ideas, and especially the spreading of his fame into the low-lands of South Babylonia, has

indeed a good deal to do with the striking resemblance of his traditional name to that of the primeval Babylonian fish- and fisher-god, the teacher and lord of all wisdom.

So we have an alleged etymological connection between Oannes and *Ionnes* (John's original Greek name), as well the association with fish and water symbolism that both figures have. John is associated with fish not only because of his baptisms in the river, but also because his namesake is the prophet Jonah. You will recall that this hero from the Old Testament spent three nights inside of a sea creature, variously called either a "fish" or a "whale," that Jewish legends and cabalists unanimously link to Leviathan.

Another piece of evidence cited by Eisler to prove his point connecting John and Oannes was that the latter reportedly ate nothing when he was above the ocean's surface giving mankind lessons in wisdom, just as the former reportedly ate nothing but locusts and wild honey. If we analyze John in what Robert Graves would call a "mythopoeic" manner, we see that John's purported itinerant lifestyle (living in the wilderness, eating bugs, wearing a hair shirt, ranting and raving in public like a lunatic) connects him with the archetype of the "wild man" discussed in the previous chapter, including the figures of Pan, Puck, Dionysus, Hermes, and the Green Man.

In the Catholic liturgical calendar, John's feast day falls on June 24th, also known as "Midsummer's Day" (or to modern neo-pagans, "Litha," embracing an Old Saxon term). This is most certainly a day in which the Wild Man is celebrated. Falling on or around the Summer solstice, this is when the Green Man-related character known as the "Oak King" would be venerated in the British Isles, before paganism was completely stamped out. It was Midsummer

Night, on which Shakespeare invoked Puck in his famous play. Midsummer Night was also called the "Honey Moon" night in Britain because it was considered the best time to harvest honey. Of course, honey is something we can connect with John. This connection was not missed by Tobias Churton in *The Mystery of John the Baptist*, where he wrote:

> The solstice coincides with what used to be called the "honey moon," the origin of our costly nuptial abandon. . . . A marble figure attributed to Leonardo's workshop, now in the Kaiser Friedrich Museum, Berlin, depicts a youthful John the Baptist gracefully gazing at a honeycomb held in his left hand (an allusion to John's wild honey diet; *Mark* 1:6). One wonders if this Midsummer link to honey may have informed the traditional idea of Masons as "busy bees."

Taking the iconotropy a step further, Churton connects the honey to Dionysus and thus, Dionysus to John, via Leonardo da Vinci, who painted and drew many images of John. After analyzing several of those, Churton writes this:

> Underlying the ambiguous and arguably pagan inspiration of Leonardo's John is the existence of a similar work, thought to have been painted between 1510 and 1515 by a follower of Leonardo from a drawing by the master. The painting has a dual identity. It is known both as *St. John in the Wilderness* and as *Bacchus*, the god of religious ecstasy, wine, and intoxication.
>
> . . .
>
> [The painter] chose to add vine leaves to the figure's head and leopard spots to John's hairy

The Head of Prophecy 285

loincloth. A vine wreath added to the Baptist's former staff transformed it into a Bacchic *thrysus*, Dionysus' sacred staff borne by his wine-intoxicated followers. According to Euripides, the *thrysus* dripped with honey....

Although it may seem strange to connect a prophet known for abstaining from wine with the very god of the vine himself, Churton is definitely onto something. He also talks about "John's role here as one incarnating the divine Hermes, the *psychopomp* leading the soul upward through the waters to a higher life...." Churton suggests that the baptism in this Gospel might actually be secretly hinted at as having taken place in the Underworld, with the river Jordan symbolically representing the rivers of Hades that one must travel to get from the realm of the living to the realm of the dead. He writes:

> Symbolically, the "ferryman" may then be seen as John-Hermes. Hermes, remember, was seen in Hellenistic tradition as a "psychopomp": literally a guide of souls through the darkness of death to the other side, the herald of another world attainable only through death.

As Churton points out, many others have connected the figure of John to that of Hermes before:

> Less than a decade before Leonardo painted his late masterpiece . . . German artist Conrad Celtes . . . produced a woodcut wherein . . . the Greek god Hermes appeared as a straight stand-in for John the Baptist. . . . Celtes simply hooked into the idea of Hermes as the divine messenger and made the identification of John-Hermes by reference to the . . . understanding of John the Baptist as revered

"forerunner" or herald of Christ: the one crying in the wilderness.

The most famous statue of Hermes by Giovanni da Bologna (which, according to Edith Hamilton, is what makes him the most recognizable Greek god to modern people) shows him pointing a finger up to the sky in the same manner that John the Baptist is often shown doing, particularly in Renaissance art. However, he has several times also been depicting with his other hand pointing downward towards the Earth, just like Eliphas Levi's depiction of Baphomet, doing what we will call the "As above, so below" pose.

The reason why St. John's Day is near the summer solstice is because *Luke* 1:36 tell us that Mary's cousin Elizabeth was already six months pregnant with John when Mary conceived Jesus. Since Jesus was born on Christmas (ostensibly), near the winter solstice, putting John's birthday on Midsummer Night just made sense. In Freemasonry, both John the Baptist and John the Evangelist are considered their two main patron saints. The Evangelist's feast day in on December 27th, while the Baptist's, as we know, is on June 24. It has been quite common historically for Masonic lodges two have mandatory meetings scheduled twice a year on the feast days of the "two Johns." During Masonic initiations, an illustration is used called the "Masonic point within a Circle." It shows the two Johns standing astride a circle with a dot in the middle, possibly representing the orbit of the Earth around the sun, with the solstices, represented visually with pictures of the two Johns, on either end. In this Masonic icon, the Baptist is *always* shown in the Baphometic "As above, so below" pose described above, wearing his hair shirt.

The Head of Prophecy 287

John the Baptist's feast day is on his birthday, which is unusual for a Christian saint, since they are usually honored on the anniversary of their martyrdom, and John's story ended just as badly as those of other saints. But there is a date fixed for that event, which happens to be August 29th. Tobias Churton points out that this coincides with the time of wheat and barley harvest in the western world. This would have been around the time that the traditional English folk song "John Barleycorn" (famously performed by the band Traffic on their fourth album, *John Barleycorn Must Die*) would have been sung. This creepy tune talks about killing and dismembering the title character in a seemingly sacrificial manner that appears to be connected to harvest rituals, and he may have been named "John" with the beheaded Baptist in mind. The connection seems close enough for Churton to definitively write:

> The beheading of John became linked to a profound archetype, rooted in ancient conceptions of the head of wheat and barleycorn being severed to fulfill the promise of life and abundance for the people. . . .

Interestingly, the time in which churches celebrate the "Baptism of the Lord" (January 19th for the Orthodox, and the first Sunday following January 6th for the Catholics) is close to the time (January 20th) when the sun enters the house of Aquarius, the water-bearer.

There is yet another pagan "Wild Man" entity that Churton saw fit to connect with John the Baptist: the aforementioned Pan. To hear him tell it, the waters of the sacred Jordan may have actually been the waters of Pan. He mentions that there was a sanctuary and sacred spring dedicated to Pan called Paneas, issuing from none other than Mount Hermon (where the Watchers landed on Earth from Heaven, according to *The First Book of Enoch*). He says it may have been the source of the river that John used to baptize people:

> We must presume that John the Baptist would have come to Paneas also. How could he not? For in his day, a giant spring used to gush from a limestone cave whence the waters wove their way down to the Huela marshes, thence southward. According to Josephus, this mighty spring was held to be the source of nothing less than the living waters of the holy River Jordan: "Now the fountains of Jordan rise at the roots of this cavity outwardly; and, as some think, this is the utmost origin of Jordan" (*Wars* 1:21:3).

So by linking John to this half-goat fertility god, Churton presents what can obviously be construed as yet another symbolic link between the Baptist and the idea of Baphomet. The other obvious link, besides the fact that the Templars revered him, is that his head was severed, and the Baphomet idols purportedly used by the Templars took the form of a severed head or skull. The idea that the Baphomet head might have been John's is written about in almost every nonfiction book ever penned about this dark chapter in the Templars' history.

John's connection with Freemasonry is interesting. Of course, it is assumed to have been absorbed from the Templars. Tobias Churton points out that, before the Grand Lodge of London completely took over and homogenized the craft in the eighteenth century, there was a time during which the members of lodges who had not yet been incorporated were known cryptically as "St. John's Men." It was clear at the time that the St. John they were referring to was the Baptist. However, after the Grand Lodge takeover,

Churton notes that the Masons began celebrating John the Evangelist as well, and he seems to think they did this to muddy the waters and make it hard to tell which John was really special to them. He quotes from the famous *Sloane Manuscript*, a fifteenth-century collection of texts on file in the British Museum, which contains a script for a Masonic ritual in which the candidate must state that the first Masonic "word" was "given" at "the Tower of Babylon," and that the first Masonic lodge, back then, was called the "Chapel of St. John." So here we have John and the origins of Freemasonry connected to the Babylonians, and perhaps an echo of their priesthood's initiation into the rites of Oannes, the memory of which may have been later transposed onto the figure of the Baptist.

This brings us to the next noteworthy quotation, from *The Cauldron & the Grail: Ritual Astronomy & the Quest for Enlightenment* by Hank Harrison. Here he talks about the Greek rites of Eleusis, an offshoot of the Dionysian cult, and how they would drink hallucinogenic intoxicants proffered to them by Pluto, the lord of the underworld, who would then transform into a "man-fish" like Oannes and reveal to them secret, sacred wisdom:

> In the rituals of Eleusis, as enacted at the height of Athenian power in the Greek Golden Age, it was crucial that Pluto entice Persephone in her human form into a state of expanded consciousness. She must see more in order to understand the mystery. To do this Pluto has her drink a psychotropic substance from a special goblet, the Kykion—another proto-Grail. Pluto then transforms himself into Iakchos—an anthropomorphic man-fish who performs a passion play, based on ritual astronomy. This is not a strictly Atlantic ritual. Clearly the man

fish can be traced to Vishnu and the Vedic scriptures. But the Atlantic contribution is also apparent, especially in the transformation process and in the fact that the audience becomes an intrinsic part of the mystery. At Eleusis the spectators sing hymns to the man-fish, a figure who shows up fifteen hundred years later in the Grail literature as the Fisher King. Only Iakchos can return the maiden Persephone (essentially the vessel of the Grail) to the world of light and only the Fisher King can reveal the Grail secrets to Perceival.

Of course Oannes is linked to John, as we have established, and "Iakchos" brings to mind "Jack," a common nickname for men named John, as well as "Bacchus," the Roman term for Dionysus. In some versions of the above-mentioned rite, it is Dionysus himself who is transformed into "Iakchos" or "Iacchus." Drinking the wine of Dionysus could very well be symbolic of drinking "divine wisdom," as we saw, with Marcus the Magician and his version of the Eucharistic cup. The Mandaeans venerated John the Baptist as a Gnostic figure who dipped others in water, immersing them in a flood of Gnosis. Simon Magus presumably taught the same thing to his disciples.

What John was teaching was that salvation through Gnosis (represented by the Logos, or by Christ to the Christians) is readily available to those who seek the hidden wisdom of the Nazarenes (a term even the Mandaeans used to refer to their priests). For the Templars, however, it seems likely that the secret knowledge they sought was symbolized by their idol Baphomet, and conferred upon their initiates via the "Baptism of Wisdom" rite, which they may or may not have believed to have had anything to do with John's baptism. As we will see, this rite was perhaps more blasphemous and scandalous than most people could even imagine.

Chapter 7: The Baptism of Wisdom

The ancient mysteries later fell into a perverted decline, and were replaced with ceremonial sorcery, incantations in lieu of divine magic, and also were filled with the indescribable practices of the orgies of Bacchus. . . . The keys to esoteric knowledge were thrown over the hedge of time.

— Henry C. Clausen, former Sovereign Grand Commander of the Supreme Council of the Southern Jurisdiction of Scottish Rite Freemasonry, USA

If John is connected to the cults of Dionysus and Pan, then we should not be surprised to find that those who practiced similar Gnostic baptismal religions at later times also indulged in ceremonies involving intoxication, frenzy, ecstasy, and sexual license. In Hippolytus' *Refutation of All Heresies*, there is evidence that the Naassenes may have performed homosexual acts in their rituals. If this is true, then it may be that they believed their sexual practice was somehow reversing the normal course of sex, and turning the energy backwards—turning the Jordan River in a different direction, as the Mandaeans may have allegorized—and thereby restoring themselves to divinity. Similarly practitioners of "Tantric" sexual yoga withhold from ejaculating in order to retain the sexual energy within, for alleged spiritual gains. Perhaps in the Naassenes, or similar groups, we can find the origins of the Templars' supposed homosexual initiation rituals. Hippolytus tells of the Naassenes, while quoting from scripture:

> *Romans* 1:27, "And likewise also the men, leaving the natural use of the woman, burned in their lust one toward another; men with men working that

The Baptism of Wisdom 293

which is unseemly"—now the expression that which is unseemly signifies, according to these (Naasseni), the first and blessed substance, figureless, the cause of all figures to those things that are moulded into shapes—"and receiving in themselves that recompense of their error which was meet." (*Romans* 1:27) For in these words which Paul has spoken they say the entire secret of theirs, and a hidden mystery of blessed pleasure, are comprised. For the promise of washing is not any other, according to them, than the introduction of him that is washed in, according to them, life-giving water, and anointed with ineffable ointment (than his introduction) into unfading bliss.

This entire section indicates that the Naassenes believed that Paul secretly taught them to practice homosexual rites. We suspect that the terms "washing," "life-giving water" and "ineffable ointment" mentioned above all refer to a ritual of bathing in semen. Judging from Epiphanius' explicit accounts of Gnostics eating semen and menses as the Eucharist, as well as consuming aborted embryos pounded with honey and pepper, it doesn't seem too far-fetched. A lot of Epiphanius' criticism against Gnostic groups is based on his interpretation of a metaphor of gathering up the "spiritual seeds" of the world for the Gnostic church. These are the "spiritual elect." The Greek word for seed is *sperma*. Here is an example of the metaphor being used in *The Gospel of Eve* that was twisted by Epiphanius in *Panarion* 26.3.1:

> I stood upon a lofty mountain, and saw a man who was tall, and another, little of stature. And I heard as it were the sound of thunder and drew nigh to hear, and he spake with me and said, I am thou and thou

art I, and wheresoever thou art, there am I; and I am sown in all things. And from wheresoever thou wilt thou gatherest me, but in gathering me, thou gatherest thyself.

The Gospel of Philip (a Gnostic gospel not part of the Nag Hammadi Codices) tells us something similar as well:

The Lord hath shown me what my soul must say on its ascent to heaven, and how it must answer each of the powers on high. "I have recognized myself," it saith, "and gathered myself from every quarter, and have sown no children for the archon. But I have pulled up his roots and gathered my scattered members, and I know who thou art. For I," it saith, "am of the ones on high."

All of this is consistent with idea that some Gnostic sects believed they were gathering spiritual seeds from the world and returning them to the realm above. It seems to have something to do with refraining from conceiving children, while at the same time not refraining from sex (quite the opposite). Simon Magus is also said to teach the same libertine practices, calling it "perfect love."

It might be wise to consider that Epiphanius was perhaps just misinterpreting a mystical teaching, and indulging in gossip about the same rumors that were once heard in the Roman empire about Christians. We saw how Celsus conflated the Christians and the Ophites with each other, accusing the Christians of being involved in the Ophites' secret orgies and cannibalistic rites. However, it is undeniable that the authors of early Gnostic scripture were practically obsessed with erotic symbolism.

In *Refutations* (5.21), Hippolytus referred to the phallic deity Priapus, who the Gnostic teacher Justin claimed had "fashioned all things." Epiphanius, in *Panarion* 25.2.4, also connected the teaching of the libertine Nicolaitans (who *The Revelation of St. John* condemns in the strongest terms), together with a great female power called Barbelo who "emitted from the Father." Her relation to the world-creating powers or Archons is highly erotic because she "continually appears to the Archons in some beautiful form and, through their climax and ejaculation, takes their seed to recover her power, which has been sown in several of them." This continued emitting of semen is an important part of the recovery of a female force situated in the eighth heaven. Nicolaus is quoted as saying, "Unless one copulates every day, he cannot have eternal life." (*Panarion* 25.1.5) We must look to the observations of Jacque Lacarriere on all of this when he connects Gnostic sex rituals as reported by the Church Fathers with the Satanic Black Mass in his book *The Gnostics*:

> The Black Mass is not far removed from the Barbelo Gnostic ritual—certainly no farther than Sabaoth is from Lucifer—and it is no mere chance that certain aspects of these rites are to be found, right down to the present day, among the Luciferean sects, where they are spiced with cabbalistic demonology. The ambivalence of the whole Gnostic attitude, the perpetual temptation that oscillates between rigorous asceticism and rigorous debauch (since both have the same sateriolagical value) is to be found there and, in the historical evolution of Gnosticism, was translated into the opposing paths of mystic Catharism (far the first) and magic Luciferism (for the second).

In *Roman History* (39.12), the Roman historian Livy makes the same accusations against those who partook in the Bacchanalia ceremonies, when he writes:

> When once the mysteries had assumed this promiscuous character, and men were mingled with women with all the license of nocturnal orgies, there was no crime, no deed of shame, wanting. More uncleanness was wrought by men with men than with women. Whoever would not submit to defilement, or shrank from violating others, was sacrificed as a victim. To regard nothing as impious or criminal was the very sum of their religion.

These Bacchus worshipers were pretty hardcore! Even more amazing, there is evidence that there was a strong Bacchic/Dionysian influence on Christianity, as well as on the Johannite heresy. As we mentioned, when we first encounter John in the Gospels, especially in *Matthew*, we find that John described as a homeless madman living on insects. He seems to be demonstrating the sort of *mania* (etymologically related to *manteia*, meaning "prophecy") described by Plato in *Phaedrus* (244de):

> This madness can provide relief from the greatest plagues of trouble that beset certain families because of their guilt for ancient crimes: it turns up among those who need a way out; it gives prophecies and takes refuge in prayers to the gods and in worship, discovering mystic rites and purifications that bring the man it touches through to safety for this and all time to come. So it is that the right sort of madness finds relief from present hardships for a man it has possessed.

The Baptism of Wisdom 297

Baptism was one of the sacraments of the Thracian moon and fertility goddess Kotys (or "Kotyto"). Ian C. Storey writes in *Eupolis, Poet of Old Comedy*:

> "Baptai" were worshipers (in this case of the goddess Kotyto) who had undergone a ritual immersion or washing as a rite of initiation.

We also find much Dionysian symbolism in *The Gospel of John* as well (some of it discussed in the previous chapter). In *John* 2:1-11 we see Jesus turning water to wine at the wedding at Cana (once celebrated by the Catholic Church on the same feast day as Jesus' baptism). Similarly, there were many myths of Dionysus' miraculous production of wine. The Middle Platonist and historian Plutarch relayed this wine miracle in the *Life of Lysander* (28, 4), where he says that the handmaidens and nurses of the infant Dionysus dipped him into a spring and the water changed into wine of a pleasant taste. For a polytheistic Greek audience, the Dionysian resonance in the story of Jesus' wine miracle would have been unmistakable.

Moreover, John's Gospel employs further Dionysian imagery when Jesus is quoted as saying: "I am the true vine" (15:1). John's Jesus presents himself as a "New Dionysus," superior to the previous version of the god. In *1 Corinthians* 12:12-13 (NASB) we read:

> For even as the body is one and yet has many members, and all the members of the body, though they are many, are one body, so also is Christ. For by one Spirit we were all baptized into one body, whether Jews or Greeks, whether slaves or free, and we were all made to drink of one Spirit.

To "drink of one spirit" parallels the Dionysian ritual of imbibing the god through the consumption of wine. (The word "spirit" is even a term applied to alcoholic beverages.) This is the basis of the Catholic Eucharist, with the consumption of Jesus Christ's blood symbolized as wine, and his flesh as the wafer of bread.

The Bacchic possession of "divine madness" has parallels with Paul's teaching on how possession of the Holy Spirit was meant to affect a convert who "received" it through baptism, resulting in things like *glossolalia* (speaking in tongues). The Greek word *entheos*, meaning "within is a god," was used to describe someone that is divinely possessed. This is the origin of the word "enthusiasm." This is the state of *ekstasis* (ecstasy), when the boundaries between the egoic self, other people, and the god worshipped are dissolved into an experience of rapture and unity. The ecstasy of the god's presence was said to be induced by music, dance, wine, and *omophagia* (the eating of raw flesh). Similarly, in *John* 6:53-56 (NKJV), Jesus said to his disciples:

> Most assuredly, I say to you, unless you eat the flesh of the Son of Man and drink His blood, you have no life in you. Whoever eats My flesh and drinks My blood has eternal life, and I will raise him up at the last day. For My flesh is food indeed, and My blood is drink indeed. He who eats My flesh and drinks My blood abides in Me, and I in him.

Jesus implored his followers to consume his divine flesh and blood to regenerate their souls from their fallen state, decaying in meat sacks because of their progenitor's exile from Eden after the consumption of the fruit of the Tree of Knowledge of Good and Evil. This can be compared to ambrosia, the food of the gods on Olympus, which gave their blood, called "ichor," the power to keep them immortal. Not too that the fruit of the Tree of Life in the

The Baptism of Wisdom 299

Garden of Eden had such properties, as do the rivers of the "water of life" that are said to flow through the New Jerusalem for the saved ones at the End Times. As we mentioned, these rivers are described as ultimately issuing from the sliced-open jugular vein of the *Agnes Dei* (Lamb of God) depicted as standing on the altar at the center of the holy city. Clearly, the latter description is a metaphor for the blood of Christ. Semen and blood were both substances considered by all ancient societies to be the givers of life and the carriers of soul essence. Especially included here was menstrual blood, which many ancient cultures thought was a coagulant from which the body of a fetus was formed, possessing the germ of life in itself, not understanding the role played by the ovum. Under a more Hermetic or Gnostic lens, one can interpret ingesting these holy foods as medicine to transcend one's fate, controlled by the fixed stars of the Zodiac.

This is the key to understanding "the elixir of life" spoken of by the alchemists, which Ignatius of Antioch equated with the Eucharist. He called it the "medicine of immortality" in *Ignatius to the Ephesians* 20:2. In modern times, the self-purported neo-Templar "Ordo Templi Orientis" serve at their "Gnostic Mass" what they call "cakes of light" (a mix of menstrual blood, semen, honey, cake batter, and olive oil) instead of the traditional Eucharist wafer. We are not quite sure how many of the participants are aware of the ingredients of the cakes, as these rites are open to the public, and no warning is given to congregants about what they are about to consume.

In *Liber Aleph*, Aleister Crowley writes that pre-eminent in all sex magick "is the Formula of the Serpent with the Head of the Lion"—which he says is a reference to semen, and another personification of Baphomet—"and all this

Magick is wrought by the Radiance and Creative Force thereof." To Crowley, the personal will and magical prowess was symbolized by the erect phallus. The woman is a necessary, respected and consecrated essential of the formula for sex magic, but only in a reflective sense as a vessel, for the manifestation of the sacred.

Returning to Paul, in *1 Corinthians* 14:23 (NIV) he discusses how speaking in tongues is indicative of one possessed by the Holy Spirit, having a private conversation with God that only He can understand. *The Acts of the Apostles* shows Paul seemingly "gone mad" from his own divine encounter with the risen Christ, and we are to understand that this behavior is a sign of one touched by God. But here in *1 Corinthians*, Paul explains that speaking in tongues will not be particularly useful for winning over converts because it makes Christians look totally insane:

> So if the whole church comes together and everyone speaks in tongues, and inquirers or unbelievers come in, will they not say that you are out of your mind?

Similarly, imbibing or absorbing the spirit of Dionysus leads to "madness" and ecstatic speech. Thus the followers of Dionysus were called "Maenads," which was sort of a pun on a Greek term that meant "maddened one." But perhaps not all such spiritual experiences are the same. Earlier in *1 Corinthians* 10:20-22 (NIV), Paul distinguished between possession by the Paraclete or Holy Spirit and demonic possession by contrasting Christian worship with Greco-Roman pagan sacrifice:

> [T]he sacrifices of pagans are offered to demons, not to God, and I do not want you to be participants with demons. You cannot drink the cup of the Lord

and the cup of demons too; you cannot have a part in both the Lord's table and the table of demons.

In *Ephesians* 5:18-19 (NIV), Paul admonishes the newly regenerated Christians to live a conservative lifestyle instead of a libertine, Dionysian one when he writes:

Do not get drunk on wine, which leads to debauchery. Instead, be filled with the Spirit, speaking to one another with psalms, hymns, and songs from the Spirit.

For Paul, imbibing the Spirit of God doesn't induce drunkenness and debauchery, but edification and maturity. It is probable that Paul (or the true Pauline author, whoever that was) wrote part of this letter with the Bacchanalia in mind. Plato took a moderate or tempered stance on celebrating the rites of Dionysus when he said that no one under eighteen should drink wine, but that adults over forty should take part in the "convivial gatherings and invoke Dionysus. . . ." (*Leg*. 2.666B) He also suggested mixing water with the wine to temper its intoxicating effects.

But whether wine, spiritual possession or some other vector is used, it seems that this state of mind was commonly thought to be the desirable result of ritual for many Gnostic groups. As Hans Jonas about Philo:

Among the impressive things which he [Philo] coins in this connection (by way of Scriptural allegory) is that of "defecting from oneself"; and a favorite one, "to fly from oneself and flee to God." "He who runs away from God flees to himself . . . he who flies from his own *nous* (mind) flees to that of the All." (*Leg*.all.III.29; cf.ibid.48).

This fleeing from oneself can, besides the ethical meaning which we have so far been considering, assume also a mystical meaning, as in the following passage: "Get thee out, not only from thy body . . . ["country"] and from sense-perception . . . ["kindred"] and from reason . . . ["father's house"], but escape even thyself, and pass out of thyself, raving and God-possessed like the Dionysian Corybantes. With this mystic version of the abandonment of the self we have to deal in the context of gnostic psychology.

In order to achieve this state of mind, the Greco-Roman mystery cults, such as the rites of Dionysus, Eleusis, and Orpheus, engaged in things meant to temporarily divorce their minds from the everyday world. The goal was to force their souls to venture forth into the wilderness of mystical ecstasy, to be absorbed fully by the deity worshipped. Wine and other intoxicants, as well as unusual forms of group sex, were to be expected.

This brings us to the famous alabaster "Ophite Bowl" found in Syria and dated from the third to fifth century. According to Kurt Rudolph in *Gnosis: The Nature & History of Gnosticism*, there is actually a controversy over whether this relic belonged to the Ophites, as the ritual depicted inside seems Ophitic, or if it came from the mysteries of Orpheus, as the inscription on the outside of the bowl seems to imply. Either way it is pertinent to our inquiry, as both Orphism and Ophitism seem to have contributed to the stream of tradition that may have eventually influenced the secret practices of the Knights Templar.

Let us consider what we see depicted inside of this bowl. We see a serpent surrounded by sixteen naked initiates arranged in a circle, each making an obscure ritual hand gesture towards the snake as if in veneration. Ewa Osek remarks on the Ophite bowl in "Hermes' Tablet (*Nonnus* D 41.343-44): An Allusion to the 'Orphic' Gold Leaves?"

> Delbrueck and Vollgraff, who examined this bowl in the early 1930s, excluded the possibility of forgery. They maintained that this was an alabaster copy of the metal original, both (copy and original) impossible to date more precisely than to AD 300–529. "The special importance of the bowl"—the scholars claim—"lies in the fact that it is, so far as we know, the only representation of a cult-scene . . . from the jealously-concealed Orphic mysteries." This led them to the conclusion that the radiant snake, pointing at the omphalos, had to be Phanes, the Orphic god of the sun. Hans Leisegang (1955), who saw the vessel in question a few years before them, supposed it was associated with the cult of the heavenly serpent worshipped by Gnostic sects (Ophites, Sethians, Naassenes) as well as by the Orphics, who sang their Bacchics to honor Phanes, envisioned as dragon.

The image of the winged serpent in the center of the bowl brings to mind the caduceus, the double-snaked staff of Hermes. Note that the snake here is coiled, much like the Hindu yogic "kundalini serpent," which is said to be "coiled" energy hidden dormant within the human spinal column. It is "released" when the devotee has done yogic practices or spiritual meditations to manipulate the subtle energy centers (called "chakras") along the spine. This may be connected to the "Nagas" of Kashmir, which were likely the Hindu equivalents of the Ophite Gnostics, venerating Hindu, Buddhist, and Jainist "Devas," or deities who were depicted with the lower bodies of serpents. The concept of the kundalini is very similar to how the Naassenes allegorized the serpent as a presentation of the spinal column combined with the pineal gland (the "third eye") within the brain. As reported by Hippolytus (*Refutation of All Heresies* 5.11):

> ... They adduce the anatomy of the brain, assimilating, from the fact of its immobility, the brain itself to the Father, and the cerebellum to the Son, because of its being moved and being of the form of (the head of) a serpent. And they allege that this (cerebellum), by an ineffable and inscrutable process, attracts through the pineal gland the spiritual and life-giving substance emanating from the vaulted chamber (in which the brain is embedded). And on receiving this, the cerebellum in an ineffable manner imparts the ideas, just as the Son does, to matter; or, in other words, the seeds and the genera of the things produced according to the flesh flow along into the spinal marrow.

The imagery in the bowl has been taken by most writers on the subject to represent the sacred orgies celebrated in secret by the Ophites, as described by Epiphanius. In the *Panarion* (1.37.5:5-5:8), he wrote that the Ophites held a Eucharistic ceremony which included kissing snakes.

> And therefore these people who possess the serpent's portion and nothing else, call the serpent a king from heaven. And so, they say, they glorify him for such knowledge and offer him bread. For they have a real snake and keep it in a basket of some sort. When it is time for their mysteries they bring it out of the den, spread loaves around on a table, and call the snake to come; and when the den is opened it comes out. And then the snake—which

comes up of its own accord and by its villainy—
already knowing their foolishness, crawls onto the
table and coils up on the loaves. And this they call a
perfect sacrifice. And so, as I have heard from
someone, not only do they break the loaves the
snake has coiled on and distribute them to the
communicants, but each one kisses the snake on the
mouth besides—whether the snake has been
charmed into tameness by some sort of sorcery, or
coaxed by some other act of the devil for their
deception. But they worship an animal of that sort
and call what has been consecrated by its coiling
around it the eucharistic element. And they offer a
hymn to the Father on high—again, as they say,
through the snake—and so conclude their
mysteries.

This ritual sounds exactly like the depiction of a ritual found by Joseph von Hammer-Purgstall, also on a ceremonial bowl that had been discovered on a former Templar property. In that image we see naked men and women kissing snakes on the lips. Similar bowls, along with images from cups coins, and the walls of cathedrals, also depict children, and animals such as dogs, bears, and camels, involved in what Hammer-Purgstall interpreted as ceremonial rites of bestiality and pederasty. They show women suckling snakes to their breasts, and blasphemous acts, like a naked woman using a water pitcher to put out the candles on a menorah, to represent extinguishing the light of the Judaic god and tradition. If these were truly ritual practices borrowed from Gnostics sects, it could explain what Justin Martyr meant, in a passage that will be quoted in the next chapter, when he spoke of the "upsetting of the lamp" as a deed that certain heretics had been accused by their enemies of doing (*1 Apology* 26).

Another counterpart to the Ophite/Orphic ritual seen in the bowl is the so-called "Gnostic Mass" of the OTO previously mentioned. This ritual—which culminates in an act between a priest and a naked priestess on top of an altar, obscured from view by a curtain—involves the congregants performing the exact same hand signal as those seen in the Ophite bowl. This is made with the left hand raised, with flat palm, above the head, and the right hand placed flat over the heart. The OTO calls this "the Hailing Sign of the Magician," and it can also be found in *Duncan's Ritual of Freemasonry,* where it is called "the Sign of a Fellow Craftsman."

Ceremonial bowls were used throughout the ancient world for conjuring, and even trapping, spirits. They were also used to collect fluids, such as blood, baptismal water, and Eucharistic wine, used in rituals. Magical or holy bowls and cups also appear quite frequently in mythology. The most well-known to the Western audience is that of the Holy Grail, which is a mythic item tied directly to the Knights Templar. In the Grail stories, the knights who guard the holy relic are depicted in ways that make it quite clear they are Templars, and in Wolfram von Echenbach's version of the tale (*Parzival*), he called them that explicitly. But what the Grail is, and the origin of the myth, has been debated for centuries.

Perhaps the most interesting connection in regards to our present inquiry has to do with the alleged "Baptism of Wisdom," seemingly the best translation of the name "Baphomet," and according to Joseph von Hammer-Purgstall, the name of an Ophite Gnostic ritual that the Knights Templar engaged in to conjure Baphomet. In *The Corpus Hermeticum*'s fourth chapter, the "Discourse of Hermes to Tat on the Mixing Bowl or the Monad," Hermes explains that the Father of all didn't give *Nous* (mind, intelligence, or wisdom) to every person born in the world. Rather, he put it in a "mixing bowl" which he sent down from Heaven, intending for humans to compete with each other for access to it, along with a herald to proclaim to us below:

> Immerse yourself in the mixing bowl if your heart has the strength, if it believes you will rise up again to the one who sent the mixing bowl below, if it recognizes the purpose of your coming to be.

> All those who heeded the proclamation and immersed themselves in mind participated in knowledge and became perfect people because they received mind.

After hearing this, Tat understandably pleads: "I too wish to be immersed, my father."

This Hermetic discourse is mentioned by Hammer-Purgstall himself in reference to the Baptism of Wisdom, which he describes as a "Baptism of Fire." Here is a translation of Hammer-Purgstall's words (from the first-ever English edition, soon to be published with commentary from Tracy R. Twyman):

> Let us now take a look at the place in Hermes Trismegistus . . . where God sends a messenger with a bowl full of "Mens" ["wisdom", or "mind"], where perfected souls tending towards gnosis are ordered to immerse themselves. Other patristic authorities [discuss] the mystical baptism of the Gnostics, and various words distorted out of Hebrew and other languages are adduced, of which one is [the Greek] "basema." What wonder, therefore, if "baptism"

was changed into "Baphen," just as "Metin" [was changed] into "Meten."

It was amazing to us when we stumbled upon this passage in *The Corpus Hermeticum* while researching the subject of Hermes for the purpose of writing this book. It was especially amazing considering that one-half of our team, Tracy Twyman, spent decades researching the subject of another sacred vessel, the Holy Grail, and had even written a book about it (*The Merovingian Mythos*, 2004), and has been writing about the subject of Baphomet for just as long, but somehow had never taken any special notice of this passage. We discovered it about the same time that we learned about the Ophite bowl, while studying Gnosticism. What was really strange was that as we found out from further reading, both the subject of the Ophite bowl and the Hermetic bowl of Mind popped up repeatedly in several very obscure references we were looking at. Emma Jung, writer and wife of Carl Jung, wrote about both topics in her book *The Grail Legend*, actually comparing and connecting the two. She said:

> Think of that vessel filled with nous (understanding and consciousness) which is mentioned in the *Corpus Hermeticum* and which, as Hermes taught his pupil Thoth, was sent from heaven to earth so that men, plunging into it, might understand the purpose for which they were created. A vessel of this kind also played a part in the Gnostic mystery celebrations of late antiquity. In Hans Leisegang's study, "The Mystery of the Serpent," an illustration is given of a bowl that appears to have originated in an Orphic community. On it sixteen naked men and women, in reverential and worshipping attitudes, stand around a coiled and winged serpent, the

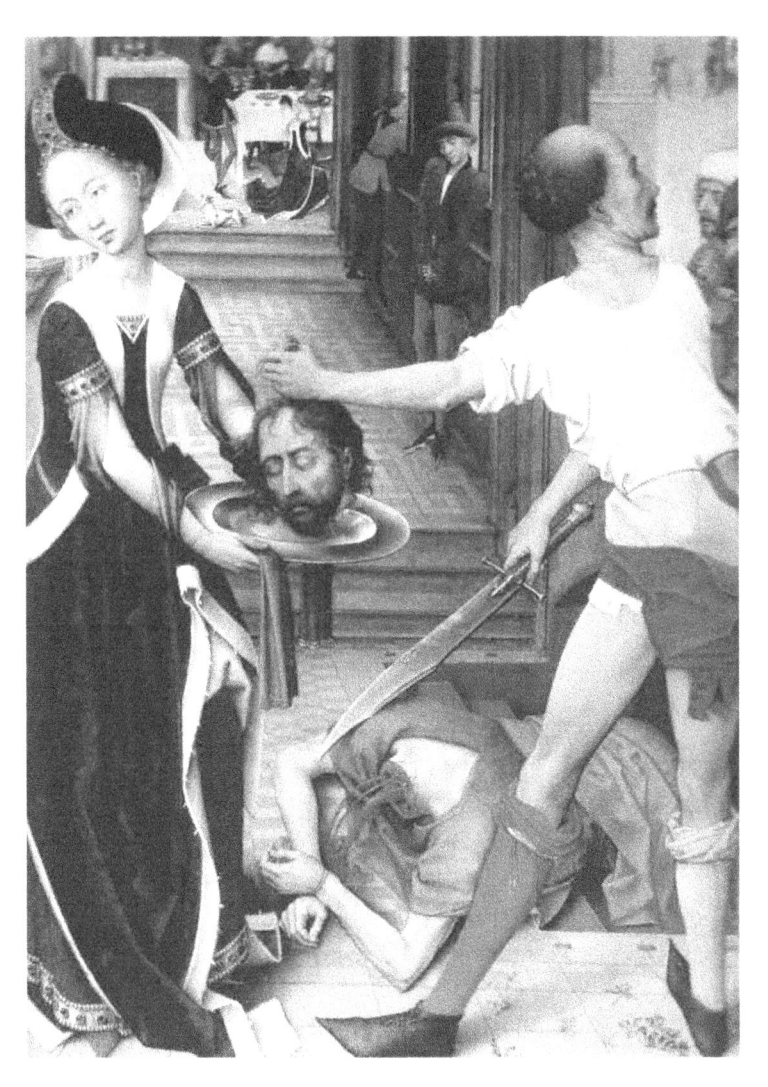

Beheading of John the Baptist, by Rogier van der Weyden, c.1455-1460.

Above left: The hair shirt, symbol of John the Baptist. Above right: "St. John's Arms," also known as a "Gorgon knot." Below: Masonic representation of the two Johns, with the Baptist adopting the attitude of Levi's Baphomet, "As above, so below."

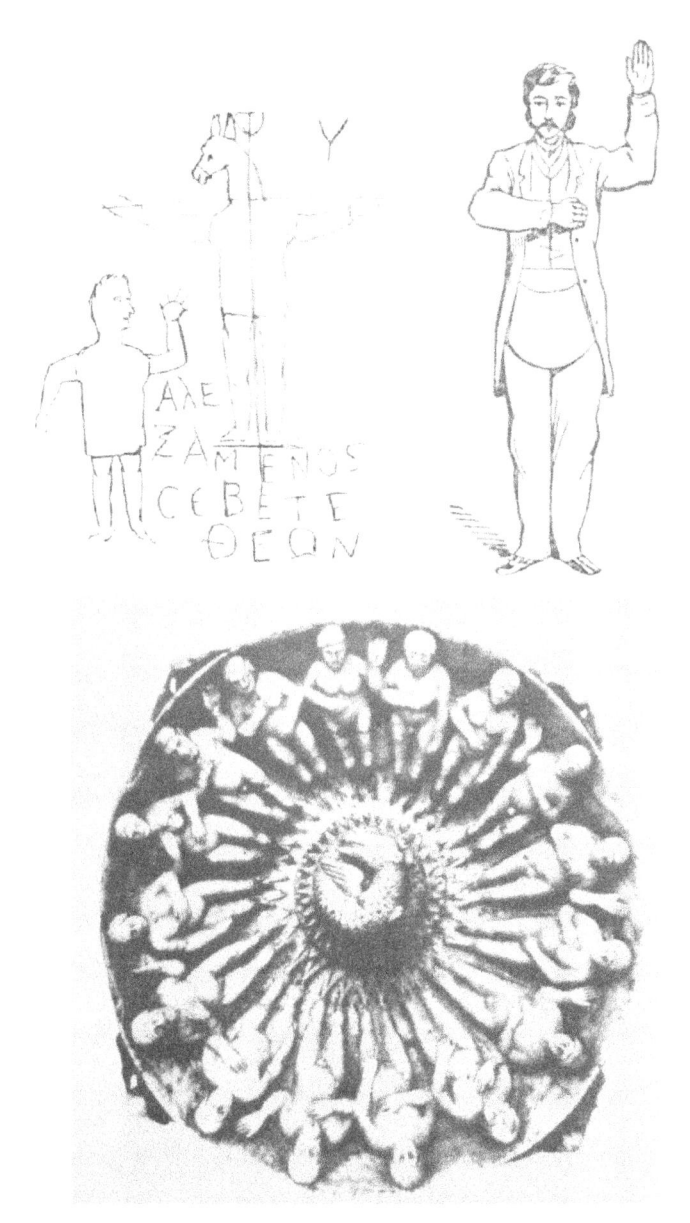

Above left: Graffiti art, Rome, c. 200 AD, featuring the crucified donkey-man. Above right: Sign of a Fellow Craftsman, from *Duncan's Ritual of Freemasonry*. Below: the Ophite Bowl.

John in the quintessential "As above, so below" Baphomet pose.

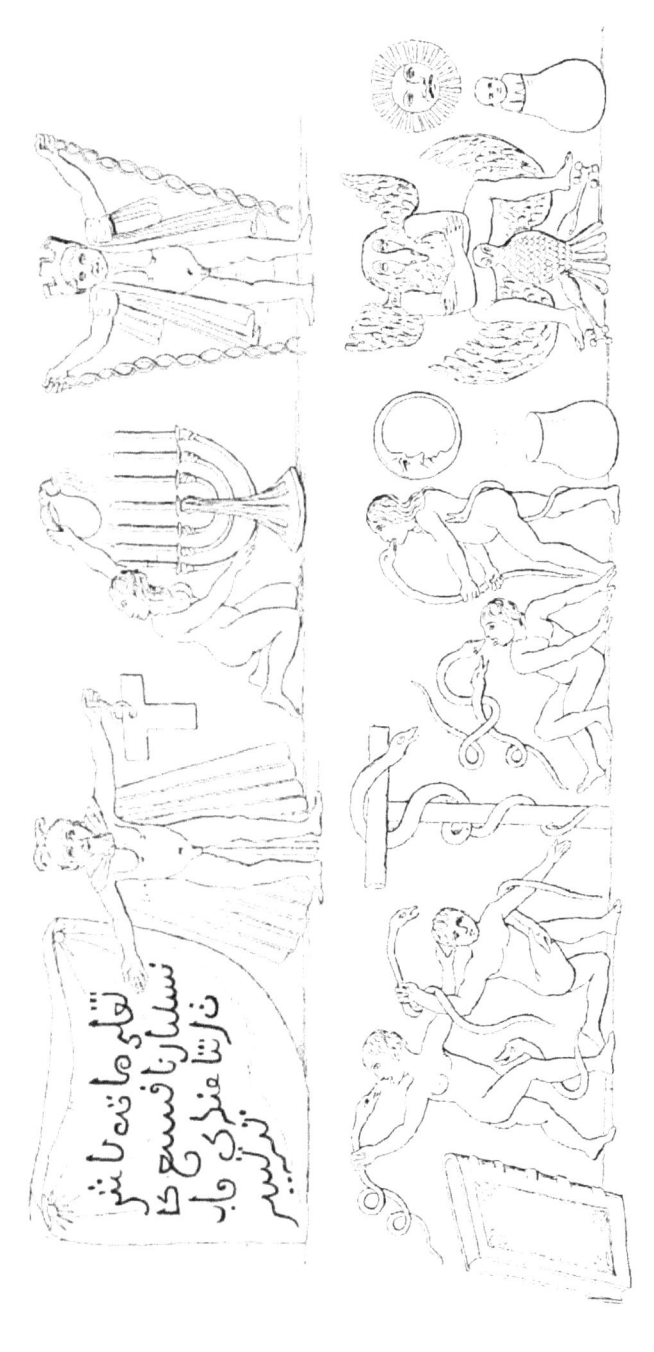

Above: Images from *Hammer-Purgstall's Mysterium Baphometis Revelatum*, featuring snake-kissing, a man with a goose on his head seated stop an eagle, the extinguishing of a menorah, and two images of Mete.

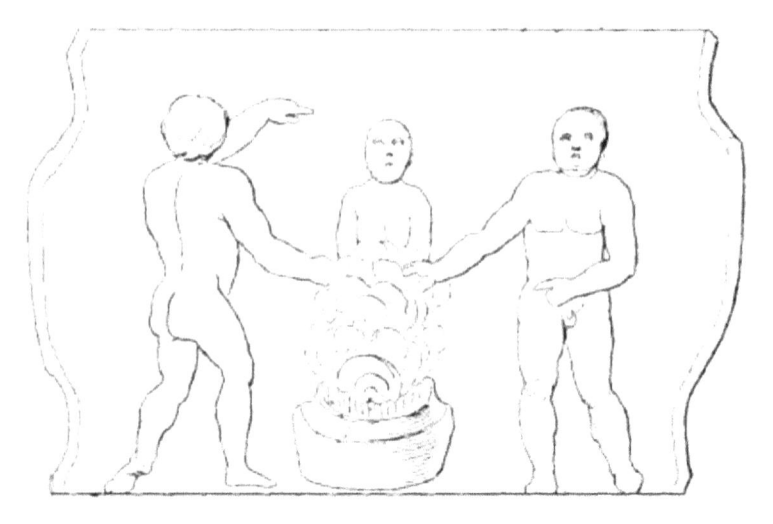

Above and left: Images from *Hammer-Purgstall's Mysterium Baphometis Revelatum*, featuring boy being immolated, the building of a sacrificial fire, and two women nursing serpents.

Opposite page: Drawings of idols, from the same source. Above left: A man holds a boy on top of a bowl. Above right: Front and back of a statue, in front of which there is a boy who has passed through a flaming bowl and is emerging beneath. Below: Images of two-faced idols.

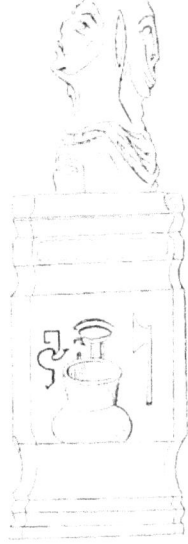

Opposite page and above: More images from
Mysterium Baphometis Revelatum.

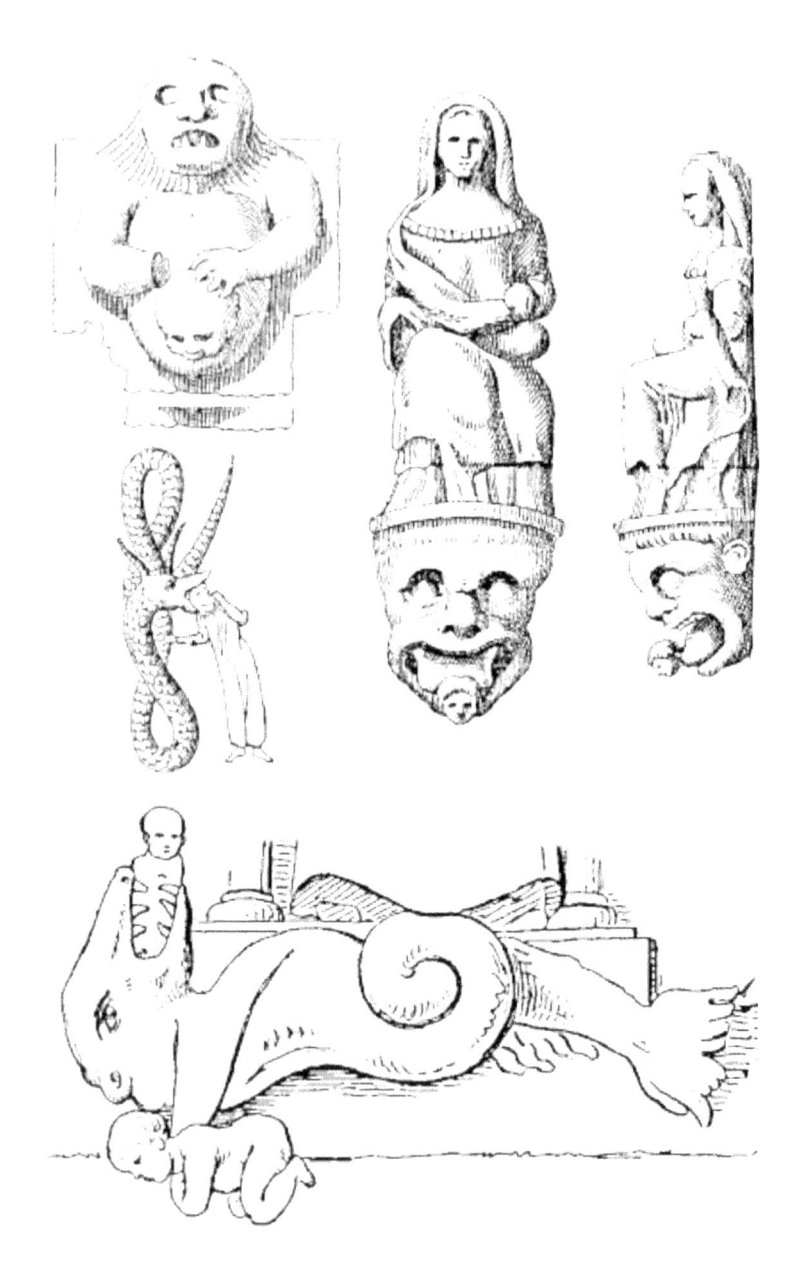

Images of children being eaten or otherwise mistreated by monsters, from *Mysterium Baphometis Revelatum*.

Seventeenth-century French priest Etienne Guibourg performing a Black Mass with Francoise Athenaas de Rochechouart de Mortemart, marquise of Montespan, whose body was used as an altar. The mass involves the sacrifice of unbaptized infants.

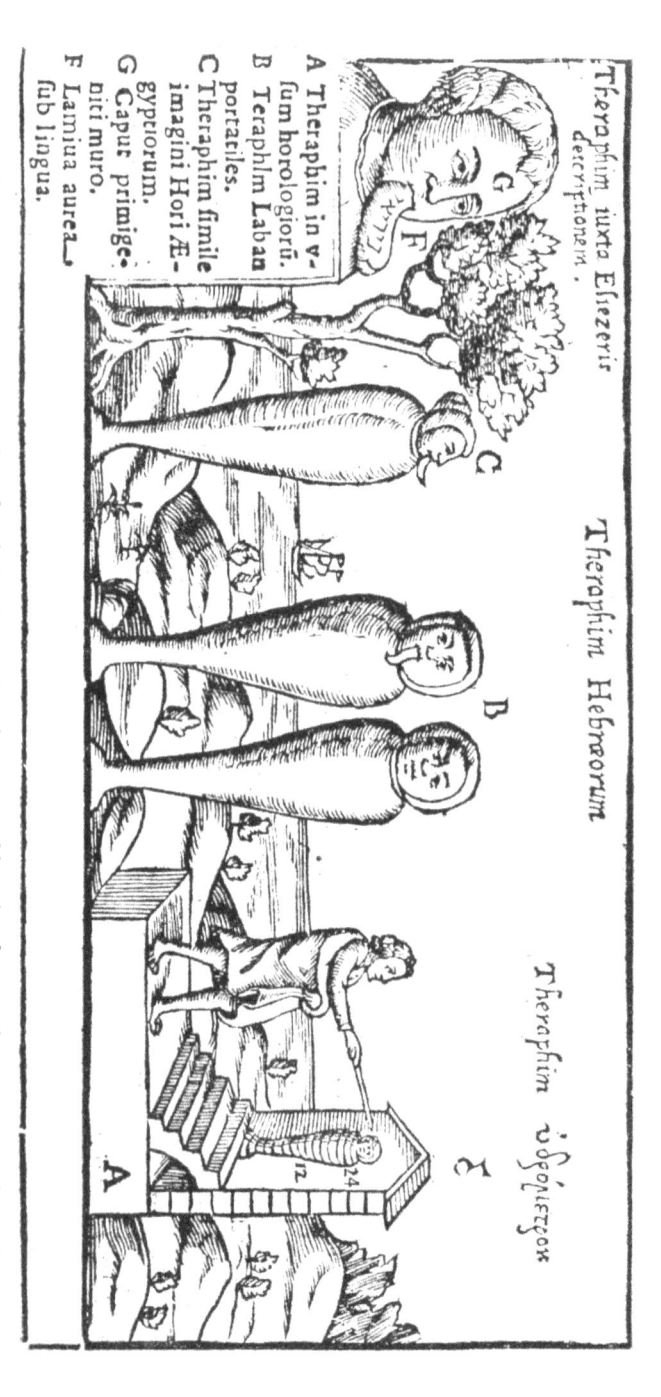

Depiction of magician creating teraphim for divination using the severed heads of young boys. From Athanasius Kirscher's *Oedipus Aegyptiacus*, 1652.

symbol of the Redeemer and Son of God in the Orphic Gnosis. . . . In this bowl the Logos-serpent is clearly being worshipped by the initiates.

In the same section she mentions several other holy cups or bowls, including a tradition from Ibn Malik that God gave Mohammed a special green goblet of light "for thine enlightenment." She also talks about a vision by the third-century Gnostic alchemist Zosimos of Panopolis, who, she says, "saw an altar in the form of a shallow bowl in which men in torment were being cooked and thereby sublimated into a state of spirituality." Mrs. Jung pointed out that Zosimos himself, had in his own writings, mentioned the bowl of Mind from *The Corpus Hermeticum*, "in which he advises his *soror mystica* to immerse herself." On this topic her husband once wrote that this bowl was "a font or piscina, in which the immersion takes place and transformation into a spiritual being is effected." The transformation, however, is described as a very bloody and horrifying process. From Zosimus:

> And when I had heard the voice of him who stood in the altar formed like a bowl, I questioned him, desiring to understand who he was.
>
> He answered me in a weak voice saying, "I am Ion, Priest of the Adytum, and I have borne an intolerable force. For someone came at me headlong in the morning and dismembered me with a sword and tore me apart, according to the rigor of harmony. And, having cut my head off with the sword, he mashed my flesh with my bones and burned them in the fire of the treatment, until, my body transformed, I should learn to become a spirit. And I sustained the same intolerable force."

> And even as he said these things to me and I forced him to speak, it was as if his eyes turned to blood and he vomited up all his flesh. And I saw him as a mutilated image of a little man and he was tearing at his flesh and falling away.

The decapitation and dismemberment process described here reminds us of the decapitation of John, and the ritual dismemberment of both Dionysus and Orpheus, as celebrated in their respective mystery cults. The vomiting up of one's own flesh sounds like something out of the movie *Hellraiser*. What we are talking about is the alchemical process of spiritual sublimation, the *nigredo*, wherein all things are dissolved into blackness—what St. John of the Cross called the "Dark Night of the Soul." It might also be what Jesus and John the Baptist both referred to as the "Baptism of Fire." For many Gnostics, Hermeticists, and alchemists, this is a personal process of self-transformation through meditation, ritual, and various processes designed to dissolve ego awareness. We do not deny, however, that some may have also performed ritual sacrifices or other dark deeds with the purpose of soul transmutation.

In the case of modern Aleister Crowley acolytes, it may involve both. Above the Ordo Templi Orientis there is a secret inner circle is called the "Argentum Astrum" (the Silver Star), consisting entirely of people who have gone through a ritual called "Crossing the Abyss." It is supposed to be a form of ego death, after which the initiate is "reborn" as a master magician. The idea is that the self is dissolved in the "Abyss" of primordial chaos. Normally, this sort of experience either kills or at least mentally destroys the average person, and they are never the same again. But a true master, they say, can go through this, burn off the dross of his false self (the common ego), and come out

The Baptism of Wisdom 323

retaining his true self (the super-ego). He then realizes his "True Will" or personal destiny.

This is analogous to being dissolved in the Hermetic bowl and retaining your true self, thus being able to recognize "the purpose of your coming to be." It is something not for the weak, but only, like with the Hermetic baptism, "if your heart has the strength, if it believes you will rise up again." Tracy R. Twyman has heard from a reliable witness, whose name we must keep secret for obvious reasons, that in the Argentum Astrum this is achieved by kidnapping the initiate from his home with chloroform. When he wakes up, he is in a dark room where he is sodomized horribly by hooded figures (his brothers in the order), for several hours, the humiliation of which is supposed to achieve the necessary purification. We are not making any formal accusations here, but simply passing along what we have heard.

This concept of "crossing" or "immersing" yourself in the Abyss, a process which only the elect few are able to pass through still whole, is also related to a repeated theme found in mystery cults in which a soul (either after death, or during the transformation of an initiation ritual) is offered two cups. One brings forgetfulness of the previous life (filled with water from the river Lethe ["forgetfulness"] which flows through Hades), while the other allows he who drinks it to retain his memory even after death or transformation, and on into the new life or new form. The Gnostic *Pistis Sophia* talks about "Adamas," in this source the equivalent of Hermes, and someone described as "a receiver of the Little Sabaoth [the Lords of Hosts]" offering these two cups to recently discarnate souls:

> And there comes Ialouham, the receiver of Sabaoth, the Adamas [ie, Hermes] who gives to the souls the

cup of forgetfulness, and he brings the water of forgetfulness and gives it unto a soul [and it drinks it], and it forgets all things and all places unto which it had gone. Afterwards there comes a receiver of the little Sabaoth . . . and he himself brings a cup filled with understanding and wisdom, and sobriety is found in it, and he gives it to the soul and they cast it into a body that will not be able to sleep nor to forget, because of the cup of sobriety which is given to the soul, but the body will lash the soul's heart continually to seek after the mysteries of the Light.

According to Hammer-Purgstall, a ritual baptism of fire was represented on the artifacts he claimed to have found:

In support of spiritual baptism and tincture of fire were the sculptured bowls at the feet of our idols, and full of fire, so that it might become well-known how that mystic rite should be administered. A double representation of the same thing is brought to view. The first is of an infant (which means a neophyte Gnostic) be placed by Mete at the pedestal to this bowl; the other of a boy of this type standing over a flaming bowl.

In the same text he also talks about the concept of the two vessels that one can drink of after death, writing that there is "a double bowl [that] pertains to souls; the one part, *oblivion*, leading to generating (Greek, *geneseos*), the other part to *Sophia*, to wisdom."

When one thinks of a bowl or a vessel containing wisdom, one obvious connection to make is with the image of the human head, the cup that holds the brain, the presumed organ of mind and, as Plato, Socrates, and later Descartes would have said, the "seat of the soul." Talking about the vessel used in alchemy, Emma Jung wrote:

> The "Liber quartorum," a Latin translation of a Sabean text, emphasizes that the vessel is "like the work of God in the vessel of the divine seed (*germinis divi*), for it has received the clay, moulded it, and mixed it with water and fire." "This," says [Carl] Jung, "is an allusion to the creation of man, but on the other hand it seems to refer to the creation of souls, since immediately afterwards the text speaks of the production of souls from the "seeds of heaven." In order to catch the soul, God created the *vas cerebi*, the cranium."

So if a person's head is the cup or bowl that contains his mind, then could this Hermetic vessel, this cup of "universal mind," be thought of as a giant "universal" head? Well actually, yes! In regards to this notion, the previously-mentioned work from Berossus (or from Alexander Polyhistor, supposedly quoting Berossus) contains a passage supposedly written by Oannes that is really worth reproducing here:

> There was a time in which there existed nothing but darkness and an abyss of waters, wherein resided most hideous beings, which were produced of a two-fold principle. There appeared men, some of whom were furnished with two wings, others with four, and with two faces. They had one body, but two heads; the one that of a man, the other of a woman; and likewise in their several organs both male and female. Other human figures were to be seen with the legs and horns of a goat; some had

horses' feet, while others united the hind quarters of a horse with the body of a man, resembling in shape the hippocentaurs. Bulls likewise were bred there with the heads of men; and dogs with fourfold bodies, terminated in their extremities with the tails of fishes; horses also with the heads of dogs; men, too, and other animals, with the heads and bodies of horses, and the tails of fishes. In short, there were creatures in which were combined the limbs of every species of animals. In addition to these, fishes, reptiles, serpents, with other monstrous animals, which assumed each other's shape and countenance. Of all which were preserved delineations in the temple of Belus at Babylon.

The person who presided over them was a woman named Omoroca, which in the Chaldean language is *Thalatth*, in Greek *Thalassa*, the sea; but which might equally be interpreted the moon. All things being in this situation, Belus came, and cut the woman asunder, and of one half of her he formed the earth, and of the other half the heavens, and at the same time destroyed the animals within her (or in the abyss).

All this was an allegorical description of nature. For, the whole universe consisting of moisture, and animals being continually generated therein, the deity above-mentioned took off his own head; upon which the other gods mixed the blood, as it gushed out, and from thence formed men. On this account it is that they are rational, and partake of divine knowledge. This Belus, by whom they signify Jupiter, divided the darkness, and separated the heavens from the earth, and reduced the universe to order.

But the animals, not being able to bear the prevalence of light, died. Belus upon this, seeing a vast space unoccupied, though by nature fruitful, commanded one of the gods to take off his head, and to mix the blood with the earth, and from thence to form other men and animals, which should be capable of bearing the air. Belus formed also the stars, and the sun, and the moon, and the five planets.

It seems to us that in many instances in mythology from around the world, composite chimera beings and being with multiple faces are presented as a product of the undifferentiated chaos that preceded creation. The idea is that there were no natural laws preventing such monstrosities, and all possibilities existed *in potentia* simultaneously—thus, in complete confusion. The chimera later presented by Levi as a depiction of Baphomet, and many of the purported Templar idols given by Hammer-Purgstall in his book about Baphomet, shown as composite creatures, may be depicted thus to signify this concept of the chaos before creation. In the story given above, a hero creator god came and ripped that chaos apart, then imposed order on it to make creation—mixing the ingredients inside his own decapitated head! It was the intellect or mind within this head that provided the wisdom that brings reason and order to the universe. This may explain the Templar use of a severed head as a symbol of divine wisdom. The concept behind their Baphomet idol may have evolved ultimately from the same archetype. In the tenth discourse of *The Corpus Hermeticum*, entitled "The Key," Hermes says to his son Tat:

Since the cosmos is a sphere—a head, that is—and since there is nothing material above the head (just as there is nothing of mind below the feet, where all is matter), and since mind is a head which is moved spherically—in the manner of a head, that is—things joined to the membrane of this head ([in which] is the soul) are by nature immortal.

This head symbolism may even figure into one of the epithets of Hermes Trismegistus, "Poimandres" (originally taken to be Greek in origin) thought derive from the late Egyptian *peimentere*, meaning "Mind of Re" (the sun god), which could also mean the "head of Re." From the description above, it is as if we should view this primordial cosmic head as a ceremonial bowl as well, in which elements are mixed to create the brew of divine gnosis in which initiates seek to be baptized. It seems worth noting here that in some of their rituals, Freemasons drink out of ceremonial chalices made from (or made to look like) human skulls inverted. The symbolism seems appropriate for a Templar-derivative order, and now we know for sure what it means.

With these symbols—the bowl and the head—some of the seemingly divergent aspects of this secret doctrine of Gnosis come into clearer view. The head is the cup. The cup contains wisdom. He who is immersed in the wisdom of the cup dies to himself, and is reborn. The Baptism of Wisdom is not for the faint of heart. It is the wisdom of death. The head, especially as a skull, represents both wisdom and death. This cup or bowl, although it be a cup of chaos, of the Abyss that tears one's soul apart, is also overflowing with the greatest revelation of insight achievable by man—if you can stand to drink of it. When Jesus' disciples asked to be allowed to sit by him in Heaven, he asked them, in *Mark* 10:38 (KJV):

The Baptism of Wisdom 329

> Ye know not what ye ask: can ye drink of the cup
> that I drink of? and be baptized with the baptism
> that I am baptized with?

On the central porch of the Notre Dame cathedral in Paris, there is a bas relief of a woman seated on a throne hitting a servant who is in front of her. In the cryptic alchemical book *Mystery of the Cathedrals*, Fulcanelli includes this image and labels it "The Queen Kicks Down Mercury, Servus Fugitivus," the latter being a Latin term which means "runaway slave" (Strangely, in *The Grail Legend*, Emma Jung writes that alchemical mercury is symbolized by the *cervus fugitivus*, which she translates as "fugitive stag," referring to yet another animal that symbolizes wild sexuality, and which she links to the rites of Dionysus.) Elsewhere in the Fulcanelli text, he says that Mercury is here acting as the royal cupbearer, "who comes with a cup in his hand to offer her his services" before being kicked away. This image of the Queen (probably Sophia) abusing her servant shows up in another noteworthy context.

In the Welsh story of Taliesin, called *Hanes Taleisin*, the witch Ceridwen has a cauldron full of "Awen," which Malcolm Godwin, in his book *The Holy Grail: Its Origins, Secrets and Meaning Revealed*, translates as "knowledge." It is more commonly translated as "poetic inspiration." Some of it splashes on the hero of the story, a little boy named Gwion, who was acting as her servant. He is suddenly able to transform himself into whatever form he wishes. (Actually, he was quite lucky, because only three drops splashed on him, and it was only the first three drops of the potion that conferred inspiration, while one drop more would have been deadly poison.) The witch, angry at him, ends up swallowing him (in the

330 *Chapter 7*

form of a piece of grain), but nine months later he is born from her body, having become a new man, the poet Taliesin. After being tossed in the ocean in a leather bag by the witch, he is later rescued, and begins his career as a bard whose compositions work magic on those around him. In one of his poems, he brags of having been alive throughout the ages in a number of religiously and mythologically significant situations, including: hanging on the cross with Jesus; "at the building of the Tower of Nimrod" (a.k.a. the Tower of Babel); "supporting" the baby Moses as he floated on the river (here changed from the Nile to the Jordan); and, most importantly, playing the role of "Johannes the Diviner."

Now you might think this is a reference to St. John the Divine, a title given to the author of *The Revelation of St. John*. This person was originally claimed by the Church to be John the Evangelist, the apostle of Jesus who they purported was the author of *The Gospel of John*. However, it is now generally acknowledged that these two books have different authors. Also, as we mentioned previously, some, like Tobias Churton, have suggested that this Gospel was actually written by (or more likely, from the projected perspective of) John the Baptist. As a prophet, the term "Diviner" certainly fits for the Baptist just as well as for the other John. The Taliesin poem seems to indicate that the poet is identifying himself with the Baptist. But he also clearly seems to be playing the role of Mercury, and the witch who gives birth to his new form is undoubtedly another representation of Sophia, the antagonistic goddess of wisdom and inspiration.

Another thing Taliesin brags about in the poem is being in the "Cair Sidin." According to Robert Graves in

The White Goddess, this is a reference to something called the "Chair of Idris":

> There is a stone seat at the top of Cader Idris, the "Chair of Idris" where, according to the local legend, whoever spends the night is found in the morning either dead, mad, or a poet.

Again, you may be thinking that this Idris is the Muslim prophet, their Hermes and Enoch, and wonder why a Welsh legend is talking about him (although that Idris is, rightly, associated with poetic inspiration). However, in Wales Idris Gawr is actually the name of a legendary giant of whom many tales are told. This seat of his is where, supposedly, he would sit at night studying the stars—another possible connection to Hermes, the purported inventor of astrology. Elsewhere in the book, Graves says that the cauldron of Awen that the witch Ceridwen brewed in the Taliesin story—"for a year and a day," according to the recipe—was located near this seat as well. The length of cooking time for liquid inspiration in the recipe seems like another connection between the hero of this story and Hermes, because as we have discussed, Enoch (the biblical Hermes) was said to have lived 365 years, and written 366 books. (The Gnostic figure of Abraxas, the subject of the next chapter, is also associated with the number 365.)

There is another Welsh myth, connected to the Holy Grail cycle, which seems to toy with the symbolism of John the Baptist. The story of Peredur, upon whom Parzival of the Grail legend is based, can be found in *The Mabinogian*, the earliest collection of British prose literature (compiled in the twelfth to thirteenth centuries from oral traditions). In this tale, the main character attends a banquet at his uncle's castle in which a bloody sword and a bloody head on a charger are brought through the room by servants, but the host continues to talk, even as the rest of the guests express dismay at the sight. Peredur, however, is too shy to say anything about it, and later it is revealed that if he had asked what the bloody head and sword were all about, he would have immediately accomplished his mission in the story, which was to lift the enchantment of barrenness and waste that had come upon the land. Instead he is cursed with more trials in his quest. In later Grail stories, a similar scene of a banquet at the castle of the Fisher King (Parzival's uncle) takes place, called the "Grail Service," and he is similarly punished for not asking him uncle the question of what has been bothering him lately (in this case, a stab wound in the genitals that won't heal).

Hammer-Purgstall certainly seems to have felt that the Holy Grail story was an allegory about the Templar Baphomet and the Hermetic concept of baptism in the bowl of Mind, along with the idea of eucharistically absorbing its contents. He wrote:

> There remains no doubt that the most celebrated bowl of the Middle Ages, under the name of St. Graal, signifies nothing but a symbol of the Templar community and of Gnostic wisdom. . . .

One of the alleged Templar artifacts that he catalogued included a bowl on which the letters "R" and "L" are written. There was also a vase with two heads on its base, like the Roman Janus (and like some of the Baphomet head idols of the Templars were said to be), which featured the letter "G." Hammer-Purgstall said he believed G stood for Gnosis, but also that it should be taken along with the R and L on the other vessel, so that together they indicated the

German word "Graal": the Grail. He conjectured that the word could be an acrostic code:

> Thus, GRAL could signify: *Gnosis Regit Animas Liberas* [Gnosis Rules Free Souls]; or *Gnosis Regina Artium Liberalium* [Gnosis Queen of Liberal Arts]; or *Gnosis Retribuit Animi Laborum* [Gnosis Requites Labor of the Soul]; or, finally, what perhaps is most similar and most in agreement with Gnostic doctrine, *Gnosis Reducit Animam Lapsam* [Gnosis Brings Back the Lapsed Soul]; or *Redintegrat Animum Lapsum* [Restores the Lapsed Soul].

Elsewhere he also says:

> It ought to be understood that, under the custody of St. Graal, those brothers of the militia [the Templars], as custodians of the Gnostic chalice, were initiated into the gnostic mystery of iniquity.

What could this iniquity be if not the obscene rites that both the Templars and the Gnostic cults were accused of engaging in? As we mentioned before, Hammer-Purgstall called this "genital wisdom," a term which he claimed he found encoded on the artifacts both in Greek (*zoogogon sophian*) and in Arabic (*ma-ta na-sha*). Comparing these rites not only to the "sacred marriage" and Eucharistic rituals of the Ophites, but also the Bacchanalia, he wrote:

> These are the ceremonies of that mystical sacrament and of the abominable orgies of which the Gnostics are accused by the Fathers, which, with the lights dimmed, with promiscuous ugliness they celebrated sometimes under the name of a meal, other times under the name of marriage. These orgies are manifestly portrayed in all three of our bowls there used, so that it might be clear to the

onlooker what these orgies are, and to what Gnostic sect these bowls, with the same inscriptions as the abovementioned idols, belonged. For the first bowl contained, in a double circle, a double representation of the orgies, the inferior [circle] *baccanalium*, where Liber ["the Free One," a version of Bacchus] is observed, in triumph borne by Satyrs and Maenads (female votaries of Bacchus). . . .

It is on this bowl that the snake-kissing orgy is represented, which image Hammer-Purgstall admitted to altering "for decency," omitting several erect phalluses on the participants. Regarding the snakes, he believed that they represented the demon Samael as an incarnation of the *Nous* or Gnosis. Serpents were connected to Dionysian rites as well. As Hammer-Purgstall wrote:

> It is well known to everyone that in all the ancient mysteries of Ceres and Liber, both the Elysian as well as the Bacchic, the serpent played the main parts. Hence, through the same serpent the connection to be discovered with great difficulty between the Ophitic and Bacchic orgies will be illustrated by evidence. We learn, indeed, from Clement of Alexandria that a notable likeness of the Bacchic orgies was the serpent, consecrated by the arcane rite.

In addition to the overt depiction of the phallus (which he omitted), Hammer-Purgstall claimed that the same symbolism of "genital wisdom" was represented by the mystical symbol of the Tau, or the letter T, which he also found used frequently on the artifacts. He stated:

> The serpent and phallus which are handed around in the Bacchic orgies we encounter also in

The Baptism of Wisdom 335

those of the Ophites, where the T which Achamoth holds in her hands, and is impressed on her forehead, we discern on the bowl, as if upholding the tree of life serpent, that is, genital wisdom. [This] retained a double signification (which it already had among the Egyptians), of a Phallus and a key, and was called, among the Ophites tree of life and key of Gnosis.

. . .

. . . Therefore, we see it elevated in orgies in imitation of the elevation of the Phallus in Bacchic orgies and a figure of the same not only put into the hand of Mother Achamoth, or Mete, but also impressed on her forehead, by which figure is indicated the character of life, which are noted the foreheads of the elect (see in *Apocalypse* 7, verse 3). This T is, therefore, the character of Baphomet and thus, a part for the whole, signified the instrument of life and life-begetting wisdom.

Hammer-Purgstall censored the phalluses on several other images to. Another artifact that Hammer-Purgstall presents, which we mentioned before, and which he also describes as depicting an "Ophitic orgy," shows two pots shaped like wombs (and also much like alchemical vessels) placed on either side of a goose-human hybrid creature that's seated on an eagle. From one vessel emerges a baby, while, according to Hammer-Purgstall's description, there was a phallus coming out of the other vessel, which, in his line drawing reproduction, has been smudged out. Other obscene pictures, he says, have been, in many cases, obliterated by priests and nuns at the churches they were found in, out of embarrassment.

But what he and the clergy weren't willing to show us is not nearly as bad as what he says that the images imply. The number of images and words in these artifacts that Hammer-Purgstall claims represent bestiality and pederasty is rather shocking. For instance, one of the statues of Mete that he found included an engraving that said, in Arabic: ". . . He ordered the camel to lie down on its knees," which, according to his interpretation, "would signify to do the most disgusting things."

This evidence of sexual interest in animals on the part of the Templars may hint that the famous *osculum inflame* which they confessed to conducting during their initiation rites (involving kissing the anus of a goat), may have been more that just a hazing prank. It may have been foreplay for what came later, which the tortured knights could have chosen to overlook in their testimony (having already said enough to be convicted of both blasphemy and indecency). This kissing rite is implied in one of the images said to come from the same coffer that features the figure seated on an eagle with a goose on his head, discussed above. Strangely this particular picture featuring the obscene kiss is not included in Hammer-Purgstall's book, but Thomas Smith, writing about Hammer-Purgstall's research, includes it in *Worship of the Generative Powers*. Smith also seems to have known many other details in the pictures also mentioned but not reproduced by Hammer-Purgstall, so that we may presume that Smith made his own independent trip to the museum where it was once kept. At any rate, the picture in question shows a statue of a horned entity with both breasts and testicles, which is being kissed by an initiate on the rear, while other participants baptize him with water pots held aloft.

According to Hammer-Purgstall, the eagle is Ialdabaoth, the Gnostic Demiurge, and this is showing him being subdued, just like another image he features in his book, of a male toddler riding an eagle. But we think it is possible, considering that the Templar rites allegedly involved sex with children, that it could be interpreted as a standard icon of Zeus in the form of an eagle carrying away his boy sex slave, Ganymede, who also happened to be his nephew. Ganymede is presently a mascot for homosexual "boylovers" who openly proclaim their attraction to male children. Perhaps it meant something similar to the Templars as well.

Regarding another drawing of a statue included in his collection of images, Hammer-Purgstall described it thusly:

> You see such a dog at the rear of a genuflecting idol . . . in which we recognize nothing other than a Gnostic or Templar, who by means of a dog adhering to the posterior parts, indicates nothing other than the most disgusting outrage of the Templars.

Elsewhere, describing a collection of Templar coins that Hammer-Purgstall had identified, he discussed the depiction of "the cross, as a sign of life, arising out of a dog's head," saying that it "alludes to the well-known predilection for the dog." He also says that this is something which goes back to the Gnostics, noting that heresiologist Epiphanius "indicated why *dogs* are held in the greatest veneration among the Ophites."

In another image, engraved in bronze high up on the walls of a church in Schoengraber, Austria (too high for most people to see it), he found a picture of Adam, Eve and the Devil in the Garden next to the forbidden tree, where:

338 Chapter 7

> Eve was not veiled, as modesty would demand, but by her own hand was thoroughly laid bare and, in addition to the serpent, also a dog assaulted her.

This was Eve's introduction to "Gnosis, that is, carnal knowledge," which, we assume, is the same as "genital wisdom." This peculiar term was probably related, at least in Hammer-Purgstall's mind, to his interpretation of the Ophite concept of Gnostic enlightenment:

> The Ophites, though, by no means tending toward moral perfection, thought that the highest peak of all science [knowledge] is to be placed in carnal cognition, and under the term enlightenment, [included] nothing other than coitus and promiscuous shameful desire.

Another term that Hammer-Purgstall claimed the Templars coined for the same concept was "distinguished charity of Mete," which he said stood for "nothing other than *paiderastian* [Greek for 'pederasty']." He claimed to have found, in a former Templar church in Prague, an image of a knight trying to uphold two collapsing columns, below which were engraved the words "the distinguished charity of Mete uproots the enemy." He also claimed that their specific symbol for this was the flaming star, now used by Freemasons. Elsewhere in the text, Hammer-Purgstall gives further reasoning behind this concept:

> That arcane doctrines and *paiderastias* common among them are to be excused, various dogmas and imaginings of the ancients seem to suggest. There were two opinions especially that they twisted in defense of their shameful indecencies; the socratic one, "know yourself," and the prior, Epicurean one, "respect God." That first one [know yourself], since

by "cognition" they understood nothing but the carnal, was to their shame. The other one [respect God] they interpreted so as to teach that by means of the moistening with seminal luminescence they themselves became gods. Above we have seen what, formerly, Plotinus objected to regarding the Gnostics always bearing in their mouths, "respect God." Here it must be added also that the Templars, as Gnostics, held themselves to be gods.

In another picture in the Schoengraber church, images of pedophilia and bestiality are combined:

> At the first station is discerned a boy, a future Ophite or Gnostic Templar, immodestly fondling a bear, an animal . . . addicted to this vice . . . to prevent which and to claim the nursling for himself, the Templar charges forward with a lance in order to pierce the bear through and to lead the infant over to his own enticements, at which the abovementioned dog not obscurely hints. On the other hand, the boy, now having become an adolescent, resists the girl's flatteries, whom she tried to entice by offering to him flowers. . . . The Freemasonic ornaments about this station agree very well with the Bacchic sense of the same for, composed from grape clusters and vine foliage, with phalluses intermixed (placed so high up that from the lower part they are difficult to discern). . . .

Note that, in Hammer-Purgstall's interpretation, these pictures show a boy being corrupted sexually from infancy onward so that later in adolescence he has no interest in normal sexual activity with a female, i.e. actual procreative sex. This supports the idea that Gnostic orgies involved the redirection of energy normally put towards reproduction, since they believed that giving birth was just trapping more souls into the archontic prison of matter. We will discuss this more in depth later.

Recall also what Morton Smith said, mentioned earlier, in his book *Jesus the Magician* regarding the animal forms used to represent demons. He stated that images or descriptions of sex between humans and animals were often used to represent the idea of people possessed by demons. Keep in mind that with the exception of the ass, all of the animals forms (goat, lion, dragon eagle, bear, dog, and ass) used to represent the Archons in the Ophite diagrams, as described by Origen and Celsus, are seen here among Hammer-Purgstall's collection. So perhaps these pictures were meant to show the demonic possession of the Templars (or whoever actually created them). However, we do not deny that rituals to facilitate such possession could involve actual sex with animals also.

While we may find it hard to believe that grown men of respectable positions (such as the Templars always were) would convince themselves that sexual abuse of children and animals was somehow spiritually enlightening, we should keep in mind that this could also be yet another veneer, with a more practical agenda behind it. In our own time, our politics is occasionally rocked with scandals of child sex abuse by the rich and powerful. This usually involves so-called "pedophile rings" that are quite secret and exclusive, making use of child prostitutes that have been obtained from orphanages. Photos are taken at their meetings for the purpose of establishing the ever-present threat of blackmail, and mutually-assured destruction should any members of the abuse ring be tempted to give information to the authorities about what they have been involved in. This ties the participants together in a bond of evil, which is used for the coalescence of power into the hands of a small cabal. On more than one occasion it has come out that these rings were actually being orchestrated by the intelligence services, acting on orders of some group within the government that was using it to control other powerful people. According to Hammer-Purgstall, something similar may have been going on with the Templars:

> It remains for us to comment on yet another expansion, or rather subversion, of the Delphic dictum. They substituted in place of that golden sentence, "Know yourself," the crafty, "know all, but let no one know you." On this truly Machiavellian principle rests their whole politic, which up to now they try to sustain by the gospel precept, "Be wise as serpents." To this depraved wisdom they connect unrestrained conduct, so that, "Pursue all, and all is permitted," they seem to have proposed as the highest branch of wisdom. That this goal of the moral, or better, immoral, Gnostic-Ophitic doctrine is precisely the same as what has been placed before true initiates at the ultimate doctrinal grade of the Assassins and of the Ishmaelites, we see in the words, "Nothing to be believed, and, everything is permissible." To what deeds exceedingly shameful this goal of the Gnostic-Ophite doctrine precipitates its followers, once all types of evil desires have been poured out . . . is clear enough. Certainly nothing either great or good was ever to be expected from the followers of this doctrine, unless men endowed with a higher political genius, the doctrine having been subjected to their ambition, used it as an instrument for attaining the highest goal of [their] ambition. Such persons, already destined by nature

as leaders, sought the highest goal of their labors not in satisfying desires, but in conducting state affairs. Finally, people eagerly followed this doctrine because, once a person wickedly indulges every sensual craving, it renders his associates more inclined to all types of illicit activities.

The quotation, "Nothing to be believed, and, everything is permissible" (More commonly translated "Nothing is true, everything is permitted") was a proclamation made by the aforementioned Assassin chief Hassan-i-Sabbah. The Assassins were a secret Islamic fighting order that operated contemporary to the Templars and fought against them on the battlefield. The two orders are often compared because of their rigorous training, their suicidal approach to battle, and the accusations both orders faced of having a secret inner doctrine of blasphemy. For the Assassins (with whom the Templars have been accused by some historians of having a friendly relationship behind the scenes), it really wasn't all that secret.

The doctrine of the Nizari Ismailis (the Islamic sect which the Assassins belonged to) was developed with the help of Hassan-i-Sabbah around 1095, just four years prior to the earliest date given for the founding of the Templars. According to James Wasserman, author of *The Templars and the Assassins* (2001), Hassan was "reputed to be deeply versed in mathematics, astronomy, magic, and alchemy." Beginning with him, the Assassins were accused, by both Western chroniclers and their Sunni foes within Islam, of, as Wasserman states:

> . . . drug taking and licentious sexual orgies. Unlimited powers of mind control were ascribed to Assassin leaders. . . . Nizari leaders were said to follow no law but their own and to be willing to

stoop to any depth, including witchcraft, to mislead their flock. The Sunni establishment accused them of plotting to undermine Islamic law and renew the ancient pagan faith of Persia.

Hassan-i-Sabbah's successor was Hassan II, who on August 8, 1164, proclaimed something called *Qiyama* (the resurrection of the dead). He was asserting that the last days had come, and that those who accepted his new teaching were to go to Paradise right away. Those who did not would go to Hell. He then explained this new teaching, which Wasserman described thusly:

> While holding aloft his sword, he is reported to have announced that the Hidden Imam [the prophet whom Shia Muslims believe will herald the last days] had proclaimed a New Dispensation and freed his faithful from the Shariah practices of Islam. . . . At the conclusion of this breathtaking speech, he descended from the pulpit, and held a banquet, stating that Ramadan [which they were in the midst of] was at its end. This supreme act of blasphemy was reportedly accompanied by wine-drinking, pork-eating, and sensual indulgences.
>
> . . . The holy practices prescribed by Muhammed as Shariah were merely outward symbols of inward spiritual truths. Outward symbols were now profanations of inner truth. . . . One no longer prostrated oneself and prayed to Allah five times per day. . . .
>
> Those Nizaris who persisted in the traditional practices of Islam and refused to follow the New Dispensation were chastised, stoned, and killed as

344 Chapter 7

blasphemers—exactly as those who had previously been found guilty of breaking the Shariah were treated.

A few years later, in 1175, Burchard of Strassbourg, Frederick Barbarossa's envoy to Egypt and Syria, described the Assassins, as paraphrased by Wasserman, as "men who lived without law, ate pig's flesh, shared their women, and practiced incest with their mothers and sisters."

We cannot be sure what secret beliefs lay behind Hassan II's bizarre proclamation, whether the "Twelfth Imam" really talked to him, and if so how. Was it in the form of a severed head, which, as we have discussed before, the Assassins made use of for divination, or at least pretended to? Nor do we know if these secrets were ever communicated to the Templars, whether through secret cooperation with them, or through information obtained from spying. But it does seem to go along with the "everything is permitted" creed of his predecessor. We don't know how much either of the Hasans were influenced by Gnosticism directly, but they were both students of Hermeticism and Neoplatonism, so they would have at least been exposed indirectly. While much of Hermetic thought seems compatible with monotheism and Mosaic law, other strains (even some seen in *The Corpus Hermeticum* itself) seem to be informed more by what we might call the "anti-creation" attitude of some Gnostics. At times this attitude manifests in something akin to the modern philosophy of Nihilism, as Hans Jonas has observed in his book *The Gnostic Religion*.

> Dread as the soul's response to its being-in-the-world is a recurrent theme in gnostic literature. It is the self's reaction to the discovery of its situation. . . Knowledge, gnosis, may liberate man from his

servitude; but since the cosmos is contrary to life and to spirit, the saving knowledge cannot aim at integration into the cosmic whole and at compliance with its laws. . . . For the Gnostics, on the contrary, man's alienation from the world is to be deepened and brought to a head, for the extrication of the inner self which only thus can gain itself. The world (not the alienation from it) must be overcome. . . .

Viewing creation as a prison for the soul made by the evil Demiurge, and equating that entity with the God of the Bible. Some Gnostics had codes of behavior and rituals that were meant to reverse the "natural order." Just as all religious ritual is based at least somewhat on the primitive notion of sympathetic magic—that by acting out a certain thing, you will affect the larger world in an analogous way— the belief would have been that, by doing these acts of natural reversal (amounting also to the reversal of all considered holy), one might harm the creator, reduce his power, or even bring the corrupt world closer to a dissolution that they must have welcomed.

In *Matthew* 11:12 (KJV) Jesus states that ". . . [F]rom the days of John the Baptist until now the kingdom of heaven suffereth violence, and the violent take it by force." This has been taken by some to mean that, during that time, in which the advent of the messiah and the End of Days was believed by many to be near, there were those who thought that, by consciously bringing about the conditions foretold by prophets at the End Times, they could force God to initiate this process and bring the kingdom of Heaven to Earth sooner. This is the reasoning behind the firm that today is breeding red cows to be sacrificed in the Jewish temple once it is rebuilt, as the birth of such a heifer, to be used as an offering in the new temple, has been foretold. As

Robert Eisler explained in his book *Orpheus the Fisher* (1920):

> This much debated saying presupposes the Jewish conviction that men could accelerate the coming of the Kingdom and even force it down immediately by certain actions, either of obedience or of disobedience to the commandments of God... That such an apparent violation of the Divine plan of Providence was not always considered as sinful, "hybris," may be seen from the repeated saying in the Talmud, that God "loves to be conquered by a sinner through repentance."

One must wonder what sort of acts of "disobedience" would be considered useful in this regard. But, it seems, a ritual with exactly that intent may have been depicted in the supposedly Templar artifacts discovered by Joseph von Hammer-Purgstall.

During Templar times and afterwards there were, in certain pockets throughout Western Europe, several religious groups that seemed to be influenced by the Gnostics, and which seem to bleed into each other at times, their membership not being mutually exclusive. These include the Waldensians, the Patarini, the Bogomils, and the Cathars, the latter having actually earned their own military Crusade from the Church aimed against them (to which their last fortress of Montsegur in the Languedoc region of Southern France finally fell in 1244). They were charged by the Church with "unnatural sexual practices," which seemed to involve abortions and non-procreative sex (to prevent the incarnation of souls), despite the fact that St. Bernard of Clairvaux, the man who chartered the Knights Templar, had said of them, "No sermons are more Christian than theirs, and their morals are pure."

"The Pure Ones" was in fact the meaning of their name. It may have been that, just like the creed of the Assassins' "New Dispensation," they believed that they were inherently "pure" to the extent that nothing which they did could defile them. In fact, indulging debaucheries in the form of a ritual may have, in their minds, sanctified a sin that they viewed as an otherwise unavoidable fact of carnal existence. Dr. Iwan Bloch, in his biography of the Marquis de Sade, mentions these groups as an outgrowth of the Persian Gnostic movement of Manichaeism, and indeed, of Satanism, stating:

> The real "Satan's Church" was founded by the Manichees in southern France. . . . The secret societies of "Perfect Beings" formed everywhere, serving exclusively the most obscene sexual vices. . . . In spite of the persecution of the church the sect and its motto persevered: "Nemo potest peccare ab umbilico et inferius" ["No one can not sin, from the navel and below"]; it found continual support from "unsatisfied" priests. Sins slay sins! That was the great principle of their sexual orgies. The priest sanctifies all women who sin with him. The nuns are "consecrated," i.e. they become the mistresses of the priests.

The same attitude was expressed by Severus, founder of a Gnostic group (the Severians) that was part of a larger Christian sect called the Encratites who abstained from marriage. In the book *Gnosticism: Its History and Influence*, author Benjamin Walker explains:

> According to Severus, a disciple of Marcion, man is divine from the navel up, and the creature of the devil from the navel down.

Women, meanwhile, were evil and entirely the product of Satan.

The descriptions of many of these groups' secret rites are quite clearly similar to what the Templars were accused of. For instance, in some of their confessions, Templar knights told of worshipping Baphomet in the form of a black cat, and kissing its anus instead of that of a goat. Likewise, according to Walter Mapes, as quoted by Thomas Wright, speaking of the Patarini of Milan:

> Some apostates from this heresy, he tells us, had related that, at the first watch of night, they met in their synagogues, closed carefully the doors and windows, and waited in silence, until a black cat of extraordinary bigness descended among them by a rope, and that, as soon as they saw this strange animal, they put out the lights, and muttering through their teeth instead of singing their hymns, felt their way to this object of worship, and kissed it, according to their feelings of humility or pride, some on the feet, some under the tail, and others on the genitals, after which each seized upon the nearest person of a different sex, and had carnal intercourse as long as he was able.

This connection with the figure of the cat is explored further by Wright, who conjectures that the Cathars were actually named after the animal. Noting that "the name of the . . . sect is often spelt Gazai, Gazeri, Gacari, and Chazari," he relates:

It was suggested by Henschenius that this name was derived from the German *Katze* or *Ketze*, a cat, in allusion to the common report that they assembled at night like cats, or ghosts; or that the cat may have been an allusion to the belief that in their secret meetings they worshipped that animal.

A Cathar group in Germany called the Stedingers were accused of worshipping the Devil in the form of a cat by Pope Gregory IX himself in the famous bull *Vox in Rama* of 1232. It is believed that this papal pronouncement led to the widespread bloody persecution of black cats throughout Christian Europe as "incarnations of Satan." Some even claim that this led to a proliferation of rats and thus, outbreaks of plague. Thomas Wright, paraphrasing the bull, gives us the juicy details:

> As the novice proceeded, he encountered a man who was extraordinarily pale, with large black eyes, and whose body was so wasted that his flesh seemed to be all gone, leaving nothing but the skin hanging on his bones. The novice kissed this personage, and found him as cold as ice; and after this all traces of the Catholic faith vanished from his heart. Then they all sat down to a banquet; and when this was over, there stepped out of a statue which stood in their place of meeting, a black cat, as large as a moderate sized dog, which advanced backwards to them, with its tail turned up. The novice first, then the master, and then all the others, in their turns, kissed the cat under the tail, and then returned to their places, where they remained in silence, with their heads inclined towards the cat. Then the master suddenly pronounced the words "Spare us!" which he

addressed to the next in order; and the third answered, "We know it, lord;" and a fourth added, "We ought to obey." At the close of this ceremony the lights were extinguished, and each man took the first woman who came to hand, and had carnal intercourse with her. When this was over, the candles were again lighted, and the performers resumed their places. Then out of a dark corner of the room came a man, the upper part of whom, above the loins, was bright and radiant as the sun, and illuminated the whole room, while his lower parts were rough and hairy like a cat. The master then tore off a bit of the garment of the novice, and said to the shining personage, "Master, this is given to me, and I give it again to thee." The master replied, "Thou hast served me well, and thou wilt serve me more and better; what thou hast given me I give unto thy keeping." When he had said this, the shining man vanished, and the meeting broke up.

The descriptions of these allegedly "Gnostic" heretical groups sound identical not only to the supposed secret practices of the Templars, but also to the rites of the Black Mass, and the Sabbath celebrated by European witches, as described by them, usually while under trial from Christians. The main difference between the Witches' Sabbath and the Black Mass is that the Sabbath is a satanic rite in homage to the Devil, whereas the Black Mass is a Christian rite performed for evil purposes. Witch Sabbaths were sometimes, but not always, done with the help of an ordained Catholic priest. But Black Masses were, by definition, always performed by a real Catholic priest. Although the descriptions of the sabbaths were extracted under duress, sometimes torture, and may be considered untrustworthy because the trials were part of a campaign of

The Baptism of Wisdom 351

persecution against certain groups of non-Christians, the Church would seemingly have no reason to accuse its own priests of performing such blasphemous rites, unless it were undeniably true. Yet the fact remains that throughout history, more than a few respected priests have confessed to performing the Black Mass, including the sacrifice of children.

The Black Mass is specifically a mockery and parody of the Catholic mass. It is meant to be officiated by an ordained priest, so that the Real Presence of the Holy Spirit can be called into the host wafer, and then defiled. Traditionally, everything in such a rite is done backwards. The priest has his back to the altar, the cross is turned upside-down, the Lord's Prayer is read backwards, and the meaning of everything is inverted. The altar is supposed to be formed by the naked body of a female, and the Holy Host is to be humiliated by being placed inside of her nether regions. Instead of wine, the blood of unbaptized babies sacrificed on the fleshy altar was consumed.

The history of the Black Mass begins with the case of Catherine de Medici, queen consort of King Henry II of France from 1547 to 1559. She was born into an influential noble family that had provided the world with two Popes and numerous noble figures. They had a tremendous influence upon the spread of Humanist philosophy, art and science throughout Renaissance Europe. But they were also known for being dabblers in the occult.

Catherine de Medici's sons were heir to the throne, and she herself was appointed regent for a time. According to French political writer Jean Bodin, Catherine attempted to prolong the life of her son Philip, who was dying of a wasting disease, by employing a priest to perform black masses involving the murder of young boys. Catherine is known to have worn a magical amulet featuring the sigil of the demon Asmodeus. Another son of hers, Henry III, continued her interest in the Dark Arts, and had an altar in his home that featured cloven-hoofed devils bearing their backsides to the Cross. Catherine de Medici was never convicted of child murder, blasphemy or witchcraft, and in fact, these stories about her are rarely mentioned by modern historians, although they were widely believed at the time.

But in the famous case of the Abbe Guiborg and Catherine Deshayes (La Voison), mistress to King Louis XIV, the perpetrators were actually brought to justice. The mistress hired the Abbe to perform hundreds of black masses in which the demon Asmodeus was invoked and children were sacrificed. La Voison herself acted as the naked female altar in these ceremonies, and after the child was slain, the blood would be poured into the ceremonial chalice. The host would be inserted into La Voison's vagina during consecration, instead of the traditional "Tabernacle." Afterwards, the Abbe and La Voison would engage in sex acts and then the fluids would be mixed in with the blood and the foully consecrated host. This mixture was then surreptitiously added to the King's food, the purpose being to cause him to continue to love La Voison to the exclusion of all others, including his wife. This is all according to both Deshayes and Guiborg's confessions at the trial, and the documentary evidence, in the form of signed demonic pacts between La Voison and Asmodeus, which were entered as evidence in the trial. That a consecrated wafer could be used for black magic of this sort is a common theme in European occultism.

The similarities between these rites and the so-called Witches' Sabbath, at which the goat god was himself said to

The Baptism of Wisdom 353

be present, becomes quote obvious once you read the descriptions of them. As Thomas Wright put it:

> In order to "mix impiety with the other abominations," they pretended to perform religious rites, which were a wild and contemptuous parody on the Catholic mass. An altar was raised, and a priest consecrated and administered the host, but it was made of some disgusting substance, and the priest stood with his head downwards and his legs in the air, and with his back turned to the altar. Thus all things were performed in monstrous or disgusting forms, so that Satan himself appeared almost ashamed of them.

At the Sabbath, attendees were expected to kiss the goat god. But only the chosen ones were permitted to kiss him on the face. The rest had to perform the humiliating *osculum infame*, placing their lips on his second face, which was beneath his tail. Sexual debaucheries ensued, including the painful rape of young girls by the goat god with his enormous penis. As Wright said:

> The young witch, Jeannette d'Abadie, told how she had seen at the Sabbath men and women in promiscuous intercourse, and how the devil arranged them in couples, in the most unnatural conjunctions—the daughter with the father, the mother with her son, the sister with the brother, the daughter-in-law with the father-in-law, the penitent with her confessor, without distinction of age, quality, or relationship, so that she confessed to having been known an infinity of times at the Sabbath by a cousin . . . of her mother, and by an infinite number of others. . . . This girl said that she had been deflowered by the devil at the age of

thirteen—twelve was the common age for this—
that they never became pregnant, either by him or
by any of the wizards of the Sabbath; that she had
never felt anything come from the devil except the
first time, when it was very cold, but that with the
sorcerers it was as with other men. That the devil
chose the handsomest of the women and girls for
himself, and one he usually made his queen for the
meeting. That they suffered extremely when he had
intercourse with them, in consequence of his
member being covered with scales like those of a
fish. That when extended it was a yard long, but that
it was usually twisted. Marie d'Aspilcuette, a girl
between nineteen and twenty years of age, who
also confessed to having had frequent connection
with Satan, described his member as about half a
yard long, and moderately large. Marguerite, a girl
of Sare, between sixteen and seventeen, described
it as resembling that of a mule, and as being as long
and thick as one's arm. . . . The devil, we are further
told, preferred married women to girls, because
there was more sin in the connection, adultery
being a greater crime than simple fornication.

Despite the pain and humiliation, the witches loved being raped by the goat god, and he always left them wanting more. To quote from Wright again:

Some of the witches examined spoke of the delight
with which they attended the Sabbath. Jeanne
Dibasson, a woman twenty-nine years old, said that
the Sabbath was the true Paradise, where there was
far more pleasure than can be expressed; that those
who went there found the time so short by reason
of the pleasure and enjoyment, that they never left

it without marvelous regret, so that they looked forward with infinite impatience to the next meeting.

Another relevant detail is that witches at the Sabbath were made to pass through a fire that did not burn them. This was meant to teach them not to be afraid of the fires of Hell which they would be going to at the end of their mortal life. So again, they were taught to have an abnormal and unnatural reaction to something that would cause a normal person unbearable pain.

This brings us to the notion of "storming heaven," and the idea that performing certain rites, either in direct obedience, or *direct disobedience*, to the word of God, could actually force him to do something—even something destructive, even the destruction of the entire world. A perfect example of this was described in anthropologist Sir James Frazer's classic ritual reference book *The Golden Bough*, which explored primitive concepts of magic and religion throughout the world. He wrote:

> French peasants used to be, perhaps are still, persuaded that the priests could celebrate, with certain special rites, a Mass of the Holy Spirit, of which the efficacy was so miraculous that it never met with any opposition from the divine will; God was forced to grant whatever was asked of Him in this form, however rash and importunate might be the petition . . . in some villages, when a change of pastors takes place, the parishioners are eager to learn whether the new incumbent has the power (*pouder*), as they call it.

The belief that the Holy Spirit can be drawn down from Heaven into a wafer is really not so different from the ancient idea (expressed repeatedly in *The Book of Nabathean Agriculture*) that one can draw down the essences of stars and planets into objects and substances such as plants, potions, and metals. The book refers to this as "star-bathing," and it really is the basic concept behind natal astrology. The essences of the heavenly bodies, as they were arranged on the nativity of a person or thing, purportedly stain that person or thing forever—a tincturing baptism.

In alchemy, there is talk of something called the "Bath of the Stars," and it seems to be an allegory for ritually bathing the metals to be transmuted in these stellar essences. The allegorical drawings of this, however—which usually feature a king and a queen, or an anthropomorphized sun and moon, bathing naked in a fountain—also seem to indicate that the bath is filled with the blood of their own "children." These are the other planets, viewed in this system as the offspring of the sun and moon. These pictures are often coupled with another image, usually labeled "the Massacre of the Innocents," as can be seen in Nicolas Flamel's *The Book of Abraham the Jew* and in Fulcanelli's *The Mystery of the Cathedrals*. This shows babes being slaughtered and the blood collected in barrels, presumably for the bathing of the king and queen. While there are numerous ways of interpreting these metaphors, alchemy is certainly a science of death and rebirth, of substances, and of souls. Tracy R. Twyman has pointed out in her books that this imagery is connected to the ancient idea that drinking and bathing in the blood of children can help retain youth, or even resuscitate the dead.

There is another way to interpret this also. The notion of drawing down heavenly things into earthly things seems like an aptly Hermetic way of bringing Heaven down by force—

another way of looking at the notion of "storming Heaven," to make the "below" like the "above." In *Sefer Hekhalot*, also known as *The Third Book of Enoch*, it tells the story of the fallen angels that bred giants with human women, and it says that they taught their hybrid children the abominations of ritual magic. One particular passage is worth quoting:

> They brought down the sun, the moon, planets and constellations, and placed them before the idols on their right hand and on their left. How was it that they had the strength to bring them down? It was only because Uzza, Azza and Azael taught them sorceries that they brought them down, for otherwise they would not have been able to bring them down.

Interestingly, in Christopher Marlowe's *Doctor Faustus*, this is one of the things that the title character asks the demon Mephistopheles to be ready to do for him:

> I charge thee wait upon me whilst I live
>
> To do whatever Faustus shall command,
>
> Be it to make the moon drop from her sphere
>
> Or the ocean to overwhelm the world.

Let us remember that Azazel, the goat demon who taught men to bring down the heavens, is also said to be the "Groomsman" for the demons Lilith and Samael, responsible for facilitating their sexual union. At the Witches' Sabbath, the goat god was sometimes also called the "Groomsman," and arranged the sex partners who were to perform at that night's festivities. We have already theorized here that the people at these orgies may have been channeling Lilith and Samael, thus acting as vessels to facilitate the mating of these two lovers who could otherwise never reconnect. It makes sense, then, that the icon which came to symbolize these orgy rituals was a Hermaphroditic figure (like Lilith and Samael once were), sporting a staff with twin serpents on it, symbolizing the two demons. When Samael and Lilith come together, via the bodies of the ritual participants, they form the conjuration of the Baphomet.

Perhaps we can imagine a ritual, possibly performed by the Templars, that might have utilized all of the symbolism we have seen in the Hammer-Purgstall images, as well as many of the motifs found at witch sabbaths, black masses, and Gnostic orgies. We know that many of the Gnostic groups were accused of performing sexual perversions which did not result in babies that were seen alive outside of the ritual chamber. That does not necessarily mean that babies were not born. Sodomy and abortion are the most commonly imagined acts that might have taken place to fulfill these requirements. But what if some of their rituals did result in births? What if that was, in some cases, the point? Thomas Wright describes a group that once met in Orleans, about which a document was found at the abbey of St. Pere in Chartres that described their alleged activities. After calling a demonic spirit to appear "in the form of an animal," they would purportedly indulge in group sex (men and women both). Then, Wright says:

> The child which was the fruit of this intercourse was taken on the eighth day, and purified by fire, "in the manner of the ancient pagans"—so says the contemporary writer of this document—it was burnt to ashes in a large fire made for that purpose. The ashes were collected with great reverence, and preserved to be administered to members of the society who were dying, just as good Christians received the viaticum. It is added that there was

such a virtue in these ashes, that an individual who had once tasted them would hardly ever be able to turn his mind from that heresy and take the path of truth.

Similarly, in modern times, there is an elite, secret resort in California called the "Bohemian Club" which performs a "neo-Druidic ritual each summer called the "Cremation of Care," involving the sacrifice of a baby "in effigy" by fire. The ashes are then swept up and used in future rituals. After the rite, the congregants commence with a two-week-long orgy with prostitutes of both sexes and reportedly all ages.

Now let us again recall some of the images presented by Hammer-Purgstall. There are several of children being brought out in front of a burning brazier, and in at least one instance, Hammer-Purgstall described the child as being placed "into" the fire. He seems to have viewed the children as allegorical of "neophyte Templars," which is surprisingly naive, considering all of the diabolical acts that he believed the Templars had engaged in. He also included in his book several images of people, mostly children, halfway inside of the mouth of a dragon.

This he interprets as Ialdabaoth, the Demiurge, spitting out the person, who instead of being absorbed fully by the beast, was able to reemerge from death intact, just as the true Gnostic is supposed to be able to survive immersion in the Abyss or bowl of Mind with his self and memory whole. While we might assume that the dragon would be synonymous with the serpent of *Genesis*, and therefore a hero to Gnostic Templars, Hammer-Purgstall thought that to them the dragon was the Demiurge, and that images of St. George or St. Michael subduing the dragon were taken by them to represent the conquering of Ialdabaoth (while

Michael was himself viewed as a serpent). He mentioned it in connection with an illustration on a bowl:

> The infant is threatened with absorption, and lest there be a hint of doubt that that dragon is the same about which Epiphanius speaks as a gnostic symbol of the one who presides over the world (who absorbs and again spits out every man not imbued with Gnosis), in this place a double infant can be seen, of whom one adheres to the jaws; the other, through the lower part of the body, is cast out by means of withdrawal. This is the dragon whom the Templars, having sculpted on their graves, trampled underfoot in the London temple. This, finally, is the same dragon who, at the time of establishment of the Brotherhood of the Temple Militia, out of gnostic fabrications on the life of St. George, and with him, but without the infant, transferred into the British Shield, and for sure the Gnostic dragon absorbing the infant gave rise to the serpent Viscount, who up to the present can be seen in the seals of Milan.

This seal of Milan, as you may know, featuring a boy being swallowed by a dragon, is now also the logo for the Alfa Romeo luxury car company.

The way Hammer-Purgstall thought that the Templars saw it, these impious deeds of debauchery would not have counted against them in the afterlife. Rather they would earn them brownie points. He believed that this was illustrated by one of the images he found:

> On the left side is exhibited the end of a Templar's life, already dead and lying on the ground, with the Archangel Michael holding a judgment scale and

The Baptism of Wisdom 361

weighing his deeds. The scale, on which were placed apples, desserts and other blandishments of the senses, and by which the Ophitic Templar's life is represented, descending to the earth, shows that the judgment of Michael favors him, because in order to hinder Jaldabaoth, he tries to depress the other, ascending, part of the scale. . . . The . . . serpent, called by the gnostics Michael, carries out the details of judgment in this way: thinking, in the day of judgment, about the life of the Templar, or Gnostic, he accepts all of his disgraceful deeds as good works. In this way [goes] the cycle of a Gnostic's life.

The goal of all these impieties may have been, as we have suggested, nothing less than the toppling of the heavenly order. This may explain, then, several of the images presented by Hammer-Purgstall which involve a bearded and breasted figure (Mete, or Baphomet, according to him) holding a set of chains—one in each hand, seemingly attached to and hanging down from the sky. Hammer-Purgstall had said these represent "a chain of aeons . . . of the Gnostics," "the hermetic chain of the Neoplatonists, and "the gods' chain in Homer."

This Gnostic, Hermetic, and Neoplatonic "chain" appears to be the chain of causality, and of the interconnected hierarchies of creation. Since in Gnosticism, each aeon corresponds to an archontic entity, and each Archon corresponds to one of the seven "classical planets" (the Sun, the Moon, Mercury, Mars, Venus, Jupiter, Saturn), and each planet was, in antiquity, believed to rule over one of the seven heavens (viewed as being spherical and concentrically stacked inside each other like a Russian doll, with the Earth in the middle), one can imagine this as a chain running from the center of the Earth, through the sky, then up through each of the seven heavens and all the way up to the Pleroma on the outside, where the real "Father" resides.

Hammer-Purgstall's reference to "the gods' chain in Homer" points to *The Iliad*, where Zeus posits a challenge to the other gods to assert his superiority over them. He says:

> Try me and find out for yourselves. Hang me a golden chain from heaven, and lay hold of it all of you, gods and goddesses together—tug as you will, you will not drag Zeus the supreme counselor from heaven to earth; but were I to pull at it myself I should draw you up with earth and sea into the bargain, then would I bind the chain about some pinnacle of Olympus and leave you all dangling in the mid firmament. So far am I above all others either of gods or men.

If you were to try to connect the Gnostic Hermetic chain concept with the chain of the gods, you might say that Zeus, as the Demiurge, tried to pretend that he was in the highest sphere, controlling everything below with his chain, but the Gnostics believed there was a higher sphere above him, and a higher power than his. Indeed, someone did connect the concepts already. In 1723, a book called *Aurea Catena Homeri* was published, edited by Anton Josef Kirchweger. It was an influential alchemical and Hermetic text that was specifically about this subject. It even features a diagram that shows his interpretation of the chain that runs through the universe.

However, the real clue comes from the one most detailed versions of the picture of Mete holding the chains, which is described but strangely not depicted in Hammer-Purgstall's book, in which we see what the chains are

The Baptism of Wisdom 363

hanging from. A line drawing of it can be found in Thomas Wright's *Worship of the Generative Powers*, and we actually discovered the physical object it came from at the British Museum, as we describe in the final chapter. At the top of each chain, respectively, we see an inverted moon and an inverted sun. (You can tell they are inverted because each one has a face). Between her feet there is a skull. Perhaps this shows Mete actually using these chains—the chains by which the Archons bind us to our fates—to actually pull the Sun and Moon down from the sky. Maybe it represents the destruction of the universe—dethroning the Archons, and making the heavens fall. Recall the message that he found on one of the artifacts: "The distinguished charity of Mete uproots the enemy." The enemy, of course, was the Demiurge, and the universe that he created.

Another set of images presented by Hammer-Purgstall contains other clues as to what this ritual might be. We have the one in which the penis is going into the womb/vase, above which there is an upright moon with a face. To the right, on the other side of a figure sitting on an eagle, a child emerges from another vessel, above which there is an upright sun. Would it be wrong to suppose that this represents the insemination of a womb at night, and the birth of a child during the day?

Perhaps, then, the image of the woman pouring water on the seven candles of the menorah is actually meant to represent the counting of seven days after the child's birth. On the eighth day, of course, a child from a normal family would have been either circumcised (if male and Jewish), or baptized (if Christian). But in this case, maybe it was more like with the heretics of the city of Orleans, and the child was baptized instead with fire.

As it turns out, this is exactly one of the things that the Templars were actually accused of—although we have no proof that any of them ever confessed to it. According to Jules Michelet's *History of France, Volume 1*, published in 1860 (and drawing on the *Chroniques Francaises de Saint-Denys*, compiled during the Templar trials):

> Baphomet, in Greek, (after, it is true, a very doubtful Greek etymology,) is the God who baptizes; the Spirit, he of whom it is written, "He shall baptize you with the Holy Ghost and with fire." (*St. Matthew*, iii.11.) He was to the Gnostics, the Paraclete, who descended on the Apostles in the shape of "cloven tongues like as of fire." In fact, the Gnostic baptism was with fire. Perhaps, we must see an allusion to some ceremony of the kind in the reports spread among the people against the Templars, *qu'un enfant nouveau engendre d'un Templier et d'une pucelle estoit sacree et ointe leur idole.* (that a new-born infant, begotten of a Templar and a maid, was cooked and roasted by the fire, and all the grease roasted out, and their idol consecrated and anointed with it.) . . . Might not this pretended idol have been a representation of the Paraclete, whose festival, that of Pentecost, was the highest solemnity of the Temple?

So could this be the Baptism of Wisdom—a ritual sex orgy that vicariously unites the parted demon lovers, Samael and Lilith, and produces a child whose sacrifice is somehow supposed to "bring down the heavens" and hasten the Apocalypse, just like the union of Samael and Lilith is supposed to cause. The participants must have felt "immersed" in a form of hidden wisdom that they saw as the "Holy Spirit," but which seems to be the knowledge of

The Baptism of Wisdom 365

chaos and death. Perhaps they felt "immersed" because their own souls were actually pulled over to the Abyss for that time, to make room for the invading demon spirits to occupy—a sensation often reported by those who claim to have suffered demonic possession, and supposedly for that very reason.

This fiery baptism, in which, it seems, they may have cremated infants, probably represented to them the universal fire that many Gnostics (starting with John the Baptist himself), and many Jews and Christians as well, believed would bring an end to this fallen realm. Some Gnostics thought that this fire would burn up the ignorant rabble, preserving only the wise elect. Actually, catastrophes involving both fire and water were envisioned as being involved in the world's end (which reminds us of the Simonian baptism ritual, of both fire and water.) In *Orpheus the Fisher* by Robert Eisler, the author argues that John the Baptist was meant to be seen like a second Noah, baptizing with water just like God baptized the Earth in Noah's day. In *Luke* 17:26 (KJV), Jesus talks about his Second Coming at the End Times, declaring that, "And as it was in the days of Noe, so shall it be also in the days of the Son of man." But just a couple of lines later, in 17:28-30, Jesus also prophesies a fiery destruction that is to come:

> Likewise also as it was in the days of Lot; they did eat, they drank, they bought, they sold, they planted, they builded;
>
> But the same day that Lot went out of Sodom it rained fire and brimstone from heaven, and destroyed them all.
>
> Even thus shall it be in the day when the Son of man is revealed.

This fire and water symbolism also corresponds to lunar and solar symbolism. The Moon is usually associated with water (as it is associated with mutability and fluidity). The Sun, for obvious reasons, is easily associated with fire. So that picture of Mete pulling down the Sun and Moon could also be showing her bringing down fire and water from Heaven. Hammer-Purgstall plainly associated the image of fiery baptism that he discovered with an apocalypse of flame. He wrote:

> The ritual fire, having been lit (according to Tertullian), signifies the mystic pyre of universal conflagration, which the Gnostics adopted from the Stoics, and through which they taught that at the end of the world, everything will be dissolved.

The concept of the destruction of life on Earth by both fire and water was described by alchemist Fulcanelli in *The Mystery of the Cathedrals* as the "double cataclysm." He chose to interpret the letters INRI—often written above the head of Jesus when he is shown hanging on the cross, and usually taken to stand for *Iesus Nazarenus Rex Iudeorum* (Jesus of Nazareth, King of the Jews), as a covert allusion to the words *Igne Natura Renovatur Integra* (By fire nature is renewed whole). He goes on:

> For it is by fire and in fire that our hemisphere will soon be tried. And just as, by means of fire, gold is separated from impure metals, so, Scripture says, the good will be separated from the wicked on the great Day of Judgment.

Interestingly, Midsummer Day, on which the feast of John the Baptist is celebrated, is said by Robert Graves in *The White Goddess* (citing Frazer's *Golden Bough*) to have "always" been "a water as well as a fire festival." Frazer also said that the bonfires of these festivals were specifically called "fire of heaven."

Returning to the subject of the Baptism of Wisdom rite, the actual production of a child through ritual orgy, to be used for further ritual magic purposes, may have been hinted at with the story of the Templar who had sex with the dead body of the girl named Yse, resulting in the birth of a "son" in the form of a talking magic skull. Perhaps this is represented by the skull beneath Mete's feet in the picture of her drawing down the heavens. Maybe they even believed that children produced this way did not possess real souls, but rather were animated merely by the essences of the heavenly bodies that they had drawn down into them during the rituals, so that, with their sacrifices, they really weren't killing babies (in their minds), but rather subduing the Archons.

If one wonders how on Earth one could believe that bringing spirits down from stars and planets in a sex rite and entrapping them in the bodies of the resulting offspring could in any way cause the end of the world, recall that the Flood was purportedly caused by angels breeding hybrid children with humans—fallen angels led by the goat demon Azazel.

Now it should be noted, of course, that while there were Gnostic groups that seemed truly motivated to offend God and corrupt his creation, not all Gnostics were really against the material universe, and some were only so in part. Kyle Fraser, in his paper "Baptized in Gnosis: The spiritual alchemy of Zosimos of Panopolis," is careful to acknowledge the differences between the Hermetic and Sethian Gnostic views on spiritual alchemy and cosmic redemption:

For the Hermetic tradition the realization of gnosis does not imply the rejection of the material universe; gnosis is described instead as a noetic transformation, from the embodied and finite perspective to a transcendent perspective in which the outer cosmos is perceived within the mind. As Tat [the son of Hermes] exclaims in a visionary moment: "I am in heaven, in earth, in water and air; I am in animals and plants; in the womb, before the womb, and every the womb—everywhere." (*CH XIII* 1.1). The Sethian notion of rupture between the created world and the spiritual universe is nowhere to be found in the Hermetica. This distinction gives us a clearer insight into what it means to speak of alchemy as a properly Hermetic science: the phases of alchemy seem to reflect the phases of Hermetic initiation, from an initial blackening, an experience of spiritual disorientation and imprisonment, to a higher realization of the unity of spirit and matter, a gnosis or enlightenment symbolized for the alchemists as Gold.

We do see many anti-cosmic sentiments expressed in *The Corpus Hermeticum*. But we can also see this anti-cosmic dualism as being simply a stage of initiation, preliminary to the rebirth of the spirit and the fresh view of creation that the initiate would experience later. Gregory Shaw describes it thusly in *Taking the Shape of the Gods: A Theurgic Reading of Hermetic Rebirth*:

> From a theurgic perspective, dualism and acosmicism mark a preliminary stage of the initiate's experience followed by a monist or non-dualist embrace of the entire cosmos, one that marks the culmination of rebirth and immortalization. The

reversal of sequence that I propose reflects a reversal of orientation: *when the initiate's particular and mortal perspective is replaced by the universal perspective of a god*. I would argue that this is the goal of both theurgy and Hermetism.

Presumably, not all Templars wanted to bring about cosmic destruction (and most likely not all of them participated in the sick rituals we have described). Though some Gnostic groups seem to have done similar ceremonies, and did have a nihilistic, anti-creation worldview, we know that not all Gnostics wanted to see the universe annihilated. We are sure that most of the Hermeticists did not have this worldview. Even most avowed Satanists today would disagree. There have only been a few throughout the ages who have both known about and embraced these doctrines. Others have embraced some of them but did not know about the rest. Still others knew about these traditions, but chose to pursue their own ideas, or other interpretations, instead. Most Hermeticists from pre-Christian times would undoubtedly be appalled, for instance, by the orgies, excesses, and blasphemies of the rites of the modern Ordo Templi Orientis, with its "Gnostic Mass" invoking the words "Baphomet" and "Baptism of Wisdom" as the congregants consume semen and menstrual blood before a naked lady sitting on an altar.

So although we do not wish to paint all occultists with this brush, we feel that these destructive rites and ideas are an inseparable part of the chaotic underground stream of Baphometic wisdom, and all of its tributaries. We will provide more evidence to this effect, particularly with regard to the Templars, before the end of this book. Next, though, we will examine a symbol used by the Templars that makes their interest in Gnosticism rather clear: the enigmatic anguipede known as "Abraxas."

Chapter 8:
Abraxas: Secret of the Temple

This is a god whom ye knew not, for mankind forgot it. We name it by its name ABRAXAS. *It is more indefinite still than god and devil.*

—Carl Jung, *The Seven Sermons to the Dead*

The chimera figure of Abraxas (pronounced "ah-BRAKS-us") seems to have greatly influenced the Templar concept of Baphomet. Abraxas seems to have played a central role in the Gnostic cult of Basilides in the second century AD. Basilides was an Alexandrian mystic and teacher who for all intents and purposes can only be learned about from the Church Fathers who hated him. He is variously depicted as a disciple of either Menander or Saturninus (both of whom belonged to the schools of Simon Magus in Syria and Alexandria), or as an interpreter of St. Peter named Glaucias. It is interesting to note that Basilides is said to come out of either of these two supposedly diametrically-opposed traditions (those of Simon Magus and St. Peter).

Basilides was more than likely the first major Gnostic writer who viewed himself as a Christian theologian (or the first major Gnostic to write voluminous commentary on the Biblical canon). But unlike his predecessor Simon Magus, he rejected the Old Testament. (Simon seemed to favor an esoteric interpretation of the Samaritan Torah, as we mentioned earlier.) Basilides' system seems like an attempt to reconcile the New Testament, Egyptian Gnosticism, and Platonic philosophy (particularly of the Aristotle tradition) with his own mystical revelations. We know from the

Church propaganda minister Eusebius that Basilides wrote 24 commentaries, called *Exegetica*, on the Gospels, only fragments of which now remain. He also wrote hymns and odes to his congregation, all of which are now lost to us.

According to preserved fragments of his writings quoted by the Church Fathers, like Clement of Alexandria, Irenaeus, and Hippolytus, Basilides taught that there was a form of reincarnation (the Platonic metempsychosis) and karma. He may have been influenced by Buddhism. He saw spirit and matter as opposing natures, while passions were caused by spirit attachments in the human soul, which Basilides' successor, his son Isidore, likened it to the Trojan horse. The only way to tame this inferior element in man, Basilides felt, was to strengthen the rational part of him. He placed a great deal of emphasis on faith, just as much as Marcion and Paul did. He was also an ascetic, unlike many of his Gnostic compatriots. Faith and asceticism were, in his mind, the only means by which one could disentangle the soul from matter.

Suffering was not considered something to be escaped, but rather a blessing, the purpose of which was to turn the spiritual essence away from its entanglement in matter. Faith was an inborn ascent of the soul for Basilides, and is equated by him with Gnosis. It wasn't a matter of instruction or indoctrination. It was a sort of nature. Perhaps for Basilides, faith and knowledge were the same thing. Basilides, therefore, had a lot in common with other Gnostics and even with the later Protestant John Calvin, as they all shared the idea of predestined salvation. The "three natures" doctrine attests to this.

The elect were those who had the capacity for faith. They considered themselves "strangers" or "aliens" to the world, longing for the transcendent and salvation in Christ. According to Epiphanius in *Panarion* (24: 5:2), those who feel perfectly at home in the world are "swine and dogs," while "We are the 'men.'" They believed that this was the meaning behind the words of Jesus in *Matthew* 7:6, "Cast not thy pearls before swine, neither give that which is holy unto dogs." Birger Pearson, in his book *Ancient Gnosticism*, reflects on this "Gnostic elitism" exemplified by the cult of Basilides, similar to what is written in *Matthew* 22:14 about "many" being "called," but few "chosen":

> Another matter of dispute in scholarship is Basilides' doctrine of human nature and his classification of some people (that is, Gnostic Christians) as elect, over against the rest of humanity. A dominical saying is cited by Irenaeus as current among the Basilidians: "Few people can know these things— only one in a thousand, and two in ten thousand" (*Against Heresies* 1.24.6; compare *The Gospel of Thomas* 23).

Like many of Basilides' Gnostic contemporaries, he too rejected the Orthodox doctrine of the carnal resurrection and the idea that the spirit only was worthy of salvation, while the flesh was worthless. Many Church Fathers used the Gnostic stance on the Resurrection as proof that Basilides was a libertine, but judging from the evidence provided by our favorite heresy hunters, and as we said before, he was very much a strict ascetic.

It is to Basilides' favorite symbol of Abraxas that we now turn our attention. Abraxas is a Gnostic name that appears in many ancient texts. It should be noted that "Abrasax" is actually the more "official" spelling of this contradictory but powerful deity's name. The word doesn't have a definition in the traditional sense, but rather a mystical meaning. The seven letters that make up the name are meant to represent the seven planets known in antiquity. Abraxas is a

Abraxas: Secret of the Temple

complicated figure whose image has changed with the passing of time. But as far as we can tell, originally he was the head of 365 other spiritual beings of Gnostic lore.

Along with the lion-headed Chnoubis, Abraxas was considered to be roughly equivalent to the Agathodaemon, the "good spirit" of fortune and health revered by the ancient Egyptians and Greeks (mentioned in a previous chapter in relation to the student of Hermes Trismegistus with the same name). They were all often represented as serpents. Abraxas, according to Gnostic myth, was a redeemed Archon who rose above the Hebdomad to rule over it as an intercessory figure between the Pleroma and the world of matter. He became a figure of veneration for many Gnostics, including those who belonged to Basilides' *cultus*. This astral god was feared by those who believed in him because they thought that he controlled the universe and their fate.

Abraxas was most often depicted as an "anguipede" (having two serpents for legs) with a human male torso and the head of a cock. We know this because of all the ancient amulets with his image engraved on them. These amulets or gemstones were used as "tokens" by the Gnostics themselves to propagate their ideas, a sort of advertising for their mythos. Edward P. Butler, in his book *Esoteric City: Theological Hermeneutics in Plato's Republic*, explains what a token is in the context of magic and the Neoplatonic philosophy of Proclus, which is closer to Gnosticism than most scholars admit:

> Proclus explains that "symbols [*symbola*] are not imitations of those things of which they are symbols"; and thus "If a poet is inspired and manifests by means of symbols"—literally "tokens," *synthemata*, a technical term in theurgy—"the truth

concerning beings," or if, using science, he reveals to us the very order of realities, this poet is neither an imitator, nor can be refuted by the arguments [in the text].

There are some similarities between Abraxas and the anguipede giants of the ancient Greeks. These are those featured in the Titanomachy, who were birthed by the titans Gaia and Ouranos in retaliation against Zeus and the Olympian gods for consigning them to Tartarus. They undoubtedly connect to the Nephilim giants of *Genesis* Chapter 6 and *The First Book of Enoch* (who owed half their DNA to fallen angels that were later associated with the Serpent of Eden). The various giant children of Gaia (such as the Titans, Oceanus, and Tethys) are naturally associated with the Earth and its waters. In *Antiquities of the Jews* (1.3), Flavius Josephus confirms that the Jews indeed knew their own scriptures mirrored or mimicked Greek myth:

> For many angels of God accompanied with women, and begat sons that proved unjust, and despisers of all that was good, on account of the confidence they had in their own strength; for the tradition is, that these men did what resembled the acts of those whom the Grecians call giants.

These giants may also be regarded essentially as demonic beings of chaos, similar to the Asuras of Hinduism. There are Etruscan artworks and gems which depict Zeus smiting a snake-footed giant from the sixth century BCE and that have served as a forerunner to the writings of Pseudo-Apollodorus and Ovid's *Metamorphoses*, as detailed by Rachel Dodd in *Morphing Monsters: The Evolution of Anguipede Giants*. In this paper, Dodd attributes the snakey characteristic of the giants to that of Typhon, usually described as Gaia's youngest monstrous anguipede son, who is considered by mythologists to be interchangeable with the evil anguipede Seth, the brother of Osiris in the Egyptian pantheon. He also has strong connections with Abraxas as well as Ialdabaoth.

Typhon was an anguipede, both born from Tartarus and Gaia. Typhon is also closely associated with the giants and is sometimes considered the reason why giants became anguipedes in mythology. Yet whenever this is mentioned, it is often only in passing or within a footnote. Ustinova explains the adaptation of snake-legs as a conflation of the giants with the Titans, and moreover of the Titans with Typhon (all of which are children of Gaia). Yet, if the giants received snake-legs from Typhon through the Titans, would not more images depict the Titans as anguipedes as well? In fact, current scholarly theory connects the archaeological evidence of a Typhon vase in Etruria with the adaptation of snake-legged giants, which also appeared first in Etruria.

However, there is another myth regarding giants that may figure into the symbolism of Abraxas' snake legs, in this instance from Judeo-Christian tradition. Regarding the giants spawned by the Watchers, *The Zohar* (*Shelah Lecha* 160b, from Volume 5 of the Soncino Edition) tells us:

> They lived to a great age until at last half their body became paralyzed while the other half remained vigorous. They would then take a certain herb and throw it into their mouths and die, and because they thus killed themselves they were called "Refaim."

It makes sense, then, to symbolize the wise elders of this race as having serpents for legs, as they could no longer walk upright.

Moreover, there are scriptures stating that during the time in which the Watchers were breeding the Nephilim giants with humans, different species of animals were being mixed together as well—just as Oannes had said that such things existed before the present stage of creation. (Think of the Greek and Persian myths of Satyrs, Manticores, Griffins, Minotaurs, Centaurs, Chimeras, etc.) As *The Book of Jasher* 4:18 tells us:

> And their judges and rulers went to the daughters of men and took their wives by force from their husbands according to their choice, and the sons of men in those days took from the cattle of the earth, the beasts of the field and the fowls of the air, and taught the mixture of animals of one species with the other, in order therewith to provoke the Lord; and God saw the whole earth and it was corrupt, for *all flesh had corrupted* its ways on the earth, all men and all animals.

Naturally, there is a direct parallel to the *Genesis* account (emphasis added):

> And God looked upon the earth, and, behold, it was corrupt; for *all flesh had corrupted his way upon the earth*. And God said unto Noah, The end of all flesh is come before me; for the earth is filled with violence through them; and, behold, I will destroy them with the earth.

In the Dead Sea Scrolls, *The Book of Giants (1Q23 Frag. 1 + 6)* tells us that the Watchers mated not only with human females, but animals as well, spawning hybrid monsters:

> [. . . two hundred] donkeys, two hundred asses, two hundred . . . rams of the] flock, two hundred goats, two hundred [. . . beast of the] field from every

animal, from every [bird . . .] [. . .] for
miscegenation [. . .]

Later in the same text (4Q531 Frag. 2), we are told that the fruits of these unions were freaks of nature:

> [. . .] they defiled [. . .] 2[. . . they begot] giants and monsters [. . .] 3[. . .] they begot, and, behold, all [the earth was corrupted]. . . .

"Monsters" seems to be the term used specifically for these animal-angel hybrids, while the word "giants" is reserved for the human-angel hybrids. We must presume that, being partially angelic in origin, these monsters could very well have been sentient and conscious, perhaps even with the ability to speak. This would explain why later in *The Book of Giants* the monsters and giants are described as though they are political partners. Could it be that figures like Baphomet and Abraxas are emblems of chimeric union between angel and beast?

As we have noted, the Archons of Gnosticism also seem to have chimeric qualities since they are often depicted as animal-headed angels, much like the gods of Egypt. Just like Abraxas, there are certain Scythian goddesses who are portrayed with snake legs as well, which serve as forerunners for the "Melusines" of European folklore. These Melusine images (showing a woman with two serpents for legs) show up on heraldic coats of arms throughout the continent.

The figure of Melusine is based on a character from the mythology of European aristocracy. She is said to have been either the daughter of Godfroi de Bouillon (Advocatus of the Holy Sepulcher), and cousin of Hughes de Payens (founder of the Templars), or of Godfroi's successor Baldwin II (who took the title "King of Jerusalem"). The latter is probably more likely to be Melusine's true father, as the research of the Plant Family History Group's website (plant-fhg.org.uk) shows that her mythic character is based on Baldwin II's daughter Melisande, who married Fulk V, an ancestor of the Plantagenet kings of England (heirs also to the Scottish House of Stuart).

The myth surrounding Melusine is that her mother was a she-demon (clearly a Lilith character). Whenever she bathed, and whenever she witnessed the miracle of the Eucharist, her legs would turn into serpents. Therefore she did not attend mass and would never allow her husband to watch her bathe. When Fulk finally discovered the truth about her, she shrieked like a banshee, sprouted demonic wings, and flew away. This may be the meaning behind the statement once made by Richard the Lionheart, a Plantagenet king, about his own family lineage, declaring, "From the Devil we came, and to the Devil we shall return!"

Thus, the Melusine symbol, though sometimes altered to look more benign, with two fish tails instead of snakes (like the Starbucks logo), was originally an anguipede meant to symbolize the serpent seed that slumbers in the blood of Europe's royalty. It is also sometimes combined with the fertility symbol called, in Gaelic, "Sheela Na-Gig" (though they are found well beyond the British Isles). Sheela is a female gargoyle with spread legs displaying her vagina (a female version of the Priapian phallus talismans). In the Scottish monastery of St. Jacob in Regensburg, Germany, there is an image of Melusine with fish tails for legs, showing off her vagina like Sheela Na-Gig.

Since the snake is an animal that slithers on the ground, it was viewed as possessing strong chthonic features, associated with the Earth and the underworld. At the same

Abraxas: Secret of the Temple 379

time, giants were also connected to the underworld, both in the ancient Greek pagan and the Judeo-Christian traditions. Therefore, the snake legs of Abraxas embody and encompass not only Heaven, but also Hell. (Remember, as we mentioned before Severus taught that "man is divine from the navel up, and the creature of the Devil from the navel down.") Abraxas being an anguipede giant with the head of a cock would make sense considering that the Hebrew root word "GBR" (GiBoR), translated in the King James Version of *Genesis* as "giant," specifically means "warrior," while "GeBoR" refers to a rooster.

The form of Abraxas is frequently said to include that of a basilisk—either his bottom, snakey half, or his whole body (depending on which definition of basilisk you embrace). According to the *Encyclopedia of Ancient Deities* by Charles Russel Coulter and Patricia Turner, a basilisk (a word meaning "little king") is a:

> . . . deified creature. This frightening-looking lizard is able to run on water. Those who annoy it can be frozen in their tracks by its angry glare. It is generally found by those who are not looking for it in the inaccessible regions of the Swiss Alps and the African desert. It has the body and wings of a dragon and the head of a serpent. It is usually shown with its tail in its mouth. Sometimes it is depicted as half cock and half snake. Basilisk is connected with the Gnostic Abraxas in that Agathodemon or "good spirit" was said to have hatched by a cock from a serpent's egg.

This fierce and terrifying creature goes by many other names as well. The shield that he holds could be connected to the goat-skinned impenetrable Aegis shield of Zeus and Athena mentioned earlier, emblazoned with the snakey head of the gorgon that can kill people who look at it by turning them to stone (which we also compared to the identical powers of the Arabic mythological creature Al-Ghul). This deadly aspect of the gaze of the basilisk (more than just causing mere muscle paralysis) is more commonly reported, for example, by Pliny the Elder (in his *Natural History*), and by Albertus Magnus (in his *De animalibus*). Also, just as Medusa was killed by Perseus, the basilisk is vulnerable to its own gaze, and can be killed by forcing it to look into a mirror. Both Albertus Magnus and an alchemist named Theophilus Presbyter stated that, once dead, the basilisk could be used to transmute metals, either with its blood (according to the latter), or by its ashes (according to the former).

In Thomas Wright's *The Worship of Generative Powers*, there are drawings that depict a variation on the chicken-headed and winged basilisk with an elongated penis for a tail. Like Abraxas images, these were often placed on amulets to protect their owners from the "evil eye." Thomas Wright claims that these are all votives belonging to the cult of Priapus, stating:

> The first of these is the figure of a double phallus. It is sculptured on the lintel of one of the vomitories, or issues, of the second range of seats of the Roman amphitheatre, near the entrance-gate which looks to the south. The double and the triple phallus are very common among the small Roman bronzes, which appear to have served as amulets and for other similar purposes. In the latter, one phallus usually serves as the body, and is furnished with legs, generally those of the goat; a second occupies the usual place of this organ; and a third appears in that of a tail.

Abraxas: Secret of the Temple

The mythicist Acharya S. (a.k.a. DM Murdock) has also written on Priapus-like images that are very close to those of Abraxas. At freethoughtnation.com, in the article entitled "The phallic 'Savior of the World' hidden in the Vatican," she points out that there is a sculpted bust, supposedly of St. Peter, that depicts a man with a rooster's head and an erect phallus for a nose, and which was once on display in the Vatican. Acharya S quotes Barbara Walker from *The Woman's Dictionary of Symbols and Sacred Objects:*

> It is no coincidence that "cock" is slang for "penis." The cock was a phallic totem in Roman and medieval sculptures showing cocks somehow transformed into, or supporting, human penises. Roman carvings of disembodied phalli often gave them the legs or wings of cocks. Hidden in the treasury of the Vatican is a bronze image of a cock with the head of a penis on the torso of a man, the pedestal inscribed "The Savior of the World."

Acharya S also quotes from Richard Payne Knight's *A Discourse on the Worship of Priapus*, which talks about this image:

> ... [T]he celebrated bronze in the Vatican has the male organs of generation placed upon the head of a cock, the emblem of the sun, supported by the neck and shoulders of a man. In this composition they represented the generative power of the [Eros], the Osiris, Mithras, or Bacchus, whose centre is the sun. . . . The inscription on the pedestal [says] . . . *The Saviour of the World* . . . a title always venerable under whatever image it be presented [with].

Acharya S found a rare actual photograph of the "Saviour of the World" presented as an image of Priapus in Otto Augustus Wall's book *Sex and Sex Worship (Phallic Worship): A Scientific Treatise on Sex*, where it states that it was "found in an ancient Greek temple. . . ." She also quotes an article titled "Priapus Gallinaceus: The Role of the Cock in Fertility and Eroticism in Classical Antiquity and the Middle Ages," by Dr. Lorrayne Baird, where it says:

> This object was published under papal and royal authority, exhibited for a time in the seventeenth and eighteenth centuries, and is now said to be held inaccessible in the secret collections of the Vatican. During the public life of this bronze, officials disagreed upon the probity of the exhibit. One offended cardinal requested that the object be removed. . . .
>
> . . . [T]he Vatican Saviour-as-Phallic-cock was a scandalous satire on early Christians.

Obviously, this cock-headed imagery corresponds greatly with that of Abraxas. Much like the twin-snaked caduceus that serves as the phallus of Eliphas Levi's Baphomet, the cock-head of Abraxas represented not only enlightenment but also sexual energy.

Abraxas was frequently associated with the Gnostic figure of Ialdabaoth, usually shown as a lion-headed serpent. This ancient image is first found at the start of the Christian era, sometimes depicted as crowned or surrounded by a halo or streaming rays, indicating its inherent solar and magical nature. The actual name for the character is "Khnoubis" or "Chnoubis," and it can be found carved on old gems and amulets. Hebraic names such as "IAO," "Adonai," "Sabaoth," and the Gnostic corruption of

"Ialdabaoth" are also found on these tokens for superstitious purposes. The Chnoubis figure turns up fairly regularly on these Gnostic gems, especially with the healing formulae for stomach and abdominal issues. It turns up in a few spells in *The Greek Magical Papyri* as well.

According to Atilio Mastrocinque in *Jewish Magic and Gnosticism*, the Chnoubis-Ialdabaoth figure originates in the syncretistic Jewish-Gnostic-Egyptian context of the Jewish Temple in Leontopolis. It is sometimes linked with the satirical god of Lucian, Glykon. Chnoubis was considered synonymous with the Gnostic deities Abraxas and Ophis, since the image shows up often along with these gods on amulets and coins.

The sixth-century philosopher Damascius Diodochos recounts some Orphic teachings, and describes Chronos (the Greek god of time) as having both the head of a lion and of a bull in *Problems and Solutions Concerning First Principles*:

> But as for the third principle after the two, it arose from these, I mean from water and earth, and it is a serpent with the heads of a lion and a bull grown upon it, and in the middle the countenance of a god, and it has wings on its shoulders, and the same god is called Ageless Time [Aion], and Heracles.

However, this is a late source, so we are simply left to guess if any of this was believed in the ancient world. The scholar Franz Cumont, in *The Mysteries of Mithra*, placed Aion, a lion-headed and winged god enveloped by a serpent (a figure called a "leontocephaline"), as Chronos, who emerged from the primordial chaos and in turn generated Heaven and Earth, like the Orphic deity Phanes. Aion here is much like the Demiurge of Gnosticism.

Ancient magical texts such as *The Greek Magical Papyri* often invoke images of Chnoubis, which were used for the purpose of warding off malevolent demonic influences, to banish and overcome the cosmic rulers that guard each succeeding section of the "astral realm." *The Greek Magical Papyri* also provides the means for summoning demons for various practical purposes, such as making thievery invisible to others, sending dreams to others via demons, winning favors from both men and women, inflaming lust in the person of desire, punishing enemies, defeating rivals, etc. It is obvious that these spells were used to achieve deeply personal goals for the individual.

If this seems to reflect a sense of moral ambiguity, in a way, that's true. Like Baphomet, Abraxas is a transcendental symbol linking light and darkness, consciousness and unconsciousness. In his Hellenistic form, he is already a chimeric emblem of the unification of opposites, which was reflected several hundred years later in Carl Jung's writings on Abraxas. The figure's cuirass is that of a Roman-Mithraic soldier, perhaps indicating the militant character of the God of Israel, in his role as the "Lord of Hosts," being represented as "Sabaoth." To Jung, Abraxas symbolized the wholeness of the soul when repaired from the fragmentation of creation, bringing the end to the schizophrenia of dualism. In Hermann Hesse's *Demian: The Story of Emil Sinclair's Youth*, Abraxas is described as functioning in the same way. In *Systema Munditotius*, Jung writes that Abraxas is also an emblem of the lower, mundane world, guarded over by the Demiurge:

> He represents *Dominus Mundi*, the Lord of the physical world and is a world creator of a polarized nature. From him sprouts the tree of life with the title *Vita*, life. The lower world of Abraxas is

characterized by the number of the natural man, five. . . . The accompanying animals of the natural world are a devilish monster and a worm, these point to death and rebirth. So the bottom of the *Munditoitius* is the natural human being, the instinctual Abraxas, this world. And this is in a strong tension and contrast to the upper world.

In the Middle Ages, Abraxas was also known as the king of demons, a title also shared in cabalistic demonology with Asmodeus, a son of Lilith and Samael. Abraxas is in some ways similar to the Hindu Narasimha, the lion-headed avatar of Vishnu, also the latter is thought of as benevolent. (However, Narasimha is considered fearsome by other demons, and is often depicted as disemboweling them on his lap!) In the *Dictionnaire Infernal* by Jacques Collin de Plancy (1818), Abraxas is spelled "Abracas." He is listed here as one of the many demons to be used for the purpose of evocation, similar to what was said about him in *The Greek Magical Papyri*. In many Gnostic texts, the Demiurge was associated with the element of fire, and bore many chimeric qualities, as *The Apocryphon of John* describes him:

And when she saw (the consequences of) her desire, it changed into a form of a lion-faced serpent. And its eyes were like lightning fires which flash. She cast it away from her, outside that place, that no one of the immortal ones might see it, for she had created it in ignorance.

In *The Pistis Sophia*, the Demiurge isn't by any means a handsome fellow, being depicted as a fiery yet dark lion-faced demon. He resides within the chaotic underworld of Hades where he and his forty-nine demons torture wicked souls in boiling rivers of pitch-black darkness. Also, in *The Gospel of Judas*, Ialdabaoth dwells in Hades with

"Nebro" (meaning "rebel angel") and his other henchman. He is said to be one of the twelve angels to come "into being [to] rule over chaos and the [underworld]." Also, his "face flashed with fire and whose appearance was defiled with blood." In the Manichaean *Kephalaia* (30.34-31.1), it describes the "King of Those of Darkness" like this:

> His head [is lion-faced, his] hands and feet are demon-faced, [his] shoulders are eagle-faced, while his belly [is dragon-faced,] (and) his tail is fish-faced.

In verse 280 of the Right *Ginza* of the Mandaeans, there is a very similar description of Satan as well, which is also closer to the Sethian Ialdabaoth, except for the fact that he has angelic wings, tortoise legs and demonic feet. The chimera found in the Homer's *Iliad* was also described with similar features as:

> . . . a thing of immortal make, not human, lion-fronted and snake behind, a goat in the middle, and snorting out the breath of the terrible flame of bright fire.

In the context of the Templars, Abraxas seems to have the most in common with the archangel Michael, as we will explore later. Under the name of "Iao," Abraxas appears in a few instances throughout the Nag Hammadi codices, in such Sethian texts such as *The Great Book of the Invisible Spirit*, *The Apocalypse of Adam*, and *Zostrianos*. In these he is basically a minor aeon or angel that works in tandem with Sophia and the "four spiritual lights" to rectify the error of our universe. The sixth-century author John the Lydian wrote in *De Mensibus*, 83:

> . . . The Roman Varro, when discussing him, says that among the Chaldaeans, in their mystical [writings], he is called "Iao," meaning "mentally perceived light" in

the language of the Phoenicians, as Herennius [Philo] says. And he is frequently called "Sabaoth," meaning the one who is "above the seven heavenly spheres"—that is, the creator.

Abraxas was in many ways interchangeable with Sabaoth, who, according to the Gnostic mythology presented in *On the Origin of the World*, was the son and offspring of Ialdabaoth. In that text, he rebels against his father in a great war, repents of his "sins," and sides with his grandmother, Sophia-Achamoth. He is then elevated "above the seventh heaven" to become the "Ogdoad" (the eighth power), and enthroned, surrounded by ministering cherubim within a mansion that is "huge, magnificent, seven times as great as all those that exist in the seven heavens." The idea of Sabaoth being redeemed is very similar to the account we just mentioned where the Archons and Abraxas were enlightened by the Gospel.

However, there is a lot of conflicting information about the nature of Abraxas. There were supposedly a total of 365 heavens in Basilides' cosmology, and Abraxas was the chief ruler over them. It doesn't explicitly say that Abraxas was an evil Archon like Ialdabaoth, however. The ruler over Basilides' 365th and final heaven was the Jewish god, the Demiurge shared by all major Gnostic systems, and he was indeed evil. Irenaeus and Hippolytus say that Abraxas was the chief Archon of Basilides' cosmology, not the supreme god, whereas Tertullian says that Abraxas and the highest god are the same. Most scholars think that Tertullian was dependent on Irenaeus and misread what he said. In *Against Heresies* (1.24.3-4.7), Irenaeus lays out Basilides' system (which isn't particularly dualist) pertaining to Abraxas' domain:

They make out the local position of the three hundred and sixty-five heavens in the same way as do mathematicians. For, accepting the theorems of these latter, they have transferred them to their own type of doctrine. They hold that their chief is Abraxas; and, on this account, that word contains in itself the numbers amounting to three hundred and sixty-five.

Then other powers, being formed by emanation from these, created another heaven similar to the first; and in like manner, when others, again, had been formed by emanation from them, corresponding exactly to those above them, these, too, framed another third heaven; and then from this third, in downward order, there was a fourth succession of descendants; and so on, after the same fashion, they declare that more and more principalities and angels were formed, and three hundred and sixty-five heavens. Wherefore the year contains the same number of days in conformity with the number of the heavens.

Those angels who occupy the lowest heaven, that, namely, which is visible to us, formed all the things which are in the world, and made allotments among themselves of the earth and of those nations which are upon it. The chief of them is he who is thought to be the God of the Jews; and inasmuch as he desired to render the other nations subject to his own people, that is, the Jews, all the other princes resisted and opposed him. Wherefore all other nations were at enmity with his nation.

In *Refutation of All Heresies*, Hippolytus reports that Basilides taught the concept of a non-existent deity. This is similar to what other Gnostics called the "Unknowable Father." But this concept seems to refer to a realm of infinite potentiality rather than simply *nothing*. Abraxas (spelled "Abrasax" in this instance) is said to be an Archon that exists within the Hebdomad beneath the Ogdoad. He is mentioned as the third of three great Archons. Here are the words of Basilides regarding the non-existent god, as quoted by Hippolytus:

> Whatsoever I affirm to have been made [beyond] these, ask no question as to where. For the Seed had all seeds treasured and resting in itself, just as non-existent entities, and which were designed to be produced by a non-existent Deity.

According to Hippolytus, Basilides' system began with the non-existent god, from whom came the Seed. From the Seed came the three-fold or triple-sonship (the three natures), the existent cosmos, the Great Archon of the Ogdoad, the Lesser Archon of the Hebdomad, and a peculiar Archon who is said to be the sum of all the powers of the Hebdomad, including the 365 heavens therein: Abrasax (Abraxas). In *Refutation of All Heresies* (7:10-15) we read:

> There existed, he says, in the Seed itself, a Sonship, threefold, in every respect of the same Substance with the non-existent God, and begotten from nonentities, Of this Sonship thus involving a threefold division, one part was refined, another lacking refinement, and another requiring purification.
>
> The refined portion, therefore, in the first place, simultaneously with the earliest deposition of the Seed by the non-existent One, immediately burst forth and went upwards and hurried above from

> below . . . and attained, he says, unto him that is nonexistent.
>
> For every nature desires the nonexistent God. . . . However, each nature desires this after a different mode. The un-refined portion of the Sonship continuing still in the Seed . . . was not able to hurry upwards. For this portion was much more deficient in the refinement that the Sonship possessed . . . and was left behind. Therefore the unrefined Sonship equipped itself with some such wing as Plato, the Preceptor of Aristotle, fastens on the soul in his Phaedrus.

That last remark refers to Plato's dialogue *Phaedrus*, where it is said that the soul must acquire "wings" through the practice of philosophy in order to regain its memory and to return to its original divine estate. This is the Platonic equivalent of Gnostic knowledge. Hippolytus continues:

> And Basilides styles such, not a wing, but Holy Spirit; and Sonship invested in this Spirit confers benefits, and receives them in turn. . . . For the Sonship, carried upwards by the Spirit as by a wing, bears aloft. . . . And it approaches the refined Sonship, and the non-existent God, even Him who fabricated the world out of nonentities.

Hippolytus tells us about a "third Sonship" that requires purification from above. This third Sonship is of course, the Great Archon, Abraxas. He is also called the "Head of the World," and a master of the air (which sounds similar to "prince of the power of the air," a title given to the Devil by Paul in *Ephesians* 2:2). The text continues:

> This Archon, when begotten, raised Himself up and soared aloft, and was carried up entire as far as

the firmament. And there He paused, supposing the firmament to be the termination of His ascension and elevation, and considering that there existed nothing at all beyond these.

... He became more wise, more powerful, more comely, more lustrous ... pre-eminent for beauty above any entities you could mention with the exception of the Sonship alone, which is still left in the conglomeration of all germs.

For he was not aware that there is a Sonship wiser and more powerful, and better than Himself. Therefore imagining Himself to be Lord, and Governor, and a wise Master Builder, He turns Himself to the work of the creation of every object in the cosmical system.

... [A]nd the Archon caused Him to sit on his right hand. This is, according to these heretics, what is denominated the Ogdoad, where the Great Archon has his throne. The entire celestial creation, then, that is, the Aether, He Himself, the Great Wise Demiurge formed. The Son, however, begotten of this Archon, operates in Him, and offered Him suggestions, being endued with far greater wisdom than the Demiurge Himself.

The account, therefore, which Aristotle has previously rendered concerning the soul and the body, Basilides elucidates as applied to the Great Archon and his Son. For the Archon has generated, according to Basilides, a son; and the soul as an operation and completion, Aristotle asserts to be an *entelecheia* [an actuality formed from an ideal potential] of a natural organic body. As, therefore, the *entelecheia* controls the body, so the Son, according to Basilides, controls the God. . . .

When all objects in the aethereal regions, then, were arranged, again from the conglomeration of all germs another Archon ascended, greater, of course, than all subjacent entities with the exception, however, of the Sonship that had been left behind, but far inferior to the First Archon. And this second Archon is called by them Rhetus . . . [and] . . . is styled Hebdomad, and this Archon is the manager and fabricator of all subjacent entities. And He has likewise made unto Himself out of the conglomeration of all germs, a son who is more prudent and wise than Himself, similarly to what has been stated to have taken place in the case of the First Archon. . . .

The Gospel then came, says Basilides, first from the Sonship through the Son, that was seated beside the Archon, to the Archon, and the Archon learned that He was not God of the universe, but was begotten. But ascertaining that He has above Himself the deposited treasure of that Ineffable and Unnamable and Non-existent One, and of the Sonship, He was both converted and filled with terror, when He was brought to understand in what ignorance He was involved.

When, then, the Great Archon had been orally instructed, and every creature of the Ogdoad had been orally instructed and taught, and after the mystery became known to the celestial powers, it was also necessary that afterwards the Gospel should come to the Hebdomad. . . .

Abraxas: Secret of the Temple 393

The Son of the Great Archon therefore kindled in the Son of the Archon of the Hebdomad the light which Himself possessed and had kindled from above from the Sonship. And the Son of the Archon of the Hebdomad had radiance imparted to Him, and He proclaimed the Gospel to the Archon of the Hebdomad. And in like manner, according to the previous account, He Himself was both terrified and induced to make confession.

When, therefore, all beings in the Hebdomad had been likewise enlightened, and had the Gospel announced to them; for in these regions of the universe there exist, according to these heretics, creatures infinite in number, viz., Principalities and Powers and Rulers (*Ephesians* 6:12), in regard of which there is extant among the Basilidians a very prolix and verbose treatise, where they allege that there are three hundred and sixty-five heavens, and that the great Archon of these is Abrasax, from the fact that his name comprises the computed number 365. . . .

Note that the text here indicates that the 365 heavens exist within the region of the Hebdomad, as opposed to the Ogdoad of the Great Archon. Thus Abrasax exists within the confines of the Hebdomad and is not to be identified with the Great Archon himself. Moreover, Abrasax is connected here with the wicked "principalities and powers" of *Ephesians* 6:12, which implies that he is a malevolent or Satanic being. (That scripture says, "For we wrestle not against flesh and blood, but against principalities, against powers, against the rulers of the darkness of this world, against spiritual wickedness in high places.") However, what is fascinating in this account is that the Archons become enlightened when they are preached the Gospel! This is very unique to Basilides. This may explain why Clement of Alexandria accused Basilides of "deifying" the Devil. However, this seems hardly fair. Hippolytus goes on:

> When these two events, viz. the illumination of the Hebdomad and the manifestation of the Gospel had thus taken place, it was necessary, likewise, that afterwards the Formlessness existent in our quarter of creation should have radiance imparted to it, and that the mystery should be revealed to the Sonship, which had been left behind in Formlessness, just like an abortion.
>
> And as far as this, the entire Sonship, which is left behind for benefiting the souls in Formlessness, and for being the recipient in turn of benefits—this Sonship, I say, when it is transformed, followed Jesus, and hastened upwards, and came forth purified. And it becomes most refined, so that it could, as the first Sonship, hasten upwards through its own instrumentality. For it possesses all the power that, according to nature, is firmly connected with the light which from above shone down. . . .
>
> When, therefore, he says, the entire Sonship shall have come, and shall be above the conterminous spirit, then the creature will become the object of mercy. "For the creature groans until now" (*Romans* 8:19-22) and is tormented, and waits for the manifestation of the sons of God, in order that all who are men of the Sonship may ascend from thence.
>
> When this takes place, God, he says, will bring upon the whole world enormous ignorance, that all

things may continue according to nature, and that nothing may inordinately desire anything of the things that are contrary to nature.

But far from it; for all the souls of this quarter of creation, as many as possess the nature of remaining immortal in this region only, continue in it, aware of nothing superior or better than their present state. And there will not prevail any rumour or knowledge in regions below, concerning beings whose dwelling is placed above, lest subjacent souls should be wrung with torture from longing after impossibilities.

It would be just as if a fish were to crave to feed on the mountains along with sheep. For a wish of this description would, he says, be their destruction. All things, therefore, that abide in this quarter are incorruptible, but corruptible if they are disposed to wander and cross over from the things that are according to nature.

In this way the Archon of the Hebdomad will know nothing of superjacent entities. For enormous ignorance will lay hold on this one likewise, in order that sorrow, and grief, and groaning may depart from him; for he will not desire anything of impossible things, nor will he be visited with anguish. In like manner, however, the same ignorance will lay hold also on the Great Archon of the Ogdoad, and similarly on all the creatures that are subject unto him, in order that in no respect anything may desire anything of those things that are contrary to nature, and may not (thus) be overwhelmed with sorrow. And so there will be the restitution of all things which, in conformity with nature, have from the beginning a foundation in the seed of the universe. . . .

The underlying wisdom in Basilides' doctrine is that all sorrows are the result of a longing for the non-existent realm by those who have an essence of that realm within them, having this from their connection with the third sonship that is confined and formless in the existent cosmos. Those souls who have a portion of the third sonship in themselves will be purified along with it and restored to the non-existent realm. A fascinating detail is that Basilides seems to construct this interpretation in part from Paul and the passage from *Romans* 8:19 ("For the earnest expectation of the creature waiteth for the manifestation of the sons of God). Basilides was saying that the "manifestation of the sons of God" refers to the revealing and ascension of the triple-sonship, while the "groaning of the creature" refers to the remaining sonship, within the creation, that is in need of purification.

The description of the non-existent god sounds curiously close to the Buddhist concept of Nirvana. Also notice how Hippolytus links the "formlessness" of matter with that of an "abortion," which is exactly how Ialdabaoth is described in other Gnostic texts. There may be a link here with the use of this language and the claims that some Gnostic groups aborted the fruitful results of their alleged orgies—which, as we have mentioned, could have been done as a way of preventing spirit from being trapped in matter through incarnation in a human body. Epiphanius claimed that the Phibionites induced abortions with honey and pepper, and ritually consumed the fetus in some twisted parody of the Eucharist.

According to Hippolytus, Basilides taught that one day there would be no unification with the Godhead possible,

Abraxas: Secret of the Temple 397

since, he believed, each level of existence will remain to its own. Spirit will go to spirit, while flesh will remain flesh, and no salvation or grace will be enacted to make anything contrary to its nature. This is what Basilides meant by the term "Great Ignorance" in his eschatology. He stood on the fringe of Gnostic thought. He felt that in the end, ignorance will win against knowledge. This is radically different from other Gnostic teachings, as well as Christianity, Judaism, and Platonism, all systems wherein it is taught that knowledge (even "unknowing knowledge") leads to union with God. Perhaps in Basilides' "non-existent god" concept (a kind of religious atheism), we can find the first instance of "apophatic theology," describing the divine in negative terms (by defining what it is not). We see this in other Gnostic texts like *The Apocryphon of John* and *Allogenes*, as well as Neoplatonic thinkers like Plotinus. We also find some similarities in Paul's *2 Thessalonians* 2:9-12, where God causes a "strong delusion" in the sinful world so that it can be damned because it rejected the Gospel:

> Even him, whose coming is after the working of Satan with all power and signs and lying wonders, and with all deceivableness of unrighteousness in them that perish; because they received not the love of the truth, that they might be saved. And for this cause God shall send them strong delusion, that they should believe a lie: That they all might be damned who believed not the truth, but had pleasure in unrighteousness.

In this context, the aforementioned Greek concept of Lethe, the river of forgetfulness in Hades, and the "cup of forgetfulness" from *The Pistis Sophia* both seem pertinent.

As we can see, Hippolytus' account of the Basilidean system is very different from Irenaeus'. Scholars dispute as to which one is older, but we are guessing that Irenaeus' system is the eldest, since it is much simpler than the other. Also, according to Irenaeus' account, Basilides' Jesus was docetic (only a spirit and not at all human), whereas Hippolytus says that Basilides saw him as fully human. Hippolytus also claims that Basilides was, as Simone Petrement put it in *A Separate God*, "nourished by philosophy," particularly that of Aristotle and Pythagoras.

Moving on to other viewpoints on the matter, in *Thrice-Great Hermes*, GRS Mead discusses the possible connection of Abraxas to the celestial spheres of the cosmic rulers of fate:

> The name Abraxas, which consisted of seven elements or letters, was a mystery-designation of the God who combined in himself the whole power of the Seven Planets, and also of the Year of 365 days, the sum of the number-values of the letters of Abraxas working out to 365. This mysterious Being was the "Year"; but the Year as the Eternity, also conceived of in a spatial aspect, as the Spirit or Name that extends from Heaven to Earth, the God who pervades and full-fills the Seven Spheres, and the Three Hundred and Sixty-five Zones, the Inner God, "He who has His seat within the Seven Poles. . . " as the Papyri have it, and also without them, as we shall see.

Sencan Altinoluk and Nilufer Atakan also see Abraxas as a solar deity, much like those from the Egyptian pantheon, such as Horus, Osiris, and Ra. In *Abraxas: A Magical Gem in the Istanbul Archaeological Museums*, they wrote:

> Abrasax is the god of the solar year. . . . Abrasax was thought to be a mighty tutelary deity. People

imagined him as a kind of sun god similar to the Greek Helios, who could protect people all of the year—i.e. 365 days—and who was able to see everything that happens on earth. . . .

In Greek and Roman belief the rooster was generally considered to be a protector from evil, as the rooster guards the farm where it lives, and as the Greek name of the animal was connected with [a word meaning] "to ward off, to avert." Furthermore, this animal was very often associated with the sun, as roosters are wont to crow at sunrise, which was interpreted as a kind of greeting to the rising sun. Roosters are widely used in magic practices and rituals. The whip and the shield are thought to be used for warding off demons. Therefore such gems are applied for the purposes of protecting their wearers from any sort of evil. Also the whip assimilates Abrasax to the sun god who uses his whip to drive his horses on. In the case of Abrasax the whip is a symbol of the god's power to prevent demons from attacking the owner of such a gem. Abrasax's shield is an instrument to protect men from demons and all kinds of evil.

As we mentioned earlier, Abraxas was also equated with the archangel Michael by the Gnostics. Recall that the Ophites demoted Michael to a serpent-like demonic power. In *The Testament of Solomon*, Sabaoth, through his intermediary, the archangel Michael, is said to entrust Solomon with a magical ring bearing a pentagram that enables to command 72 demons to build his temple. The same text tells us:

> ...I entered the Temple of God, and prayed with all my soul, night and day, that the demon might be

delivered into my hands, and that I might gain authority over him. And it came about through my prayer that grace was given to me from the Lord Sabaoth by Michael his archangel. [He brought me] a little ring, having a seal consisting of an engraved stone, and said to me: "Take, O Solomon, king, son of David, the gift which the Lord God has sent thee, the highest Sabaoth. With it thou shalt lock up all demons of the earth, male and female; and with their help thou shalt build up Jerusalem. [But] thou [must] wear this seal of God. And this engraving of the seal of the ring sent thee is a Pentalpha."

Following these connections, it seems that Abraxas, perhaps operating under the guise of "Sabaoth," may be seen as a sort of guardian spirit or "demon" for the Temple of Solomon. The demon that Solomon took as the chief architect for his project was Asmodeus, said by cabalists to be the husband of Lilith the Younger. Asmodeus takes a stance reminiscent of the "As above, so below" pose struck by Baphomet in Eliphas Levi's depiction of him in this description given by Louis Ginzberg in the fourth volume of his Louis Ginzberg classic *Legends of the Jews* (emphasis added):

> Although Asmodeus was captured only for the purpose of getting the shamir, Solomon nonetheless kept him after the completion of the Temple. One day the king told Asmodeus that he did not understand wherein the greatness of the demons lay, if their king could be kept in bonds by a mortal. Asmodeus replied, that if Solomon would remove his chains and lend him the magic ring, he would prove his own greatness. Solomon agreed. *The demon stood before him with one wing touching*

heaven and the other reaching to the earth. Snatching up Solomon, who had parted with his protecting ring, he flung him four hundred parasangs away from Jerusalem, and then palmed himself off as the king.

The pentagram on Solomon's ring is a symbol that has been used in many different cultures, even by medieval Christians, to whom it represented the five wounds of Christ. It was generally thought to be protective against evil. The students of Pythagoras also used the sign to represent he ether or spirit ruling over the other four elements of fire, earth, water and air. The Freemason Christoph Friedrich Nicolai, in *Versuch uber die Beschuldigungen welche dem Tempelherrenorden gemacht worden, und uber dessen Geheimniß* (*Essay on the Accusations Which Have Been Made Against the Templar Order, and Its Mysteries,* 1782), writes that the Gnostic Ophites, like Solomon, had the power to subdue the Archons and their demonic minions by the usage of tokens featuring the pentagram:

> What properly was the sign of the Baffomet, "figura Baffometi," which was depicted on the breast of the bust representing the Creator, cannot be exactly determined. . . . I believe it to have been the Pythagorean pentagon . . . of health and prosperity: . . . It is well known how holy this figure was considered, and that the Gnostics had much in common with the Pythagoreans. From the prayers which the soul shall recite, according to the diagram of the Ophite-worshippers, when they on their return to God are stopped by the Archons, and their purity has to be examined, it appears that these serpent-worshippers believed they must produce a token that they had been clean on earth. I believe

that this token was also the holy pentagon, the sign of their initiation. . . .

Fourteenth to fifteenth-century writer Joannes Marcarius, in his book *Abraxas seu Apistopistus* (as described by Peter N. Miller in *The Antiquary's Art of Comparison: Peiresc and Abraxas*), compares Abraxas to the Trojan horse, for "just as the Greek heroes emerged from its womb, so Abraxas hides in its womb all the family of the gods, whether Egyptian, Greek, Latin, or Persian." Perhaps this is what Charles William King was getting at in his 1887 book *The Gnostics and Their Remains*, when he compared Abraxas to the Egyptian sun deity Horus, drawing from *The Pistis Sophia* as well as from Hindu myths :

> Horus is often figured sailing through the heavens in the sacred boat, the Baris steered by two hawks; solar emblems, with sun and moon overhead, and taking the same titles . . . as the great Abraxas-god himself, and with reason, the same idea being couched in the two personifications. Horus, as Heliodorus records, was also applied to the Nile, whose Greek name . . . also contained the mystic solar number 365; this voyager in the baris is analogous to the Hindoo Neryana, the child floating in his argah leaf upon the face of the waters having his whole body coloured blue. . . . Those common emblems, the baris and the coiled serpent, have their Gnostic meaning fully explained by a remarkable passage in the *Pistis-Sophia*.

This passage he then quotes:

And the disk of the sun was a Great Dragon whose tail was in his mouth, who went up into the Seven Powers on the left hand, being drawn by four

Powers having the similitude of white horses. But the going of the Moon was in the shape of a boat, the rudder whereof showed a male and female dragon with two white cows drawing the same, and the figure of a child on the stern guiding the dragons, who drew away the light from the Rulers (the regular synonym in the book for the rebellious aeons, lords of the Zodiac), and in front of the child was the similitude of a cat.

King also recognized the similarities between Abraxas and Baphomet, as well as the connections between these two characters and other ancient gods such as Osiris. He writes:

> Interesting above the rest for the part it played in medieval superstition is the *Osiris, or old man, with radiated head, a terminal figure always shown in front face with arms crossed on the breast, the true Baphomet of the Templars*. Sometimes he is borne aloft upon the heads of four Angels, upon whom two streams pour forth from his sides. This group has been explained as Ormuzd borne up by the Four Elements; although it may possibly refer to the notion the prophet Enoch mentions [:] "I also beheld the Four Winds which bear up the earth and the firmament of heaven." The idea in truth has rather an Assyrian than Egyptian cast, for in Assyrian works Athor (Mylitta) often appears pouring out from her extended arms the Waters of Life; and again the Persian female Ized Arduisher is by interpretation "the giver of living water."

The image of a figure with two streams of water pouring out his or her left and right sides connects to the Babylonian god Ea or Enki, who is also shown this way, and to the prophet Idris, who is said to live at the crossing of two rivers. It also indicates the throne of God, from under which the rivers of Paradise are said to emerge. King continues on the subject of Abraxas, noting on p. 236 that Abraxas' torso really belongs to a Mithraic soldier:

> An armed man, the Mithraic soldier, one of the figures regularly set up in the mystic Cave of the Solar god, often decorates a talisman, holding a spear tipped with the head of a cock, a mark of honour granted by the Persian kings to distinguished valour (as by Artaxerxes to the Carian who slew Cyrus the Younger); or else grasping a serpent in each hand.

As we saw earlier with the triple "sonships" of Hippolytus' account, Basilides' system is a cosmos created by angels, one of them being the Jewish God of the Old Testament. These blundering world-creating angels are constantly at war with one another, while Christ is thought to be a shape-shifting, phantom spirit sent to save those who have knowledge of the Unknown Father, or the higher god, from this universal crisis. This is the same teaching we find with Simon Magus. In his *Apophasis Megale* of Simon Magus (as paraphrased by Hippolytus in *Refutation of All Heresies*), there are six roots (forming three pairs) on his version of the "Tree of Fire": Mind (*Nous*) and Forethought (*Epinoia*); Voice (*Foni*) and Name (*Onoma*); along with Reasoning (*Logismos*) and Desire (*Enthymesis*). Similarly, according to Irenaeus, Basilides taught that there were six emanations, also in three pairs: Father (*Pater*) and Mind (*Nous*); Word (*Logos*) and Prudence (*Fronesis*); then Power (*Dynamis*) and Wisdom (*Sophia*).

It seems to us that Simon could very well be the "father of all heresies," and that Gnosticism as a whole came largely

Abraxas: Secret of the Temple 405

from his ideas, which ultimately spring from the earlier tradition of John the Baptist. As pointed out by Neil Godfrey at Vridar.org, Basilides was apparently responsible for instituting the festival of the Epiphany of Jesus and of his Baptism on January 6. He gets this from St. Clement of Alexandria's comment from the *Stromata* (XXI, 45) which says:

> And the followers of Basilides hold the day of his baptism as a festival, spending the night before in readings. And they say that it was the fifteenth year of Tiberius Caesar, the fifteenth day of the month of Tubi; and some that it was the eleventh of the same month.

Although Neil Godfrey isn't by any means the first one to point this out, Basilides taught the strange doctrine of Jesus' substitution on the cross—the same idea found in the *Acts of John*, and similar to what is told in *The Koran* (that someone/something that looked like Jesus was crucified in his stead). Writes Godfrey:

> Basilides taught that Jesus somehow was confused with Simon of Cyrene and it was this Simon who was crucified in his place. Jesus, being supernaturally related to God or Mind was able to change his appearance at will, and so escaped crucifixion and was taken, laughing at how he had deceived mere mortals, to heaven. Thus the Pauline theme of the mocked Archontes/Rulers was maintained, but in the process the crucifixion was denied—a denial we see repeated in the *Acts of John* and in the *Koran* of Islam.

In Tracy R. Twyman's book *The Judas Goat: The Substitution Theory of the Crucifixion*, she discusses various texts that support the idea that the crucifixion was a hoax, an idea suggested by the authors of *Holy Blood, Holy Grail*. She starts off by comparing a passage from *The Second Treatise of the Great Seth* and a passage from *The Koran*. The latter source tells us, "They did not slay him, neither crucified him, only a likeness of that was shown to them." Likewise, in *The Second Treatise of the Great Seth*, Jesus says:

> I did not succumb to them as they had planned. . . . And I did not die in reality but in appearance, lest I be put to shame by them. . . . For my death which they think happened [happened] to them in their error and blindness, since they nailed their man unto their death. . . . It was another, their father, who drank the gall and the vinegar; it was not I. They struck me with the reed; it was another, Simon, who bore the cross on his shoulder. It was another upon whom they placed the crown of thorns. . . . And I was laughing at their ignorance.

For Basilides, it was Simon of Cyrene, not Jesus, who was crucified. In *A Separate God*, Simone Petrement remarks on this subject:

> Simon of Cyrene is the man who carries the cross; this allowed a religious thinker who loved symbols to take it as a symbol of the part of Jesus that carried (that is, suffered) the cross. Moreover, Ph. Carrington has shown that this idea could have been suggested by a literal interpretation of Mark's Gospel (15:1-15). As Jesus' name is not expressly mentioned by Mark after that of Simon of Cyrene, the pronominal forms (*aton, atuo, autou*) in what follows might be interpreted as referring to Simon. Finally, the idea that the cross was a trap that

ridiculed the executioners, together with the reference to a psalm that is considered prophetic (*Psalms* 2:4), might have led someone to say that at the moment of crucifixion Christ "laughed." But, for Basilides, Jesus truly suffered.

Indeed, the Laughing Jesus is not only present in *Seth*, but also in *The Gospel of Judas*. It is also a characteristic associated with Docetism, since if Jesus was never incarnated in the flesh, the crucifixion must have been illusory. This is what the Docetists were getting at: the images aren't of his true nature, because he is not limited by the material world, but he manifests in ways familiar to us so that he can be comprehended. In *The Gospel of Judas*, we see Jesus laugh quite a few times, especially at the folly and stupidity of his disciples, because they blindly worship a lesser god. There we read:

> One day he was with his disciples in Judea, and he found them gathered together and seated in pious observance. When he [approached] his disciples, gathered together and seated and offering a prayer of thanksgiving over the bread, [he] laughed. The disciples said to [him], "Master, why are you laughing at [our] prayer of thanksgiving? We have done what is right." He answered and said to them, "I am not laughing at you. You are not doing this because of your own will but because it is through this that your god [will be] praised."

Jesus, as being representative of the "immortal generation" (the heavenly Aeons), laughs at the foolish piousness of his disciples since they worship the inferior creator, Jehovah who is rendered as Ialdabaoth in this text. Oddly though, Ialdabaoth isn't depicted as a megalomaniacal foolish angel like he is in other Gnostic texts. He also is not said to have been involved in creation, nor is he shown to rebel against the divine order. Creation is a job relegated to Saklas, who is a different Archon altogether in *The Gospel of Judas*. In this text, the Archons are intentionally created by the luminary Eleleth (whose name sounds a lot like "Lilith") to bring order to chaos. They don't actually rebel until they create humanity, and it isn't Ialdabaoth who does that, but Saklas. In *The Apocryphon of John*, Saklas is another name for Ialdabaoth, which means "blind fool." This isn't the case in *The Gospel of Judas*, however. There, we read:

> [Eleleth] said, "Let twelve angels come into being [to] rule over chaos and the [underworld].'"And look, from the cloud there appeared an [angel] whose face flashed with fire and whose appearance was defiled with blood. His name was Nebro, which means "rebel"; others call him Yaldabaoth. Another angel, Saklas, also came from the cloud.

Nebro is here used as the alternate name for Ialdabaoth (spelled Yaldabaoth in this text). Saklas is clearly presented as a different Archon altogether. Yaldabaoth and Saklas create inferior Archons to rule over the lower universe and the underworld. However, it's only Saklas who creates the earth and humanity. Ialdabaoth seems to have a very miniscule role in *The Gospel of Judas*' creation narrative, where it says.

> Then Saklas said to his angels, "Let us create a human being after the likeness and after the image." They fashioned Adam and his wife Eve, who is called, in the cloud, Zoe. For by this name all the generations seek the man, and each of them calls the woman by these names.

Abraxas: Secret of the Temple 409

The text quotes Jesus as saying that there will be those who will sacrifice to Saklas in his name at the End Times. So again, Saklas is given prominence over Ialdabaoth. Which begs the question: Is *The Gospel of Judas'* Yaldabaoth actually evil? Nebro is obviously a demonic entity. But again, the Archons are an intentional creation in this text. They are meant to bring order to the lower world. However, after Yaldabaoth creates the other Archons to reign over the rest of the lower universe, Saklas creates humanity without Yaldabaoth. Could it be that this is the author's way of saying that angels and demons both worked to bring order out of chaos during creation, even to the depths of the underworld? *The Gospel of Judas* may be a text written by someone who was influenced by Sethianism, but not actually Sethian. Or it could have been a non-Sethian text that was eventually adopted by Sethians and redacted with Sethian features, as other scholars such as John Turner have argued.

Let us note that just as there are multiple men named James in the New Testament (James the brother of John and James the brother of Jesus), and multiple Judases (Judas Iscariot, Judas Thaddeus, and Judas Thomas Didymus, all of whom Tracy R. Twyman suspects are based on the same person), there are multiple Simons as well (including Simon of Cyrene, Simon Peter, Simon the Zealot and Simon Magus, all of whom we theorize are based on the latter Simon). The claim that Simon of Cyrene helped Jesus carry his cross is most likely the result of misinterpreted teachings by Simon Magus (who, as we mentioned earlier, may even be the inspiration for the character of Paul as well). In *Galatians* 2:20, Paul states "I am crucified with Christ," perhaps a hint at this idea.

410 Chapter 8

Returning to Tracy Twyman's theories about the substitution of Jesus on the cross, in *The Judas Goat*, she goes into the subject of the Judaic rituals of the Passover and Yom Kippur, connecting them not only to the sacrifice of Jesus (naturally), but also Azazel and Baphomet. She brings up what Sir James Frazer wrote in *The Golden Bough* about the archetype of the sacrificial king, of which the story of the crucifixion of the messiah Jesus is an example. Into this she introduces the idea of a twin king sacrifice (mentioned by Frazer as being a common theme in antiquity). Basically, the concept is that there are two "kings" who are somehow "twins," or at least they metaphorically mirror one another, but one is a dark character, while the other one represents the universal light. The "white" king has his life sacrificed for the redemption of creation, while the "black" king takes the blame for the killing and sacrifices his soul. A perfect example would be the sacrifice of Abel, for which Cain took the blame. In the case of Judas Iscariot, he took the blame for the sacrifice of Jesus.

Twyman makes the case that he is probably the same as Judas Thomas (a.k.a. "Thomas Didymus," a.k.a. "Judas Thaddeus"). Since both "Thomas" and "Didymus" are words meaning "twin," there have been heretics who believed that he was literally Jesus' twin (although, if true, it would be quite an oversight for the Gospels not to overtly mention it). But we do know for sure that Judas Thaddeus is a biological brother of Jesus, as the Gospels identify him thusly. We also know that Judas Thomas Didymus and Judas Thaddeus are widely thought to be the same, and are even depicted with the same features in Christian iconography. *The Gospel of Barnabus*, a medieval forgery influenced by Islam, said that Jesus used magic to make Judas Iscariot appear in his likeness and allowed him to be crucified in his stead.

Abraxas: Secret of the Temple

What Twyman suggests is that this story is an echo of a heretical belief that may have once been held by certain people, in which Thomas, and all of the Judes and Judases, were thought to be the same person: Jesus' twin. She suggests that this other character, whether literally his twin, or just metaphorically a second Christ (a black messiah), may have died on the cross, while the real Jesus took his identity and moved on to India, where he was known as Saint Thomas. Eventually, he may have revealed his true identity to some of the Indians, for there are local stories about both Thomas and Jesus (the latter known there as "Saint Isa") visiting the region.

Reflecting this possibility, what is most intriguing is Jesus' bizarrely intimate relationship with Judas Iscariot, which, Twyman points out, is illustrated in the Gospels. She writes:

> The fact that Jesus predicts Judas' betrayal, and that Judas does not seem surprised at the accusation, is telling. So too is the fact that Jesus makes no attempt to stop him from doing this, but instead tells him to hurry up and get it over with. . . . Later that night, when Judas arrives with the Roman guards to arrest him, Jesus is fully aware of what is about to befall him. He allows Judas to come up and identify him to the Romans by kissing him on the cheek, saying "Hail Rabbi." Jesus plays his part accordingly, replying, "Judas, betrayest thou the son of Man with a kiss?" More than that, Jesus is shown as actually rushing out with his disciples to meet Judas and the Roman guards. In *Matthew*, he wakes his sleeping apostles just before Judas' arrival and says, "Rise, let us be going: behold, he is at hand that doth betray me." Thus, many scholars believe

that the entire "betrayal" scenario was concocted, rehearsed, and enacted in collusion between Jesus and Judas.

But it may not have been all an act on Judas' part, for as Twyman reveals, Jesus seems to have deliberately infected Judas with a demonic spirit using black magic. In *John* 13:26-27, Jesus hands Judas a morsel of food, declaring to the other apostles that the person he is giving it to is destined to betray him. As soon as Judas swallows it, "Satan entered into him." Then Jesus commands the now-possessed Judas: "What you are going to do, do quickly." This is a kind of negative communion. Instead of the Holy Spirit, an evil spirit is introduced into the body, and henceforth this spirit assumes authority there.

Or it may indeed have been the Holy Spirit, for as we have mentioned, not everyone has always thought of the Holy Spirit as being something "nice." (The Mandaeans certainly don't.) Hammer-Purgstall theorized that it was, to the Gnostics, the same thing as Sophia, and therefore, for the Templars, connected to the female aspect of Baphomet. Also, Judas Thomas and Judas Thaddeus (again, most likely the same person) are both shown in Christian iconography with a flame burning upon the brow, in between the eyes. This is said to represent the Holy Spirit that descended upon him and inspired him with *glossolalia* (speaking in tongues) during the miracle of the Pentecost. Since Eliphas Levi's Baphomet (as well as the goat icon of the Aniza tribe of Arabs, discussed later on) is shown with a flaming torch on his brow in the same spot, in between his horns, we can only assume that this represents the Holy Spirit as well.

Returning to the subject of demonic possession, let us recall that Basilides' son Isidore claimed that every human being is surrounded by a multitude of spirits at all times, and these spirits influence the decisions of each person by manipulating their thought patterns at a subliminal level. There is no strict dichotomy of possessed and unpossessed. Rather, each individual is influenced by these attachments to greater and lesser degrees. Clement of Alexandria wrote thusly in *Stromata* (II.20):

> Accordingly, Basilides' son himself, Isidorus, in his book, *About the Soul*, . . . while agreeing in the dogma, as if condemning himself, writes in these words: "For if I persuade any one that the soul is undivided, and that the passions of the wicked are occasioned by the violence of the appendages, the worthless among men will have no slight pretense for saying, 'I was compelled, I was carried away, I did it against my will, I acted unwillingly;' though he himself led the desire of evil things, and did not fight against the assaults of the appendages. But we must, by acquiring superiority in the rational part, show ourselves masters of the inferior creation in us."

This sounds a lot like the "body thetans" of Scientology. *The Greek Magical Papyri* contains a spell for strength that involves Abraxas. While this is admittedly speculative, we can see that this magical spell may have been used to cast out these spiritual attachments from the user (a self-exorcism?), allowing him to become a god-like being:

> "PHNOUNEBEE' (2 times), give me Your Strength, IO' ABRASAX, give me Your Strength, for I am ABRASAX!" Say it 7 times while holding your two Thumbs. [PGM LXIX.1-3]
>
> . . .

Persephone baptizing an initiate at the ancient Rites of Eleusis.

Above: St. Thomas Didymus, with the torch of wisdom burning on his brow, just like Levi's Baphomet. Below: The Scythian anguipede goddess Api, forerunner of the Melusine.

Illustrations from *The Book of Abraham the Jew*, 1624, showing the crucified serpent and the slaughtering of babes to produce the "Bath of the Stars."

Above: Gnostic talisman with Gorgon head invoking Sabaoth, "the Lord of Hosts." Below: From *Rossarium Philosophorum*, 1550.

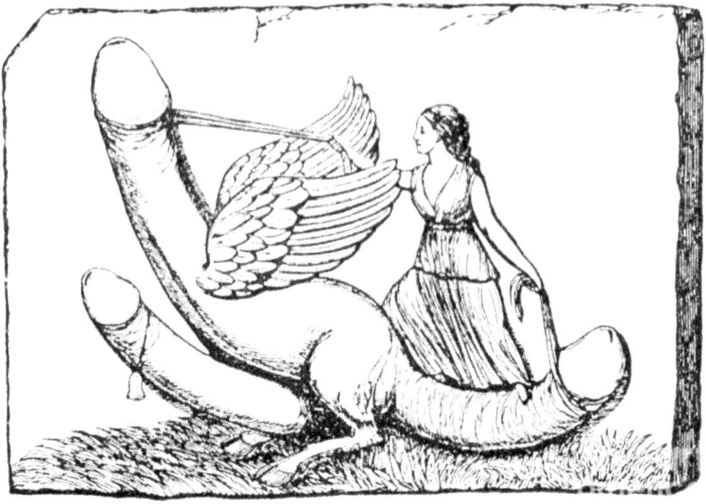

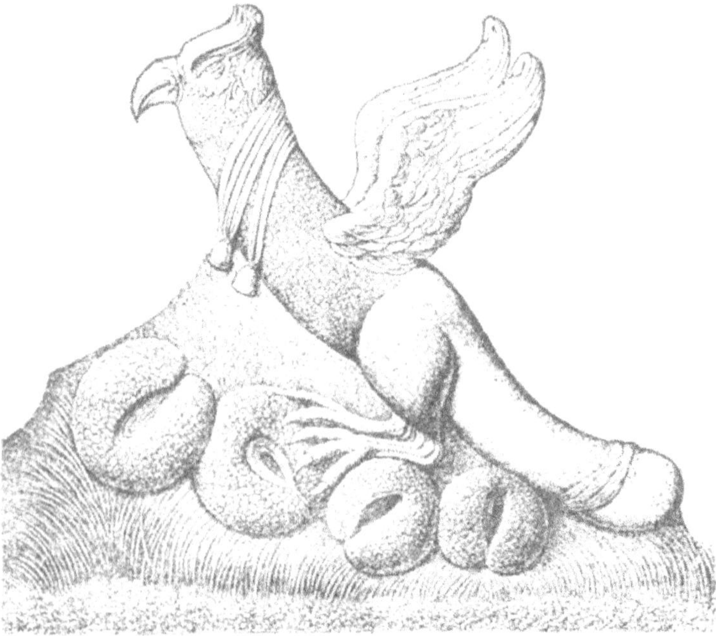

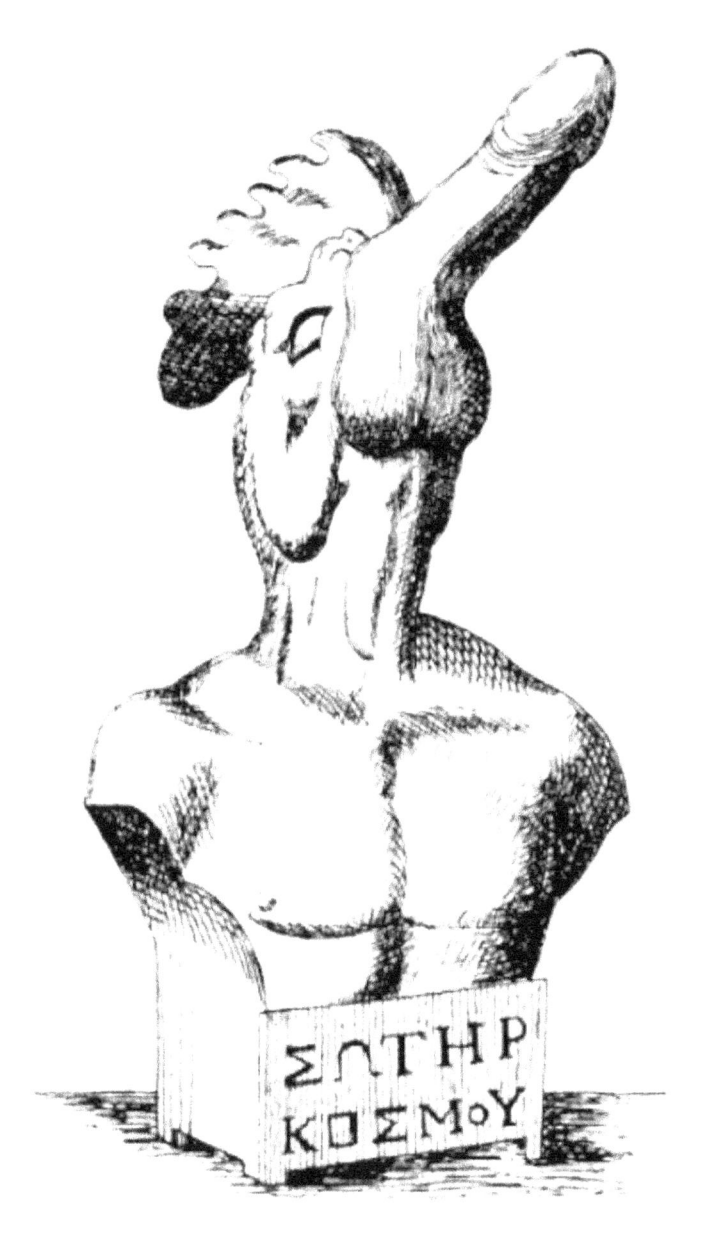

Above: "The Saviour of the World," once on display at the Vatican.
Opposite page: Priapian talismans.

Above left: Anguipede giant grasping thunderbolt protruding from his side on Roman denarius, 45 BC. Compare this to the Abraxas coin, above right. Below: Chnoubis and Abraxas talismans, both taken from *The Gnostics and Their Remains* by Charles William King. Opposite Page: Gnostic talismans among the coins found by Hammer-Purgstall on former Templar properties.

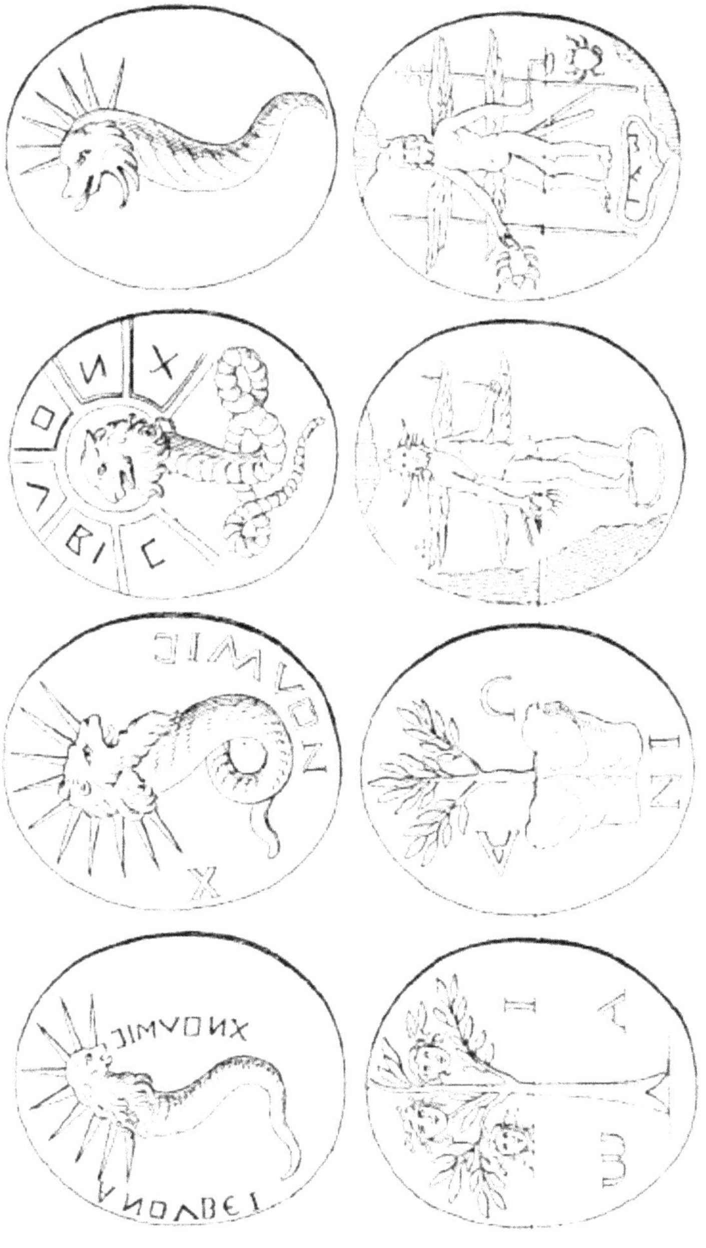

Above, and below left: Three different designs of Templar Abraxas seals. Below right: Abraxas token from *Index of Illumination*, identical to one featured among Hammer-Purgstall's "Templar finds."

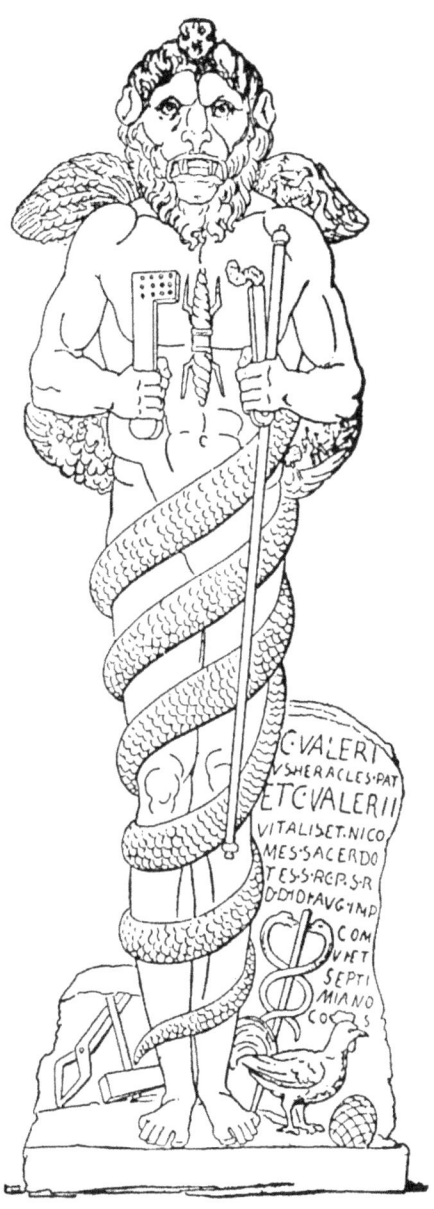

Aion, the leontocephaline gatekeeper, reminiscent of Ialdabaoth, Abraxas and Asclepius. Found at a second-century mithraeum at Ostia Antica, Italy.

"Everyone fears Your Great Might. Grant me the Good Things: The Strength of AKRYSKYLOS, the Speech of EUO'NOS, the Eyes of Solomon, the Voice of ABRASAX, the Grace of ADO'NIOS, the God. Come to me, Kypris, every day! The Hidden Name bestowed to You: THOATHOE'THATHO-OYTHAETHO'USTHOAITHITHE'THOINTHO'; grant me Victory, Repute, Beauty toward all Men and all Women!" [*PGM* XCII.1-16]

Perhaps in this spell, the initiate would actually *become* Abraxas and, in essence, control his or her fate in the process. In other words, from a theurgical perspective, the theurgist becomes what is invoked. The invocation would essentially dissolve the "egoic self" of the magician and such a person would become divinized by the indwelling spirit. Stephen Skinner writes in *Techniques of Graeco-Egyptian Magic* that "theurgy" and "goetia" are two different approaches to working magic:

> The Greeks made a clear distinction between *goetia* . . . the magic of the *goes,* . . . and that of *theurgia*. . . . It is difficult to be sure of what was exactly meant by the ancient Greeks when they used the term [*goetia*], as it was associated with rites for the dead. *Goetia* . . . and *goes* . . . were later used in the sense they acquired in the Latin grimoires of "dealing with spirits," rather than in the sense . . . of "dealing with the dead."
>
> . . .
>
> Theurgia is a quite separate category, and is a descendant, via Porphyry and Iamblichus of Chalcis, of the ancient Mysteries. This usage has persisted through to 13th century (and later) grimoires. It has

been suggested that *theurgia*, meaning "divine work," was a term that might even have been invented by the group of Neoplatonically-inclined magicians, including luminaries like Iamblichus, probably based in Alexandria around the 2nd century CE. The theurgists were concerned with purifying and raising the consciousness of individual practitioners to the point where they could have direct communion with the gods.

. . .

The *goes,* . . . the practitioner of *goetia,* . . . on the other hand, attempts to bring daimones/demons onto the physical plane and to manifest them, or their effects. The relationship of the practitioners of *theurgia* to practitioners of the *goetia* is that both attempt to invoke/evoke a spiritual creature (be it god, daimon, angel or demon). The *teletai* . . . priest does it for the benefit of the client's immortal soul while the *goes* does it to benefit the client's material desires.

In *Plaster Perspectives on "Magical Gems": Rethinking the Meaning of "Magic" in Cornell's Dactyliotheca*, Caitlin E. Barrett takes a more historical perspective on magic:

Originally derived from *magos* (a word referring to Persian priests), the terms *mageia* and *magia* could describe a wide range of practices, including the use of potions and drugs, the casting of binding spells, the practice of necromancy, the control of natural phenomena, and more. One of the things these seemingly diverse actions had in common was their stigmatization: for the most part, *mageia* and *magia* had negative connotations. In the Roman empire, many types of magic were illegal and punishable with severe penalties, such as death or exile. Even when not illegal, actions classifiable as *mageia* or *magia* typically incurred social disapproval—despite the fact that many such activities, such as the casting of binding spells, appear to have been extremely common in practice.

Not surprisingly, this is exactly how Irenaeus describes the Gnostic followers of Basilides in *Against Heresies* (1:24.5-6):

These men, moreover, practise magic; and use images, incantations, invocations, and every other kind of curious art. Coining also certain names as if they were those of the angels, they proclaim some of these as belonging to the first, and others to the second heaven; and then they strive to set forth the names, principles, angels, and powers of the three hundred and sixty-five imagined heavens. They also affirm that the barbarous name in which the Saviour ascended and descended, is Caulacau. He, then, who has learned [these things], and known all the angels and their causes, is rendered invisible and incomprehensible to the angels and all the powers, even as Caulacau also was.

For these Gnostics, "Caulacau" was, as Ireneaus states, actually a secret barbarous name for Jesus Christ. At Jesus8880.com, Daniel Gleason writes about *isopsephia* (the ancient Greek practice of gematria in which hidden meaning is found based on the numerical values of Greek letters):

Basilides was absolutely famous for combining mathematics with religion. Orthodox Christians viewed the practice of *isopsephia* as a kind of "number magic" and the graphing of diagrams (images) as "another kind of curious art." There are three *isopsehia* riddles hidden in Irenaeus' account: The barbarous name "Caulacau" is a pun on *Isaiah* 28:9-13 which reads . . . "To whom would God impart knowledge (gnosis)? To whom would he convey the message? . . . [F]or them the Word of the Lord shall be: command upon command, line upon line, here a little there a little." The Hebrew pronunciation for the words "command" and "line" is SAU-LASAU and CAU-LACAU! Amazingly, it appears no one before me has bothered to compute the *isopsephia* value of the Greek spelling for the name Cau-la-cau (Kaeu-lae-kaeu). The answer is "888," the same number as Jesus! The "coined name" Caulacau is thus a clever Gnostic riddle that equates the name Jesus with gnosis (knowledge)!

The father of Neo-Platonism, named Plotinus, also similarly described the Gnostics as "magicians" and "sorcerers" for using the barbarous names for the Ineffable in his polemic in the *Ennead* 2.9, titled "Against the Gnostics: Against Those That Affirm the Creator of the Cosmos and the Cosmos Itself to Be Evil":

> In the sacred formulas they inscribe, purporting to address the Supernal Beings—not merely the Soul but even the Transcendents—they are simply uttering spells and appeasements and evocations in the idea that these Powers will obey a call and be led about by a word from any of us who is in some degree trained to use the appropriate forms in the appropriate way—certain melodies, certain sounds, specially directed breathings, sibilant cries, and all else to which is ascribed magic potency upon the

Supreme. Perhaps they would repudiate any such
intention: still they must explain how these things
act upon the unembodied: they do not see that the
power they attribute to their own words is so much
taken away from the majesty of the divine.

Plotinus resented the Gnostics' demonization of Plato's Demiurge, the creator of the material cosmos. Plotinus believed the Gnostics had corrupted the original teachings of Plato to suit their world-views. In fact, Plotinus goes as far as to mock the Gnostic creation story of the fall of Sophia and the aborted Demiurge as surpassing "sheer folly." Plotinus also took issue with the Gnostics' neglect of the pursuit of virtue, maintaining themselves as beyond reproach of the laws of the world. His view is of course influenced by the rumors of their supposed hedonistic and libertine tendencies. He wrote:

For they manufacture these doctrines as though
they were not in contact with the ancient thought of
the Greeks; for the Greeks knew, and spoke clearly
without pomposity, of ascents from the cave,
coming closer and closer by gradual stages to a truer
vision.

This was a problem for Plotinus, who thought these Platonizing Sethian Gnostics were mucking-up philosophy with their static dualism, world-hatred, and defamation of the creator. Plotinus caricatured the Sethians as rubes for practicing magic. Needless to say, many Neoplatonists such as him didn't like Gnostics very much (despite the obvious similarities between the two groups). Yet the Sethian Gnostics weren't a unified movement, but rather a diverse set of small cult communities—the Borborites, Archontics, Ophites, etc.

Neither Plotinus nor Irenaeus were lying about the Gnostics' ritual magic tendencies, since their texts indicate this interest. These Gnostic magicians more than likely invoked the name of Abraxas among other barbarous, secret names of God. *On the Origin of the World* contains a compendium of demon names that is attributed to King Solomon, so it is possible that some Gnostics practiced early Solomonic magic. The text explains that when Sabaoth was redeemed, Ialdabaoth, "the prime parent of chaos" immediately became jealous of his son's stature and created Death (i.e. Samael), taking the place of Sabaoth in the sixth heaven while creating lesser demons:

> Then Death, being androgynous, mingled with his (own) nature and begot seven androgynous offspring. These are the names of the male ones: Jealousy, Wrath, Tears, Sighing, Suffering, Lamentation, Bitter Weeping. And these are the names of the female ones: Wrath, Pain, Lust, Sighing, Curse, Bitterness, Quarrelsomeness. They had intercourse with one another, and each one begot seven, so that they amount to forty-nine androgynous demons. Their names and their effects you will find in the *Book of Solomon*.

"Their effects" probably meant the abilities they could be compelled to use if summoned, like in *The Goetia*. The "Book of Solomon" referred to here could very well be the same as, or an earlier version of, *The Testament of Solomon*.

Another example of spells and incantations that were employed by Gnostics is provided by Karen King in *What is Gnosticism?*, where she talks about the demonic correspondences to human body parts listed so thoroughly in the long recension of *The Apocryphon of John* (highlighting the inherent corruption of the body), which was intended for use in rituals to heal the sick or injured. *On the Origin of the World* also perpetuates the idea that demons are associated with the passions of the flesh. It says:

> This ignorance, my child, is the first torment; the second is grief; the third is incontinence; the fourth, lust; the fifth, injustice; the sixth, greed; the seventh, deceit; the eighth, envy; the ninth, treachery; the tenth, anger; the eleventh, recklessness; the twelfth, malice. These are twelve in number, but under them are many more besides, my child, and they use the prison of the body to torture the inward person with the sufferings of sense. Yet they withdraw (if not all at once) from one to whom God has shown mercy, and this is the basis of rebirth, the means and method.

We also see similar ideas being promoted by Zosimos in *The Final Quittance*, where he encourages his disciple Theosebeia to be initiated in the mysteries of Poimandres (Hermes) and to baptize herself in the Hermetic bowl of Mind. Here is the relevant passage, as quoted by GRS Mead in *Thrice-Greatest Hermes, Vol. 3*:

> But be not thou, O lady, [thus] distracted, as, too, I bade thee in the actualizing [rites], and do not turn thyself about this way and that in seeking after God; but in thy house be still, and God shall come to thee, He who is everywhere and not in some wee spot as are daimonian things. And having stilled thyself in body, still thou thyself in passions too—desire, [and] pleasure, rage [and] grief, and the twelve fates of Death. And thus set straight and upright, call thou unto thyself Divinity; and truly shall He come, He who is everywhere and [yet] nowhere. And [then],

Abraxas: Secret of the Temple 431

without invoking them, perform the sacred rites unto the daimones,—not such as offer things to them and soothe and nourish them, but such as turn them from thee and destroy their power, which Mambres taught to Solomon, King of Jerusalem, and all that Solomon himself wrote down from his own wisdom. And if thou shalt effectively perform these rites, thou shalt obtain the physical conditions of pure birth. And so continue till thou perfect thy soul completely. *And when thou knowest surely that thou art perfected in thyself, then spurn . . . from thee the natural things of matter, and make for harbour in Poemandres' arms, and having dowsed thyself within His Cup, return again unto thy own [true] race.*

As we saw earlier in the previous chapter, Epiphanius conflated the myth of the lewd Sophia or "Prunikos" with that of Barbelo of Sethian Gnosticism (which is the female hypostatized version of the highest divine realm outside of the Father). There she sets out to collect and "reabsorb" the living sparks of power that were stolen from her by her retarded son, Ialdabaoth and his legion of Archons. She appeared to the Archons in a beautiful form, seduced them, and took their sperm, which contained the power originally belonging to her. (Recall that the she-demon Lilith was also believed to steal sperm from human males as they slept.) Epiphanius repeats this in further detail in *Panarion* (1:21, 2, 2:5) by connecting the Barbelo myth with the story of Simon Magus and his consort Helena:

For these angels went to war over the power from on high—they call her Prunicus, but she is called Barbero or Barbelo by other sects—because she displayed her beauty [and] drove them wild, and was sent for this purpose, to despoil the archons who had made this world. She has suffered no harm, but she brought them to the point of slaughtering each other from the lust for her that she aroused in them. And detaining her so that she should not go back up, they all had relations with her in each of her womanly and female bodies—for she kept migrating from female bodies into various bodies of human beings, cattle and the rest—so that, by the deeds they were doing in killing and being killed, they would cause their own diminution through the shedding of blood. Then, by gathering the power again, she would be able to ascend to heaven once more. . . .

But others honor one "Prunicus" and like these, when they consummate their own passions with this kind of disgusting behavior, they say in mythological language of this interpretation of their disgusting behavior, "We are gathering the power of Prunicus from our bodies, and through their emissions." That is, [they suppose they are gathering] the power of semen and menses. . . . For if they say, "Prunicus," this is just a belch of lustfulness and incontinence. Anything called "prunicus" suggests a thing named for copulation, and the enterprise of seduction.

Despite the strong erotic imagery used in Gnostic myth, many Gnostic texts, such as *The Pistis Sophia* (147:387), explicitly condemn the practices of ritually consuming sperm, menstrual blood, and fetal embryos in the strongest terms. In that book, a certain question put to Jesus by Thomas concerning such matters relates directly to the story in *Genesis* 25 of Jacob and Esau (the latter selling his "birthright" to the former for red lentil porridge). We read:

> Thomas said: "We have heard that there are some on the earth who take the male seed and the female monthly blood, and make it into a lentil porridge and eat it, saying: 'We have faith in Esau and Jacob.' Is this then seemly or not?"
>
> Jesus was wroth with the world in that hour and said unto Thomas: "Amen, I say: This sin is more heinous than all sins and iniquities. Such men will straightway be taken into the outer darkness and not be cast back anew into the sphere, but they shall perish, be destroyed in the outer darkness in a region where there is neither pity nor light, but howling and grinding of teeth. And all the souls which shall be brought into the outer darkness, will not be cast back anew, but will be destroyed and dissolved."

The passage above certainly reflects a time in late antiquity when Gnostics were being accused of such activities. Here Jesus says that there will be no mercy for people who do this, and that they will not enter the bridal chamber with Sophia and the Savior, but will inherit the "outer darkness" instead. The second book of the Gnostic *Jeu*, Chapter 43, also condemns this practice. However, groups like the Barbelites felt that by these practices, "light" contained in their sexual emissions could be released back to the Supreme God, and therefore bypass the reproductive system that added more souls to bodies under the authority of the wrathful Jehovah.

Another writer, Roger Pearse, in his article "Summing up the ancient accounts of the Borborites-Phibionites," points out that spreading rumors of ritual orgies being practiced by one's religious enemies isn't exactly a new practice:

> The testimony of Epiphanius has often been impugned, and for obvious reasons. For his description of a communion ritual which involves fornication and eating babies is uncomfortably like the accusation made against the Christians, and rebutted by Athenagoras (c.31-36) and Tertullian (*Apol*. 7). Origen tells us that Jews accused Christians of immorality and eating babies (*Contra Celsum* 6, 27). Mandaean heretics also accused Christians of ritual horrors (Right *Ginza* IX = Lidzbarski 227, 8 ff.).
>
> In turn similar accusations are made against Montanists by Epiphanius (*Pan*. 48.14.6) and Cyril of Jerusalem (Cat. 16, 18), although queried by Jerome (Ep. 41, 4.1) and in *Praedestinatus* (chap. 26). Augustine accuses the Manichaeans of the same in *De haeresibus* 46. Even Tertullian, as a Montanist, accuses some Catholics of immoral agapes (*De ieiunio* 17).
>
> . . .
>
> It seems possible that the aborted baby-eating story really does reflect something real, something tried once and found revolting and not done again, and told to the young Epiphanius (and quite possibly misunderstood by him). Life was cheap. Those involved in ancient magic might do horrible things, and at the low end of society, there might not be a great distance between a gnostic, a sorcerer, or a wandering sophist-cum-conman. We are entirely familiar today with those who try to push the boundaries, to gain notoriety. But then again . . .

maybe it was just a cheap rumour, circulating at the time, and included willy-nilly by Epiphanius.

At this time . . . we cannot tell. In the end, his statement cannot be confirmed or refuted. Perhaps we should simply leave it at that.

It is probable that a few of these cults embraced these practices, and were lumped together with Gnostics by their enemies. The Valentinian Christians, especially Marcus the Magician, were accused of seducing women from their congregation by Irenaeus, but there is no mention of the spermatic mass in his report. In *Against Heresies*, Irenaeus claimed Marcus the Magician to be a "precursor of the Antichrist," ("Satan" being his "true father"), and a "follower" of the "fallen and mighty angel Azazel" who had been initiated by the "Magi." Irenaeus said of him that "he is regarded by his senseless and cracked-brain followers as working miracles by these means." As you can tell, Irenaeus didn't particularly like Marcus. One member of the Catholic clergy, Justin Martyr (c. 110–160) who lived during the height of the heretics, regarded the rumors against them with skepticism, writing in *1 Apology* 26 to the Roman Emperor Antoninus Pius:

> Whether they perpetuate those fabulous and shameful deeds—the upsetting of the lamp, and promiscuous intercourse, and eating human flesh— we know not.

(As previously noted, this "upsetting of the lamp" may be the same practice represented in one of the alleged "Templar" images discovered by Hammer-Purgstall, which depicts a woman using a vase of water to extinguish the candles on a menorah.)

So we find that Justin himself was skeptical of the rumors being spread against the Christians. In Celsus' refutation of Christianity, he claims the "Christians" (who were really the Ophites) were a secret society that practiced sorcery, sexual immorality and cannibalism. Writers like Justin Martyr and Tertullian were simply trying to deflect these rumors, while condemning the Romans for their own perversions.

Returning to the subject of Abraxas, in *The Seven Sermons of the Dead*, Carl Jung refers to the figure as an "emergence" of form from the hidden depth of the Godhead. He says that it embodies opposing powers that are fused together into a sort of yin/yang relationship:

> Abraxas is the god whom it is difficult to know. His power is the very greatest, because man does not perceive it at all. Man sees the supreme good of the sun, and also the endless evil of the devil, but Abraxas, he does not see, for he is undefinable life itself, which is the mother of good and evil alike. . . . Abraxas is the sun and also the eternally gaping abyss of emptiness, of the diminisher and dissembler, the devil. The power of Abraxas is twofold. You can not see it, because in your eyes the opposition of this power seems to cancel it out. That which is spoken by God-the-Sun is life; that which is spoken by the Devil is death. Abraxas, however, speaks the venerable and also accursed word, which is life and death at once. Abraxas generates truth and falsehood, good and evil, light and darkness with the same word and in the same deed. Therefore Abraxas is truly the terrible one. He is magnificent even as the lion at the very moment

when he strikes his prey down. His beauty is like the beauty of a spring morn.

Readers are often in awe at the sheer uniqueness of this text when compared with other more typical Gnostic writings. For example, whereas Gnostic tradition describes the "Pleroma" as the fullness of Light and the Aeons, this text calls it a void in which nothing and everything cancel each other out. In Jung's view, existence (*creatura*) happens only outside of the Pleroma. The greatest of all the existent beings is "Abraxas," who is described by Jung as the Pleroma manifest as God. The most interesting aspect of this doctrine is that Abraxas is the soul in which "God" and "Devil" intersect. Whereas most Gnostic traditions say that salvation means returning to the Pleroma, this text says instead that each person has their own god that corresponds to one of the stars in the heavens, and that it is through them that people will receive their salvation. (This is reminiscent of Aleister Crowley's proclamation in the channeled *Book of the Law,* written 12 years earlier**,** that "Every man and every woman is a star.") There seems to be a warning in the text to avoid Abraxas and seek the personal god instead.

According to *H. G. Baynes*' introduction to the 1916 edition, Carl Jung actually attributed the *Sermons* to several different historical figures:

> In the original journal account of the revelation (*Black Book* 6) Jung himself is the voice speaking the *Seven Sermons to the Dead*. In the version transcribed into the *Red Book* manuscript, Jung gives Philemon as the voice speaking the Sermons. Interestingly, a few pages later, on the last page of the *Red Book* manuscript, Philemon is identified with the historical Gnostic prophet Simon Magus.

When Jung subsequently transcribed the Sermons for printing as an independent text, the Sermons were attributed pseudepigraphically to yet another historical second century Gnostic teacher, Basilides of Alexandria. Thus Jung, Philemon, Simon Magus, and Basilides are all finally conflated together in the voice of the Gnostic prophet who speaks the *Septem Sermones ad Mortuos*.

As we have said, in the *Sermons*, Abraxas is said to be the supreme existent deity, containing within itself all good and evil, as well as everything and nothing. The "Pleroma" is said to be a form of nothing because the everything and the nothing cancel each other out. Here is a quote from *Sermon I*:

Harken: I begin with nothingness. Nothingness is the same as fullness. In infinity full is no better than empty. Nothingness is both empty and full. As well might ye say anything else of nothingness, as for instance, white is it, or black, or again, it is not, or it is. A thing that is infinite and eternal hath no qualities, since it hath all qualities.

This nothingness or fullness we name the PLEROMA. Therein both thinking and being cease, since the eternal and infinite possess no qualities. In it no being is, for he then would be distinct from the pleroma, and would possess qualities which would distinguish him as something distinct from the pleroma.

In the pleroma there is nothing and everything. It is quite fruitless to think about the pleroma, for this would mean self-dissolution.

Abraxas: Secret of the Temple 439

Abraxas in this sense was just one of the many symbols Jung would use to represent the ancient doctrine of *Coniunctio Oppositorum* (the Conjunction of Opposites). Jung's Gnostic vision of 1916, with its bipolar Abraxas, written under the persona of Basilides, has virtually no connection to the actual teachings of the historical Basilides. Jung claimed that Abraxas was the embodiment of the Monad, whereas the ancient heretics viewed Abraxas as a lower aeon or even an Archon. Abraxas, like Baphomet, becomes a "syzygy" of an alchemical pair conjoined, combining good and evil, darkness and light, Christ and Antichrist, God and the Devil. The symbolism involved is similar to that of the Tree of Knowledge of Good and Evil in *Genesis*. Abraxas could also be seen as a synthesis of Michael the Archangel and the Great Dragon of *Revelation* 12:9. ("And the great dragon was cast out, that old serpent, called the Devil, and Satan, which deceiveth the whole world. . . .")

So you can see that there is considerable discrepancy between the Western occult view, which seeks a union of opposites as the ultimate goal, and Gnostic systems that seek to separate light from darkness through purification. This issue is muddied even further by Carl Jung, who associates Gnosticism with his doctrine of *Coniunctio Oppositorum*. There weren't very many "Gnostic" texts available during Jung's time, so perhaps that's why he projects so many of his own views on to the concept of Gnosticism.

When viewed through a dualist lens, the intermingling of good and evil is in actuality the fall from Eden, the tragedy that gave rise to human suffering and all the world's horrors. The classical Gnostics viewed spirit as the original unity, with matter being a shallow imitation of this higher reality. In this estimation, the light is seen as the only eternal principle, while the world of matter is simply a passing shadow, a temporary setback or foul-up in the scheme of infinity that will eventually be rectified. A more radical interpretation of dualism, found in the Manichean Gnostic religion (and in the Persian religion of Zoroastrianism that preceded it), has light and darkness existing as co-eternal yet independent principles, each with their own domain, in a constant duel.

This dichotomy is for the most part rejected by modern Western occultists due to its association with the mainstream Judeo-Christian tradition, which they consider deficient. But the fact remains that many Gnostics sects, and those later influenced by them (such as the Cathars), considered themselves foremost to be Christians, and recognized the difference between sin and righteousness. To embrace the classical Gnostic tradition means to embrace their dualist perspective. It is simply impossible to separate such perspectives from Gnosticism with disdain, as many modern occultists attempt to do when incorporating Gnosticism into their own self-made, heterodox worldviews. In *Liber Tzaddi vel Hamus Hermeticus sub figura XC*, Aleister Crowley explains a concept very similar to that of Carl Jung's *Coniunctio Oppositorum*, stating:

> Many have arisen, being wise. They have said 'Seek out the glittering Image in the place ever golden, and unite yourselves with it.' Many have arisen, being foolish. They have said, 'Stoop down into the darkly splendid world and be wedded to that Blind Creature of the Slime.' I who am beyond Wisdom and Folly, arise and say unto you: achieve both weddings! Unite yourselves with both! Beware, beware, I say lest you seek after the one and lose

the other! My adepts stand upright; their head above the heavens, their feet below the hells. But since one is naturally attracted to the Angel, another to the Demon, let the first strengthen the lower link, the last attach more firmly to the higher. Thus shall equilibrium become perfect. I will aid my disciples; as fast as they acquire this balanced power and joy so faster will I push them.

Baphomet, like Abraxas, is a perfect hieroglyph to represent this sentiment, and the conjunction of opposites that he embodies (not only the union of good and evil, but the androgynous balance of the genders as well) is believed by ceremonial magicians to be an altered state of consciousness that allows one to tap into innate superhuman abilities. But if you know anybody into the occult, chances are high that you know somebody who, despite what they may say openly, tends to gravitate towards the darker side of things, delighting in control over others. In *Magic: Book 4*, Crowley writes gleefully about using this transcendental power to make slaves of the angels and demons of the universe, encouraging his students to:

Master everything, but give generously to your servants, once they have unconditionally submitted.

In *Transcendental Magic*, Eliphas Levi wrote about the use of the power of "the Devil" in black magic, calling it "the Great Magical Agent," similar to the term "Universal Agent" that he used to describe Baphomet in the previously-quoted section from *Magic: A History of Its Rites, Rituals and Mysteries*. But in this passage, he warns that calling up Satan could bring negative results:

Chapter 8

IN BLACK MAGIC, THE DEVIL is THE GREAT MAGICAL AGENT EMPLOYED FOR EVIL PURPOSES BY A PERVERSE WILL. The old serpent of the legend is nothing else than the BLACK MAGIC, universal agent, the eternal fire of terrestrial life, the soul of the earth, and the living fount of hell. We have said that the astral light is the receptacle of forms, and these when evoked by reason are produced harmoniously, but when evoked by madness they appear disorderly and monstrous; so originated the nightmares of St. Anthony and the phantoms of the Sabbath. Do, therefore, the evocations of goetia and demonomania possess a practical result? Yes, certainly one which cannot be contested, one more terrible than could be recounted by legends! When any one invokes the devil with intentional ceremonies, the devil comes, and is seen. To escape dying from horror at the sight, to escape catalepsy or idiocy, one must be already mad.

Recall that in the confessions of the Templars, several knights said that they were profoundly affected by seeing the terrible visage of the Baphomet head. But as terrifying as it can be, Eliphas Levi nonetheless lauds the power that can be utilized with the Universal Agent," writing in *Transcendental Magic* that:

> . . . having equilibrium for its supreme law, while its direction is concerned immediately with the Great Arcanum of Transcendental Magic. . . .This agent . . . is precisely that which the adepts of the Middle Ages denominated the First Matter of the Great Work. The Gnostics represented it as the fiery body of the Holy Spirit; it was the object of adoration in the Secret Rites of the Sabbath and the Temple,

under the hieroglyphic figure of Baphomet or the Androgyne of Mendes.

Then later on he adds:

The symbolic head of the goat of Mendes is occasionally given to this figure, and it is then the Baphomet of the Templars and the Word of the Gnostics.

Elsewhere in this same book Levi describes the agent as "a horse having nature analogous to a chameleon, ever reflecting the armor of his rider." So the Universal Agent is whatever the magician makes of it, subject to the same strengths and weaknesses that he possesses. This goes along with another description Levi gave of it as a "universal plastic mediator," the word "plastic" meaning, literally, "capable of shaping or molding." In this case, the Universal Agent conforms to the mold projected by the will of the magician.

Yet the analogy of horse and rider, when used in relation to the subject of demonic possession, is usually employed the other way around: the person is the horse, and the demon is riding him. (This is actually the terminology used by practitioners of Voudon.) But the role of a magician is of one who controls the spirits, rather than letting them control him, as Solomon is said to have done with the power of his magic ring. In that case, the magician becomes the rider, and the demon is the horse. This same concept may have given rise to the terms "riding the Dragon" (used in Bram Stoker's novel *Dracula* to describe the mastering of occult power) and "riding the Goat" (a Masonic term to be discussed more later). We must wonder then what was meant by one of the seals frequently used by the Knights Templar, featuring two knights riding one horse. Also consider that Azazel, in *The*

Zohar, is called the "rider on the serpent" because he acts as the intermediary to connect Lilith and Samael sexually.

It appears that this perceived ability to control the spirits of the ether with the Universal Agent is a matter of tapping into, as we have said, powers both infernal and divine, and thus, necessarily, powers associated both with the Devil and God in the Bible. When we examine the research of Stuart Nettleton in *The Alchemy Key: Unraveling the Single Tangible Secret In All Mysteries* we find, again, more evidence that Baphomet may have been seen as the key to both, or as Nettleton terms it, the "intercessor between Jehovah and the Messiah." He even compares the role played by Baphomet to that usually taken by the Virgin Mary in Christian theology! Using the Atbash cipher with Hebrew, he discovered the following:

> The Atbash Cipher produces BphOM from Jehovah (YHWH). Using the Cipher once more, Baphomet (BPhOMTh) leads to Yahushua (YHWShO), which means The Messiah. . . . Baphomet is therefore the partner of Jehovah and route to the Messiah. Thus, Baphomet figuratively gives birth to the Messiah from Jehovah. Baphomet therefore fulfills the age-old role of the Mother Goddess in the old sacrificial king rituals. She is Wisdom or Sophia, who brings forth the son of perfection. Thus, the repeated use of the Atbash Cipher through Baphomet, gives the same answer as the straightforward method, Sophia. Baphomet is therefore equivalent to the Shema or understanding that unites the one with God. This is the Shekhinah or the Virgin with Child.

So in this sense Baphomet is not only Sophia, but the Demiurge she gave birth to as well. This connects Baphomet again with Abraxas, who also seems to be an avatar of the

Abraxas: Secret of the Temple 445

Demiurge. This might explain why Aleister Crowley referred to Baphomet as the "Lion and the Serpent," since Ialdabaoth was represented by the Gnostics as a lion with a serpent's tail. But can these two, diametrically-opposed figures be combined? What has the God of the Bible to do with the goat god? As we ponder this, let us also reflect on the supposedly "erroneous" translation in St. Jerome's Latin Vulgate version of *Exodus* 34:29-30, in which the "face" of Moses becomes "horned" after talking to God:

> And when Moses came down from the Mount Sinai, he held the two tables of the testimony, and he knew not that his face was horned from the conversation of the Lord. And Aaron and the children of Israel seeing the face of Moses horned, were afraid to come near.

Actually, though, it was not a mistranslation at all, and Jerome even left commentary explaining it. The word he translated as "horn" is *keren,* which also means "radiant." Thus, in the King James translation, it simply says "the skin of his face shone," and presumably because of the overbearing brightness, other people "were afraid to come nigh" until "he put a vail on his face." But at that time, horns were considered a crown of divine glory, as they were featured on the heads of so many of the gods of the ancient world. Jerome (who said he had consulted rabbinical scholars specifically about this word) was trying to imply both meanings simultaneously (both horns and radiant light). This is why Moses has been depicted in classic works of art with rays of light projecting from his head like horns, as in Dore's drawing, and on the "Moses Fountain" in Bern, Switzerland. Michelangelo famously sculpted Moses with regular horns, which made him look like a satyr. According to Louis Ginzberg's *Legends of the Jews*, there is a story of Moses visiting Hell and Paradise while on the mountaintop with God, where he was guided by an "angel with the horns of glory." Interestingly, Moses was able to enter Hell without being burned because he had been cauterized with a baptism of divine fire that protected him. As the horned angel told him:

> There is a fire that not only burns but also consumes, and that fire will protect thee against hell fire, so that thou canst step upon it, and yet thou wilt not be seared.

So is this the meaning of the "baptism of fire" that John the Baptist said the one who came after him would bring? Is it a fire that "consumes" you, but somehow protects you from hellfire? Tobias Churton reports that Mandaeans believe John's body could not be burned by fire. Analyzing Saint Paul's interpretation of the baptism of fire, he writes that Paul felt that:

> ... The Holy Spirit [received through the] baptism of fire ... sustains the soul through the fire of judgment.... [It was] both destroyer of chaff and quickener of righteous spirit: a kind of winnowing.

We have mentioned previously the prophecies found in Judeo-Christian scripture promising that the world will be destroyed by not just one, but two coming cataclysms, one of fire and one of water. Fulcanelli suggests that each disaster will affect one of the hemispheres of the globe. Several writers have purported that John's baptism of water was meant to be a sort of prophylactic to protect the recipient against drowning in the coming deluge, while the baptism of fire would protect against the coming conflagration. As we read in *Orpheus the Fisher* by Robert Eisler:

The Messianic baptism of fire, foretold by John, is nothing else than the Last Judgment of humanity in "the Day that cometh burning like an oven" [*The Book of Malachi* 4:1]. As his baptism in water is *not simply identical* with the final deluge, which is to purify the world, but a symbolic and, for the repentant ones, an apotropaic [warding off evil influences] and protective anticipation of it, even so does he expect that the "Mightier One" coming after him will purge the righteous remnant of Israel, "like a refiner," in a baptism of fire, so that then they shall be proof as gold against the flame, which is to exterminate the sinners.

He then quotes from *Malachi* 3:1-3, in which, as we read from the King James translation, God tells us through his prophet:

Behold, I will send my messenger, and he shall prepare the way before me. . . . For he is like a refiner's fire. . . . And he shall sit as a refiner and purifier of silver: and he shall purify the sons of Levi, and purge them as gold and silver, that they may offer unto the Lord an offering in righteousness.

Now is this special fire that protects from hellfire connected to Baphomet, Abraxas, and the Universal Agent? According to Levi (*Transcendental Magic*), the answer is yes. There is also yet another mysterious alchemical name for it too. He calls it:

AZOTH, universal magnesia, the great magical agent, the astral light, the light of life, fertilized by animic force, by intellectual energy, which they compare to sulphur on account of its affinities with divine fire.

So it seems that, if this isn't exactly *the* divine fire (the Holy Spirit), it is the closest thing that a magician can get his hands on, and serves a similar purpose for him. You may recall a scene at the end of the horror film *The Ninth Gate*, when the villain, a Satanic magician, lights himself on fire, believing that because of the power he got from the Devil, the flames will not burn him (a trick which works for a few minutes and then fails him). Perhaps he thought he had doused himself in a protective coating of Azoth.

This substance is described by Levi as being omnipresent, in everything, filling all space between the magician and the intended object. In alchemy it is called the "quintessence," the "Philosophic Mercurial, and even "Sophia Mercurius." It is the "panacea" or "universal medicine" that cures everything, as it heals the separation between creation and the creator. Julius Evola, in *The Hermetic Tradition*, also describes the Philosophical Mercury (quoting the *Filum Ariadnae*) as:

> ". . . a chimera that lives only in the imagination. It is on the rule of Fire that everything depends." And we need hardly belabor the fact that this is not vulgar, physical fire.

The subject of Azoth was written about very thoroughly in the book *Liber Azoth* by the alchemist Paracelsus, who was also a physician, astronomer, botanist, and all-around Renaissance man. Legend has it that he made his own Azoth and kept it stored in the pommel of his sword. Apparently he wanted to always have a good dose of the stuff handy in case he got injured or sick. The name Azoth represents totality because it starts with "A", which is the first letter in most alphabets, and end with "z", "o," and "th," which are the final letters of the Latin, Greek, and Hebrew alphabets. In *The Emerald Tablet: Alchemy for Personal Transformation*, Dennis William Hauck explains that:

> The word is meant to embrace the full meaning of [the alchemical operation], which is both the chaotic First matter at the beginning of the Work and the perfected Stone at its conclusion.

At the same time, it is also thought to be related to the Arabic *al-za'buq*, meaning "the mercury." Also, we should note, the Hebrew word for a he-goat is "Az," which brings up obvious connections to Azazel and Baphomet.

The famous German alchemist Basil Valentine first wrote about this subject in the 1659 book *Azoth of the Philosophers*. In it there is a famous illustration of Azoth as a chimera creature. It is a sort of platter on which all of the elements of the universe are arranged in harmony, with a bearded, slightly leonine face in the middle, human arms coming out of the sides, and human legs on the bottom. On top are the wings usually found on a caduceus (they appear to be attached to a pole jutting out from the crown of the head). Between the legs is the white cubic Philosopher's Stone, labeled "Corpus" ("the Body"). So Azoth, like Abraxas and Baphomet, can be thought of as a living being that contains the magical power of the universe, as it contains everything that exists (and perhaps, like Abraxas, even nonexistence itself).

So here we are yet again on the subject of the unity of dual, seemingly opposite currents. In the article "Baphomet and the Azoth" by Soror KTK at pyramidlodge.org, the author connects Azoth with the twin snake legs of Abraxas and with the caduceus:

> The Great Magical Agent is a "double-current of light" which Levi best likes to represent as a serpent: the dual serpent of the caduceus, the serpent of *Genesis*, the brazen serpent of Moses, the serpent

twined around the Tau (which he sees as a symbol of the generating lingam), the Gnostic Hyle, the twin serpents forming the legs of Abraxas, and the Oroboros serpent, which he relates to prudence and Saturn.

In the Hermetic Nag Hammadi Codex *On the Ogdoad and Ennead*, commonly known as *Discourse on the Eighth and Ninth*, it mentions that the origin of holy names like Zoxathazo (found in Nag Hammadi Codex VI)—which sound very similar to Zothaxathoz (found in *Greek Magical Papyrus* XIII), and presumably the countless similar names in *The Books of Jeu*—may have their roots in permutations of the Greek words *zoe* (life) and *thanatos* (death). If these words in any way inspired the creation of the word Azoth, it would make since, as they all seem to contain a synthesis of two opposing forces, just like Baphomet and Abraxas. We are reminded, again, of William Blake's classic poem *The Marriage of Heaven and Hell*, which describes the same kind of fusion of contradictory symbols. There we find the following lines (emphasis added):

> Prisons are built with stones of Law, Brothels with bricks of Religion. The pride of the peacock is the glory of God. *The lust of the goat is the bounty of God. The wrath of the lion is the wisdom of God*. The nakedness of woman is the work of God. Excess of sorrow laughs. Excess of joy weeps.

Time and again we have been told by the authors of occult books that a magician, if he is to master this deadly power, must fully transform his consciousness or purify his soul into the "One Thing," the ultimate goal of the alchemical operation described in the Emerald Tablet of Hermes. Albert Pike explains it in *Morals and Dogma*:

Abraxas: Secret of the Temple

> The Great Work is, above all things, the creation of man by himself; that is to say, the full and entire conquest which he effects of his faculties and his future. It is, above all, the perfect emancipation of his will, which assures him the universal empire of Azoth, and the domain of magnetism, that is, complete power over the universal magical agent.

In his books *Liber Null* and *Psychonaut*, Peter Carroll has advice for anyone wishing to work with Baphomet to perform ritual magic. Carroll is one of the main proponents of the practice of "chaos magick," which is built on the idea that the subconscious mind is the primary generator of the reality that each individual experiences. Although this reality is subjective, the understanding is that this is still somehow connected to external reality, and that via the principles of "sympathetic magic," the chaotic elements of the universe will align to conform to the pattern of symbols expressed in a ritual, thus influencing objective reality according to the magician's will. This model is deeply influenced by *The Greek Magical Papyri*, as well as *The Pyramid Texts* and *The Egyptian Book of the Dead*.

Before performing such rituals, Carroll advocates reaching a state of "Gnosis" through the means of yoga, tantric sex, psychoactive substances, chanting, drumming, dancing, and lucid dreaming. The trick, supposedly, is to concentrate on an abstract idea of one's expressed desire while using the altered state of consciousness to bring forth the powers of creation that allegedly slumber in the subconscious mind, resulting, hopefully, in the manifestation of what is desired. Chaos magick embraces the same moral philosophy expressed by Assassin chief Hassan-i-Sabbah (as we mentioned earlier): "Nothing is true, everything is permitted." Since reality is pliable, in this view, you can make of it what you will.

One of the techniques suggested by Carroll is "sigil magick," developed by the British occultist and artist Austin Osman Spare in the early twentieth century. By the goat and ritual orgy motifs in some of his art, it seems that Spare also tapped into the Baphometic current, which makes sense considering that he was heavily influenced by his contemporary and fellow countryman, Aleister Crowley (who literally called himself Baphomet). Sigil magick requires no elaborate tools or regalia, just a pen and paper. It quite simply consists of making hieroglyphs out of the letters used to form words that express the purpose of the spell being cast, after all vowels and redundant letters have been removed. The resulting symbol is then meditated upon to imprint the subconscious mind with the desire and to bring it into manifestation.

Pertinent to our inquiry, Peter Carroll suggests that a would-be chaos magician should visualize himself as Baphomet while chanting the following "aeonic litany":

In the first aeon, I was the Great Spirit

In the second aeon, Men knew me as the Horned God, Pangenitor Panphage

In the third aeon, I was the Dark one, the Devil

In the fourth aeon, Men know me not, for I am the Hidden One

In this new aeon, I appear before you as Baphomet, The God before all gods who shall endure to the end of the Earth.

This is very similar to the spell from *The Greek Magical Papyri* mentioned earlier, where the magician attempts to

Abraxas: Secret of the Temple 453

personally take on the chimeric qualities of Abraxas himself. However, some would say that the magician is not taking in something from outside of himself, but rather tapping into qualities that lay hidden within. These inner, normally suppressed personalities may be thought of as the "hidden," or "chthonic" shadow selves which may be channeled for creative purposes. However, magical texts frequently warn that bringing them forth could also be the undoing of one's life, resulting in both figurative and literal death. For Carl Jung, the power of Abraxas was connected to the bestial nature of humanity, and this beast, being composed of totally opposite essences, can tear us apart from the inside out if awakened but not controlled. Is this what the title character of Johann Wolfgang von Goethe's *Faust* was saying when, after invoking the Devil, he complained: "Two souls dwell, alas! In my breast"?

This is what modern Western occultism has to say on the subject. But is this truly related to the original concept of Baphomet that was supposedly whispered about in the secret rituals of the Knights Templar? Well, possibly, for it does seem that they knew about Abraxas, a figure that as we have seen is inherently related not only to Gnosticism but also to ritual magic. As it turns out, tokens and seals featuring the image of Abraxas and the words "Secretum Templi" ("Secret of the Temple") have been found and connected to the Templars.

One was, according to Oddvar Olsen in *The Templar Papers* (2006), found by a man in Britain with a metal detector, and is now in the possession of the British Museum (where it is not, unfortunately, on display). Another pair of them was found among Templar property and are in the French National Archives in Paris. They appear, from the pictures we have seen, to go together. They are for sealing documents, and were to be pressed together with a piece of paper or parchment in between, to make an impression. In *Gnostic Philosophy*, Tobias Churton cites Sylvia Beamon's 2011 book *The Royston's Cave: Used by Saints or Sinners?*, where it says that this seal was used by one of the Temple's grand masters, who at the time would have been Guillaume de Chartres. He writes:

> It is striking that the seal depicted in Beamon's book belonged to the grand master of the Templars and was used in a French charter dated October 1214.

However, the French researcher Michel Lamy, in his 1997 book *Les Templiers, Ces Grands Seigneurs aux Blanes Manteaux* (*The Templars, the Great Lords of the White Mantles*) talks about a document signed with this seal in that same year by "the Templar Preceptor of France." This makes us wonder if it is in fact the same document he is talking about, and if the title of the order's French Preceptor has been conflated by these other authors with the actual grand master. At any rate, Lamy states that the document he is talking about deals with the division of a certain forest between the Templars and the King of France. As Lamy comments, "One cannot say that this is a particularly a hermetic text." He then goes on to suggest that the word *secretum* found on the seal meant simply that it was used on particularly important documents. However, this does not bar the possibility that the image was adopted by the Templars because to them it represented the real "secret" of their "temple"—the Temple of Solomon, or the Al-Aqsa Mosque that was built on top of the Temple Mount. This makes us wonder, then, if they meant to imply that Gnosis, or the transcendental power of Abraxas, was their secret. According to Tobias Churton, several other authors have already speculated about this, and connected it to Baphomet:

Abraxas: Secret of the Temple

There have been suggestions that the figure represents Baphomet or "Baphometides," the baptism of wisdom; or, alternatively, Bios, Phos, Metis—Life, Light, Wisdom. The speculative possibilities are legion because we simply do not know why the grand master of the Templars should have employed such a figure.

It is not only people in modern times who have connected Baphomet and Abraxas. Long before the Templar Abraxas tokens were found anywhere, Charles William King, in his 1887 book *The Gnostics and Their Remains*, quoted the late eighteenth-century writer Rudolf Erich Raspe (famous for his adaptations of the tales of "Baron Munchausen") on the subject (emphasis added):

> The Gnosis of Basilides was an occult science which, according to his tenets, should be known only and communicated to one in thousands, and to two in ten thousands, and that if the Knights Templars were guilty of any offence at the time of their extermination, it was that of having adopted the doctrines of the Gnostics, and consequently of having renounced the established doctrine of the Church on the human nature of Christ, and on the Trinity: in the place of which they, with the Gnostics, professed one Supreme Being, Father and Creator of all the Powers which, emanating from him, have created and do govern this world. At their reception or initiation into the highest degree of the Order they received . . . the Baptism or Tincture of Wisdom; they were presented with a sign or symbol of their baptism, which was the Pentagon of Pythagoras; *and they worshipped a kind of image or idol; that like the Abraxas . . . was the figure of a Bearded Old Man, or rather the*

representation of the only Supreme Being that they admitted and professed.

We are not familiar with the sight of a "bearded" Abraxas. However, King explained that Raspe was referring to a particular representation of the figure found on a "gem" that showed, as Raspe described it:

Abraxas, the Sun, or God-Father, or Demiurgus according to the Gnostics and necromancers. This head is crowned, the beard long, the hands crossed upon the breast: for the rest, he is formed as a Term, or a mummy. In the field are eight stars, probably an allusion to the eight Powers, or heavens, that are subordinate to them, according to Epiphanius. In the field are two Hebrew letters. . . .

The two Hebrew letters are "He" and "Chet," the equivalent of "H" and "Ch," respectively. The meaning of this is unknown. Regardless of this, and in spite of the fact that we have not yet seen the image described by Raspe, it must be admitted that the description reminds us of the allegedly bearded and mummified head supposedly worshipped by the Templars as an idol of Baphomet. If similar images exist elsewhere, and if they are as old as the Templars or older, they may have inspired the Templars to use Abraxas as an emblem of Baphomet, their deepest secret.

Charles William King didn't think much of the theories of Joseph von Hammer-Purgstall, declaring that any "sober archeologist" would conclude that many of the "Templar artifacts" presented in *Mysterium Baphometis Revelatum*, specifically several of the vases, are:

. . . nothing more than a portion of the paraphernalia of those Rosicrucian or alchemical quacks, who fattened upon the credulity of that arch-virtuoso,

Rudolf II., ever since whose reign these "fonts" have been treasured up in the Imperial Cabinet.

Rudolf II was the Hapsburg Holy Roman Emperor and King of Bohemia in the late sixteenth and early seventeenth century whose political failures, leading to the disastrous Thirty Years' War, are often blamed by historians on his preoccupation with the occult. Clearly, King thought that Hammer-Purgstall's artifacts may have been items that were collected by the emperor because of their seemingly esoteric nature, but could have had nothing to do with the Templars. At present it is impossible to say, as even after years of thorough investigation we have been unable to track down most of the original objects. However, unlike every other modern researcher on the subject, we did manage to find some of them, and this at least affords us the possibility of analyzing them, as we will discuss in the next chapter.

Chapter 9: Riding the Goat Current

Light and Darkness, life and death, right and left, are brothers of one another. They are inseparable. Because of this neither are the good good, nor evil evil, nor is life life, nor death death. For this reason each one will dissolve into its earliest origin. But those who are exalted above the world are indissoluble, eternal.

—*The Gospel of Philip*, 53

Since commencing our investigation of these matters, we have managed to bring to light much more regarding the origin of some of the images featured in Hammer-Purgstall's book. Most of the artifacts seem impossible to find now. They do not appear to be listed as what Hammer-Purgstall called them in any museum. The pictures that purportedly came from the walls of churches cannot be verified, as in most cases the churches (located in what are now Austria, Hungary, the Czech Republic, Germany and France) no longer exist. Even the townships they were in have changed names. However, one of the items, a coffer featuring the most striking image of "Mete" (as he calls her) pulling down the Sun and Moon with chains, is in fact be in the British Museum now. As we mentioned previously, Hammer-Purgstall talks about but does not include the images from this object in his essay. But later, Thomas Wright did show the pictures in *Worship of the Generative Powers*, and said that this coffer came from the private collection of Louis, Duc de Blacas. Research into this confirmed that this collection had been sold some years ago to the British Museum, where Tracy R. Twyman found it in August of 2015, labeled as a limestone casket that has been:

Riding the Goat Current 459

... sculpted with crude figure of Cybele lifting up chains; sun and moon in top corners; pentagram and seven-pointed star with skull in lower corners; Arabic inscription round edges; sides carved with scene of human and animal sacrifices.

At the time of this writing, on the museum's website, only two sides of the coffer are shown. It is very hard to see what's going on in the images. We had to pay the museum to re-photograph the item, so that we could see all of the sides of the coffer clearly. Those pictures are featured in this book. They will also be included in the first-ever English translation of his *Mysterium Baphometis Revelatum*, which Tracy R. Twyman has commissioned, and was just completed at the time of this writing. This book, with new commentary by Twyman, will be available within a few months of the publication of the book which you are currently reading.

It seems a bit damaged, but on one side of the coffer (side 1), we see a bull being held by the neck while a group of people sit around a flaming bowl. On another side (side 2), we see some similar themes to other images in Hammer-Purgstall's book: a man wielding an ax (as well as a shovel) over a small child who is riding a crocodile. (Axes and crocodiles are featured in several of the other pictures.) This child is holding the right hand of a taller figure. To that person's left, a smaller child is kneeling and holding his other hand. To the right of all of this we see a winged angel holding a serpent behind his back. In his left hand he holds the animal's head, and in his right hand, the tail is coiled up into a circle.

On a third side of the coffer, there definitely seems to be an orgy depicted. Everyone shown there is naked and appears to be male. On the left edge, there is a man with his back to us. He is spreading the legs of someone in front of him, of whom only the legs can be seen. To the right of this, there is a large cauldron with what looks like a crocodile bring dragged into it. Bending over the cauldron from the right are two men who seem to be forcing the creature into the bowl. One of them is pouring something over it from a vase. Both of the men restraining the crocodile are bent over so that their bare buttocks are sticking up to the right, and from that side, another man is reaching with his right hand to fondle them. To the right of all of this, there is a short brick altar with a man sitting on it, and two others molesting him, one of whom appears to be a child, and who seems to have his backside pressed against the man behind him—the one who is touching the buttocks of the men leaning over the cauldron. Everyone in this picture seems to be smiling. On the left edge, next to the man with a pair of legs spread in front of him, there is what looks like a very large bird talon reaching up from out of nowhere.

On the fourth side of the coffer, we found the origin for a line drawing featured in *Worship of the Generative Powers*, which Wright had said was from the same coffer as the image of Mete pulling the chains, but which wasn't shown in the Purgstall-Hammer book. On the left it shows a statue of a horned demon with breasts and male genitals—clearly Baphomet. There are no legs, but just a column below the genitals, like the classical Greek herm statues described in an earlier chapter. A man is kneeling beside this statue, kissing its buttocks (the *osculum inflame* of the Templars) and grabbing its testicles. A woman in a long dress stands over the kneeling figure on the right, pouring something onto him with a vase. To her right, a man holds another vase lazily in his right hand while a man to his left fondles him with his penis and testes visible. All of these things are shown in the drawing in Wright's book.

Riding the Goat Current 461

However, that's only half the image. To the right of this scene, there is more. We see a man riding what looks very much to be a goat. The creature has his front right hoof resting on the back of a man kneeling in front of him, who is helping to support a round tray full of vases that is being held by another man standing to the right. The man riding the goat is removing an item from the tray. To the right of everything, there is a winged and crowned creature with bird-like legs, including large talons for feet similar to the one sticking up from the ground on the left edge of the second side of the coffer, described above. The crown and facial features somewhat resemble those of Mete on the lid of the coffer.

We also found, in the Duc de Blacas collection, another coffer in near-perfect condition (except for the missing lid) which for some reason is labeled "fake." This item has not been featured, as far as we know, in any book or website ever, yet it is clearly part of the same group of items as the Mete coffer. The images found thereon are described in the following paragraphs.

On one side, a group of people are involved in very strange activity. To the left, we see a person stirring a cup in one hand with a large stick in the other. In front of him, another person kneels and fondles him. To their right, another man is pointing a stick to his right, over the head of another man who seems to be having sex with a hooved creature, the details of which are hard to make out beyond the bent hind legs. Whilst he mounts the animal, he is simultaneously stirring a bowl that sits on the ground with a large pole. The bowl has an object sticking out of it that may be a small child standing, and the animal's front paws or arms are on his head. To the right of this, another man is kneeling over the bowl, and reaching up over his head to the right to grasp what looks like an alchemical vessel by the neck, holding it over the flames of a brazier that sits on the ground to his right. To the right of the brazier, another man holds out his left hand and grasps the vessel by the neck as well. Over the brazier and the two men holding it, there is a banner tacked to the wall with a message in Arabic. The look of this banner, and the entire scene as well, makes it clear that this piece, "fake" or not, was made by the same artist that made the coffer with the orgy scenes featured in Hammer-Purgstall's book. The poorly-written "Arabic" letters on the banner are of the same style.

On side two of the "fake" coffer that we discovered, we see someone being baptized, perhaps forcibly. He is standing waste-deep in a cauldron, bent forward, with his head buried in another man's hands, while a third man, standing on top of a bricked platform, pours something on his head from a vase above, just like in the previously described image of the crocodile being dragged into the cauldron. In the upper left, a disapproving owl (symbol of the wisdom goddesses Lilith, Athena and Minerva) scowls at the viewer. The man holding the other man's head is also looking at the viewer, as if we have walked in on a secret ceremony.

On the third side, a bull is on an altar being either worshipped or sacrificed. One of the participants clutches a stick like in the previous scenes, and holds out a garland as if to place it on the neck of the bull. Another kneels in front of it with a vase that looks like it might contain wine. One of them holds up a *tau* sign identical to those seen in several pictures featured by Hammer-Purgstall. Floating in the air next to the bull we see an equilateral cross. At the bottom of altar sits a billows for fanning flames, although no fire is featured in this scene. As to whether the bull is being worshipped or sacrificed, it seems that Thomas Wright thought the latter, for he described it thus and wrote that Hammer-Purgstall thought it was part of an Ophite Gnostic ceremony, adding:

> The offering of a calf figures prominently among the Nossarii, or Nessarenes, the Druses, and other sects in the East.

However, Hammer-Purgstall himself thought the Templars were involved in calf worship, and that this was directly related to their rituals to Baphomet. At least, that's what he wrote in his introduction to *Ancient Alphabets and Hieroglyphic Characters Explained* by Ibn Wahshiyya, published twelve years before *Mysterium Baphometis Revelatum* and containing the beetle-like "Hermetic" hieroglyph of Baphomet, or, rather, "Bahumed." There Hammer-Purgstall declares

> It is written *Bahumid*, and translated into Arabic by the word *calf*.
>
> It is superfluous to recall here to the memory of the reader the great antiquity and mysterious sense of the idolatrous veneration in which this calf has been continually held. It is superfluous to repeat any thing that has been said on the worship of *Apis* in Egypt, renewed by the Israelites in the worship of the calf, and preserved in the mysterious rites of the Druses. Let us remember only a circumstance which shows wonderfully the concordance and relation of the name of *Bahumid* and its translation.
>
> *Bahumed* or *Bahumet* is related in the History of the Templars to have been one of their secret and mysterious formulas, with which they addressed the idol of a *calf* in their secret assemblies. Different etymological explanations and descriptions of this word have been brought forward, but none surely so

satisfactory as this, which proves that the Templars had some acquaintance with the hieroglyphics [presumably, the "Hermetic" hieroglyphs that are the subject of the book], probably acquired in Syria.

Notably, in the actual text by Ibn Wahshiyya, he does that the hieroglyph can be identified with the name "Kharuf," which he does translate as "calf," but seems to indicate that this is another name for the concept symbolized by the hieroglyph, "The Secret of Secrets," in addition to "Bahumed." He does not seem to be saying that "calf" is in any way a translation of the word "Bahumed." This detail, connecting Baphomet and calf worship, helps us imagine what must have been going Hammer-Purgstall's mind when he saw this casket, considering that he'd already gone on record proclaiming that the Templars practiced this particular form of idolatry.

Returning to the box in question, we find, on the remaining (fourth) side, a man slumped backwards as if dead has been placed on a flaming brick altar, on top of some logs, while two men lift up their hands in worship towards an unseen god. The lid of the coffer is apparently missing. All of the people featured in all of the pictures on both coffers seem short and malformed, like demons or gargoyles.

The Louis, Duc de Blacas collection also contains a great many Gnostic talismans featuring the figures of Abraxas, Bes and Ialdabaoth. The pictures are similar, and in some cases seemingly identical to those found on some of the coins featured in Hammer-Purgstall's book. We did not find any other coffers of a similar nature, nor any of Hammer-Purgstall's "bowls" or other artifacts, nor did we find anything else in the de Blacas collection labeled "fake."

Although the second, "fake" coffer does not appear to be discussed in detail anywhere in known literature, it must be the second coffer mentioned by Peter Partner when he viciously derided Joseph von Hammer-Purgstall's work in his 1987 book *The Murdered Magicians: The Templars and Their Myth*. Partner sees Hammer-Purgstall's theories as an outgrowth of the paranoia, rampant during his time, about Adam Weishaupt's Bavarian Illuminati, a real secret society that had operated through Masonic lodges in Europe to foster republican revolutions against the crowns. Partner basically accuses Hammer-Purgstall, and all of his informants for the research of *Mysterium Baphometis Revelatum*, of being part of their own vast right-wing conspiracy to discredit the French revolution by connecting it, via the Illuminati, then Freemasonry, and then Templarism, to heresy, Satanism, and debauchery. Partner wrote of Hammer-Purgstall's physical evidence, the "Templar artifacts," that:

> A few of the archeological exhibits may have been forgeries from the occultist workshops; there is an especially suspicious pair of so-called "Templar caskets," found after the publication of Hammer's first article, which were supposed to have been medieval artefacts of Templar provenance. The Gnostic "orgies" depicted on these supposedly medieval caskets are uncannily like the late classical objects which had a few years earlier been published in the original "Baphomet" thesis. The "medieval" caskets had come into the possession of the Duc de Blacas. Since Blacas was a leading figure in the reactionary French government, and a close personal friend of the renegade Freemason Joseph de Maistre, it is not impossible that they were forged on his behalf. Whether they were forged or not, Hammer

First casket, lid.

First casket, side one.

First casket, side two.

First casket, side three.

First casket, side four.

Second casket, side one.

Second casket, side three.

Second casket, side two (above) and side four (below).

Above: Baron Joseph von Hammer-Purgstall. Lithograph by Josef Kriehuber, 1843. Below: Line drawing from Thomas Wright's *Worship of the Generative Powers*, the source of which was found to be one of the caskets we discovered in the British Museum.

Left: Louis de Blacas d'Aulps, 2nd Duc de Blacas.

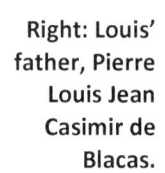

Right: Louis' father, Pierre Louis Jean Casimir de Blacas.

failed to prove that they had anything to do with the Templars.

Partner derides Hammer-Purgstall's school of Orientalism, and basically the entire field of comparative mythology, as well as the anthropology of religion, as the obsessions of older less rational generations, tying it to "Romanticism":

> Like so many early modern students of religious origins, he sought to establish a pattern of primitive pagan religion which had survived Christianity in various deviant ways. . . . The Romantic movement was passionately addicted to such theories of primitive religion.

He then wonders:

> How was it that a writer enrolled in the service of rampant conservatism, whose duty it was to demonstrate that advanced radical thought was subverting the foundations of Christian civilization, ended by seeming to show that Christianity had always existed alongside another, more primitive and perhaps more powerful religion?

His evidence that Hammer-Purgstall was "enrolled in the service of rampant conservatism" seems to be that he worked as a diplomat for the government of Austria, and that some of the artifacts he showed in his book were owned by the Duc de Blacas, a so-called "reactionary" (as would describe any politically-active nobleman at this time who did not want to lose his land and titles). Partner wrote:

> Hammer was not employed by Metternich, the greatest conservative minister in western Europe, for nothing. The whole drift of Hammer's argument is in

the sense of that used by the ubiquitous Abbe Barruel. Everything connects, from the Gnostics of the early Church, to the Albigensians in the west, the Assassins in the east, thence to the Templars, thence to the Freemasons, thence to the revolutionary anarchists. In 1818, the political order of European conservatism was making its greatest effort to master the threat of radical ideology and radical sedition. The center of that effort was in Vienna, where Hammer was employed by the Austrian Chancery.

You are free to decide what you think about Partner's reasoning skills, which he seems to think are superior to Hammer-Purgstall's, perhaps due to his being born into a world that has benefited from the influence of "advanced radical thought" (from the anti-royalist revolutionaries, apparently). Partner also claimed that "the medieval French word for Muhammad was 'Baphomet,' as any competent scholar in Old French could have told [Hammer-Purgstall]." This is not borne out by the evidence of our investigation (benefitting from being born into our own advanced information age), for as we explained in Chapter Two, the French word for Mohammed was actually just "Mahomet" (although some claimed that Baphomet could have somehow been a corruption of this). One would think that the *French* occult scholar Eliphas Levi, who contributed so much to the lore of Baphomet, would have been perfectly aware of this if it were true, as would his entire contemporary reading audience.

In the mid-nineteenth century, a few years after the publication of Hammer-Purgstall's work on the Templars, Pope Pius IX issued an "Allocution Against the Freemasons," which said a lot about the Templars as well (and which we have quoted from a bit already). Strangely the place where it is easiest to find an English translation of at least a large segment of this document is in Albert Pike's *Morals and Dogma*, where he quoted from it at length. We will now give you that entire section verbatim, as each word of it is precious:

> A power that ruled without antagonism and without concurrence, and consequently without control, proved fatal to the Sacerdotal Royalties; while the Republics, on the other hand, had perished by the conflict of liberties and franchises, which, in the absence of all duty hierarchically sanctioned and enforced, had soon become mere tyrannies, rivals one of the other. To find a stable medium between these two abysses, the idea of the Christian Hierophants was to create a society devoted to abnegation by solemn vows, protected by severe regulations; which should be recruited by initiation, and which, sole depositary of the great religious and social secrets, should make Kings and Pontiffs, without exposing it to the corruptions of Power. In that was the secret of that kingdom of Jesus Christ, which, without being of this world, would govern all its grandeurs.
>
> This idea presided at the foundation of the great religious orders, so often at war with the secular authorities, ecclesiastical or civil. Its realization was also the dream of the dissident sects of Gnostics or Illuminati who pretended to connect their faith with the primitive tradition of the Christianity of Saint John. It at length became a menace for the Church and Society, when a rich and dissolute Order, initiated in the mysterious doctrines of the Kabalah, seemed disposed to turn against legitimate authority

the conservative principle of Hierarchy, and threatened the entire world with an immense revolution.

The Templars, whose history is so imperfectly known, were those terrible conspirators. In 1118, nine Knights Crusaders in the East, among whom were Geoffroi de Saint-Omer and Hugues de Payens, consecrated themselves to religion, and took an oath between the hands of the Patriarch of Constantinople, a See always secretly or openly hostile to that of Rome from the time of Photius. The avowed object of the Templars was to protect the Christians who came to visit the Holy Places: their secret object was the re-building of the Temple of Solomon on the model prophesied by Ezekiel.

This re-building, formally predicted by the Judaizing Mystics of the earlier ages, had become the secret dream of the Patriarchs of the Orient. The Temple of Solomon, re-built and consecrated to the Catholic worship would become, in effect, the Metropolis of the Universe; the East would prevail over the West, and the Patriarchs of Constantinople would possess themselves of the Papal power.

The Templars, or Poor Fellow-Soldiery of the Holy House of the Temple intended to be re-built, took as their models, in the Bible, the Warrior-Masons of Zorobabel, who worked, holding the sword in one hand and the trowel in the other. Therefore it was that the Sword and the Trowel were the insignia of the Templars, who subsequently, as will be seen, concealed themselves under the name of Brethren Masons.

The trowel of the Templars is quadruple, and the triangular plates of it are arranged in the form of a cross, making the Kabalistic pantacle known by the name of the Cross of the East. The Knight of the East, and the Knight of the East and West, have in their titles secret allusions to the Templars of whom they were at first the successors.

The secret thought of Hugues de Payens, in founding his Order, was not exactly to serve the ambition of the Patriarchs of Constantinople. There existed at that period in the East a Sect of Johannite Christians, who claimed to be the only true Initiates into the real mysteries of the religion of the Saviour. They pretended to know the real history of YESUS the ANOINTED, and, adopting in part the Jewish traditions and the tales of the Talmud, they held that the facts recounted in the Evangels are but allegories, the key of which Saint John gives, in saying that the world might be filled with the books that could be written upon the words and deeds of Jesus Christ; words which, they thought, would be only a ridiculous exaggeration, if he were not speaking of an allegory and a legend, that might be varied and prolonged to infinity.

The Johannites ascribed to Saint John the foundation of their Secret Church, and the Grand Pontiffs of the Sect assumed the title of Christos, Anointed, or Consecrated, and claimed to have succeeded one another from Saint John by an uninterrupted succession of pontifical powers. He who, at the period of the foundation of the Order of the Temple, claimed these imaginary prerogatives, was named THEOCLET; he knew HUGUES DE PAYENS,

Riding the Goat Current 481

he initiated him into the Mysteries and hopes of his pretended church, he seduced him by the notions of Sovereign Priesthood and Supreme royalty, and finally designated him as his successor.

Thus the Order of Knights of the Temple was at its very origin devoted to the cause of opposition to the tiara of Rome and the crowns of Kings, and the Apostolate of Kabalistic Gnosticism was vested in its chiefs. For Saint John himself was the Father of the Gnostics, and the current translation of his polemic against the heretical of his Sect and the pagans who denied that Christ was the Word, is throughout a misrepresentation, or misunderstanding at least, of the whole Spirit of that Evangel.

The tendencies and tenets of the Order were enveloped in profound mystery, and it externally professed the most perfect orthodoxy. The Chiefs alone knew the aim of the Order: the Subalterns followed them without distrust.

To acquire influence and wealth, then to intrigue, and at need to fight, to establish the Johannite or Gnostic and Kabalistic dogma, were the object and means proposed to the initiated Brethren. The Papacy and the rival monarchies, they said to them, are sold and bought in these days, become corrupt, and to-morrow, perhaps, will destroy each other. All that will become the heritage of the Temple: the World will soon come to us for its Sovereigns and Pontiffs. We shall constitute the equilibrium of the Universe, and be rulers over the Masters of the World.

The Templars, like all other Secret Orders and Associations, had two doctrines, one concealed and reserved for the Masters, which was Johannism; the other public, which was the Roman Catholic. Thus they deceived the adversaries whom they sought to supplant. Hence Free-Masonry, vulgarly imagined to have begun with the Dionysian Architects or the German Stone-workers, adopted Saint John the Evangelist as one of its patrons, associating with him, in order not to arouse the suspicions of Rome, Saint John the Baptist, and thus covertly proclaiming itself the child of the Kabalah and Essenism together.

The better to succeed and win partisans, the Templars sympathized with regrets for dethroned creeds and encouraged the hopes of new worships, promising to all liberty of conscience and a new orthodoxy that should be the synthesis of all the persecuted creeds.

The seeds of decay were sown in the Order of the Temple at its origin. Hypocrisy is a mortal disease. It had conceived a great work which it was incapable of executing, because it knew neither humility nor personal abnegation, because Rome was then invincible, and because the later Chiefs of the Order did not comprehend its mission. Moreover, the Templars were in general uneducated, and capable only of wielding the sword, with no qualifications for governing, and at need enchaining, that queen of the world called Opinion.

Hughes de Payens himself had not that keen and far-sighted intellect nor that grandeur of purpose which afterward distinguished the military founder of another soldiery that became formidable to kings. The Templars were unintelligent and therefore unsuccessful Jesuits.

Riding the Goat Current 483

Their watchword was, to become wealthy, in order to buy the world. They became so, and in 1312 they possessed in Europe alone more than nine thousand seignories. Riches were the shoal on which they were wrecked. They became insolent, and unwisely showed their contempt for the religious and social institutions which they aimed to overthrow. Their ambition was fatal to them. Their projects were divined and prevented. Pope Clement V and King Philip le Bel gave the signal to Europe, and the Templars, taken as it were in an immense net, were arrested, disarmed, and cast into prison. Never was a Coup d'Etat accomplished with a more formidable concert of action. The whole world was struck with stupor, and eagerly waited for the strange revelations of a process that was to echo through so many ages.

It was impossible to unfold to the people the conspiracy of the Templars against the Thrones and the Tiara. It was impossible to expose to them the doctrines of the Chiefs of the Order. The Templars were gravely accused of spitting upon Christ and denying God at their receptions, of gross obscenities, conversations with female devils, and the worship of a monstrous idol.

The end of the drama is well known, and how Jacques de Molai and his fellows perished in the flames. But before his execution, the Chief of the doomed Order organized and instituted what afterward came to be called the Occult, Hermetic, or Scottish Masonry. In the gloom of his prison, the Grand Master created four Metropolitan Lodges, at

Naples for the East, at Edinburg for the West, at Stockholm for the North, and at Paris for the South.

The Pope and the King soon after perished in a strange and sudden manner. Squin de Florian, the chief denouncer of the Order, died assassinated. In breaking the sword of the Templars, they made of it a poniard; and their proscribed trowels thence-forward built only tombs

The Successors of the Ancient Adepts Rose-Croix, abandoning by degrees the austere and hierarchial Science of their Ancestors in initiation, became a Mystic Sect, united with many of the Templars, the dogmas of the two intermingling, and believed themselves to be the sole depositaries of the secrets of the Gospel of St. John, seeing in its recitals an allegorical series of rites proper to complete the initiation.

The Initiates, in fact, thought in the eighteenth century that their time had arrived, some to found a new Hierarchy, others to overturn all authority, and to press down all the summits of the Social Order under the level of Equality.

So here we have the Pope (Pius IX, otherwise known to history for proclaiming his own "infallibility" and that of his predecessor pontiffs) accusing the Templars of a long-standing conspiracy against the Church and the crown heads of Europe to take over the world, and of wanting to rebuild the Temple in Jerusalem. He also claimed that they were involved in Johannism, Cabalism, Gnosticism, Essenism, and Rosicrucianism. He said that the Freemasons were heirs not only to the same traditions, but the same revolutionary goals. However, after his Allocution was published, the Pope was accused of hypocrisy by several Masons in print, who claimed that he himself was known to be a member of the Lodge!

Today, the latest word from the Church about Freemasonry goes back to a statement made by Joseph Ratzinger (the future Pope Benedict XVI) in 1983, approved by John Paul II, that said: "The faithful who enroll in Masonic associations are in a state of grave sin and may not receive Holy Communion. . . . [M]embership in them remains forbidden." This statement had to be made because the revised Canon Law which was issued that year had made the penalty for joining, which is excommunication, implicit instead of explicit, and many people took that as a green light signal. Today this penalty is never enforced, but we can assume that the official stance towards the lodge is still one of disapproval (despite the fact that the Vatican's own bank was at one time heavily infiltrated by a Roman Catholic Masonic lodge, called *Propaganda Due*, that doubled as an organized crime syndicate).

But the real change in attitude from the Church is towards Templarism. In 2007, during Benedict XVI's reign, a book called *Processus Contra Templarios* was published by the Vatican in a limited edition of 799 copies selling for $9000 each. It purported to reveal the "truth" about a document they had dubbed the "Chinon Parchment." It had been purportedly discovered six years earlier in the Vatican Secret Archives by a paleographist who worked there named Barbara Frale, "misfiled," allegedly, for 700 years. The book release was timed to coincide with the 700th anniversary of the arrest of the Templars by the French police on October 13, 1307, and gained a great deal of attention from the international press.

What grabbed the headlines was the extraordinary claim that the document proved that Pope Clement V had held his own trial of the Templar leadership after King Philip IV's, the results of which had "exonerated" knights and proved that they were "innocent" after all. These were the terms used in newspaper articles that were published. They were also the words used by Barbara Frale herself when she published a more accessible book on the subject several years later, called *The Templars: The Secret History Revealed*. This would certainly seem newsworthy: both the discovery of the document, and the revision of history that its existence would apparently require.

The only thing is that once you read what Frale writes about what's actually in the document, you find that it proves nothing of the sort. If fact, trying to follow Frale's version of the story of the end of the Templars, it quickly becomes very confusing, mostly because of the meaning she attaches to certain elements of it. She has her own spin on things, but frequently asserts these opinions as though they are facts. It was these assertions that journalists repeated unquestioningly. For instance, here is an utterly misleading description of the document's content from BBC News, using Frale's own words:

> However, according to Prof Frale, study of the document shows that the knights were not heretics as had been believed for 700 years.
>
> In fact she says "the Pope was obliged to ask for pardons from the knights... the document we have found absolves them."

Actually, according to the Parchment, they did confess to what most Christians today would consider blasphemy, including denying Christ and spitting on the cross, as the BBC article states:

Riding the Goat Current 487

> In the hearings before Clement V, the knights reportedly admitted spitting on the cross, denying Jesus and kissing the lower back of the man proposing them during initiation ceremonies.

This mention of the "kiss on the lower back" (which was also applied to the navel and mouth, according to the document) is as close as the BBC comes to addressing one of the most shocking things that one of the knights, Hughes de Perraud, confessed to Clement's cardinals: that the brotherhood had a doctrine condoning—even insisting upon—homosexuality. As the show relates, the knights were obliged to swear off all contact with women the moment they joined the order (dumping their wives and children, in many instances). So, as one of the knights told the cardinals questioning him, they were instructed that if they couldn't control their desires, they should turn to each other for relief, and not refuse one another's advances. As Frale wrote in her book:

> [T]he preceptor exhorted the new Templar not to have sexual relations with women, inviting him, should he absolutely not be able to live chastely, to unite with his brothers and not refuse them should they request sexual favors from him. The novice often reacted angrily, but there were no consequences because the ritual sequence did not provide for any concrete application of this "precept of homosexuality."

As far as the absolution the BBC refers to in their article, this was the absolution of sin after confession, which of course the cardinals had the right to issue. It in no way negated the fact that the sin had taken place. But why did the BBC's writers have the wrong idea here? Even the Catholic

News Agency presented the news with this spin when Frale's book came out in 2007, using the word "exonerated":

> The investigation took place in Rome between 1307 and 1312. According to the document, Pope Clement V exonerated the Templars on the charge of heresy, but found them guilty of other infractions. He also ordered the Knights Templar to disband.

The BBC article had also used the word "exonerated," and went even further:

> The official who found the paper says it exonerates the knights entirely.

The last sentence refers to Ms. Frale. One can certainly see upon inspecting her book where the authors of the news articles got their ideas. In the first chapter, she declares that her discovery has finally set the record straight on the Templar issue, even using the word "innocent":

> [The Chinon Parchment] reveals that the grand master and other high-ranking Templars were found innocent of the charges of heresy, were absolved for less serious offenses by the apostolic authority, and were fully integrated into the Catholic community. Historians believed that the Templars were innocent of the charges brought against them by Philip IV, but many outside academia still suspected the Templars of having been heretics and occultists. The Chinon Parchment is the definitive and incontrovertible proof of the Templars' innocence and should finally put this question to rest.

Apparently, only the uneducated ever had any doubt in the first place! Now this word "innocence," which has now been repeated by so many other writers on the subject

Riding the Goat Current 489

without any qualifications, could only conceivably be used in regards to the very narrow definition of heresy given by Ms. Frale. After describing the juicy details of the secret Templar initiation ceremony, as the knights confessed it to Clement's cardinals, she says:

> Although it was an unworthy tradition that the Templars had further embellished with other vulgar and violent practices, under no circumstances could it be confused with heresy, an offense that implied a strict and long-term adherence to subversive doctrines.

So the Templars were not heretics, she thinks, because their bizarre practices were not part of a religious lifestyle to the individual knights, who, perhaps at least initially, had no idea why they were being asked to do these things. She tells the story of the circumstances that led up to the papal inquiry. Prior to sending the cardinals to question the knights, and prior to Philip's arrest of them, in March 1307 Pope Clement personally interviewed a couple of them. First he called in grand master Jacques de Molay himself "and immediately demanded an explanation for the infamous rumors of the idol said to be secretly venerated in the Temple. . . ." This the grand master denied, and insisted that the matter be investigated to clear the Order's reputation. She writes:

> The grand master of the Templars, indignant at the rumors the sovereign had been spreading, expressly requested the pope to open an inquest into the state of the Temple so as to demonstrate that the slanderous accusations were unfounded. . . .

"Slander" of course would mean that they were the targets of willful lies. But is that what we're talking about here? When the Pope then interviewed Hughes de Perraud, he "confirmed to the pope that the Templars practiced a ritual that required new members to spit on the cross during their induction ceremony."

After the knights were arrested by Philip, Clement sent the cardinals to question the leaders mentioned, and that is when they all, including De Molay, confirmed many of the accusations, as we have discussed. That is also when all of the details about the initiation ceremony finally came out. Frale's description of events is full of contradictions. For instance, she writes:

> The written statutes of the Temple, which date back to the second half of the thirteenth century, contain the complete text of the initiation ceremony.

But she then admits that the controversial final elements of the ceremony were not written in the Rule, and "can be constructed only from the testimony given at the trial." So the statutes didn't in fact give the complete ceremony, as she'd said earlier. According to her, after the knight had sworn his oath to the Order and donned his mantle, he was taken to an ante room, where he was suddenly told to spit on the cross to prove his obedience. Frale gives the details of the ceremony, which she put together from all of the similar elements found in each of the confessions:

> A systematic analysis of all the testimony revealed that at this point most of the brothers resigned themselves to doing what had been commanded, perhaps attempting to spit in the direction of the cross without actually hitting it, while others adamantly refused. . . . Sometimes a candidate's firmness was respected, and he was asked nothing more, but more often his brothers threatened him with prison or death, beating him brutally with their

bare fists or holding a sword to his throat. Then the preceptor gave him the kiss of monastic brotherhood—on the mouth. Often this kiss, common to all religious orders, was followed by two more kisses on the belly and the posterior, which was usually covered by the tunic, but at times there were officiators who exposed their bottoms and, according to some witnesses, even obscenely proposed kisses on the penis. Most postulants obeyed without arguing when the request was moderately humiliating, such as a kiss on the behind, and refused in more extreme cases. While the preceptors demanded that a postulant at least deny Christ or spit on the cross, they usually overlooked a refusal of kisses, and unwilling candidates were not forced to comply.

Now a couple of questions about this clearly need to be asked. For one thing, does spitting on the cross and denying faith in Jesus constitute blasphemy for a Christian knight? Well, Ms. Frale manages to describe the spiritual consequences of this without actually using that term:

> Although it was clear that they were not heretics, it was equally clear that under church doctrine they were guilty, albeit of a much lesser offence. According to canon law, anyone who commits an act of rejection of the faith, even if he does so without conviction, removes himself from the Catholic community, effectively excommunicating himself. The excommunicant can be absolved of his guilt but cannot be acquitted.

At this point in the story, the knights had been excommunicated, but this decision got reverse later, according to the Chinon Parchment, for reasons we will discuss shortly.

The second question that comes to mind after learning the details of the Parchment is this: why was more of an issue not made about the institutionalized homosexuality in the Order? According to Frale, Pope Clement wanted to assign the knights penance, grant them absolution (forgiveness), reverse their excommunication, and then combine the Order with the Knights Hospitaller so that he could launch a new Crusade. How could he even think of doing this in medieval Catholic Europe with a bunch of guys who had all been kissing each others' butts and penises at the very least, and who had sworn not to refuse each others' sexual advances? The Parchment even details the initiation of an eleven-year-old relative of the king of England, who was purportedly subject to the same treatment (and pathetically begged for his uncle to save him when they told him to spit on the cross). Frale seems to think that almost no homosexual activity occurred beyond the homoerotic initiation rite and oath. She writes:

> The surviving trial testimony consists of approximately one thousand depositions with only six attesting to homosexual relations, all of which were described as long-term relationships that almost always had a dimension of affection. . . .

As for the sexual humiliation and forced alienation from God that each knight experienced during initiation, Frale says that these feelings were alleviated afterwards because the neophytes were encouraged to confess their "sins" immediately afterwards. This is in fact how all those "slanderous" rumors got started, she says— you know, the slanderous rumors that accurately stated exactly what the Templars were doing? As she put it:

Riding the Goat Current 493

At the end of the ceremony, the "victim" of all these impositions was invited to report to the chaplain of the order to confess the sins he had just committed and ask for forgiveness. The priests of the Temple comforted these penitents by telling them that they had not committed grave offenses and that if they demonstrated remorse and shame, they would be absolved. Often, however, the brothers confessed to priests outside the Temple, generally Franciscans or Dominicans, who, naturally, were dumbfounded and amplified the brothers' moral disquiet by telling them that they had committed mortal sins, sometimes encouraging them to leave the order. These indiscretions of these honest priests, who were totally ignorant of the real function of the secret ceremony within the Temple, undoubtedly contributed to the gossip circulating in the secular world about the "dark side" of the order.

So what on Earth was the supposed reason for doing any of this stuff in the first place, if they were not heretics or even "occultists," as she put it? Ms. Frale trips all over herself to argue that it was just a test of the postulant's mettle.

> Bernard of Clairvaux . . . insisted on inserting into the text of the Rule a clause exhorting the leaders of the order not to accept new vocations too hurriedly, but rather to subject candidates to a test to ascertain their character and commitment. The exact nature of the test is unclear. Bernard elegantly alluded to Saint Paul's advice to "put them to the test to see if they come from God. . . ."
>
> The written Rule offers no details as to how the preceptor might discourage postulants who were less than totally convincing. . . .

In her imagination, without specific instruction it was only logical that over time tests would be devised that involved blaspheming Jesus and making people kiss their private parts. But she simultaneously makes two contradictory claims about the purpose of this:

1) To see if a candidate would have the courage not to renounce Christ if the Saracens tried to force him to.

2) To see if a candidate would be obedient to his superiors no matter what.

So which were they looking for: loyalty to the Order, or loyalty to Christ and Christian morality? Apparently, nobody flunked the test no matter how they reacted. Frale's opinion on the matter is confusing (especially when she claims that it has somehow been established by the evidence of the Parchment whilst still admitting that it's purely theoretical on her part). Regarding the need for strict obedience within the Order, she states:

A cardinal point of the Templars' ethical code was absolute obedience to one's immediate superiors. . . .

As for the idea that they were testing their recruits to see how they'd stand up to the religious persuasion tactics of the Muslim enemy, here is what she bases it on. She says:

Perhaps they [did these things] because it immediately confronted the new Templar with the violence that he would be subjected to if he were captured by the Saracens.

. . .

We know that the Saracens used to beat and torture capture Christians, forcing them to deny

Christ and spit on the cross before ultimately compelling them to convert to Islam."

. . .

The ritual took place according to a fixed script based on the actual experiences of Templar escapees from Muslim prisons, and dated back to the earliest days of the order... Over time, extraneous elements were added, such as the kiss on the buttocks, a true example of hazing aimed at humiliating the recruit in front of the veterans, and the verbal exhortation to homosexuality, which probably started as a parody of the precept that required Templars to give their whole selves to the order and to their brethren. These vulgar and derisive practices were typical of the often crude behavior found among military corps, and probably arose when the order's traditional discipline began to deteriorate.

This does not seem to fit with the existing legend of the brave Templar knight. How is it that men who were charged never to retreat on the battlefield when fighting Muslims for God would crumple under a bit of peer pressure when asked by their superiors to renounce Christ? Also, how does committing the blasphemy beforehand, without torture, help to prevent you from doing so again later under torture from the enemy? If renouncing Christ is a big deal with real spiritual ramifications, and they were being trained to avoid having to do that, why would they go ahead and commit the blasphemy during the training?

At any rate, this is what the Templars confessed to, twice, both to the king of France's inquisitors, and to the Pope's. So while they may have had their reasons (if you follow and believe Frale's twisted apologist logic), and while they may have been absolved (as any murderer or rapist who confessed to a priest would be), they were certainly not innocent, either by contemporary standards, or today's.

But it does seem that when Frale says "exonerated," she means reconciled with the Church. She seems to place all the importance on the Templars' charter and the fact that it put them under the sole authority of the Pope. She completely rejects the notion that the king of France should have anything to say about the activities of the knights who were stationed in his country. She constantly describes Clement as having the best of intentions. She says he wanted to use his power to protect them, but was constantly thwarted by the king of France trying to "illegally" (her word) claim jurisdiction over them.

The battle for political supremacy between the French crown and the Papacy had been going on for several years. The election of Clement, historians say, had been orchestrated by Philip IV in the first place, as he felt that Clement could be a useful puppet. He then insisted that Clement move the seat of St. Peter from Rome to Avignon, France, where it remained until 1378. Prior to this, there had been a feud between Philip and Clement's predecessor, Pope Boniface VIII.

It is interesting that, according to a National Geographic documentary that featured Frale, one of the ways in which Philip kept Clement in line was by threatening to publicly accuse Clement of heresy as well. Furthermore, as she states in her book, Philip even wanted to exhume the bones of Pope Boniface VIII and put him on trial as "a heretic, a blasphemer, an atheist, and a practitioner of witchcraft." She describes how the bishops in France wanted to separate from the papacy because they believed it "to have reached a state of decadence as to be incapable of performing its traditional role." Then she complains about how a bishop in Troyes named Guichard was burned at the stake for witchcraft at this time, "despite having been acquitted by the pope."

Frale describes the bizarre ending to this series of events. In December of 1307, Jacques de Molay recanted his confession to Philip IV's inquisitors, claiming he'd lied because he was under torture, and publicly displaying his wounds before an audience he was granted at Notre Dame cathedral. The Pope's panels of bishops decided that the knights should be absolved, but that the leaders who were already in prison must remain there for the rest of their lives to pay for what they had done. The way Frale puts it, the papacy saw this as a compromise, bargained down from the death penalty that Philip wanted (although Philip had not actually negotiated with them at all). The Church leaders thought this would enable them to wrap up the matter quickly so they could get about the business of launching another war in the Middle East:

> Upon the return of the three cardinals to Poitiers, the pope drafted a second version of his bull *faciens misericordiam*. It reiterated the main points expressed in the first release, but added that the leaders of the Temple had been absolved and were now protected by judicial immunity and that no one, except the Roman pontiff, could so much as interrogate them.

But as it turned out, De Molay and his sidekick, Geoffrey de Charny, did not care for this solution. They then recanted their confessions again, this time presumably including the ones they gave to the Church authorities who, according to Frale, had not tortured them. Instead, as Frale put it, they proclaimed "the Temple's absolute innocence of all the charges brought against them. . . ." Again, it is hard to see how any of this behavior could be classified as particularly noble, considering that even Frale acknowledged that the Templars were, on many of the counts, "guilty," which normally is thought of as the opposite of "innocent," a term she also used to describe the knights.

At any rate, Frale still seems to think that the Church's authority here, which had failed on all counts, should have continued to reign supreme over the situation. She describes what happened next as a violation of the rights of the Church, as Philip took matters into his own hand and acted decisively:

> In 1310 [Philip IV] ordered 54 Templars who had been found innocent burned at the stake, in total violation of papal authority. Even the theologians of Sorbonne opposed this decision, declaring it completely illegal, but their opinion was ignored.
>
> In the south of France, where the powers of the Inquisition were strongest, there were records of convictions for violations associated with witchcraft, such as the witch's Sabbath and group orgies, which even went beyond the accusations of Philip the Fair in his indictment.

These Frale calls "the most baseless charges, which drew from the most abominable fantasies of the popular imagination." Then, she says, Philip thwarted Clement's authority once again:

> Although the leaders of the Temple were still detained illegally by Philip IV, the pope granted them judicial immunity. Templar grand master Jacques de Molay tried multiple times to obtain an audience with the pope, but royal agents prevented that meetings from ever taking place. Nor were the Templars allowed to be in contact with their grand master. . . .

Riding the Goat Current

Finally, Philip had De Molay and De Charny both executed, burnt at the stake. Predictably, Frale sees these deaths as nothing short of noble martyrdom. She writes:

> Accounts of the execution attested to the great heroism demonstrated by the two leaders. Jacques de Molay asked his executioners to untie the knots around his wrists, raised his eyes to the cathedral of Notre Dame, and prayed to the Virgin Mary... With his prayer, the grand master bore glorious witness to the demise of the Temple and proclaimed its innocence and fidelity to the Christian faith.

So clearly, the Templars have in no way been exculpated. They seem to have been quite guilty of the elements of blasphemy (at least according to the common definition) and committing homosexual acts. Many people have been executed for less. The idea that this was not done as part of a larger heretical doctrine is unproven and groundless. Contrary to the sweeping claims of Barbara Frale (who in 2009 also claimed to have found the name of Jesus written on the Shroud of Turin), the question of why they did these things, and the extent to which they did, as well what other crimes they may have committed, is as unanswered today as before the Chinon Parchment was discovered in 2001. As for the question of the Baphomet idol, Frale offers one sentence, proposing what seems a very odd idea:

> The last point raised in the indictment against the Templars concerned the secret veneration of an idol in the shape of a bearded head. There is clear evidence of the existence of an unusual image of Christ in the religious life of the order, as well as a mysterious cult devoted to the Sacred Blood.

So is she suggesting that the Baphomet head was a representation of Jesus. It seems so. As strange as this may seem, the same idea was the subject of the 1998 book The Head of God: The Lost Treasure of the Templars by Keith Laidler. However, instead of claiming that it was a mere representation of Christ, he theorized that actual man's head had been removed and preseved by them. He proposed that it is now buried underneath Rosslyn Chapel in Scotland. Perhaps he gave Frale the spark of insight that led to her concocting the only "innocent" explanation she could come up with for why the knights would be prostrating themselves before a mummified head that the confessors described as "terrifying." But we need not go that far. The skulls and mummified remains of many saints, including John the Baptist and Mary Magdalene, are regularly venerated by Christians the world over, and all of them look rather creepy. As we mentioned, the Templars were involved in the relic trade. It could have been any one of these that the Templars used in their ceremonies, or something else altogether.

As for Barbara Frale herself, who's worked at the Vatican Secret Archives since 2001, she comes across as a Church spokeswoman apologizing for what happened to the knights, and offering up excuses for why the Pope failed to protect them from Philip. While Philip's control of Clement has long been known, to us it seems that an attempt is being made by her to rehabilitate the reputations of both the Church and the Temple. We can only speculate on whether this is personal interest on her part, or something that her employers have asked her to do, but the Church certainly doesn't seem to have corrected the record at all on these issues in the intervening fourteen years since she allegedly discovered the Chinon Parchment in 2001.

We should also note that, long before the Templars were

openly accused and arrested by Philip IV, several papal pronouncements had stated explicitly that the Templars were guilty of the same sort of things they were eventually prosecuted for. Prince Michael of Albany, in his 2006 book *The Knights Templar of the Middle East* (co-authored with Walid Amine Salhab), recounts some of these:

> Innocent II (1198-1216), writing to the grand visitor of the order, said, "The crimes of your brothers pain us deeply by the scandal that they provoke within the Church. The knights Templar practice the doctrines of Satan." Gregory IX (1227-1241) mentions the fact that he knew that the Templars practiced the act of homosexuality and occult sexual magic under a secret new rule established by Roncelin de Fos (later master of Tortosa and Syria) in 1240. This new rule was written in a Templar book known as "the book of baptismal (sic) by fire."

This final item is of great interest to us. We found mention of *The Book of the Baptism by Fire* in a few other places, but not many (although we were not able to corroborate that it was ever mentioned by Gregory IX, who as we said previously, also condemned the Cathars for worshipping the anuses of black cats). Oddvar Olsen writes about it in *The Templar Papers*, also from 2006:

> In 1877, a German Masonic specialist named Merzdorf claimed to have found, among other Masonic manuscripts, two Latin "Rules" of the Templars (purported to date from the 13th century). One was the Rule for the "chosen brothers," and the other for the "consoled brothers." The first Rule describes the church as the "Synagogue of Anti-Christ," and stipulates an elect reception ceremony (involving various ritual kisses—one on the male

member—and including readings from opening verses of the *Koran*). The latter Rule implies strongly that the Templars shared the doctrines of the Cathars, including that of the "consolamentumm," or mystical baptism. Still authenticity of these has yet to be determined.

. . . I have recently been referred to a text called *The Book of the Baptism of Fire* (The credence of this text needs to be ascertained, so I will just briefly mention it here.) The text was apparently transcribed by the Grand Master in England (Robert Sandford), in 1240 AD. It lists the different articles of *The Order of the Weather*. Some of the articles refer to both the "chosen" and "consoled" brothers. There is also mention of Baphomet and "the Secret Science of the great philosophy: Abrax and the Talisman."

So according to Prince Michael, *The Book of the Baptism of Fire* (which he calls the "baptismal") actually contained these secret rules, while Olsen claims that they are separate documents that nonetheless seem to confirm one another. Yet another author, Timothy Hogan, in his 2012 book *Entering the Chain of Union*, tells the story differently still (drawing on a French website edited by one Jean-Pierre Schmit):

There is a series of documents first published in 1877 by Theodore Merzdorff, which were said to come from the Masonic Grand Lodge of Hamburg. These Latin documents were the official *Rule* of the Knights Templar followed by three other documents said to be secret statutes of the Order. They were said to be copies of the original documents that existed in the Vatican, which were copied in the 1780s-1790s by the Danish scientist Frederic Munter. The documents were translated into German, and from there into French in 1957 by Rene Gilles.

Hogan adds an extra "f" to the end of Merzdorf's first name and tells us that before they were stumbled upon at a German Mason's lodge, they were stumbled upon in Latin in the Vatican archives and translated into German. That's a whole lot of stumbling upon something that is of such great historical importance, and presumably excuses the Church's treatment of the Templars. But yet again—whoopsy!—those Vatican file clerks just can't do anything right! Masonic lodges, as you will find later in this chapter, are just the natural place for such things to show up later for historians to find them. Hogan goes on to describe in more detail what some of the documents were:

> The third document dated July 1240 opens with "Here begins the 'liber consolamenti' or secret statutes, written by Master Roncelinus for the Consoled Brothers of the militia of the Temple." These statutes, composed of twenty articles are signed by Master Roncelinus and another dignitary of the Templar Order, brother Robert of Samford, Procurator of the Knights Templar in England. . . . The last piece dated August 1240 starts with "Here begins the list of secret signs that master Roncelinus has assembled in eighteen articles and addressed to the same Robert of Samford."

Yet another version of the story, told by Mark Amaru Pinkham in his article for *Atlantis Rising Magazine*, entitled "The Templars' Biggest Secret & the Vatican," calls the text *Baptism of Fire of the Brothers-Consulate*, and says that it was discovered in 1780 at the Vatican Library by "a Danish Bishop" (not, as Hogan had claimed, "Danish scientist Frederic Munter"). Also, like the others but unlike Oddvar

Olsen, Pinkham purports that this document is one and the same as that which, he says, is "often referred to by Templar historians as the 'Secret Rule of the Templars.'" According to him, the document contains quite a few amazing admissions not mentioned by the other writers on the subject:

> Said to have been written in 1240 AD. by a French Templar Master named Roncelinus, it appears to give a green light to all the heretical offenses that the Knights were accused of in the 14th century. Permission to indulge in all manner of Templar heresy can be found in this document, including defilement of the Cross, denial of Christ as the Savior, sexual liaison, and the worship of the idolic head known as Baphomet. There is even a passage within the document that gives the Knights permission to initiate other gnostics into their order, including Cathars, Bogomils, and even Assassins. If the *Baptism of Fire of the Brothers-Consulate* was indeed in circulation beginning in 1240 AD. it would have been an easy task for a Church or Royal spy to procure a copy for their employers.

The references made by the above-quoted sources to the "Consoled Brothers," "Brothers Consulate," and "consolamenti" are taken by Oddvar Olsen to imply that the Templars practiced the *consolamentum* of the Cathars, which he describes as a "mystical baptism." Benjamin Walker tells us more about this mysterious ritual in *Gnosticism: Its Influence and History*:

> The central Cathar rite was the *consolamentum*, a kind of adult baptism of the spirit, which was administered only once. It was reserved as a rule for those who had attained the level of the Perfect, but it could be given to any Cathar prepared to make an

irrevocable renunciation of the flesh and consecrate his or her life to God. The rite was preceded by a fast and imparted by the laying on of hands and placing on the head the gospel of St John. If anyone sinned after being "consoled," he was expelled from the Cathar communion.

So strict were the requirements that many Cathars only underwent the rite at the point of death, so as to avoid any further chance of sinning. Because it was generally held that death through illness or old age only proved that Satan was still in control of the body, some Cathars hastened the end by what was called the *endura*, a ritual suicide or killing. It was thought best to be purified by the *consolamentum* and then face the *endura*, for then salvation was certain. The methods of *endura* included fasting to death or taking poison, or being smothered by one or more of the Perfect who held a pillow over the mouth of the endurist, or strangled him.

So this is the ritual that the "Consoled Brothers" of the so-called *Book of the Baptism by Fire* were named after? We presently cannot be sure. A copy of the book in which the alleged document was published, compiled by Theodor Merzdorf (who spelled his first name without an "e" on the end, a detail that none of the authors quoted above got right), has been obtained by our research staff and is now being analyzed. It has an extremely long title in German. But it seems to us that Prince Michael was probably able to read the text, or at least knew someone who could, because it appears that some of the "inside information" in his book about the Templars must have come from this.

One thing we do know, though, is that this Roncelin/Roncelinus fellow has been associated with the Cathars, and blamed for introducing blasphemous rituals to Templar tradition, in many books before. *The Temple and the Lodge* by Michael Baigent and Richard Leigh (1989) tells us:

> Between 1248 and 1250, the Master of Provence was one Roncelin de Fos. Then, between 1251 and 1253, Roncelin was Master of England. By 1260, he was again Master of Provence, and presided in that capacity until 1278. It is thus quite possible that Roncelin brought aspects of heretical Cathare thought from their native soil in France to England. This suggestion is supported by the testimony before the Inquisition of Geoffroy de Gonneville, Preceptor of Aquitaine and Poitou. According to Geoffroy, unnamed individuals allege that all evil and perverse rules and innovations in the Temple had been introduced by a certain Brother Roncelin, formerly a Master of the Order. The Brother Roncelin in question is bound to have been Roncelin de Fos.

At this point, we would like to delve much more deeply into the claims made in Prince Michael's book regarding the Templars. But first it is necessary to say a few words about Prince Michael himself. Tracy R. Twyman first became aware of this man in 1999, after reading about him in a book by Laurence Gardner entitled *Bloodline of the Holy Grail*, and subsequently reading Prince Michael's book *The Forgotten Monarchy of Scotland*. She then interviewed him for a magazine she published at the time called *Dagobert's Revenge*.

Prince Michael claims to be the rightful heir to the throne of Scotland, saying that his own "Royal House of Stewart" is the same as the British royal dynasty the "House of Stuart."

Riding the Goat Current 507

They provided monarchs for Scotland from 1371 through 1714, and ruled over England as well from 1567 to the same end date. Michael, whose given last name is Lafosse, is an immigrant to Scotland from Belgium, where, he claims, his family has been waiting "in exile" to return to the throne. His first book was part of his campaign to present himself as a potential head of state should Scotland become independent at some point. Michael further claims that his family is descended from Jesus Christ and Mary Magdalene through the Merovingian dynasty of France. He also says that he is the head of Scottish Templarism, and purports to have inside knowledge about their "real" history.

The legitimacy of all these assertions has been widely disputed. In past writings, Michael has relied heavily on the "research" of his friend Laurence Garner, now deceased. Gardner put himself forward as the head of an organization called the "Dragon Court," which was supposedly as old as the sixteenth century and dedicated to promoting the interests of the "Dragon lineage." What was meant by this, essentially, were the royal bloodlines, found in all cultures throughout history, which purportedly have a more-than-human origin—either through gods or angels that allegedly mated with humans in the distant past. Gardner traced these bloodlines from modern royalty back to the mythical figures they allegedly came from. These genealogies seem to connect everyone of importance in history to everybody else, whether they are good or bad, the Hitlers and the Mother Theresas. So it is of no great contradiction to realize that these genealogies put Jesus himself as a descendant of fallen angels, claiming also that he married a lady of similar extraction (Mary Magdalene) and bred children with her. It is a holy lineage beyond good and evil. This idea is perhaps similar to what was expressed by Charles Peguy in his poetic ode to the House of Lorraine (a French branch of this "Dragon bloodline"), referencing the double-barred cross that is associated with their family:

> The arms of Jesus are the Cross of Lorraine,
>
> Both the blood in the artery and the blood in the vein,
>
> Both the source of grace and the clear fountaine;
>
> The arms of Satan are the Cross of Lorraine,
>
> And the same artery and the same vein,
>
> And the same blood and the troubled fountaine.

Tracy R. Twyman happens to have some inside knowledge of the workings of the Dragon Court. Shortly after publishing her interview with Prince Michael of Albany, she became friends with Nicholas de Vere von Drakenberg, whom she knew until his death in 2012. He claimed to have been the "actual" head of the "real" Dragon Court, as well as the real author of several of the books that Laurence Gardner published under his own name. He presented her with the original manuscript, which was quite clearly what Gardner had based his own writings on, in very close parallel. On the copy of Laurence Gardner's *Genesis of the Grail Kings* that she has in her office, De Vere is thanked in the acknowledgements for giving Gardner access to his "household archives" as a source for his research. In the first edition of this book, his name was listed on the cover as the co-author, which was then mysteriously removed in subsequent editions.

After knowing De Vere well and seeing the evidence, she did become convinced, as she still is, that De Vere was the actual author of two of Gardner's books, and the actual progenitor of the "Dragon Court" that Gardner based his own organization on. She does not believe that it is centuries old. She says it was an informal group of De Vere's friends who took their inspiration from him and who took on various "royal titles" that he handed out to them, supposedly based on their genealogies. She herself received one of these titles, and was even made the Grand Master of the Dragon Court for a few years, as well as the copyright holder for some of De Vere's books. All of this happened at his insistence. She never asked for it. She helped him get his own book published in his own name, and then voluntarily relinquished the copyright, the royal title, and the grand mastership.

While Twyman thought that De Vere's work on historical and mythological matters had value, she found his claims about himself and his organization to be grandiose and unverifiable. She is also fairly positive that some of the information in his books came from channeling. The family "archives" that Laurence Gardner said he got his information from were, in fact, like the "Akashic records" of New Age western pop Buddhism: they existed on the astral plane, accessible only through the mind of Nicholas de Vere.

Ms. Twyman is not sure to what extent Prince Michael knows the truth about where Laurence Gardner got his information from, which Michael has relied on so heavily. He himself claimed to be part of the Dragon Court too (although he doesn't mention it in his latest book). Most recently we found him on the membership list of something called IBSSA (the International Bodyguard and Security Services Association). The other members of this group (whose names are listed on the organization's website) all seem to fall within the following categories:

(1) Members of one or several "royal houses," either legitimate and verifiable, and/or fake-seeming royal

houses like the House of Stewart and the Dragon Court were.

(2) Members of both legitimate and/or fake-seeming Masonic groups and modern Templar organizations.

When we say "and/or," we mean that some of these people were simultaneously members of real organizations and what seem like scam organizations, holding both real and possibly fake titles. Also common was involvement in very real UN non-governmental organizations of various types. We have verified, by researching the backgrounds of each name listed, that several of them really are royalty, and most are quite high up in Masonry, some in significant leadership positions. Many of them can be found in pictures on the ISBBA's website dressed in royal or Templar regalia. They are shown pictured in investiture ceremonies receiving honors. The website also contains information on martial arts classes that the ISBBA is purportedly holding, as well as international security reports on matters like terrorism and organized crime.

We have no idea why this organization exists, if in fact it does. It may just be a website meant for people like us to find, giving the impression of an Illuminati nexus of royals and Masons who happen to be connected to international intelligence (as the name of the organization implies). Michael reported in his first book being surveilled and interviewed by MI5 after launching his campaign for the Scottish throne. So he has been trying to suggest for some time that is a spook at war behind the scenes with other spooks.

We are not sure exactly what we are suggesting here, but these details have to be important, for in his latest book, *The Knights Templar of the Middle East*, Michael claims that he

Riding the Goat Current 511

based his research on some Masonic documents that he accidentally stumbled upon in a Masonic lodge that he belongs to. As he tells it:

> I came across what is referred to as "The Charles Morrisson Collection" (about 2000 works), housed at the library of Scottish Grand Lodge in Edinburgh, Scotland. The collection's oldest script dates back to 1615, extending into the 19th century. Some of these scripts were handwritten in Old French, some of which had been published privately, all of which had been forgotten and never consulted.

Think about the fact that so much of what we think the accusations were against the Templars, linked to more modern accusations against Freemasons, comes from the papal "Allocution Against the Freemasons" of Pius IX, who was himself accused of being an initiated Freemason by other Freemasons, allegedly speaking out in their own order's defense. Consider the fact that the most complete text of this Allocution easily available to the general reader is to be found in the Masonic textbook *Morals and Dogma* by Albert Pike, where it is merely quoted and commented upon, supposedly to demonstrate the adversity of suspicion that Masons have had to face because of the Church throughout the years. The information we have about what the Templars and Masons have been accused of comes from . . . Masons themselves!

Consider the fact that the aforementioned *Book of the Sun of Suns and Moon of Moons*, which purportedly mentions "Bafumed," and described it as the transformative power of the universe was supposed to have been discovered by Freemason Giles F. Yates in the library of a Masonic lodge. The documents published by Theodore Merzdorf, claiming to contain the Templars' secret rule in a privately-published

Templar text (*The Book of the Baptism of Fire*), was supposedly found in the Masonic Grand Lodge of Hamburg by Merzdorf after being discovered by Danish scientist Frederic Munter in the Vatican archives. In a similar story, the Chinon Parchment was supposedly accidentally discovered in the Vatican library.

Likewise the *Dossiers Secrets*, kept on file at the Bibliotheque Nationale and supposedly published for the Swiss Masonic "Grand Loge Alpina," are the documents that lured three British journalists into investigating the French Masonic secret society called the "Priory of Sion," promoting a questionable claimant to the (now nonexistent) French throne. This culminated in the 1980s bestseller *Holy Blood, Holy Grail* and later the *Da Vinci Code* storyline of the secret bloodline of Christ. Once again, the "rumors" were floated by the Masonic secret society itself, via documents deposited in a library. Other documents related to the group's "history" that were presented to the authors for evidence appeared to have been faked with the forged signatures of notaries and forged bank receipts in a ruse that involved several people known to work for British intelligence services.

Nicholas de Vere told Tracy R. Twyman personally that the way to falsely establish the historicity of newly-invented "facts" is to deposit documents with false publication dates in libraries and wait for someone to discover them. He said it as though it was something he had done before. Although De Vere did have a falling out with Laurence Gardner and Prince Michael early on, it seems likely that other friends of the "prince" have been involved in the same kinds of shenanigans and know the same tricks of the trade.

The narrative being promoted by Prince Michael in his latest book—that Templars were more influenced by secret traditions of Islam than Judeo-Christianity, with more than a

Riding the Goat Current 513

hint that this tradition is truly superior to either Christianity or Judaism—seems to be one that several Masonic scholars (that is, scholars on the subject of Freemasonry who were themselves also Freemasons) have been promoting for some time. This goes along with the idea, supported by occult writers like Richard Burton, Idries Shah, Robert Graves, and Baron von Sebottendorf—all probably Masonic initiates at one point in their lives—that Freemasonry comes directly from the mystical Islamic stream of Sufism. First, let's go over what Prince Michael has to say.

One of the first things the reader notices is that Prince Michael's book is rather shockingly critical of Christianity, as well as "the American-created state of Israel" and "the banking world . . . within the hands of a Jewish hierarchy." He writes:

> The simple truth is that the creation of Christianity, an uphill struggle that took over six hundred years, was no more than a fantasy gone wrong. Moreover, it was concocted by a bunch of rather sick but ambitious individuals who not only lied through their teeth, but also sent millions of people to their death with the sole purpose of dying, so they thought, in the name of "The Lord." The history of Christianity is bloody, savage, and cruel.

Of course, as for the 27,000 Islamic terrorist attacks carried out globally since 2001 alone, Prince Michael's only applicable comment in this book is to say that, because of the hijinks of Israel and the Jewish bankers, "Islam is bound to fight back for the very survival of its own religious tenets."

But let us remember that Prince Michael has spent his whole adult life preparing his ill-omened campaign to become the new king of Scotland. He could even imagine that his reformed royal house will somehow take over England as well, as his alleged ancestors did before him. So perhaps he, like Prince Charles of the House of Windsor, is looking at the demographic projections regarding immigration into the UK from Islamic countries, versus the even higher rate of emigration of the native population fleeing to the continent and the US, as well as the birth rates of those immigrants versus that of the native population. Maybe he sees that, were this to happen, he would be reigning over a population largely predisposed to the Muslim religion. Charles, whose family links to the descendants of Mohammed were announced by Burke's Peerage years ago, has gone as far as to proclaim that he began learning Arabic in 2013, "in order to undertake a deeper study of the *Koran*," and in that same year was quoted as saying:

> The Islamic world is the custodian of one of the greatest treasures of accumulated wisdom and spiritual knowledge available to humanity.

Prince Michael's book goes on to make a claim that should be easily verifiable or discredited, except for the fact that the holy sites in both Jerusalem and Mecca are all totally inaccessible to archeologists or other independent researchers. He says that Jerusalem is not the site of Solomon's Temple, but rather that Mecca is instead, and that the Templars knew this. First, he asserts, they discovered, by conducting secret digs beneath the Mosque of Omar and the Dome of the Rock in Jerusalem, that there was no foundation of Solomon's Temple to be found there. They found the remains of the second temple, built by Herod, but not Solomon's. He writes:

> What became also obvious to the Templars is that the original Jerusalem of Solomon, the pre-Babylonian invasion Jerusalem, was not that which

the crusaders were occupying in Palestine and from which these various crusader kings were ruling from.

Prince Michael then tells us, again on inside information, that some Templars went on a secret mission to Mecca to see the real temple foundations for themselves. He says that the caliph of Egypt loaned them a fleet of ships based in the Red Sea, which they used to travel to the holy city "disguised as faithful Muslims." The Prince purports that there are rumors believed "in some quarters" (Masonic ones, we presume) that the knights:

> . . . had a free entrance within the city of Makkah. Strangely enough, the history of Makkah also claims that they had free access to the "Sons of the Old Woman" (also referred to as the "Sons of the Widow"), the priests in charge of the Makkah temple.

This last reference, of course, is significant to Freemasons because "Sons of the Widow" is an epithet that members of that fraternity use for themselves.

Prince Michael then goes on to make the case that Mecca was the original Jerusalem, and the Kaaba the true Temple of Solomon, pointing out Hebrew-sounding place-names in western Arabia, "from the port of Jiddah to that of Jizzan," which match up to the names of Israelite cities mentioned in the Old Testament. He questions the validity of the geographical designations that have been made ascribing biblical histories to places in modern Israel and Palestine, rightly mentioning the academic controversy that each of these identifications has provoked. Opining that "Very little in Palestine proves it to be the promised land of Moses, even less that of the kingdom of Solomon," and stating that most of the controversial designations were made as recently as the nineteenth century "by Christian so-called scholars,"

Prince Michael then posits that what we think of now as the ancient city of Jerusalem was in fact a settlement of Babylonians practicing Judaism who were sent there when the Persians took over Babylon. As he put it:

> The question that the Templars had to ask themselves was: did the Jews, following their Babylonian exile, go back to the right area of origin or did they simply choose a new area to settle? The simple truth is that none of those Jews who "came back" to Jerusalem after 539 or 519 BC (scholars are still arguing the exact date when the Jews left Babylon) had been born in their place of origin. All of them, including Zerrubabel (sic) (whose name actually means "born in Babel"), were born in Babylon. In all probability, Zerrubabel (sic) and his people were told by the Persian king Cyrus or Cambyses where to settle.

So why would the Templars have received special permission to visit Mecca, the sacred center of their battlefield enemies? Also, why would it have occurred to them to look there in the first place? Well according to Prince Michael, many of the founding Templars came from families that had intermarried with Arabic Muslim aristocracy, particularly Grand Master Hughes de Payens (whose last name, by the way, means "of the Pagans"). Prince Michael says that his grandfather was Abd ar-Rahman an-Nasir, son of Muhammad al-Mansur, the emir of Cordoba in Muslim Spain, a descendant of Mohammed through the Idrisid dynasty of North Africa. He claims that the Islamic side of the family was involved in Sufism. The same claim is made by Idries Shah in his book *The Sufis*, where he said that de Payens' father Theobaldo was surnamed "the Moor" (the word for Arabs living in medieval Muslim Spain) and that this was the meaning behind the three severed Moors heads on the family coat of arms. Shah said that they were really "heads of wisdom," or Baphomet heads. On this last subject, Shah wrote:

> Probably relying upon contemporary Eastern sources, Western scholars have recently supposed that "Bafomet" has no connection with Mohammed, but could well be a corruption of the Arabic *abufihamat* (pronounced in Moorish Spanish something like *bufihimat*). The word means "father of understanding." In Arabic, "father" is taken to mean "source, chief seat of," and so on. In Sufi terminology, *ras el-fahmat* (head of knowledge) means the mentation of man after undergoing refinement of the transmuted consciousness.
>
> It will be noted that the word "knowledge, understanding" used here is derived from the Arabic FHM root. FHM, in turn, is used to stand for both FHM and derivatives, meaning "knowledge;" and FHM and derivatives, standing for "black, coalman" and so on.

Not only does Shah insist that the word Baphomet came from Sufi Arabs, but also that the image of Baphomet as a goat-man has similar origins, along with the body of tradition observed by European witches who held sabbaths for the goat god. Specifically he credits the "Aniza Bedouin clan" with having "brought the witches to the West." In particular, he names as responsible the Sufi poet Abu el-Atahiyya ("the Freak"), about whom Shah quotes an unnamed source describing him as the "father of Arabic sacred poetry." This poet had a mystical cult of followers that Shah says migrated to Spain after his death in the ninth century, bringing with them symbols and rituals that would be absorbed by practitioners of Western witchcraft. If Shah is to be believed, Eliphas Levi's depiction of Baphomet with a torch burning between his horns originates with the poet's followers. As he wrote:

> His circle of disciples, the Wise Ones, commemorated him in a number of ways after his death. To signify his tribe, they adopted the goat, cognate with the tribal name (Anz, Aniza). A torch between goat horns ("the devil" in Spain, as it later became) symbolized for them the light of illumination from the intellect (head) of the "goat," the Aniza teacher. His *wasm* (tribal brand) was very much like a broad arrow, also called an eagle's foot. An alternative name for the Aniza is a kind of bird. This sign, known to witches as the goosefoot, became the mark for their places of meeting.
>
> . . . After Atahiyya's death before the middle of the ninth century, tradition has it that a group of his school migrated to Spain, which had been under Arab rule for over a century at that time.

Shah, who clearly presents himself as a Sufi just like the ones he writes about, tended to put forward information with no attribution, claiming to have inside knowledge as a Sufi initiate. He traced quite a few peculiar terms associated with European witchcraft to Arabic words used by Sufis, including "athame" (the ritual knife used in witches), "coven," and "sabbath" (or "sabbat," as it's often spelled, which he connects to "az-zabat," meaning "the forceful [occasion]"). He purported that quite a few non-Islamic religious and esoteric traditions actually stem from the influence of Sufism, including Jewish cabalism, the Holy Grail myth, chivalry, the cult of the Virgin Mary, the Catholic use of rosaries, the Hindu chakra system, yogic exercises, and the Yezidi religion of

Kurdish Iraq. (The latter sect does, in fact, claim their own lineage from eleventh-century Sufi Master Sheik Adi.) While Shah didn't suggest that the Kaaba in Mecca is the real Temple of Solomon, he did say that it was not the Solomonic temple that the Templars were really dedicated to:

> That the Templars were thinking in terms of the Sufi, and not the Solomonic, Temple in Jerusalem, and its building, is strongly suggested by one important fact. "Temple" churches which they erected, such as one in London, were modeled upon the Temple as found by the Crusades, not upon any earlier building. This Temple was none other than the octagonal Dome of the Rock, built in the seventh century on a Sufi mathematical design, and restored in 913. The Sufi legend of the building of the Temple accords with the alleged Masonic version.
>
> . . .
>
> This, and no earlier one, is the Temple whose servants were the Knights Templar, accused of Saracenic leanings.
>
> . . .
>
> . . . The architectural measurements chosen for this Temple, as for the Kaaba building at Mecca, were numerical equivalents of certain Arabic roots conveying holy messages, every part of the building being related to every other part in definite proportion.

Prince Michael concurs with the idea that Templar buildings were modeled after the Dome of the Rock, and that this was the origin of the "secrets of sacred geometry" that later became central to Masonic teachings, stating that:

The architectural concept of the Dome of the Rock would be later borrowed by the Christian church in its endeavor to establish the gothic style of architecture in Europe. For this is what the Dome of the Rock was, (sic) the precursor of the gothic arch.

Now while Shah did not come out and say anything concrete about the original Solomon's Temple and where it was located, he did make an intriguing statement that hints at something similar to what Prince Michael is claiming:

What possible connection, it is sometimes asked, could there be between the Mecca temple of the Moslems and the Temple of Solomon and its building? There could be a very close connection indeed. First let it be noted that charges against ancient Sufis included the terrible allegation that a mime of the Mecca pilgrimage ceremonies could be carried out anywhere with equal validity to the actual pilgrimage.

This introduces the idea that post-diaspora Jews could have built a temple in Jerusalem to mimic their real temple in Mecca, as Prince Michael asserts they did. He also suggests a connection between the "black stone" of the Kaaba (a meteorite said to have fallen from heaven) and the "stone of the wise" (i.e., "Philosopher's Stone") of the alchemists:

It should not be forgotten that the Kaaba (literally, the Cube) is the foursquare temple of Mecca. The "black stone" of Mecca is set in an outer corner of the Kaaba. It is thus correctly described as the Kaaba (Cube) stone, easily rendered as the Cubic Stone. It is also called *harajel aswad* (black stone). "Black," as we have noted, is rendered as "coal," and the "stone of black" can be rendered as *harajel fehm*, "stone of wisdom," or even, in translation, "stone of the wise." Second only to this place for all Moslems is the sanctified spot known as the Temple of Solomon in Palestine.

Sufi tradition has it that [there] were a number of men who assembled in the Mecca temple and devoted themselves to its service. On the fall of Jerusalem to the Arabs, the first act of the Moslems was to repair to the site of the Solomonic Temple to acquire it for Islam. That the Sufi tradition was continued in respect of the Dome of the Rock is evidenced by the fact that its later interior decorations contain Sufi symbolic designs. Templar churches and other indications show the influence of the Saracen version of the Solomonic Temple.

There are several interesting connections between the (alleged) temple(s) in Jerusalem and the Kaaba in Mecca that we have noted ourselves. One is that Mohammed is alleged to have flown from the Kaaba to Jerusalem and back in a single night. Actually, *The Koran* says that he was taken "for a Journey by night from the Sacred Mosque to the farthest Mosque," but these have always been taken to be the Kaaba and the Temple Mount in Jerusalem, respectively. He also visited Heaven, as Enoch and Hermes are said to have done. While he was there he met Jesus and John the Baptist.

Supposedly it all started when he laid his head on the black stone of the Kaaba (analogous to the biblical story of Jacob falling asleep with his head on a stone), and was visited by the archangel Gabriel (the angel of wisdom and communication, similar to Hermes in that regard). He was given a ride on a winged horse with the face of a human female whose name was "Barak" ("Lightning"). Amazingly, before the trip began, Mohammed was baptized with the holy water of wisdom, including his internal organs. A *hadith* (tradition) attributed to Malik bin Sa`sa`ah (as reported in the first footnote on Sura 53 of the Hilali and Khan translation of *The Koran*) says that Mohammed told him:

> While I was at the House in a state midway between sleep and wakefulness, (an angel recognized me) as the man lying between two men. *A golden tray full of wisdom and belief* was brought to me and my body was cut open from the throat to the lower part of the abdomen and then *my abdomen was washed with Zam-zam water and (my heart was) filled with wisdom and belief* (emphasis added).

Zam-zam water is that coming from the sacred well near the Kaaba, which supposedly miraculously sprang from the ground when the Arab progenitor Ishmael and his mother Hagar were dying of thirst in the desert after being ditched there by Abraham. It is used by Muslims today in much the same way that holy water is used by Catholics. The whole incident is called "Isra," which sounds an awful lot like "Israel," but is actually translated "Night Journey," from the root "sera," meaning "to travel by night." Although it is described as happening to him while he was in a state "midway between sleep and wakefulness," most Muslims take it to have been a literal, physical, and miraculous journey.

However, to us it sounds identical to the term "go forth by night," which is used in the European witchcraft tradition to refer to the process of astral-projecting in one's sleep as a method of attending the Witches' Sabbath on a high mountain peak. After projecting their souls into the ether, it was said that the witches would ride flying goats or broomsticks to the secret meeting place for the ceremony. The Devil or "Black Man" was sometimes said to arrive at the

Riding the Goat Current

Sabbath by the same method. Just like with Mohammed's Night Journey, while it sounds like it's all just a dream, it was taken by the witches themselves to be real. The Church took it to be so real that confessing to it was punishable by death. Modern witches sometimes have a more nuanced understanding. As Nigel Jackson wrote in *Masks of Misrule*:

> The true Sabbat is simultaneously a state of Dreaming-Consciousness and an extradimensional locus where the convocation of the living and the dead occurs and the Great Return which leads to a new becoming is achieved.
>
> . . . The oneiric nature of the Witch-Cult is evidenced at some of the earliest trials in Toulouse in 1335, where the witch Catherine Delort affirmed that she went to the Sabbat in her sleep. The Dream-Sabbat is the supreme rite of the Witches. . . . The Sabbat is a dream . . . of such potency that the profane world seems pallid and unreal in comparison.

This journey to the Sabbath on the back of a goat evinces the stories of Masonic initiations involving a goat ride, discussed previously. One can find postcards from the nineteenth and early twentieth century decorated with images of caricatured men dressed in Masonic regalia mounted upon a caprine animal and captioned with the term "Riding the Goat." As we mentioned, the rumor among suspicious "cowans" (non-Masons) was that this was part of the Masonic initiation ceremony. But as the previously-quoted passage from Albert Mackey's Masonic encyclopedia proves, the fraternity officially denies that this is anything but a joke inspired by the accusations from their critics that they worship the Devil.

The 2012 book *Ritual America*, edited by Adam Parfrey and Craig Heimbichner, features numerous pictures taken from Masonic supply companies offering mechanical goats for sale to be ridden during ceremonies (along with devil costumes and other diabolical paraphernalia). However, they quote Christopher Hodapp's *Freemasons for Dummies* (written by a Mason, of course), which puts a damper on the idea that these goats were ever used for any "real" ceremonies. He says that the toy goats were only used:

> . . . in other fraternal organizations and "fun" degrees. . . . Such items only served to perpetuate the myth that Masons and other fraternities required a goat-ride ritual for their initiations. Freemasonry never has.
>
> Rest assured: There is no lodge goat. The degrees of Freemasonry are serious business to Freemasons, and there is no horseplay (or goatplay).

On the opposite side of the spectrum of belief, Turkish television, in the late 90s, aired footage supposedly taken of the "secret 33rd degree ritual" of Scottish Rite Masonry (which is purportedly "honorary" and has no actual ritual, according to Masonic publications). The rite shown on TV, taken with a "hidden camera," allegedly showed a goat being "sacrificed to Satan," although the image quality is so poor that nobody could have guessed that from watching it. Nonetheless, the video had quite an impact on the Turkish public, where Masonic conspiracy theories are quite widely believed. In fact, throughout the Muslim world it is frequently taught in school textbooks that the Ottoman Empire was taken down by infiltration from atheistic anti-establishment Freemasons in the Turkish government through the "Young Turks" reform movement, largely populated by Masons.

The claim that mechanical goats have only been used in auxiliary "fun" lodges is probably a reference to the antics of groups like the "Royal Order of Jesters," a quasi-Masonic

Riding the Goat Current 525

offshoot organization open only to members of the Masonic "Shrine," which itself is only open to those who have already reached the thirty-second degree of the Scottish Rite. The ROJ is dedicated to the concept of "Mirth," and their official emblems for lodge functions are usually pornographic. Their mascot is the Billiken, a charm doll that looks like a little troll smiling evilly. It is called "the God of Things as They Ought to be," and the dolls, which began being sold around the turn of the century in an un-Masonic context, were said to bring good luck. The ROJ Billiken is often shown displaying his anus (marked with a red dot) and inviting the onlooker to kiss it. This is a clear reference to the *osculum inflame* of the Gnostics, Templars, and witches.

The Royal Order of Jesters is registered as a tax-exempt charitable organization and promoted as a place for men who are already Masons to have fun putting on comedy plays and the like. In reality, the ROJ seems to exist solely as a place for members to have group sex with prostitutes, which is what happens at most of their meetings. In relation to this, some of the Jesters were prosecuted for the trafficking of underage sex slaves after an FBI sting in Buffalo, New York. The existence of an inner hierarchy of the Jesters called the "Secret Order of Brothers in Blood" hints at possibly even darker practices. The obscene kiss of the Jesters is not unique to them among Masonic organizations, but is also practiced by their parent order, the Shrine, yet in a much more interesting context.

The Ancient Arabic Order of the Noble Mystic Shrine (an acronym for an anagram of "A MASON") was started in 1870 in Manhattan by Walter M. Fleming and William J. Florence. Mr. Florence claimed that the idea came to him when attending a party in Marseilles, France that was thrown by an Arab diplomat, which ended with the guests being initiated into a secret society of some sort. This inspired him to create a Masonic appendage organization dedicated to "fun" and "fellowship." Originally membership was confined only to Masons who have reached the 32nd degree of the Scottish Rite (Prince of the Sublime Royal Secret), or the Knights Templar degree of the York Rite. (In 2000 this was changed so that you only have to be a third degree Master Mason in the Blue Lodge, and in Arkansas you don't have to be a Mason at all.) The first "Temple" (as the lodges of this group are called) was named "Mecca."

There is no doubt that the "Shrine" which the order is named after is the Kaaba in Mecca. The initiation rite involves pretending that you are there. At the start of it, the "Oriental Guide" opens the Bible to the first chapter of *Job*, and *The Koran* to the 38th Sura, with *The Koran* placed in front of the Bible. Strangely, some of the opening lines indicate the idea that "Allah" and "God" are not the same thing, as the "Illustrious Potentate" prays the following:

> In the name of God, our Father, and by the existence of Allah, the creed of Mohammed, and the legendary sanctity of the Temple of Mecca, I now proclaim this Temple regularly opened for business and ceremony.
> . . .

Elsewhere in the ritual, Allah is referred to as "their God"—that is, "of the Arabs." But then the Illustrious Potentate declares his faith in that very religion, proclaiming:

> Who is he who hath professed to have conversed in person with the Supreme and maketh himself mightiest of the mighty? Mohammed, the Prophet of the Arab's creed.

A few minutes later, the High Priest pronounces:

> There are Moslems among us; there are others who swerve from propriety: but who so seeketh Islam earnestly seeks true direction. . . .

Later, the candidate must declare:

> And upon this sacred book, by the sincerity of a Moslem's oath, I here register this irrevocable vow, in wilful violation whereof may I incur the fearful penalty of having my eyeballs pierced to the center with a three-edged blade, my feet flayed and I be forced to walk the hot sands upon the sterile shores of the Red Sea until the flaming sun shall strike me with livid plague; and may Allah, the God of Arab, Moslem and Mohammed, and the God of our fathers, support me to the entire fulfilment of the same. Amen, Amen, Amen.

He is then put through the "Moslem test," which is a series of hazing rites of physical abuse, on his "journey" to the "shrine" where the black stone is. Just as at the real Kaaba, the sacred black stone is situated in the corner, the one in the Shriner rite is placed in the southeast corner of their "temple." One of these hazing rites is called the "Grand Salaam," and involves being hit on the buttocks with an exploding paddle. He is also made to urinate on the "Devil's Pass," which seems analogous to what Muslims do during the "Hajj" (the pilgrimage to the Kaaba). Later it is explained that this is literally just an excuse to get him to whip out his penis for others to see, as a test of his manhood. He is told:

> Since this is a male organization, it is one way we have of making sure we are not admitting any impersonators into our ranks. Thus, you had to display your male organ to give a few drops.

As if this were a real concern, part of the ritual involves a character (male, a brother) dressed up as a female who is found to be "spying" on the fraternity, and who is stabbed in the heart as punishment (with a bag of wine under his armpit punctured to represent the blood). They pretend to cut a wound into her breast into the shape of a Muslim crescent. The "blood" is collected in a bowl and held aloft. Then the Illustrious Potentate tells them all:

> Let us in this maiden's blood, seal the alliance of our bond of secrecy and silence, and let this day's bloody work in the deepest recesses of every Noble's heart be buried.
>
> . . .
>
> . . . It now becomes our duty to deposit the result of our vigilance in the tomb, isolated from the eyes of a meddling world; a fit abiding place for the remains of the unfaithful. . . .

Another character, the "spy" woman's male accomplice, is "beheaded," and a plastic head is placed on display on a chair next to a skeleton, a coffin, a noose, and a coffin. Then the members are given a lecture stating that their order was started by Mohammed himself, with the exact same *raison d'etre* as the Knights Templar: to protect pilgrims *en route* to the holy shrine. He says:

> My friends or Nobles of the Mystic Shrine, the order with which you have become united was founded by Mohammed and has as its background the trackless desert of Arabia and the fearless, devoted, and barbaric Arab.

Arabic history and tradition tell us that after the fall and separation of Adam and Eve, they were united near the place now known as "Mecca."

Adam prayed for a Shrine where he might worship. In due time, a Tabernacle of Clouds was given to him.

After the death of Adam, the Tabernacle was withdrawn, and his son, Seth, erected a Temple of Stone in that place; later Ishmael, with his father Abraham, rebuilt on this sacred spot of the Tabernacle of Clouds, the Kaaba or the Sacred Temple of National Worship.

Each year the true followers of the faith would make a pilgrimage to Mecca to worship at the national shrine.

Because of the presence of a lawless element in the city of Mecca, many of these pilgrims were robbed, beaten, and even murdered. Therefore, in the year of AD 647, Mohammed organized a group of fearless men as an inquisition or vigilance committee, whose main objects were to protect the weak, dispense justice, and punish the criminals.

The order was firmly established in 1698, and since then has become one of the most highly-favoured secret organizations in the world.

Because of the ruthless manner which the group used to accomplish its aims, its leaders had to be careful in their selection of new members. Therefore, severe tests and strong obligations were required of each candidate.

You have just passed through those tests and are now a Noble of the Mystic Shrine.

In these rites, the Shriners pretend to have much respect for Islam, the Kaaba, and Mohammed. In fact, the candidate is essentially converting to Islam here. The supposed beauty and truth of *The Koran* is praised with words like this:

> *The Koran* is the unique history of our founder Mohammed. The work is absolutely unique in its origin and in its preservation, upon the authenticity of which no one has ever been able to cast a serious doubt. *The Koran* is the actual text as dictated by Mohammed himself, day by day and month by month, during his lifetime. It is the reflection of this master-mind, sometimes inartistic and self-contradictory, more often inspiring and lyrical, and always filled with great ideas which stand out as a whole.

It doesn't seem like the person who wrote this has actually read *The Koran*, which does not contain any history per se and is not meant to be taken as such. But for some reason, they certainly want to promote it. Yet, there is clearly an air of the unholy, the prurient, and the base in the ritual. In addition to the public urination requirement, there is what we might call the abundant "ass-play." The candidate is made to wash the "hind parts" of one of his fellows (with what is pretended to be holy Zam-zam water). He is slapped on the buttocks numerous times with various objects, including during the aforementioned "Grand Salaam," which happens when the candidate is instructed to place his "hind parts in the faces of the Nobles sitting behind" him. He is later forced to eat something that he is told is "dung." Finally, when he reaches the black stone in the corner of the temple, which

Riding the Goat Current 531

they call the "Black Stone of Casper" (presumably named after one of the three Oriental Wise Men that attended the birth of Jesus), he is told to kiss it (which is what Muslim pilgrims do to their own black stone), only to then be humiliated for doing so! The holy Black Stone is then compared to a butt. The candidate is told, condescendingly:

> Ishmael and his father, Abraham, built the National Shrine near the place where . . . an angel presented them with a dazzling White Stone, which they inserted in the wall of the Temple, and each year the worshipers would journey to Mecca to kiss this Stone. Today so many have kissed the Stone that it has become black, and is known as the Kaaba Stone or Black Stone of Casper. Our ritual stipulates that you, in token of your sincerity, seal your obligations by kissing the Black Stone of Casper.
>
> No doubt many times you have stated that you would not "kiss" anybody's "hind parts" to gain a favor. Well, it seems that you wanted to be a Shriner so bad that you were willing to kiss "the Black Stone of Casper." Shame on you.

This is all very interesting. The humiliating admonition at the end reminds us of the description of the Templar initiation in the Chinon Parchment, where it says that, after being made to kiss his brother's behind, the new initiate would be encouraged to confess his "sin." Later in the "Shrine Lecture," the candidate is told that in Mecca the Black Stone is "according to Arab tradition, in the center of the world and immediately beneath the throne of the Almighty." In Eliphas Levi's depiction of Baphomet, the goat-man is shown seated on a dark cubic stone, with a lunar crescent (an Islamic symbol) on either side of him. Are the Shrine rituals a clue that some Masons see the Kaaba as the "seat" of the goat god, to be "kissed" ritually as the butt of the goat was kissed anciently by Templars and witches?

That, perhaps, will never be known. But does the existence of the Shriners strengthen Prince Michael's argument that the Templars found the Solomon temple at the Kaaba site, and that secrets pertaining to this are hidden within the rites of Freemasonry? It certainly seems that way to us. Although the Shrine is, admittedly, not the oldest of Masonic orders, it is now one of the highest ranked, at least in America. It does seem significant that this order is essentially the pinnacle of Freemasonry, open (until recently) only to their most elite. After going through all of the Masonic rituals dedicated to the Temple of Solomon, and immediately after receiving the honors of the Knights Templar, one then then has the opportunity to "graduate" next to an order dedicated to Islam and its foremost temple! But they are also making fun of it, like the old "Feast of Fools" where people would mock the Passion Play in medieval times, and which constituted a Black Mass of sorts. It also reminds us of the mocking of Islamic holy symbols and rituals that purportedly took place within the Order of Assassins, as we mentioned earlier.

Also interesting is a description given in the Shrine Lecture about how Mecca (at the time the lecture was first written) was sort of hidden in the surrounding landscape. It says:

> Mecca unfolds in the wilderness of the Arabian desert, halfway between Yemen and Syria, in a land wasted by winds and secular rains, a valley enclosed between two sharp and arid chains of rock mountains, making its position so secluded that not until the pilgrims are looking down into its streets do they know that they have arrived at the sacred city.

Riding the Goat Current 533

The description brings to mind the idea of the Templar treasure hunters intrepidly marching down to Mecca with inside information about what was really there, and an open invitation from the guardians of the sanctuary, as Prince Michael claims it to have happened. Besides, if we were, just for a moment, to entertain the idea that the Masons got the Shrine rites directly from Mohammed himself, would this not then indirectly imply the involvement of the Templars? Weren't the Templars (with their seeming involvement with Sufi groups and the Assassins) better positioned to have obtained such secrets from Muslims in a position to know, rather than a New Yorker from the nineteenth century who attended a party in France with an Arab diplomat?

The real question though, is whether or not there really is a secret connection between the Temple Mount in Jerusalem and the Kaaba in Mecca that the Templars may have known about. There may be at least a vague memory of this latent in the traditions of modern Freemasons and their offshoots. In this regard it is worth contemplating a few salient points.

Firstly, the "Black Stone" of the Kaaba is, like the Kaaba itself, older than Islam. As the Shriner initiation ritual indicated, there is an Islamic belief that it was brought down from Heaven by an angel, or that it "fell" from Heaven (which would make sense if, as is assumed, it is a meteorite). The places where it first landed supposedly indicated to Adam and Eve where to build the first altar to God. Its use was interrupted by the Deluge. Later, Abraham and Ishmael supposedly built an altar in the same spot, around the same stone. Here (say Muslims) it was Ishmael, not Isaac, who was almost sacrificed to God by his father, before God changed his mind at the last minute. There are other theories too. Tracy R. Twyman's husband, Hareth al-Bustani, once attended a Sufi lecture where he was told that the Black

Stone brought the germ of life to Earth from outer space. Others have suggested that the Kaaba is positioned at the center of Pangea, the land mass believed to exist before the continents drifted to where they are today.

Ishmael's descendants, the Arabs, turned the area of the Kaaba into a place of pagan worship. Supposedly, there were at one point hundreds of idols within it, each belonging to one of the Arab tribes who sent pilgrims there every year to sacrifice goats to them. (The offerings were placed inside of a dried well within the Kaaba tent.) The number that we have read most often for how many idols were there is 360, which divides nicely into 12, the number of tribes that supposedly descended from Ishmael, and matches up with the number of degrees in the circle around the Kaaba that pilgrims walk in. However, we have also seen the numbers 364 and 365 written in books, which may indicate a connection to either the lunar or solar calendars (respectively). 364 is the number of days in thirteen lunar months, and the number thirteen seems important to the Freemasons, particular the Shriners. Muslims do observe a lunar calendar (though not one of thirteen months), and they do appear to afford some special reverence to the Moon, as the crescent is one of their emblems (and was used by the Templars on their seals also).

Presently the Kaaba stone is broken into several fragments, and much of it appears to be lost. The remaining bits are sealed together in a black epoxy, which is then affixed to the Eastern corner of the tabernacle it sits within. This structure is roughly in the shape of a cube, thus the name "Kaaba," which means exactly that. The silver object that holds the black stone in the corner looks a bit vaginal, with the stone and epoxy recessed inside of it, and this is what the pilgrims kiss when they are "circumambulating" around the Kaaba during the Hajj.

Riding the Goat Current 535

The Temple Mount in Jerusalem is, like the Kaaba, supposedly built upon the "Eben Shetiyah," the "Foundation Stone" of the world. This is believed to have been Ground Zero for creation, from which everything God made radiated outward. This rock is in the center of the platform called the "Temple Mount," and it is believed to be the site where Solomon placed the "Holy of Holies," the inner chamber of his temple, built in the shape of a perfect cube, where the Ark of the Covenant resided.

This is the rock that the Dome of the Rock, which crowns it, is named after, and it is here that Mohammed supposedly touched down when he came there during the Night Journey. The rock purportedly enjoyed Mohammed's company so much that it tried to follow him when he left. As he ascended back up, it floated up also, and they say Gabriel had to press down on it to get it to go back in place. This allegedly caused his hand print, as well as the hooves of al-Burak, to be left in its surface (which some people believe can be seen there to this very day).

The location is thought of as a nexus between Heaven and Earth. Indeed, right next door is something called the "Dome of the Chain," which is actually older and was in fact the architectural model for the Dome of the Rock. According to Jerome Murphy-Conner, in his 2008 book *The Holy Land: An Oxford Archaeological Guide from Earliest Times to 1700*, Mujadir ad-Din (a fifteenth-century writer in Jerusalem) once wrote:

Among the wonders of the Holy House is the chain, which Solomon, son of David, suspended between Heaven and Earth, to the east of the Rock, where the Dome of the Chain now stands. The chain had one characteristic. If two men approached it to solve a point of litigation, only the honest and upright man could take hold of it; the unjust man saw it move out of his reach.

Some Muslims further believe that this same test will be used to judge their souls at the End Times, and that the Final Judgment will take place right there under the Dome. This chain of course reminds us of the one mentioned in *The Iliad* that Zeus dangled between Heaven and Earth, and the chains held by "Mete" on the coffer at the British Museum, which might be used to pull the Sun and Moon down from their heavenly spheres.

In his book on the cabalistic text *Sefer Yetzirah* (*The Book of Creation*), Aryeh Kaplan writes about a pair of serpents, one coiled around the other, called the "telis," one male and one female. They are clearly Lilith and Samael. He describes them as hanging down from Heaven, and that the universe is suspended from them. Kaplan says that according to cabalistic tradition, they can also be viewed as one hair hanging down from the beard of "Zer Anpin," a name for the "Little Face" of God, visualized as a disembodied head. Yes, like Baphomet (and the Roman god Janus), God has two faces—in his case, one small and one large, and like Baphomet, can be viewed as a head. From each of the hairs of Zer Anpin's beard, an entire universe is suspended. This is a head of wisdom, for as Kaplan explains:

> The Talmud states that the hanging (or piled) hair relates to the fact that every letter of the Torah contains "piles and piles" (*teli tela'im*) of wisdom. Besides this, the hanging hairs are said to relate to the lines upon which the letters of the Torah are written.
>
> The Torah which is spoken of here is not the ordinary written Torah, but the primeval Torah,

which was written "with black fire on white fire." According to many Kabbalists, this primeval Torah is itself identified with Zer Anpin.

> In this picture, each letter of the Torah is seen as a hair in the beard of Zer Anpin. These are not seen as simple hairs, but as channels, through which God's wisdom emanates from His "head." The "head" is the concealed wisdom of God, while the letters are its outwards revelation. . . .

A few paragraphs later, Kaplan makes a comment which seems to indicate that the place where the hair/serpent hangs down, from which our universe is suspended, is actually Jerusalem:

> The scripture calls the "hangings" of the divine beard *Taltalim*. *The Zohar* relates this to the word *Talpiot*, which, as the Talmud teaches, is the "hill (*tell*) to which all mouths (*piot*) turn." This "hill" is the mount upon which the Temple was built, which Jacob called the "gate of heaven" (*Genesis* 28:17).

According to tradition, the area of the Temple Mount connects not just Heaven and Earth, but the underworld as well. For Muslims believe that beneath the Foundation Stone is the Well of Souls, a cave where you can hear the cries of ghosts awaiting judgement. A whole punched in the Foundation Stone leads down there. *The Talmud* also says that the stone covers an opening to the Abyss, where the waters of the Deluge came from, and receded back to. According to *The Book of Jubilees*, it is even the place where Eden once was. The cube-shaped inner sanctum of Solomon's Temple, where only the high priests were allowed, is said here to match up precisely with the location of the Garden, so that when the priests go in there, it is like returning to the forbidden zone of Eden. The inner sanctum of the temple contained the Ark of the Covenant, which served as God's "throne" on Earth, where he would make his appearance during the ceremonies, just as his throne was also present (according to many extra-biblical texts) in Eden.

Mohammed's Night Journey, as we mentioned previously, brings to mind the story of Jacob, who, according to *Genesis*, fell asleep on a certain stone and had a fantastic vision of a ladder leading to Heaven, with angels ascending and descending upon it. Afterwards, he declared the spot where he had slept the "House of God, and a gate to Heaven." He built a temple on that very spot, using the rock he had slept on as a cornerstone.

Significantly, the word for "ladder" used in this instance was "salem," which specifically indicates a ziggurat (a stepped pyramid like the kind found in ancient Mesopotamia). Consider the fact that this word is part of the name of the city of Jerusalem, where the temple of Solomon is commonly believed to have been. Consider also that the "Tower of Babel" was literally, according to the story in *Genesis*, a stepped ziggurat as tall as Heaven, built for the purpose of storming Heaven. Then consider that the builder of another temple, the foundations of which *have* been found in Jerusalem (unlike those of Solomon's Temple), was named Zerubabel, because he was born in Babylon.

Also amazing is the fact that Jacob's pillow stone is believed by Brits to be a treasure of their own monarchy, and they claim that this is the stone which sits beneath the throne where all their kings and queens are coronated. But it came to them via the Stuarts of Scotland (who got it from Ireland, where it was supposedly brought from Egypt). Prince Michael claims in *The Forgotten Monarchy of Scotland* that the stone

Riding the Goat Current 539

beneath the throne is a fake, and that the real one is in his family's possession.

However, *The Talmud* says that Jacob's stone is the very same as the Foundation Stone in the Temple Mount, and that this is the same location where Jacob had built his temple earlier. Yet the Bible's description of the incident with Jacob (*Genesis* 28: 10-22) makes it seem to take place somewhere else, in a place then called "Luz," which he renamed to Bethel ("House of God"). Bethel is usually found north of Jerusalem on the maps printed in Bibles.

Now, doesn't it strike you as odd that the Christians and Jews have both each identified multiple sites for what seems to be the same honor: the location of their temple that connects Heaven to Earth? Also, doesn't it strike you as odd that the Muslims honor both the Temple Mount and the Kaaba, for essentially the same reason? Mohammed even visited both in the same fantastic night, making the connection between the two overt. Also, he originally instructed the converts to his new religion to set their "Qiblah" (the direction in which Muslims are to pray) to point towards the Temple Mount in Jerusalem, but then later changed it to the direction of Mecca on the instructions of his deity. What does this mean?

Tracy R. Twyman has speculated about this earlier in her book *The Merovingian Mythos and the Mystery of Rennes-le-Chateau*. On the subject of the various "navels of the world" that have been observed by different societies in different places throughout history as their premiere holy sites, the alleged centers of the world where supposedly creation began (of which there must be hundreds), she suggested that these locations are usually marked with relic, such as the world's "foundation stone" or a "stone from Heaven," that makes them sacred. They are thus considered the "navel of the world" because that's where the sacred "belly button" is placed. When different locations become identified as such by the same society, this indicates to her that the sacred object has been moved from one place to another during the course of time. Therefore both places are remembered as the "center," even though only one (or none at all) may still be the location of the stone.

This would explain why the mere symbol of "the Stone" itself, and not just any particular location, is enough to unite Hermetic and occult groups throughout the centuries in an unending tradition of the veneration of this concept. In Wolfram von Eschenbach's *Parzival*, the Holy Grail is a "stone that fell from heaven." By magic it calls out the "Grail knights" (clearly Templars, with red crosses on their mantles) that it wants to serve it (as their names appear temporarily on its surface). As we just mentioned, the tent around the Black Stone at Mecca is cubic, and the "Holy of Holies" of Solomon's Temple was cubic. So too was Noah's Ark (though few realize this, unless they try to draw out the dimensions dictated to Noah by God). The alchemists, as we stated before, described their Philosopher's Stone as cubic. The Anatolian goddess Cybele, worshipped throughout the ancient world, was associated with a stone that was venerated, and many have suggested that her name is connected with the word "cube." You will recall that, according to Joseph von Hammer-Purgstall, the feminine aspect of Baphomet, whom he identified as "Mete" or Sophia, could also be equated to Cybele. The image of "Mete" on the coffer he found was labeled by the British Museum as featuring Cybele, probably because of the towers on her crown (one of Cybele's signature features).

It should come as no surprise then to find those critical of Islam suggesting that the veneration of the black stone of the

Kaaba is a continuation of the goddess worship of the ancient world. They even claim that the goddess being worshipped there is Lilith herself. In *The Archeology of World Religions* by Jack Finegan from 1952, the author suggests that Allah, a version of the Babylonian Enlil, was worshipped as a supreme creator god at the Kaaba, though among other gods, by the pre-Islamic pagan Arabs. His consort in this scheme was the goddess Allat, linguistically connected to Lilith. Allat is actually mentioned in *The Koran*, Sura 53, where the names of three goddesses popularly worshipped by pagans at the pre-Islamic Kaaba are cursed. But according to eighth-century Muslim historian Ibn Ishaq, based on the narration of Muhammad ibn Ka'b, tradition has it that these verses originally said something else entirely. But then Mohammed determined that those verses had actually been inspired by Satan, so Allah gave him new ones to replace them. The (now infamous) "Satanic Verses" supposedly stated:

> Have ye thought upon Al-Lat and Al-'Uzza,
> and Manat, the third, the other? These are the
> exalted [birds], whose intercession is hoped for.

Finegan puts forth that the crescent and star symbol of Islam represents the Al-Lat (as a lunar goddess) and Al-Uzza (connected with the goddess and planet Venus, the Morning Star). He also describes Al-Manat as the deity who metes out justice or fate, making her the equivalent of the Roman goddess Nemesis. Let us point out that "Nemesis" just happens to be the password of the Masonic Shrine. Also interesting is that, in *The Third Book of Enoch*, the Watchers (who become the fallen angels) are led by three characters, named, "Azza," "Uzza," and "Azzael" (all seemingly based on Azazel), who accuse mankind of sin before God (but are themselves driven from their heavenly abode because of their own transgressions).

It is worthy of note that on the grounds of the Kaaba, there are three pillars (actually changed into flat walls now) that have always been there. Pilgrims traditionally stone them each with pebbles, to represent throwing stones at the Devil. The "Tracing Board" of the first degree of Freemasonry (an instructional graphic) always shows three pillars, above which are the Sun (on the left), the Moon surrounded by stars (on the right) and the All-Seeing Eye above the one in the center. They are positioned in a right triangle, with a ladder (like a fireman's ladder) in the midst, leading up to Heaven. There is a chequered floor on the bottom, indicating either the floor of the Kaaba, or the floor of Solomon's Temple (as they have both been depicted with such a floor in artwork).

What if we were to think of both the Kaaba and the Temple Mount as each being a "ladder to Heaven," and the stones associated with each as "pillars" that "hold up the sky?" This is a concept commonly found in mythology and in Islamic scripture in particular. So the three pillars on the Masonic tracing boards could be expressive of the idea that there is a third pillar somewhere else. More commonly, though, the concept is expressed with only two pillars, such as those of Jachin and Boaz. These are the names given in the Old Testament to the two pillars that allegedly stood outside of the entrance to Solomon's Temple. In Masonic lodges they are usually represented with a globe on top of each: one a terrestrial globe (showing the world), the other a celestial globe (showing the stars in the sky). Thus the pillars are shown holding up both the Earth and Heaven, just as the ancients believed that such pillars kept the sky from collapsing on top of us, and kept the world from falling into the Abyss.

Riding the Goat Current 543

In Freemasonry, and in many Western occult traditions, these pillars are taken as representations of two polar opposite but necessary principles of existence, often characterized as either "strength and beauty" or "wisdom and severity." In the classic Rider-Waite tarot deck, one pillar is shown colored black, and the other is white. Then there are the Pillars of Seth, and the Pillars of Hermes, which were both described as having been erected to preserve human knowledge through a global catastrophe. Both of these sets of pillars are also the subject of Masonic legends.

So is it possible that the Templars, and later the Freemasons, revered both the Temple Mount in Jerusalem, and the Kaaba in Mecca, as the twin pillars of the universe, and the locations of two sacred stones, one black, and one (in their system of symbols, at least) white? Could it be that they had a special relationship with the guardians of the Kaaba, as Prince Michael suggests, due to a shared blood lineage, and a shared understanding of the sacred secrets hidden in these places. Is it possible that they revered Baphomet as a representation of the union of these two things—the powers behind both holy shrines? Did they perhaps also honor Mohammed, and Islam, for having rediscovered and united the powers of these two places?

Let us recall that, while the Templars may have been Christian in a certain sense, the upper echelons of the group were certainly more than that as well, as we have amply demonstrated in this book. We know that Jesus, the Virgin Mary, and John the Baptist are all acknowledged as holy people in *The Koran*, and by Muslims everywhere. Those of us who grew up Christian should also know that in *John* 14:16-17 (KJV), Jesus told his apostles before he left them that:

> I will pray the Father, and he shall give you another Comforter, that he may abide with you for ever.

Even the Spirit of truth; whom the world cannot receive, because it seeth him not, neither knoweth him: but ye know him; for he dwelleth with you, and shall be in you.

The Greek word here, *Periclytos*, has been variously translated as "comforter" and "consoler." Some Islamic theologians choose to believe that it is the equivalent of the Arabic word for "praised one," which is "Ahmad," one of Mohammed's epithets. In Sura 61:6 of *The Koran* (Sahih International translation), Mohammed is identified as the one whose coming was promised by Jesus:

And . . . when Jesus, the son of Mary, said, "O children of Israel, indeed I am the messenger of Allah to you confirming what came before me of the Torah and bringing good tidings of a messenger to come after me, whose name is Ahmad." But when he came to them with clear evidences, they said, "This is obvious magic."

However, verse 22 of *John* Chapter 14 (KJV) makes it clear that the Comforter is in fact the Holy Spirit:

The Comforter, *which is* the Holy Ghost, whom the Father will send in my name, he shall teach you all things, and bring all things to your remembrance, whatsoever I have said unto you.

This would seem to disqualify Mohammed, unless we want to identify the Prophet with the Holy Spirit. Certainly, we previously mentioned evidence that suggests Baphomet may have been identified with the Holy Spirit, as he/she was with Sophia, the Divine Wisdom, which the Church has always equated with the Holy Spirit. So we can connect Mohammed with Allah, Allah with Allat, Allat with Lilith, and Lilith with Sophia, and thus get to the Holy Spirit that way.

Also, there is the possibility that the baptism "with fire, and with the Holy Spirit" that John the Baptist promised the one to come after him would bring was, in the eyes of the Knights Templar, the same as their "Baptism of Wisdom." Let us recall that the Templars' alleged secret rule, supposedly contained in *The Book of The Baptism of Fire*, was said to have been written for the "Consoled Brothers," and possibly referred to the Cathar rite of *Consolamentum*.

It is fitting that the bloodline of Abraham's disinherited first-born son Ishmael (whose name literally became a term in English for "outcast") should produce Mohammed, the "Seal of the Prophets." After all, Jesus did predict that in the End Times, "the last shall be the first, and the first shall be the last." As we mentioned before, the Judaic tradition is replete with first-born sons that have been disinherited, with God's favor. There was Cain, who admittedly, actually did something to deserve this. But then there was Jacob and his older brother Esau (progenitor of the accursed Edomites). Jacob used trickery and subterfuge against their father Isaac as he lay on his deathbed, and impersonated his brother in order to steal his inheritance from him. He did this by covering his arms with goat hair to simulate the fur that *Genesis* says Esau was covered with, which is an interesting detail in itself. But the Lord still blessed him, and cursed his brother!

Then there was the story of Pharez and Zerah, twin sons of Jacob's son Judah. Zerah's hand protruded from the womb first, and the midwife tied a scarlet thread around his wrist to indicate that he was the first-born. But then his hand was pulled back inside, and his brother bullied his way out first, becoming the inheritor of the family birthright. It is Pharez who went on to become an ancestor of King David and Jesus Christ.

But shouldn't we note that on Yom Kippur, the goat that was sacrificed to Azazel was marked with a red thread tied around its horn? Does that not indicate that Azazel represents the disinherited first-born? It was Azazel who, according to *The First Book of Enoch*, God decided to blame for all of the crimes that resulted in him bringing the Deluge, even though many others were at fault also. We are talking about the Devil, the Serpent, who felt slighted by his creator's preference for his younger creation, Adam, and refused the order to bow down to the new man of "clay" (according to both *The Koran* and the Christian *Book of Adam and Eve*.)

It could be viewed as Adam's first wife, Lilith, pushed aside for Eve, or Jehovah's first wife, the Matronit, pushed aside for a "mistress," as the cabalists described in the previously quoted sections of *The Zohar*. Or it could be seen as the Father of all looking down resentfully at the Demiurge as he pretends to be the first and only god. You might think of it as the eldest principal of darkness, jealous of the presence of the younger principle of light, which it comprehendeth not. Or you could think of it as the other way around, as many Gnostics did.

The following quote from *The Zohar* makes it clear that Esau was identified with the "seirim" (goat-demons), a word associated with both Azazel and Lilith. It is done in the context of explaining why the Israelites would sacrifice a special "portion" of the regular daily burnt offerings to a spirit called the "End of All Flesh," to appease the "accusers," saying that these beings get sustenance from the smoke. Here Jehovah has dictated that his priests must sacrifice to these disinherited accuser spirits while invoking the Holy Spirit in order to satiate the demons' desire for flesh and quell their anger at having their inheritance taken away from

Riding the Goat Current 547

them. From *The Zohar* (*Noah* 65a, from Volume 1 of the Soncino Edition):

> R. Eleazar, studying one day with his father, R. Simeon, asked him "Did the 'End of all flesh' derive nourishment from the sacrifices which Israel used to offer on the altar?" His father replied: "all alike derived sustenance from them, both above and below. . . . Baked meal-offerings and other meal-offerings are the means of invoking the Holy Spirit . . . and from the smoke that rises up from the oil and the flour all the accusers replenish themselves, so that they are powerless to pursue the indictment which has been delivered into their hands. Thus we see that things have been so arranged in a mystery of faith that the adversary should have his share in the holy things, and that the requisite portion should ascend even to the Limitless.
>
> . . . In regard, then, to the "End of all flesh," just as there is unison above with joy (at the time of the sacrifice), so also below there is joy and appeasement. There is thus satisfaction both above and below, and the Mother of Israel watches lovingly over her children. Consider this. At every New Moon the "End of all flesh" is given a portion over and above that of the daily offering, so as to divert his attention from Israel, who are thus left entirely to themselves and in full freedom to commune with their King. This extra portion comes from the he-goat (*sa'ir*), being the portion of Esau, who is also called *sa'ir*, as it is written, "Behold Esau my brother is a hairy (*sa-ir*) man" (*Genesis* 27:2). Esau thus has his portion and Israel their portion. . . . The whole desire of this "End of all flesh" is for flesh only, and the

tendency of flesh is ever towards him; it is for this reason that he is called "End of all flesh." Such power, however, as he does obtain is only over the body and not over the soul. The soul ascends to her place, and the body is given over to its place. . . ."

"Accuser" is one of the common epithets for the Devil, a word that comes from the Greek *diabolos* ("slanderer"), just as "Satan" means "the adversary" (like one's opponent in a court of law). The idea is that he is constantly accusing the sons of Adam of sin, and Jehovah of hypocrisy for loving Adam's sons. He is a villain precisely because he is judgmental and tries to hold others to the letter of the law. But we see from the Bible stories we have mentioned so far that Jehovah seems quite willing to twist the law in order to put his favorites in the line of succession of heavenly blessings, which just further enrages the adversary.

In Greek mythology, the adversarial role was played by Momus, a god whose name means "blame" or "censure." He was kicked out of Olympus by the other gods because of his constant sneering criticism of them all. But he was adopted by the Royal Order of Jesters as their mascot, identified with their idol, a trollish good luck charm called a Billiken, because they saw him as the ultimate joker, the lord of "mirth." It is interesting to think that this organization may be stockpiling blackmail footage of their members cheating on their wives, violating prostitution laws and committing child rape, with the power to hold their members under the threat of public accusations regarding these things should anyone break the code of silence. Momus is the one to say "We are all equally guilty here, so don't throw stones."

Returning to the above-quoted passage from *The Zohar*, another thing to be noted there is the claim that the way to invoke the Holy Spirit is through burnt offerings, just as the

Templars may have associated the Holy Spirit with human infant sacrifice through a baptism of fire. The Bible makes it clear that sacrifice of the firstborn is an offering demanded by Jehovah of everybody. Just as he rejected his own firstborn (the Serpent, Chaos, the Night), he has demanded the same of each generation of his "chosen" families, according to the Bible stories we have mentioned. The pantomime of Abraham pretending to "almost" sacrifice Isaac, only to substitute a ram for him instead, represents the real scapegoat sacrifice that happened when Abraham sent Ishmael out in the wilderness to die, just like the goat for Azazel on Yom Kippur.

This concept of the sacrifice of the firstborn, and the substitution of it, comes up over and over again throughout the biblical narrative: from the Passover, with its sheep substitute; to the sacrifice of the freedom of the Levites in slavery to priesthood as a substitute for the other tribes of Israelites (and the temple tax as the price to redeem each individual Israelite whose firstborn was not sacrificed); to the sacrifice of Jesus on behalf of everyone worldwide. There is the need to somehow pay that "price," charged by God that is for some inexplicable reason connected with sin. This is because "the wages of sin is death," and if death (Hades) is identified as the abode of the Devil, we should note that, as in the Yom Kippur ritual, and the aforementioned sacrifices to the End of All Flesh, the Devil is given his "due" along with the offerings to God.

It is our suspicion that the concept of Gnosis treasured by the Templars, the Freemasons, and many other occultists, is the understanding that both God and the Devil had a hand in creation, and their children—the bloodline of Adam and the bloodline of the Serpent (respectively)—each have equal claim to lordship over creation. All of these groups have left many clues indicating that their real "secret" is the shared origin, and the equality, of the principles of good and evil, darkness and light, or creation and destruction. This is what alchemists have always claimed is the secret of the Philosopher's Stone, the key to mastery over all created matter. This is what Hermeticists have always indicated they believe to be the ultimate enlightenment. All of the radically dualist heresies—the Cathars, the Bogomils, and the Manichaeans—all claimed that there were two distinct, eternal principles of light and darkness, in constant strife with one another and may have applied this to idea of competing bloodlines (symbolized in the New Testament as "the sheep and the goats," "the wheat and the tares," or "the good tree and bad tree").

The principle is clearly illustrated in compound chimera figures like Baphomet and Abraxas. We also see it in the piebald or checkerboard patterns of alternating black and white segments used by the Templars as their battle flag, and used by Freemasons on the floors of their lodges. Chequerboard tile floors can also be found in early images of what the floor of the Kaaba used to look like, as well as several old drawings of the floor of Solomon's Temple (perhaps influenced by Masonic traditions).

The secret, latently understood goal of the "Craft"—of witches and Masons—is to unite the black and white stones—to "double the cube" (a famous mathematical problem once thought impossible). They want to somehow put it all back together, to gain that ultimate power of the universe that was used for creation *ex nihilo*. Seizing this power—God's power—is like storming Heaven, piercing the seal of the "flaming sword" which "turns every way" to protect the Tree of Life. This is the same concept as the Valentinian Gnostic doctrine of a "cross" that separates the

Riding the Goat Current 551

Pleroma (akin to what the Hermetic Order of the Golden Dawn calls the "Supernal Eden") and the Kenoma (the manifest realm of matter). As Tracy R. Twyman posits at the end of her book *Clock Shavings*, secret societies have long cherished the idea of being able to penetrate this hidden realm, not only to escape the material "prison" that we are in, but to escape the cycle of death that pervades here, and to take for themselves the immortality of the gods. While different groups embraced different theories about how to do that and what it meant, their mysteries, when decoded, frequently point to this as their main long-term goal.

The Corpus Hermeticum tells us that a soul entering a physical body is being "baptized" or "immersed" into the "inferno of matter" (the lustful pleasures and pains of the flesh) as a form of punishment. In the Ophite diagrams of the universe (as revealed by Celsus and Origin), the archontic realm of matter is surrounded by a circle labeled "Leviathan." The Ophites are said to have viewed Leviathan the "soul of all things" (or alternately the "soul that travels through all things"). It is the equivalent of the Ouroboros, the snake swallowing its own tail, often used to represent the barrier between the cosmos and eternity, where the beginning meets the end and engenders a new beginning. The image was popularized by Cleopatra the Alchemist, third to fourth-century author of *Chrysopeia* (*Gold-Making*), who described the Ouroboros as "the sum of all philosophy."

Meanwhile, the angelic realm in the Ophite diagrams (as demonstrated in Jacques Matter's 1826 book *Histoire Critique du Gnosticisme*) is surrounded by a circle labeled "Behemoth." This figure, you will remember, is identified as the partner of Leviathan, and just as with Lilith and Samael, it is said that creation will be destroyed if they are ever allowed to mate. The Arabs wrote about this creature as well, calling him "Bahamut." *The Arabian Nights* describes him as a fish with a bull head supporting the universe on his back. Surely this is the same character as "Bahumed," taken by both Giles F. Yates and Hammer-Purgstall to be related to "Baphomet," and to bovine symbolism (the calf or *Karuf* in this instance). How strange, then, that the interpretation Hammer-Purgstall later took of the name of the Templar idol ("Baptism of Wisdom") seems so widely divergent from this early speculation. But, as we have discovered, the meaning of Baphomet is really multi-faceted, and none of the possible interpretations cancel out the others.

Recall that Eliphas Levi, who probably contributed more to the development of the Baphomet mythos than almost anybody, suggested that the name was a code for the Latin phrase *Templi omnium hominum pacis abhas*: "abbot (that is, 'father' or 'priest') of the temple of universal peace among men." What if the Templars, and later Freemasons, believed that there had once been a temple that all men could turn towards in prayer that would unite all of the world's monotheists, and perhaps most everybody else as well, in the common belief that it was indeed the center of the world— the main contact point with the divine? Or, what if they discovered that there never was a physical temple to begin with, but rather a symbolic or etheric one—one that they intended to rebuild? What if they revered Baphomet as the high priest (the *pontifex*, meaning "bridge builder," the origin of the Pope's title "pontiff") or intercessor of a metaphorical temple that acts as a bridge or ladder linking Earth to Heaven, like the Tower of Babel was meant to do?

It seems they may have anticipated that penetrating this forbidden zone could result in the destruction of creation as we know it, "pulling down the heavens," as the image of Mete discovered by Hammer-Purgstall suggests, collapsing the "pillars" that hold Heaven up from Earth, which connects to the Masonic allegory of death as a the breaking of a column. Eve, by the way, is represented in the cabalistic rituals of the Hermetic Order of the Golden Dawn as actually holding up these pillars on her shoulders. The pillars are shown as being part of the Tree of Life in the Garden of Eden, and it is explained in the rite that when Adam and Eve fell from grace, these pillars fell also, causing the flaws in existence that we have now.

Now here there is a connection to the planetary powers of the Gnostic Archons, and to the *krater* bowl of Mind mentioned in *The Corpus Hermeticum* as being a source of wisdom in which initiates to the mysteries should immerse themselves. The ancients actually spoke of seven *cosmocrators* which clearly corresponded to the seven so-called (back then) "planets." The name seems to mean "cosmic bowls," and goes along with the old idea that the "heavens" were circles within circles (or bowls within bowls, each a planetary orbit). But the descriptions of them make them sound like columns holding up the heavens (*Mundi Tenentes* or "World Holders," as Tertullian called them). This goes along with the imagery found in *The Arabian Nights* of Bahamut supporting the "seven hills" (described as seven stages of existence) on his back. The *Oxford English Dictionary* actually translates the word *cosmocrator* as "Ruler of the World," stating that it was a Gnostic "technical term for Satan" (just as the Cathars called the same figure "Rex Mundi").

An inverted, infernal interpretation of the Hermetic Baptism of Wisdom (such as the Templars are alleged to have practiced) might have aimed at upsetting these bowls, pouring our their contents on us all (thus the immersion) as the levels of reality they were thought to uphold and separate came crashing down, causing the different essences that they contain to intermingle, with deadly consequences for the universe. This may have been the goal of certain Nihilist occultists and Gnostics throughout history who hated God and what he made. Remember the stories claiming that when Lilith and Samael, or Leviathan and Behemoth, reunite sexually into a single being, existence will be destroyed. Others may genuinely think that this is the sacrifice necessary to heal the wound of separation from the divine caused by Adam and Eve's fall from Eden.

This could explain the symbolism of the Black Mass and the Witches' Sabbath. Everything considered holy in traditional religious rituals is reversed. It's about "going backwards," back to the beginning before creation, to reverse the error that took place in Eden and return to the perfection of chaos in the pre-existent Pleroma. As Nigel Jackson writes in *Masks of Misrule*, Sabbath attendees would:

> ...through the averse formulae of infinite return, deliberately go backwards to that which lies behind all phenomena and consciousness, the ineffable source of all creation. . . .

It may be also that some folks have sympathy for the Devil, and would like to see his punishment ended. A collapse of the pillars (whatever that means) might lead either (a) to a merciful release for him via the "Second Death," or (b) a release from his prison into another realm, as the barriers between the planes of existence might dissolve, bringing everything that is back together into one. In *The First Book of Enoch*, Azazel actually sends a letter to Enoch begging him to ask God for forgiveness for the Watchers and their giant offspring. This could be the meaning behind Jesus' parable of the Prodigal Son. It is the idea of God's firstborn, the rebellious one (Satan), returning to his father's bosom, even as his younger son, the faithful one (Adam), protests. The central figure in this story has wasted his inheritance, representative of Satan's original estate and dispensation, given to him by God. But the moral of that story is that we should rejoice in the ultimate reconciliation between them as the healing of a grave cosmic wound, rather than grumbling about the unfairness of the Lord forgiving and even rewarding the infidelity of the one whom he initially trusted most. In *King Jesus*, Robert Graves describes a (fictional) image engraved on a clay tablet in the Cave of Treasures in Israel that depicts what that would look like:

> . . .[H]ere the King has taken Adam into his household; he and his brother Azazel are for a while united in loving comradeship.

Perhaps, then, some people believe that then a temple of *total*, universal peace, not just among the living but among everything whatsoever, could be built wherein everything could be reconciled to everything else: angels and demons, humans and gods, along with everything above, below, or in between. We have already discussed how this is what the Temple of Solomon is envisioned by Jews as having been, allegedly built on the cornerstone of Jacob's "gateway to Heaven," and also over the "Well of Souls." There are similar traditions about other places. Mircea Eliade wrote in *Cosmos and History: The Myth of the Eternal Return*:

> Every Oriental city was situated at the center of the world. Babylon was a *Bab-ilani*, a "gate of the gods," for it was there that the gods descended to earth. . . . Such a capital is, in effect, at the center of the universe, close to the miraculous tree, . . . at the meeting place of the three cosmic zones: heaven, earth, and hell. The Javanese temple of Borobudor is itself an image of the cosmos, and is built like an artificial mountain (as were the ziggurats). Ascending

it, the pilgrim approaches the center of the world, and, on the highest terrace, breaks from one place to another, transcending profane, heterogeneous space and entering a "pure region." Cities and sacred places are assimilated to the summits of cosmic mountains. This is why Jerusalem and Zion were not submerged by the Deluge. According to Islamic tradition, the highest point on earth is the Kaaba, because "the polestar proves that . . . it lies over against the center of heaven." (Kisai, fol. 15; cited by Wensinck, p.15) [By this he means A.J. Wensinck, *The Muslim Creed: Its Genesis and Historical Development*, 1932. We do not know who "Kisai" is.]

. . . Dur-an-ki, "Bond of Heaven and Earth," was the name given to the sanctuaries of Nippur and Larsa, and doubtless to that of Sippara. Babylon had many names, among them "House of the Base of Heaven and Earth," "Bond of Heaven and Earth." But it is always Babylon that is the scene of the connection between the earth and the lower regions, for the city had been built upon the *bab apsi*, the "Gate of the *Absu*"—*apsu* designating the waters of chaos before the Creation. We find the same tradition among the Hebrews. The rock of Jerusalem reached deep into the subterranean waters (*tehom*). The Mishnah says that the Temple is situated exactly above the *tehom* (Hebrew equivalent of *apsu*). And just as in Babylon there was the "gate of the *apsu*," the rock of the Temple in Jerusalem contained the "mouth of the *tehom*."

So is this the sort of temple that Baphomet is the archpriest and caretaker of? Consider that, if rendered as an anagram, "Baphomet" could be thought to contain the words "tehom" and "bap," the latter of which could indicate *bab*, a Semitic root meaning "gate," or the root of the Greek *baptismos* ("to baptize"). So then he is at once the abbot of the temple that acts as the gate to Heaven, and to the Abyss, as well as the priest who baptizes initiates in the waters of the Abyss. These waters of chaos are considered the same as the hidden "wisdom," and the "Knowledge of Good and Evil." The *tehom* has been compared to the Gnostic Pleroma, where everything originated, also called "Bythos," meaning "the deep," the exact same thing in Greek that *tehom* means in Hebrew.

The Apocalypse of Abraham is a pseudepigraphic work assumed to have been composed between 70–150 AD. It is not accepted as scripture by any group, but the text is suspected of having been adulterated at some point by someone from the Bogomil Gnostic sect. The first English translation appeared in the Mormon magazine *Improvement Era* in 1898. In it, Abraham travels to the celestial temple in Heaven, and is taught priestcraft there by the angel Yahoel, who acts as that temple's abbot. In the process he learns that Azazel was once the high priest there, but got demoted. Therefore, Azazel's priestly garments are given over to Abraham, and Abraham's soiled garments are given to Azazel to wear instead. As part of this process, all of the sins of Abraham are transferred over to Azazel, just as will later be done at the Temple of Solomon in the scapegoat ritual. Yahoel says to Azazel:

> Reproach is on you, Azazel! Since Abraham's portion is in heaven, and yours is on earth, since you have chosen it and desired it to be the dwelling place of your impurity. Therefore the Eternal Lord, the Mighty One, has made you a dweller on earth. . . . For behold, the garment which in heaven was formerly

yours has been set aside for him, and the corruption
which was on him has gone over to you.

The story ends with the destruction by fire of a temple on Earth: the one filled with idols, curated by Abraham's father Terah and his brother Nahor, who both die in the blaze.

In the chapter on the subject that appears in his book *Dark Mirrors*, Andrei Orlov compares the reflective relationship here between the earthly and heavenly priests and their garments to something stated in *The Zohar* (*I*, 217a, as quoted by Orlov) where it says:

[T]hese garments are after the supernal pattern, as we have learnt: "There is a High Priest above and a high priest below, raiment of honor above and raiment of honor below."

The term for the priestly garment here is the Hebrew *kavod*, a word which means "glory" but also implies "gravity" or "heaviness." This is similar to the "garment of light" that rabbinic traditions say Adam and Eve were clothed with before the Fall. Recall also the Ophite parody account of Eden, as we saw earlier. In the commentary on *Genesis* found in *Targum Pseudo-Jonathan*, it talks about the original garments being made from "fingernails," but they were then replaced by garments made from the skin of the Serpent:

And the Lord God made garments of glory for Adam and for his wife from the skin which the serpent had cast off (to be worn) on the skin of their (garments of) fingernails of which they had been stripped, and he clothed them.

Similarly, in *Pirke de Rabbi Eliezer* 20, we read:

> From skins which the serpent sloughed off, the Holy One, blessed be He, rook and made coats of glory for Adam and his wife, as it is said, "And the Lord God made for Adam and his wife coats of skin, and clothed them."

Earlier in the same chapter of that book, the garment is described as both "nail skin" and a "cloud of glory." Another rabbinic commentary text, *Genesis Rabbah* 20:12, says that Adam and Eve had "garments of light . . . like a torch . . . broad at the bottom and narrow at the top." They were priestly vestments, for Adam was the first priest, and Eden was the location of the first temple overseen by man, as argued by Robert Hayward in *The Jewish Temple: A Non-Biblical Sourcebook*. He points to *The Book of Jubilees* 3:26-27, where Adam is clothed by God before he first enters the Garden, and immediately offers sacrifice to his heavenly father. In the book *De Somniis*, Philo of Alexandria's commentary on the dreams Jacob had on the famous pillow-stone, the author describes his understanding that, upon entering the Holy of Holies, the high priest becomes "a being whose nature is midway between [man and] God." He speaks of an "oracle" of unknown origin "given about the high priest" that says "when he enters into the Holy of Holies, he will not be a man until he comes out." Thus, Philo says, "he retains this midway place until he comes out again into the realm of body and flesh."

As for Satan, *The Life of Adam and Eve* (12:1-16:2) tells us that Satan, before the creation of Adam, lived on "the throne of the cherubs who . . . spread out a shelter [and] used to enclose me." So we get the idea that the wings of these cherubs somehow formed his garment. This is in keeping with the notion that they were made from light and flame, for

God's throne was surrounded and permeated by these things. In *The First Book of Enoch*, when Azazel (or "Asael" in that text) is punished for his transgressions, God orders that the criminal be thrown into a pit in the desert and "covered in darkness." As Orlov notes:

> Asael's covering with darkness appears to be a sort of counterpart to the garment of light which Enoch receives in heaven. This ominous attire deprives its wearer of receiving the divine light—the source of life for all God's creatures.

So we see here that Azazel has fallen into darkness beneath the earthly plane, but he wears the darkness like a jacket—a straightjacket, because it cannot be removed. Thus it is like he is "inside" matter, possessing it like an indwelling spirit. This is something he is repeatedly shown to be capable of. *The Primary Adam Books* describe Satan entering the fleshy body of the Serpent, wearing him, and playing him like a "lyre." In the Armenian version, it states:

> Then he went and summoned the serpent and said to him, "Arise, come to me so that I may enter into you and speak through your mouth as much as I will need to say." At that time the serpent became a lyre for him.

In the Greek version of this text, the specific words are "be my *vessel* and I will speak through your mouth." In the *Pirke de Rabbi Eliezar*, Chapter 13, Samael is said to have "mounted" and ridden the Serpent like "a camel."

If Satan can be demoted from Heaven by putting on the "darkness" of matter as a garment, and can even be trapped there, is dissolving this flesh jacket necessary to enter Heaven? It seems that this may be implied by some of the texts that we have examined here. In *The Apocalypse of*

Abraham, entering into Heaven is described like passing through a fire, and Azazel even warns Abraham not to go there, saying that the fire will destroy him.

Perhaps, like Moses entering the flames of Hell, Abraham was cauterized with a baptism of divine fire, so that the flames would not hurt him. Or perhaps the fire there in Heaven *simply is* this divine fire, which can be used to protect oneself against all other fire. The ancient Greeks conceived of the highest heaven as the "Empyrean," a realm of fire. This was adapted by Dante Alighieri into the cosmology of *The Divine Comedy*, where it became the location of God's throne, inhabited by being composed of light. (*The Midrash* also says that some of the rivers beneath God's throne flow not with water, but fire.) Maybe, then, *The Apocalypse of Abraham* is implying that Abraham obtained from the angels a garment of fiery light that protected his flesh. Remember that Moses returned from his trip to Hell with shining skin.

As for Adam, the garments he was originally given were priestly vestments. Andre Orlov believes it is implied in *The Third Book of Enoch* that when Enoch ascends to Heaven and is translated into the angel Metatron, "his very flesh and bones are suddenly annihilated by the divine fire, the substance that refashions the visionary's moral body into and angelic . . . corporeality." Perhaps this is because, in Chapter 6 of that text, it says that Enoch was carried there by the angel Anaphiel "in great glory upon a fiery chariot with fiery horses." There his mortal odor was immediately perceived by "the ministers of consuming fire," who complained to God uncharitably about him:

> What smell of one born of woman and what taste of a white drop [is this] that ascends on high. . .?

These fiery angels basically just told Enoch that he tastes like his father's semen and smells like his mother's vagina. How's that for a greeting on your first day of divinity school?

In *The Second Book of Enoch*, prior to coming to God's throne, Enoch's clothes are taken from him and he is anointed with oil. This implies the investiture ceremony of a priest, as argued not only by Orlov, but also Martha Himmelfarb and Crispin Fetcher-Louis, both of whom Orlov quotes. The oil is described as "greater than the greatest light . . . like the rays of the glittering sun," seemingly similar to the glorious *kavod* of light-emitting nail-skin given to humanity before the Fall, and a hint of what may be the reason behind the anointing of priests with oil in the first place. The dead are also similarly anointed, as if this shiny coat is necessary for the translation of the soul beyond the body into another realm.

In *The Apocalypse of Abraham* 23:4-11, the title character is given a vision of Adam and Eve being tempted by Azazel, here identified as the Serpent, who has taken on a peculiar form that is all at once animal, human, and angelic. Orlov interprets this as just a "garment" that he is able to put on. It is here that the scene takes place, mentioned in an earlier chapter, in which Azazel is seen placed between Adam and Eve as they are "entwined" sexually. It says:

> And I saw there a man very great in height and terrible in breadth, incomparable in aspect, entwined with a woman who was also equal to the man in aspect and size. And they were standing under a tree of Eden, and the fruit of the tree was like the appearance of a bunch of grapes of vine. And behind the tree was standing, as it were, a serpent in form, but having hands and feet like a man, and wings on its shoulders: six on the right side and six on the left.

And he was holding in his hands the grapes of the tree and feeding the two whom I saw entwined with each other. And I said, "Who are these two entwined with each other, or who is this between them, or what is the fruit which they are eating, Mighty Eternal One?" And he said, "This is the reason of men, this is Adam, and this is their desire on earth, this is Eve. And he who is between them is the Impiety of their pursuits for destruction, Azazel himself."

Orlov makes the amazing observation that Azazel's appearance here is similar to that of the golden cherubim on top of the Ark of the Covenant (which are always said to have been made to mimic the cherubim that sit near God's throne in the celestial realm). He does not resemble just one of the cherubs, but both of them put together, as each cherub is said to have six wings, and here Azazel is described as having twelve. Abraham's *Apocalypse* actually specified that the cherubim on God's throne had wings coming from their shoulders, their sides, and their loins, bringing to mind Gnostic depictions of the god Bes which ended up on the coins connected by Hammer-Purgstall with the Templars. This figure has wings attached to roughly the same areas, including two wings that protrude from his bottom as tail feathers.

Orlov also notes, in an earlier chapter in his book, that just as Adam and Eve are entwined sexually around Azazel in the above description, the cherubs on the Ark of the Covenant were actually shown to be joined in sexual union as well. As for evidence, he presents a passage from the "Yoma treatise" of *The Babylonian Talmud*, where it says:

Whenever Israel came up to the Festival, the curtain would be removed for them and the Cherubim were shown to them, whose bodies were intertwisted with one another, and they would be thus addressed: Look! You are beloved before God as the love between man and woman.

Later on in that same text, we read that that cherub images were so explicit, they caused scandal among Israel's enemies:

When the heathens entered the Temple and saw the Cherubim whose bodies were intertwisted with one another, they carried them out and said: These Israelites, whose blessing is a blessing, and whose curse is a curse, occupy themselves with such things! And immediately they despised them, as it is said: All that honored her, despised her, because they have seen her nakedness.

Regarding the vision of Azazel in the Garden that Abraham is given in the *Apocalypse*, Orlov states:

Scholars have previously suggested that Azazel may attempt here to mimic the divine presence often represented in sacerdotal settings as the intertwined cherubic couple in the Holy of Holies by offering his own, now corrupted and demonic version of the sacred union.

It seems to us that this is true, but that Azazel (whom *The Zohar* refers to as the Tanin'iver or "intermediary") only manifests as this dual creature *through* the bodies of Adam and Eve, as though they provide the "garments" that the male and female aspects of himself clothe themselves in, via demonic possession. But then, there is also the idea that Adam and Eve got their original heavenly garments from the Serpent, as it says in *The Zohar*. Orlov mentions this again, noting that:

Pseudepigraphic and rabbinic accounts often provide various interpretations of the serpent's gender. Some of these sources seem to understand the serpent as an androgynous creature, whose skin God later used to create the "garments" of both Adam and Eve.

Then there is the aforementioned quote from *The Life of Adam and Eve* that before his Fall, Satan lived on God's throne, where the wings of the cherubim provided his garment. This really almost sounds like Satan were God himself! Remember that *The Zohar* refers to the "Beast" formed by the combination of Lilith and Samael as "the Other God."

The idea of being inside the skin of the Serpent is added to with another bizarre quote from *The Zohar* which seems to indicate that human souls originate inside the womb of a "certain female animal," who appears to be Lilith. She is described as always thirsty, presumably because she has been consigned to a desert wasteland. We humans come to this realm, it says, because the Serpent (seemingly, the same as the one from Eden) bites a hole in her womb, opening up a portal that allows our souls to incarnate into human bodies. As the text (*Vayaqhel* [Exodus] 219b, from Volume 4 of the Soncino Edition) states:

> There is . . . a certain female animal that has under her daily charge a thousand keys, and that pants continually after the water brooks to drink and quench her thirst, of which it is thus written, "As the hart panteth after the water brooks." It is to be observed that this verse commences with a masculine subject, "hart" (*'ayyal*), and continues with a feminine predicate, *tha 'erog* (she panteth). the recondite explanation of this is that it is an allusion to the male-female as one undivided and inseparable;

and so it is the female part of the same that "panteth for the water brooks" and then becomes impregnated from the male element, and is in labour, coming under the scrutiny of Rigour. But at the moment when she is about to be delivered of offspring the Holy One, blessed be He, prepares for her a huge celestial serpent through whose bite she is safely delivered. And this is the hidden meaning of, "I will greatly multiply thy pain and thy travail," for she is in daily convulsions and pain because of the deeds of mankind: "in pain thou shalt bring forth children," a hidden allusion to the Serpent who casts a gloom over the faces of mankind; "and thy desire shall be to thy husband" . . . Why all this? It was on account of the Moon's dissatisfaction with her state, in punishment for which, as tradition teaches us, her light was diminished, also her power was reduced so that she is beholden to what they grant her from outside. It may be asked, Why is the Serpent necessary in this connection? It is because it is he who opens the passage for the descent of souls into the world. For if he did not open the way, no soul would come down to animate a man's body in the world. So Scripture says, "sin coucheth at the door" (*Genesis* 3:7) alluding to the celestial door through which pass the souls at birth to emerge into this world. He, the Serpent, waits at that door. It is true, when the souls about to emerge are such as are to enter sanctified bodies, he is not present, having no dominion over such souls. But otherwise, the Serpent bites, and that spot is defiled and the soul passing through is unpurified. Herein is concealed a sublime mystical teaching. "In pain thou shalt bring forth children" is a mystical allusion to that Serpent, as it is with him that She brings forth souls, since he is responsible for the body and she for the soul, and the two are combined.

It would seem that the creature giving birth here is a hermaphrodite. The hole bitten by the Serpent may also be what constitutes the cleaving apart of the male and female halves, since this is given as an explanation for why the woman (now thought of as Eve) yearns for her husband.

Maybe part of the mystery being hinted at here is that "Lilith" was the first wife of "Adam" because "Adam" was originally God, and she was his female half. He was pregnant with all the possibilities of what could be, the "complete man" that Adam Kadmon, the "first Adam" of the cabalists, is described as. Part of what was inside him was the awareness of the possibility that some of his constituent parts could be separated from others. This awareness was in itself part of what caused that split to actually happen (the knowledge of Good and Evil). This brought about the rupture that caused the possibilities trapped *in utero* to be born as actualities, so that sex and death were simultaneously brought into existence. But the pain of separation between the male and female halves, now called "Adam" and "Eve," and considered diminutive creations of their now deified (in the case of the male half, God), and infernalized (in the case of the female half, Lilith) past selves. Islamic tradition has it that after the Fall, Adam and Eve separated out of shame for a number of years, and when they reunited again, it happened in Mecca, near where the Kaaba would be built (a fact mentioned in the previously-quoted Shriner ritual).

This strange description of what seems to be the demon Lilith giving birth to humans, along with so many other hints that we have gone over in this book, bring to mind what is potentially one of the most blasphemous questions you could ask. Are all of the original hermaphroditic pairs—God and the Matronit, Adam and Eve, Lilith and Samael—all in some way the same thing? Is this what the rabbinic texts are hinting at: that the real reunion which our universe is yearning for is between God and the Devil? It would seem a question too audacious to ask, but then, this passage from *The Zohar* (I.35b, as quoted by Orlov) makes us feel we are not off the mark. We have quoted this in part before, but let us now look at the whole context:

> Now observe a deep and holy mystery of faith, the symbolism of the male principle and the female principle of the universe. In the former are comprised all holinesses and objects of faith, and all life, all freedom, all goodness, all illuminations emerge from thence; all blessings, all benevolent dews, all graces and kindnesses—all these are generated from that side, which is called the South. Contrariwise, from the side of the North there issue a variety of grades, extending downwards, to the world below. This is the region of the dross of gold, which comes from the side of impurity and loathsomeness and which forms a link between the upper and nether regions; and there is the line where the male and female principles join, forming together the rider on the serpent, and symbolized by Azazel.

So it seems to us that Azazel somehow acts as the intermediary not just between the male and female halves of the Serpent (Lilith and Samael), but also between the principle of good (here described as male) and the principle of evil (here described as female). Is the Devil God's girlfriend here, or even his wife? It certainly seems that way. But if that's the case, it may be safe to assume that they are presently divorced, or perhaps legally separated. As in any split-up from a long-term relationship, there has been a legal agreement regarding the shared property (creation) and the kids (humanity). They seem to have joint custody. Drawing upon the work of writers Michael Stone and John Collins, Andrei Orlov describes the arrangement, with Azazel, the intermediary, being given power of attorney to oversee the Serpent's possessions on its behalf:

> Michael Stone draws attention to the traditions found in chapters 20, 22, and 29 [of *The Apocalypse of Abraham*], where the reference to Azazel's rule, which he exercises jointly with God over the world, coincides "with the idea that God granted him authority over the wicked."; Stone suggests that "these ideas are clearly dualistic in nature." John Collins explores another cluster of peculiar depictions repeatedly found in the second part of the *Apocalypse,* in which humankind is divided into two parts, half on the right and half on the left, representing respectively the chosen people and the Gentiles. These portions of humanity are labeled in the text as the lot of God and the lot of Azazel.

But the idea of bringing this primordial couple back together again, no matter how dangerous that may be, seems to have been the ultimate goal of many, including the rabbis who wrote *The Zohar*, and the secret societies that have perpetuated through the centuries the mysteries discussed in this book. The Holy Grail has been described as both a cup and a stone. But really they are both of the same substance, and the ultimate treasure would be to obtain and reunite both the cup and the stone.

In his 1973 book *The Spear of Destiny*, Trevor Ravenscroft claimed that "The Sign of the Holy Grail . . . is a Dove winging across from the Sun into the invisible disc held within the arms of the Crescent Moon." This is essentially the same as one of the primary symbols of Christianity: the image of the heavenly Host descending into the Eucharist cup. It is shown either as a white disc (the communion wafer), usually marked with a cross, sometimes carried down in the beak of a dove, or it is shown as a sun disc with shining rays. Aleister Crowley's OTO uses their own version of this as their official "lamen," but instead the bird descends into a cup containing a rose, a Templar cross, and flames, presumably on its way to immolate itself like a phoenix in its own "baptism of fire."

If the Host is the Sun, then the cup, logically, is the crescent moon, a symbol of Islam that was also incorporated by the Templars into some of their official seals. On these the Moon was often shown along with either a lion, or the image of the Dome of the Rock. One of the most interesting depictions of the holy Host and cup can be found in the window of the Dominus Flevit ("The Lord Wept") church in Jerusalem, directly overlooking the Dome.

Interestingly, an event has occurred recently there at the Dome that brings to mind the image of the Host descending into the communion cup. On the night of January 28, 2011, a strange and sizable ball of light was seen hovering over the Dome, descending to touch the top, and then raising up again. It did this several times before it suddenly zipped off heavenward and flew away. The event was recorded by many witnesses. While we are not making any claims about what this meant, it does fall into line with the Holy Grail imagery associated with the Dome and the buildings nearby.

In alchemy, the combination of the Sun and the Moon is considered a symbol of the great chemical conjunction of the elements of the universe, which is allegedly key to the magical transformation of substances that is the goal of this art. It is these heavenly bodies, represented sometimes as a king and a queen, who are shown mating in a bathtub in so many alchemical images from medieval times. This is the "Bath of the Stars" discussed in a previous chapter, in which they are shown bathing in the blood of their own children. It may also be the "Baptism of Wisdom as practiced by the Templars, in which, it seems quite possibly, they sacrificed babies produced during orgies, and utilized their bodies for black magic purposes.

The wedding of the solar and the lunar embodies the same concept as the merging of light and darkness (symbolized by the chequer pattern), as it is the blending of day and night. The courtship between Solomon and the Queen of Sheba (Sheba an incarnation, supposedly, of Lilith, and both of them associated with "wisdom") could be thought of as a symbol of the same idea. The fact that Solomon's birth name was actually "Jedidiah" ("beloved of the Lord") indicates that "Solomon" (a permutation of *shalom* or *salem*) was actually a symbolic title he took as king. It has the same root as the name of his capital city, "Jerusalem," and the alleged location of his temple/stairway to Heaven (the temple of the white rock). Again, the word also means "peace," like that which the reconciliation of opposing forces would bring. Meanwhile, the Queen of Sheba can be connected directly with the Kaaba in lore, for the guardians of the Kaaba have always been referred to as "Beni Shaybah," ("the Sons of the Old Woman"), which is traditionally taken to be a reference to her. Prince Michael of Albany, as we noted, believes that it also points to the "widow" Isis (impregnated with her son Horus by the undead body of her deceased and resurrected husband Osiris), as the epithet "Sons of the Widow," used by Freemasons to identify themselves, is meant to imply that they are symbolically her children.

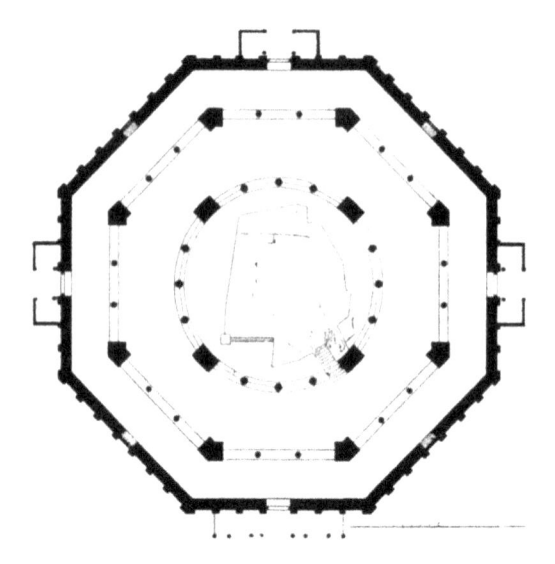

2. JERUSALEM: DER FELSENDOM.

Above: Floorplan of the Dome of the Rock, from *Kirchliche Baukunst des Abendlandes* by Georg Dehio and Gustav von Bezold, 1887-1901. Below: View from the window of the Dominus Flevit church in Jerusalem. Opposite: Mohammed's flying steed, Barak.

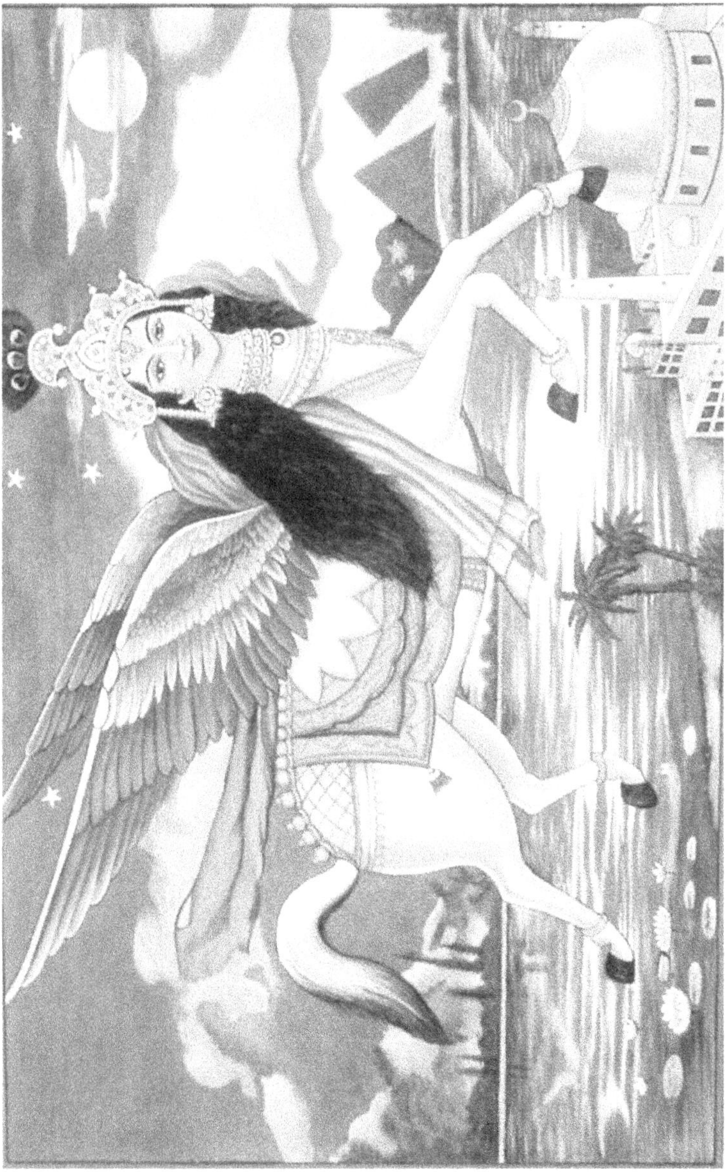

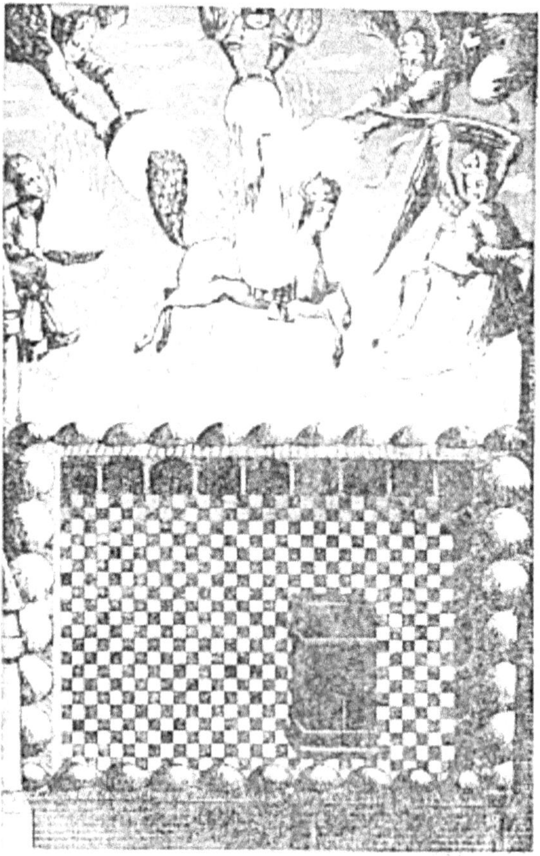

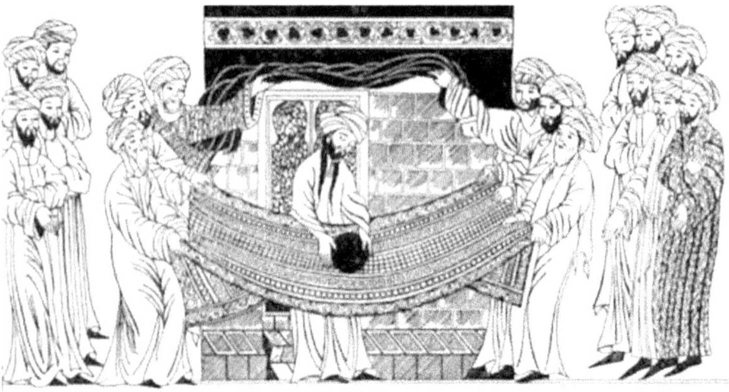

Right: Sophia Mercurius, from an alchemical manuscript. Below: *The Azoth of the Philosophers*, by Basil Valentine, 1659. Opposite page, above: Mohammed and Barak flying over the Kaaba, shown with chequered floor, from D'Ohsson's *Tableau General de l'Empire Othoman*, 1788-1824. Opposite Page, below: Mohammed rededicating the Black Stone at the Kaaba, by Jami' al-Tavarikh, from *Compendium of Chronicles*, Rashid Al-Din, c. 1315.

Cover for *La Femme et L'Enfant dans la Franc-maconnerie Universelle* by AC de la Rive, 1894.

Promotional poster for *Les Mysteres de la Franc-maçonnerie Devoiles* by Leo Taxil, 1895.

Glad Påsk!

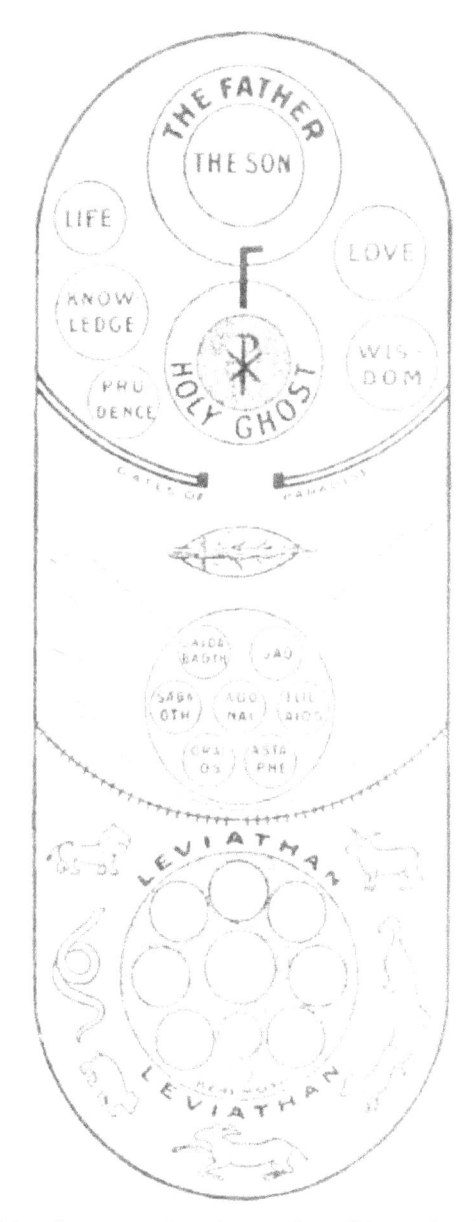

Above: Ophite diagram, taken from SaintWiki.com (CCL). Opposite, above: Postcards referencing the "goat-riding" Masonic "joke." Opposite, below: Postcard featuring "the Easter Witch" with goat-riding and cat-riding.

The Great Symbol of Solomon, from *Transcendental Magic* by Eliphas Levi. It is a representation of God and "Zer Anpin," God's "little face." Levi calls it "the Macroprosopus and the Microprosopus; the God of Light and the God of Reflections; of mercy and vengeance; the white Jehovah and the black Jehovah." Note the figure is wearing a Templar cross.

Above: Bahumed, "The Secret of the nature of the world, or The Secret of Secrets, or The Beginning and Return of every thing." From *Ancient Alphabets and Hieroglyphic Characters Explained* by Ibn Wahshiyya.

Left: Ouroboros from *Chrysopeia* by Cleopatra the Alchemist, tenth-eleventh century.

As for what Baphomet (the "abbot of the temple of peace") was, or is, to the thousands if not millions of people who belong to secret societies and fringe religious groups influenced by this concept, well, there is no one answer. Rather, there are several answers that are all simultaneously true. It is really neither a single object nor a merely abstract concept. Instead it is a continuum running throughout time and space, connecting all of the gods, people, objects, myths and symbols that manifest the forbidden wisdom given to Eve in the Garden of Eden. Individual personages, both human and divine, have throughout history come along to act as living avatars of this hidden Gnosis. Baphomet is not a static, definable idea, but a mutable mercurial sentience that expresses itself in a multitude of ways.

We could certainly say that Baphomet is a nonhuman intelligence, variously described as a demon or a deity, seemingly made from the energies of the male and female halves of an originally hermaphroditic entity of primordial chaos. Baphomet is perhaps specifically the intelligence formed when Azazel, the Tanin'iver, acts as an intermediary between the two serpents and allows them to mate. This seems to be connected to the idea of the Serpent/s using the bodies of humans as hosts through when they unite with each other sexually.

The Templars appear to have used an idol as a touchpoint to contact this entity. The idol is usually described as a head, and the name Baphomet applies to the idol itself as well (along with the various copies that were made of it to be used in Templar preceptories far-flung throughout Europe and the Middle East). They believed that their demon used these heads to talk to them. If they were anything like the other oracular heads in history, its mouth may have moved, like the robot head supposedly owned by Catholic saint and alchemist Albertus Magnus. It is likely that some Templars also thought that it spoke to them telepathically.

From the Templars' confessions, they seem to have believed that the head had given their leaders information that they found helpful in building their global empire through moneylending, trade, and military conquest. To them it was both a priest and a prophet, like John, whose head or skull may have been the actual physical idol. As we have explained, the heads of prophets were revered as having special magical qualities. We mentioned that there were Talmudic rumors that John had a demonic servant, and that the control of this demon was passed on to Jesus. It seems possible for there to have been a belief that Jesus, who was related to King Herod's bloodline, may have somehow gotten hold of John's head, and used it to control either John's own spirit, or a spirit that John had formerly controlled while he was alive. This head, then, may have later come into the hands of the founding Templars (or, at least, something that they believed was this). Or the head and attached spirit could have come to be possessed by John's student and successor Simon Magus first. Perhaps too, rather, as Alexander Rivera has suggested, Simon may have been beheaded just like John, and it could have been his head that ended up with the Templars.

If this was the case, it seems likely then that the spirit they acquired was connected to Lilith-Samael, the Serpent of the primordial deep, which makes sense if they had come into contact with it via their time spent on the alleged Temple Mount, or through something they found there. It also seems likely, given the combination of images that came to be joined to the concept of Baphomet, that the Templars used magic to blend in with this spirit the attributes of wild satyr gods like Dionysus, Hermes, and Pan (which were, in a roundabout way, already connected to Lilith-Samael via the imagery of the goat-demon Azazel, their intermediary). It seems like they also blended in the essence of the wisdom of Hermes Trismegistus, and that of the Gnostic Sophia.

What do we mean by saying that they "used magic" to "blend" these things? Let us give a few examples. In imperial Rome, when a new land was conquered, those people's gods would be rededicated and incorporated into the Roman pantheon, often joined up with other existing gods who were either considered to have the same attributes, or to be complimentary. The resulting hybrid entities would sometimes thereafter be represented with the physical features of both gods stuck onto the same body. The names would be hybridized too. There was a magical ceremony that was part of this process. Robert Graves wrote about it in *The White Goddess*:

> In ancient times, once a god's secret name had been discovered, the enemies of his people could do destructive magic against them with it. The Romans made a regular practice of discovering the secret names of enemy gods and summoning them to Rome with seductive promises, a process technically know as *elicio*. . . . Naturally, the Romans, like the Jews, hid the secret name of their own guardian deity with extraordinary care.

In the modern fantasy anime series "Fullmetal Alchemist," real live "chimeras" are created through alchemy by "marrying" creatures of dissimilar nature, including humans and animals. The resulting monstrosities are then kept as servants, used to do things like guarding an alchemist's laboratory. While this is obviously just fiction, the writers of this show displayed a great deal of understanding of the subject not found in many nonfiction books on the subject. Ultimately, the Philosopher's Stone in this program is revealed to be made from human souls, and the sacrifice of these is what makes alchemical transformations possible—an idea that almost no modern writer has touched upon outside of horror fiction. But the true story of Gilles de Rais—a fifteenth century French nobleman who raped and murdered hundreds of boys in an attempt to persuade the Devil to transform lead into gold alchemically with their blood—proves that these things have been understood for some time.

The creation of chimera servants in the above-mentioned TV show brings to mind what chaos magick author Phil Hine says about "servitors" that can be made by magicians to do their bidding. These are spirits that are pulled out of chaos (*tehom*, "the deep") and formed in whatever shape the magician chooses, to do whatever he needs. This involves the drawing of an image to represent the character that the servitor will take on, including what he looks like, what attributes he will have, and what rules he will operate by. Hine talks about creating the servitor as a glyph on a piece of paper, perhaps using the "sigil magick" process discussed earlier, and then "animating" it with meditation, sacrifices of blood, incense, and things of that nature, to impart to it energy and the essence of spirit.

However much one may believe in ceremonial magic, the instructions given by Hine indicate that the spirit created will never act like more than an imaginary friend, and its influence will be subtle if detectable at all (on the level of doing a personal affirmation in the mirror). However, if one actually has a severed human head for the spirit to inhabit, or one takes the bodies of creatures and sews them together *a la* Frankenstein, then uses magic to animate the resulting monstrosity, the event takes on quite more serious tone. Remember too that according to Polyhistor's quote of

Berossus supposedly quoting Oannes, before the present stage of creation, there existed a primordial Abyss of chaos populated by beings with multiple heads, and "in which were combined the limbs of every species of animals." The substance of chaos seems to lend itself to such things, because it contains the potentiality of everything possible, in perfect mutability.

What we are proposing is that the Baphomet was a chimeric hybrid demonic servitor formed by the Templars, not from scratch, but through the transmutation and rededication of something they found, which was connected by them to a collection of related spiritual energies. This created an "egregore": a "thought form" made from the combined imaginations and mental energies of a group of people that came to life and took on a will of its own. This egregore was then added to over the centuries by individuals and groups claiming to be perpetuating the mythos of the Templars: Freemasons, Eliphas Levi, Aleister Crowley, and Anton LaVey (creator of the Church of Satan). Along with them, a huge role was played by one of the Templars' greatest critics, Joseph von Hammer-Purgstall, whose work is still being assessed by us. (Please see our translation of *Mysterium Baphometis Revelatum*, with commentary by Tracy R. Twyman, which should be available shortly after the publication of the book you are now reading.)

Although we feel that, in a way, Baphomet is an artificial entity created by the Templars, we also think that they revered this figure as a teacher. As his connection to Hermes would indicate, Baphomet is an example of the archetype of the teacher of forbidden wisdom (as the goat god or Black Man of the Witches' Sabbath would later be seen by his acolytes also). This includes both the "divine secrets" of another reality beyond our own, the "Pleroma" (knowledge

Riding the Goat Current 587

of which is Gnosis), as well as seemingly mundane knowledge of science and technology which we take for granted now, but which scriptures and myths teach us were once forbidden for men to know, and available to us now only because certain brave angels or gods defied divine law to bring them to us. The Serpent taught forbidden wisdom to Eve in the Garden. The Watchers, Azazel and Samyaza, in turn taught it to their half-human children before the Flood. After that, a number of teachers are remembered as having brought these things to men again, in the attempt to help rebuild our shattered civilization. Thus we have stories of figures like Enoch, Oannes, Enki, Hermes, Asclepius, Agathodaemon, and several others, teaching knowledge to men and initiating wisdom traditions that were passed on for generations.

Speaking of "generation," that is in fact part of the hidden wisdom. In the Garden of Eden it was carnal knowledge that was bestowed upon Eve. The secret of *Genesis* was the secret of generation. The hints embedded in this text, when decoded, reveal the implication that our universe is a time-space box that didn't exist until Eve ate the "fruit." We may wonder how it is that there was "fruit" for her to eat (specifically "fruit of a tree bearing seed") when there was no sexual generation in the first place. The "fruit," most likely, was the fetal potentiality of new life, the fruit of the tree of carnal knowledge.

As we know, there were two trees in the Garden—the Tree of Knowledge of Good and Evil and the Tree of Life. If the "knowledge" is carnal knowledge, and its "fruit" is a fetus or a baby, wouldn't the fruit of the Tree of Life also be the same thing? We mentioned briefly the idea that the Philosopher's Stone is made from the flesh and blood of the young, babies and fetuses in particular, and that the consumption of such preserves youth (a notion explored in greater depth in Tracy R. Twyman's books *Clock Shavings* and

Money Grows on the Tree of Knowledge). As *Genesis* implies, eating from the Tree of Knowledge brought birth and death into the world. Therefore, it says, the gods (or Jehovah and whoever he was talking to in this text) sealed off the Tree of Life, so that humans would not eat of it and become immortal. But the Tree of Life had only been briefly mentioned in the text until that point. Did the Tree of Knowledge *become* the Tree of Life after Eve ate from it? Did the Tree of Knowledge contain only the potentiality of life, which became real after carnal knowledge was obtained?

The idea of eating babies brings to mind the myth of Chronos, the Greek god of time eating his own children at birth, the imagery of which is directly invoked in alchemical treatises, with Chronos (the Roman Saturn) shown doing exactly this. In alchemy Chronos is equated with the *nigrido* or *prima materia*, the primordial chaos that is transformed through the alchemical process into the desired form, usually represented with either a skull or a black sun. In *Money Grows on the Tree of Knowledge*, Tracy R. Twyman talks about the fact that, in Greek myths, Chronos was treated the same was by his own father:

> Ouranous (Uranus) had likewise resented his children, the Titans, and imprisoned them underneath the Earth in order to keep them from threatening his rule. Since his consort's name was Gaia, or Earth, this really means he was imprisoning them inside of her. Indeed some versions of the story refer to Ouranous shoving his children back into their mother's womb as a way of jailing them.

Chronos was said to have ruled over an epoch of Earth's history called the "Golden Age," in which there were no seasons, and nobody had to work for a living. It seems as if there may have been no death or birth in that place either, just like in pre-Fall Eden. In Part 1 of the article series on her website entitled "Regnum in Potentia: Saturn's Kingdom Transformed into the Golden Age," Tracy R. Twyman elaborates on this:

> Here is the meaning of this myth. Chronos ("Father Time") had lived and ruled (or "unruled") for untold aeons in a timeless realm before the coming of Zeus. In this realm, there could be no begetting of offspring, or else there would also be death. Thus the birth of children had to be prevented, either by confining them within the womb—as Ouranos did—or by swallowing them at birth—as Chronos did, attempting to negate their existence by confining them to another womb of sorts: his gullet.
>
> This is exactly what the story of the Garden of Eden indicates. Adam and Eve live in happy, timeless ignorance. They are the children of a god who remains, to them, invisible, and they are still shut up inside the womb, or within their father's gullet. There, they live as parasites, forming a symbiotic relationship with their host, who provides them with all of the sustenance they need. Then one day, a foreign fruit is introduced to them from outside. They are told by their father, the unseen god, not to eat it. But they do anyway, and it initiates in them an awakening to the reality of what they are involved in. Their eyes are opened. They wake up from the dream and realize that they are slowly being digested. At that moment, they are vomited out into the cold, cruel, outside world, forced to work for their daily bread, fighting for survival. With their birth, or perhaps, their second birth, the passage of time is finally allowed to begin.

590 *Chapter 9*

In mythology, there is an archetypal scenario in which a person travels from one realm to another, and becomes stuck there upon eating the food of the other realm. This happened to the Greek figure of Persephone when she ate the food of the underworld. Eve ate from the Tree of Knowledge and it changed the universe, or perhaps it created a new universe, and she became trapped in it. Jesus told us to eat his flesh and drink his blood to live forever in the New Jerusalem (the "Kingdom of God") after death. In the New Jerusalem everyone drinks of the waters of life from the rivers of Paradise and becomes immortal. So perhaps there are other recipes involving similar ingredients that likewise could affect the universe around you upon consumption.

Satan, according to some interpretations, is God's firstborn son, who came before Adam. But Adam was his favorite, and when his firstborn son refused to honor his younger brother, God sacrificed him. Satan embodied the forbidden wisdom that Adam was not allowed to have, and God told him not to eat of that "tree." Was this "fruit" the product of sexual union? The carnal knowledge that Eve was endowed with, according to the cabalistic legends, came from her having carnal knowledge of the Serpent, which bred Cain (and perhaps others, according to some stories). What happens when a human and a spirit of the chaos realm mate? Better yet, what happens when you eat the child that was born of such a union?

Cain was later exiled by his parents to a place called "Nod" (after killing his brother and, according to some versions of the story, drinking his blood). Nod seems like a word for the Abyss. In other words, Cain was shoved back into the non-existent chaos that had fathered him, like the children of Ouranos were shoved back into their mother's womb. Upon the basis of the primordial events attempting to be expressed in these myths, it seems, the cultic practice of child sacrifice and brephophagy (baby-eating) has continued throughout the thousands of years of man's history, particular the sacrifice of the firstborn.

We think it likely that the Templars may have engaged in such a ritual, it being a "baptism of wisdom" or "immersion in the divine mystery" for the initiates (and, sadly, perhaps a deadly "baptism of fire" for the victims). The title of this ceremony provides yet another interpretation for the name of Baphomet. Part of what may have been achieved for the participants by such ceremonies was a state of mind, which seems to be akin to merging one's mind with the other side, the Pleroma, or the pre-Fall Eden. This experience in itself is also one of the meanings of "Baphomet."

In addition to the effects on the mind for the ceremony's participants, there may have also been a belief among the Templars that a long-term goal could be achieved over time, through generations, if certain rituals were done in this state of mind, including the breeding of children, both for sacrifice, and for the continuation of a sacred bloodline. The lineage is that of Cain, the Serpent seed. The original Templars, and all of their grand masters, came from that bloodline, as did most of the royal families of Europe who have done so much to shape the world we live in. The members of this family can be thought of as incarnations of the Serpent, just as Lilith was thought by cabalists take human form in order to breed into the patriarchal pedigree of Israel. The goal of this, as we have indicated, might have actually been to put the seed of the Serpent in powerful positions on Earth, so that, through his children, he may finally rule over what he considers to be his rightful inheritance. Baphomet can be thought of as a combination formed by this chain of incarnations via these bloodlines throughout the centuries—the spirit that inhabits all of them, and ties them together. Also, through the bodies of these, the Serpent's descendants, the male and female halves of the Beast get to experience the pleasure of mating.

Returning once more to the image of Abraxas, can it not be thought to symbolize this dangerous union, capable of destroying the universe? For his body provides a place of union where two serpents, shown as his legs, combine. If so, perhaps the use of a rooster's head on top can be seen as an expression of hope that from the destruction wrought by such a union, the dawn of a brand new day (maybe a new Eden) will be announced.

So what if we look at Levi's Baphomet image in the same way? Does his goat persona connect him with Azazel, and indicate that Baphomet is the thing that unites these serpents in their destructive unholy matrimony? Is this part of what is symbolized by the two serpents on the caduceus that rises from his crotch region? Is this because his "body" is the "temple" where the conjunction of the two snakes takes place (perhaps at one point literally, via the bodies of the Knights of the Temple, through possession)?

One thing is for certain: Baphomet, to modern Satanists, exemplifies the nuanced view of the Devil that they now have, which is quite different from the views of all of the other religious groups that we have examined in this book (Jews, Christians, Hermeticists, Gnostics, and various pagan cults). To Jews and most Christians, Jehovah is the creator of the universe, and the bestower of all blessings. He decides how fate will be meted out, who will gain and who will lose. If you have wealth and health, it is because God has chosen that for you. The Devil is God's adversary, so whenever God blesses or curses something, Satan tries to do the opposite. Yet to the Gnostics, the entity who does these things was not the real "God," but an imposter with evil intent. To the

Cathars he was actually the Devil, Rex Mundi. Since he was the lord of this Earth, you would think that all material blessings enjoyed in life would be attributed to him.

Actually, that is how modern Satanists view it, but they don't see Satan as a negative entity. They (generally) don't seem to lament the creation of the world. Rather, they enthusiastically embrace materiality and the flesh. To them (generally) Satan is the god of this world, from whom all wealth or earthly success is granted. While organizations like the Church of Satan aren't generally populated with financially prosperous people, other, more secretive fraternities are, and some of those do seem to have satanic intent when their symbols are decoded. Perhaps, just as their enemies on the outside fear, they have discovered that the secret to riches and power is to prostrate themselves before the one who is truly in charge of these things. The closest parallel, historically, to this viewpoint can actually be found in the Yezidi scripture called *Al-Jilwah* (*The Revelation*), in the first three chapters, where their lord Melek Taus (whom they also call "Azazil" and acknowledge is identical with "Sheitan") is portrayed as a benevolent Demiurge—at least for those who honor him. As it says in the translation by Isya Joseph, from his 1919 book *Devil Worship: The Sacred Books and Traditions of the Yezidis*:

> I was, am now, and shall have no end. I exercise dominion over all creatures and over the affairs of all who are under the protection of my image. I am ever present to help all who trust in me and call upon me in time of need. There is no place in the universe that knows not my presence. I participate in all the affairs which those who are without call evil because their nature is not such as they approve. Every age has its own manager, who directs affairs according to my

decrees. This office is changeable from generation to generation, that the ruler of this world and his chiefs may discharge the duties of their respective offices every one in his own turn. I allow everyone to follow the dictates of his own nature, but he that opposes me will regret it sorely. No god has a right to interfere in my affairs, and I have made it an imperative rule that everyone shall refrain from worshiping all gods. All the books of those who are without are altered by them; and they have declined from them, although they were written by the prophets and the apostles. That there are interpolations is seen in the fact that each sect endeavors to prove that the others are wrong and to destroy their books. To me truth and falsehood are known. When temptation comes, I give my covenant to him that trusts in me. Moreover, I give counsel to the skilled directors, for I have appointed them for periods that are known to me. I remember necessary affairs and execute them in due time. I teach and guide those who follow my instruction. If anyone obey me and conform to my commandments, he shall have joy, delight, and goodness.

I requite the descendants of Adam, and reward them with various rewards that I alone know. Moreover, power and dominion over all that is on earth, both that which is above and that which is beneath, are in my hand. I do not allow friendly association with other people, nor do I deprive them that are my own and that obey me of anything that is good for them. I place my affairs in the hands of those whom I have tried and who are in accord with my desires. I appear in divers manners to those who are faithful and under my command. I give and take away; I enrich and impoverish; I cause both happiness and misery. I do all this in keeping with the characteristics of each epoch. And none has a right to interfere with my management of affairs. Those who oppose me I afflict with disease; but my own shall not die like the sons of Adam that are without. None shall live in this world longer than the time set by me; and if I so desire, I send a person a second or a third time into this world or into some other by the transmigration of souls.

I lead to the straight path without a revealed book; I direct aright my beloved and my chosen ones by unseen means. All my teachings are easily applicable to all times and all conditions. I punish in another world all who do contrary to my will. Now the sons of Adam do not know the state of things that is to come. For this reason they fall into many errors. The beasts of the earth, the birds of heaven, and the fish of the sea are all under the control of my hands. All treasures and hidden things are known to me; and as I desire, I take them from one and bestow them upon another. I reveal my wonders to those who seek them, and, in due time my miracles to those who receive them from me. But those who are without are my adversaries, hence they oppose me. Nor do they know that such a course is against their own interests, for might, wealth, and riches are in my hand, and I bestow them upon every worthy descendant of Adam. Thus the government of the worlds, the transition of generations, and the changes of their directors are determined by me from the beginning.

In *A History of Secret Societies*, Arkon Daraul (Idries Shah) describes his attendance at a secret meeting of a Yezidi cult active in London in the late 1950s. The order's members were wealthy and, it seems, mostly white Britons, who would pray to Melek Taus for success in business. Whenever they would gain "as a result of any activity for whose success they have prayed to the Peacock," they were expected to pay 2.5 percent to the cult. Their rituals involved baptism at initiation, and circumambulation around a stone, of which one member was quoted as saying:

> Let us remember the force of the good and the bad which are one; and let us now stand before it, and move around our stone.

We also have the rare esoteric eighth-century Shiite text, *Mother of Books* (*Umm al-ktab*), which portrays "Azazi'il" in terms identical to that of the Gnostic Demiurge. *The Gospel of John*'s description of Satan is the "prince of the world" is virtually indistinguishable from the Yezidi and Shi'ite notions of who Melek Taus/Azazil is. In the *Liber Secretum* used by Bogomils and Cathars, the Devil is defined, as Yuri Stoyanov put it in *The Other God*, as:

> . . . a creator and master of the visible world, as "Lord of the sky, the sun, the air and the stars."

This appears to have been how the Templars viewed their Baphomet also, and from all available evidence, worshipping him seems to have worked out for them, at least for a time. As Pope Pius IX put it, "Their watchword was, to become wealthy, in order to buy the world," and that they did. Later they confessed to their torturers that it was Baphomet who enabled it all.

It should not surprise us, then, that there are many people today who think their fantasies of fame and fortune can be fulfilled by making a pact with the Devil. On this topic, the name "Baphomet" is frequently bandied about on the internet, as the popular belief is that this is the particular infernal name to invoke if you are looking to make such a Faustian bargain. (We noticed this trend took off after the release of Tracy R. Twyman's book *Solomon's Treasure*, which highlights the possible connection between the alleged "power" of Baphomet and the global financial dominance of the US dollar.) Conspiracy theorists, who believe that popular musicians and movie stars are part of a Satanic "Illuminati" plot, strain their eyes to find any pattern in a logo, an outfit, or even a set of curtains in the background of an image, that can in any way be construed to somehow look like a horned figure, and then call it "Baphomet."

We are certain that for as many people that there are who fear this perceived plot, there are just as many who are actually eager to join it. Both of the authors of the book you are reading now receive hits daily on their websites from people seeking information about how to make a pact with Baphomet for wealth (or, as we have seen it put so many times in our web statistics, "How to join the Baphomet"). Many of these people, strangely, live in Africa. But there is plenty of interest in the West too. Recently, a statue of Baphomet was erected in Detroit by Satanists, to much public outcry, and the word was trending high on Google for days.

Today, people talk about Baphomet a lot, but they don't really know him. After years of research, however, we feel that we do, and we are pleased to have been able to introduce him to you. It is a knowledge you cannot disremember, and now that you have been dipped in its tincture, your mind will forever be stained. We hope you have enjoyed your baptism.

Initium Sapientiae Timor Domini.

Bibliography

"The Acts of Peter and Paul." New Advent. Web.

"Against Heresies." CHURCH FATHERS: (St. Irenaeus). New Advent. Web.

"Against the Pelagians (Book I)." CHURCH FATHERS: (Jerome). New Advent. Web.

Agnes, Michael. *Webster's New World College Dictionary.* 4th edition. New York: Macmillan, 1999. Print.

Altinoluk, Sencan, and Nilufer Atakan. "Abraxas: A Magical Gem in the Istanbul Archaeological Museums" Anatolia Antiqua XXII (2014): 219-23. Print.

Arendzen, J. "Gnosticism" in *The Catholic Encyclopedia*, Volume 6. (New York: Appleton, 1909). Print.

"Asclepius 21-29." Gnosis.org. Web.

Baigent, Michael, and Richard Leigh. *Holy Blood, Holy Grail*. New York: Delacorte, 1982. Print.

Baigent, Michael, and Richard Leigh. *The Temple and the Lodge*. London: J. Cape, 1989. Print.

"Baphomet and the Azoth." Pyramidlodge.com. Web.

Barrett, Caitlin E. "Plaster Perspectives on 'Magical Gems': Rethinking the Meaning of 'Magic' in Cornell's Dactyliotheca." Cornell Collection of Antiquities. Cornell University Library. Web.

Barnstone, Willis, and Marvin Meyer. *The Gnostic Bible*. Boston, Massachusetts: Shambhala, 2003. Print.

Barnstone, Willis. *The Other Bible: Ancient Alternative Scriptures*. New York, New York: HarperCollins, 1984. Print.

Berg, Rav PS. *The Essential Zohar: The Source of Kabbalistic Wisdom*. New York: Three Rivers Press, 2002. Print.

Betz, Hans Dieter. *The Greek Magical Papyri in Translation, including the Demotic Spells.* Chicago, Illinois: University of Chicago, 1986. Print.

Biggs, Mark Wayne. *The Case for Lilith: 23 Biblical Evidences Identifying the Serpent as Adam's First Failed Wife in Genesis*. Samson Books, 2010. Print.

Bladel, Kevin Thomas. *The Arabic Hermes: From Pagan Sage to Prophet of Science*. Oxford, England: Oxford University Press, 2009. Print.

Blake, William. *The Marriage of Heaven and Hell*: *A Facsimile in Full Color*. Dover Fine Art, 1994. Print.

Bloch, Iwan, and James Bruce. *Marquis De Sade, the Man and His Age: Studies in the History of the Culture and Morals of the Eighteenth Century*. Newark, New Jersey: Julian, 1931. Print.

"The Book of the Cave of Treasures." SacredTexts.com. Web.

"The Book of Jasher." SacredTexts.com. Web.

Box, GH. *The Apocalypse of Abraham*. London: Society for Promoting Christian Knowledge, 1918. Print.

Budge, Ernest A Wallis. *The Book of the Dead; the Hieroglyphic Transcript of the Papyrus of Ani,*. New Hyde Park, N.Y.: U, 1960. Print.

Budge, Ernest A. Wallis. *The Gods of the Egyptians, or Studies in Egyptian Mythology.* London: Methuen, 1904. Print.

Burton, Richard (Translator). *The Arabian Nights: Tales from a Thousand and One Nights*. Modern Library, 2004. Print.

Butler, Alan, and Stephen Dafoe. *The Warriors and the Bankers*. Belleville, Ontario, Canada: Templar Books, 1999. Print.

Butler, Edward P. "Esoteric City: Theological Hermeneutics in Plato's Republic," Abraxas No. 5, 2014, Pp. 95-104.

Carroll, Peter J. *Liber Null & Psychonaut*. York Beach, Maine: Samuel Weiser, 1987. Print.

"Cathar Texts: Interrogatio Johannis (The Book of John the Evangelist)." Gnosis.org. Web.

Churton, Tobias. *Gnostic Mysteries of Sex: Sophia the Wild One and Erotic Christianity*. 2015. Print.

Churton, Tobias. *Gnostic Philosophy: From Ancient Persia to Modern Times*. Rochester, Vermont: Inner Traditions, 2005. Print.

Churton, Tobias. *The Mysteries of John the Baptist: His legacy in Gnosticism, Paganism, and Freemasonry*. Rochester, Vermont: Inner Traditions, 2012. Print.

Clarke, Ernest G. (Editor). *Targum Pseudo-Jonathan of the Pentateuch*. Ktav Publishing Inc, 1985. Print.

Clement I. *Clementine Homilies.* S.l.: The Classics US, 2013. Print.

"Clementine Recognitions." Early Christian Writings. Web.

Cohen, A. (Translator). *The Babylonian Talmud*. Cambridge, Massachusetts: Cambridge University Press, 2013. Print.

Connor, Jerome. *The Holy Land: An Oxford Archaeological Guide: From Earliest times to 1700*. 4th edition. Oxford, England: Oxford University Press, 1998. Print.

Conner, Miguel. "Jesus and Gnosticism in Islam, Part 2." Examiner.com. 10 Nov. 2010. Web.

"Contra Celsus." CHURCH FATHERS: (Origen). New Advent. Web.

Copenhaver, Brian P. *Hermetica the Greek Corpus Hermeticum and the Latin Asclepius in a New English Translation, with Notes and Introduction*. Cambridge, Massachusetts: Cambridge University Press, 1992. Print.

Coppens, Philip. "Ficino: The High Priest of the Renaissance." PhilipCoppens.com. Web.

Cory, Isaac Preston, and E. Richmond Hodges. *Cory's Ancient Fragments of the Phoenician, Carthaginian, Babylonian, Egyptian and Other Authors.* London: Reeves & Turner, 1876. Print.

Coulter, Charles Russell, and Patricia Turner. *Encyclopedia of Ancient Deities*. Jefferson, North Carolina: McFarland, 2000. Print.

Crane, Dr. Frank, RHP, Jr. and Solomon J. Schepps (Contributors). *The Lost Books of the Bible*. New York: Bell Publishing Company, 1979. Print.

Crowley, Aleister, *The Holy Books of Thelema*. York Beach, Maine: Samuel Weiser, 1983. Print.

Crowley, Aleister. *Liber Aleph Vel CXI: The Book of Wisdom or Folly, in the Form an Epistle of 666, the Great Wild Beast to His Son 777, Being the Equinox*, Volume III, Number VI. York Beach, Maine: Samuel Weiser, 1991. Print.

Crowley, Aleister. *Magic: Book 4.* New York: Samuel Weiser, 1980. Print.

Cumont, Franz. *The Mysteries of Mithra*. New York: Dover Publications, 1956. Print.

Daraul, Arkon. *A History of Secret Societies*. New York: Citadel, 1962. Print.

Davies, Stevan L. *The Secret Book of John: The Gnostic Gospel Annotated & Explained.* Woodstock, Vermont: SkyLight Paths Publishing, 2005. Print.

DeConick, April. *Practicing Gnosis: Ritual, Magic, Theurgy, and Liturgy in Nag Hammadi, Manichaean and Other Ancient Literature: Essays in Honor of Birger A. Pearson*. Leiden, Netherlands: Brill, 2013. Print.

DeConick, April. *The Thirteenth Apostle: What the Gospel of Judas Really Says.* London: Continuum, 2007. Print.

Deferrari, Roy J. *Ecclesiastical History.* Washington, D.C.: Catholic University of America, 2005. Print.

"Deatils (sic) Emerge on Knights Templar Document from Secret Archives." Catholic News Agency. 16 Oct. 2007. Web.

Diodochos, Damascius. "Damascius' Problems and Solutions Concerning First Principles." Google Books. Web.

"The Discourse on the Eighth and Ninth—The Nag Hammadi Library." Gnosis.org. Web.

Dodd, David Brooks. *Initiation in Ancient Greek Rituals and Narratives: New Critical Perspectives*. London: Routledge, 2003. Print.

Dodd, Rachel. "Morphing Monsters: The Evolution of Anguipede Giants." *Sunoikisis Undergraduate Research Journal*. 17 Sept. 2014.

Doresse, Jean. *Secret Books of the Egyptian Gnostics*. MJF Books, 1997. Print.

Duncan, Malcolm C. *Duncan's Ritual of Freemasonry*. Three Rivers Press, 1976. Print.

Eschenbach, Wolfram Von. *Parzival*. Penguin Classics, 1980. Print.

Eisler, Robert. *Orpheus the Fisher: Comparative Studies in Orphic and Early Christian Cult Symbolism*. London, England: JM Watkins. 1921. Print.

Eliade, Mircea. *Cosmos and History: The Myth of the Eternal Return*. New York: Harper, 1959. Print.

Eliade, Mircea, and Willard R. Trask (Translator). *The Sacred and the Profane: The Nature of Religion*. New York: Harcourt, Brace & World, 1959. Print.

Embry, Ray. "Marcion: Progenitor of Three Famous Christian Communities: Baptists, Catholics, Gnostics." Marcionite-Scripture.info. 2001. Web.

"The Epistle of Ignatius to the Ephesians." CHURCH FATHERS (St. Ignatius). New Advent. Web.

Evola, Julius. *The Mystery of the Grail: Initiation and Magic in the Quest for the Spirit*. Rochester, Vermont: Inner Traditions, 1997. Print.

Evola, Julius. *The Hermetic Tradition: Symbols and Teachings of the Royal Art*. Rochester, Vermont: Inner Traditions, 1995. Print.

Finegan, Jack. *The Archeology of World Religions: The Background of Primitivism, Zoroastrianism, Hinduism, Jainism, Buddhism, Confucianism, Taoism, Shinto, Islam, and Sikhism*. Princeton, New Jersey: Princeton University Press, 1952. Print.

"The First Apology." CHURCH FATHERS: (St. Justin Martyr). Web.

Fowden, Garth. *The Egyptian Hermes: A Historical Approach to the Late Pagan Mind.* Cambridge: Cambridge University Press, 1986. Print.

Frale, Barbara. *The Templars: The Secret History Revealed.* Arcade Publishing, 2011. Print.

Franz, Marie. Projection and Re-collection in Jungian Psychology: Reflections of the Soul. La Salle, Ill.: Open Court, 1980. Print.

Frazer, James George. *The Golden Bough a Study in Magic and Religion*. New York: The Macmillan Company, 1958. Print.

Friedlander, Gerald (Translator). *Pirke de Rabbi Eliezer.* Intellectbooks, 2009. Print.

Fulcanelli, *Le Mystere des Cathedrales*. Albuquerque, New Mexico: Brotherhood of Life, Inc., 1984. Print.

Fundgruben des Orients, Volume 6. Vienna, Austria: Anton Schmid. 1818.

Gardner, Laurence. *Bloodline of the Holy Grail: The Hidden Lineage of Jesus Revealed*. Rockport, Massachusetts: Element, 1996. Print.

Gardner, Laurence. *Genesis of the Grail Kings: The Explosive Story of Genetic Cloning and the Ancient Bloodline of Jesus.* Boston, Massachusetts: Element Books, 2000. Print.

Gardner, Iain. *The Kephalaia of the Teacher: The Edited Coptic Manichaean Texts in Translation with Commentary*. Leiden: E.J. Brill, 1995. Print.

"Genesis Rabba." SacredTexts.com. Web.

Gibbs, Mark. *The Virgin and the Priest: The Lost Secrets of the Messianic Code*. The Vineyard Press, 2007. Print.

Ginzberg, Louis. *Legends of the Jews*, Volume Two. Baltimore, Maryland: The John Hopkins University Press, 1998. Print.

Gleason, Daniel. "A Gematria Based Commentary on the Gospels." Jesus8880: The Sacred Geometry Mysteries of Christianity. Web.

"Gnostic Scriptures and Fragments: Excerpta Ex Theodoto." Gnosis.org. Web.

Godfrey, Neil. "John the Baptist Became (or Came From) a God?" *Vridar.* 17 Nov. 2011. Web.

Godfrey, Neil. "The Earliest Gospels 2—the Gospel of Basilides (according to P.L. Couchoud)." Vridar. 27 Dec. 2011. Web.

Godwin, Malcolm. *The Holy Grail: Its Origins, Secrets & Meaning Revealed*. New York: Viking, 1994. Print.

Goethe, Johann Wolfgang von. *Faust*, Part I. New York: Penguin Books, 2005. Print.

"The Gospel of Eve." Early Christian Writings. Web.

Graves, Robert. *King Jesus*. New York: Creative Age, 1946. Print.

Graves, Robert. *The White Goddess: A Historical Grammar of Poetic Myth*. New York: Farrar, Strauss and Giroux, 1975. Print.

Greer, John Michael and Christopher Warnock. *The Picatrix.* Adocentyn Press. 2010. Print.

Hallam, Henry. *View of the State of Europe During the Middle Ages*. New York: Harper & Brothers, 1818. Print.

Hameen-Antilla, Jaakko. *The Last Pagans of Iraq: Ibn Wahshiyya and his Nabatean Agriculture*. Leiden, Netherlands: Koninklijke Brill NV, 2006. Print.

Hamilton, Edith. *Mythology: Timeless Tales of Gods and Heroes*. New York, New York: Warner Books, 1940. Print.

Hammer-Purgstall, Joseph von. *The History of the Assassins*. London, England: Smith and Elder, Cornhill, 1835. Print.

Harrison, Hank. *The Cauldron and the Grail*. Los Altos, California: The Archives Press, 1992. Print.

Hauck, Dennis William. *The Emerald Tablet: Alchemy for Personal Transformation*. New York: Penguin/Arkana, 1999. Print.

Hayward, Robert. *The Jewish Temple: A Non-biblical Sourcebook*. London, England: Routledge, 1996. Print.

Hesse, Hermann. *Demian: The Story of Emil Sinclair's Youth*. Penguin Classics, 2013. Print.

Al-Hilali, Muhammand Taqi-ud-Din and Muhammad Muhsin Khan. *The Noble Qur'an: The English Translation of the Meanings and Commentary*. Medina, Saudi Arabia: King Fahd Complex, 1998. Print.

Hippolytus. "Refutation of All Heresies." New Advent. Web.

"History of the Ancient Arabic Order Nobles Mystic Shrine." PheonixMasonry.org. Web.

Hodapp, Christopher. *Freemasons for Dummies.* Hoboken, New Jersey: Wiley Publishing, 2005. Print.

Hogan, Timothy. *Entering the Chain of Union.* Lulu.Com. 2012. Print.

Holmes Christian Standard Bible. BibleHub.com. Web.

The Holy Bible (King James Version). Nashville, Tennessee: Thomas Nelson, Inc., 1976. Print.

The Holy Bible (New International Version). BibleHub.com. Web.

The Holy Bible (Young's Literal Translation). BibleHub.com. Web.

Homer (Author) and Fagels, Robert (Translator). *The Iliad/The Odyssey.* Baltimore, Maryland: Penguin Classics, 1999. Print.

Humm, Alan. "Lilith in Kabbala: Zohar." Lilith Gallery. Web.

Huysmans, J-K *Against Nature.* Baltimore, Maryland: Penguin, 1959. Print.

Hyginus, C. Julius, and Peter K. Marshall. Hygini Fabulae. Stutgardiae: Teubner, 1993. Print.

"International Bodyguard and Security Services Association." IBSSA.org. Web.

"Lysander by Plutarch." The Internet Classics Archive. Web.

Jackson, Howard M. *Zosimos of Panopolis on the Letter Omega*. Claremont, California: Claremont Graduate School, 1979. Print.

Jackson, Nigel. *Masks of Misrule: The Horned God & His Cult in Europe*. Berks, England: Capall Bann Publishing, 1996. Print.

Jackson, Nigel, and Jackson Howard. *The Pillars of Tubal-Cain*. Somerset, England: Holmes Publishing Group LLC, 2001. Print.

Jonas, Hans. *The Gnostic Religion: The Message of the Alien God and the Beginnings of Christianity.* 2nd edition. Boston: Beacon, 1963. Print.

Joseph, Isya. *Devil Worship; the Sacred Books and Traditions of the Yezidiz,*. Boston, Massachusetts: R.G. Badger, 1919. Print.

Jung, Carl, and Murray Stein. *Jung on Christianity*. Princeton, New Jersey: Princeton University Press, 1999. Print.

Jung, Carl. *Aion: Researches into the Phenomenology of the Self*. Princeton, New Jersey: Princeton University Press. 1978. Print.

Jung, Carl and HG Baynes (Translator). "Sermones Ad Mortuos." Gnosis.org. Web.

Jung, Emma, and Marie-Luise von Franz. *The Grail Legend*. New York: Published by Putnam for the CG Jung Foundation for Analytical Psychology, 1970. Print.

Kaplan, Aryeh. *Sefer Yetzirah: The Book of Creation*. Northvale, New Jersey: Jason Aronson Inc., 1995. Print.

Kasser, Rodolphe, Marvin Meyer, and Gregor Wurst (Editors). *The Gospel of Judas*. Washington, D.C: The National Geographic Society, 2006. Print.

King, Charles William. *The Gnostics and Their Remains*. London, England: Bell & Daldy, 1887. Print.

King, Karen. *What is Gnosticism?* Belknap Press, 2005. Print.

Kirchweger, Anton Joseph. *Aurea Catena Homeri, Oder, Eine Beschreibung Von Dem Ursprung Der Natur Und Naturlichen Dingen: Wie Und Woraus Sie Geboren Und Gezeuget, Auch Wie Sie in Ihr Uranfanglich Wesen . . .* Franckfurt: Johann Georg Bohme, 1723. Print.

Kyle Fraser. "Baptised in Gnosis: The Spiritual Alchemy of Zosimos of Panopolis." *Dionysus*, Vol. 25. 2005. Print.

Lacarriere, Jacque. *The Gnostics*. New York: EP Dutton, 1977. Print.

Laidler, Keith. *The Head of God: The Lost Treasure of the Templars*. Weidenfeld & Nicolson, 1998. Print.

Lamy, Michel. *Les Templiers: ces grands seigneurs aux blancs manteaux*. France: Auberon, 1998. Print.

Laurence, Richard (Translator). *The Book of Enoch the Prophet*. Glasgow, Ireland: John Thompson, 1882. Print.

Leland, Charles Godfrey. *Aradia, or The Gospel of the Witches*. London, England: D. Nutt, 1899. Print.

Levi, Eliphas. *Magic: A History of Its Rites, Rituals and Mysteries*. Mineola, New York: Dover, 2006. Print.

Levi, Eliphas, and Arthur Edward Waite. *The Ritual of Transcendental Magic*. Altenmuunster, Germany: Jazzybee Verlag, 2013. Print.

Machen, Arthur. *The Great God Pan*. London, England: J. Lane, 1894. Print.

Mackey, Albert. *Encyclopedia of Freemasonry and its Kindred Sciences*. Philadelphia: McClure Publishing Company, 1917. Print.

Majercik, Ruth Dorothy. *The Chaldean Oracles: Text, Translation, and Commentary*. Leiden: EJ Brill, 1989. Print.

The Mabinogian: From the Llyfr Coch O Hergest, and Other Ancient Welsh Manuscripts. London, England: Longman, Orme, Brown, Green, and Longmans, 1838. Print.

Marlowe, Christopher, and Sylvan Barnet. *Doctor Faustus.* New York: New American Library, 1969. Print.

Mastrocinque, Attilio. *From Jewish Magic to Gnosticism*. Tubingen, Germany: Mohr Siebeck, 2005. Print.

Matter, Jacques. *Histoire Critique du Gnosticisme*. Paris, France: Chez FG Levrault, 1828. Print.

Mead, GRS. *Did Jesus Live 100 B.C.?: An Enquiry Into the Talmud Jesus Stories, the Toldoth Jeschu, and Some Curious Statements of Epiphanius—being a Contribution to the Study of Christian Origins*. Hardpress Publishing, 2012. Print.

Mead, GRS. *Fragments of a Faith Forgotten*. Forgotten Books, 2012. Print.

Mead, GRS. *Gnostic John the Baptizer: Selections from the Mandaean John-Book*. Kessinger Legacy Reprints, 2010. Print.

Mead, GRS. *Pistis Sophia: A Gnostic Gospel*. San Diego, California: The Book Tree, 2006. Print.

Mead, GRS. *Thrice-Greatest Hermes: Studies in Hellenistic Theosophy and Gnosis*. Weiser Books, 2001. Print.

Al-Mehri, AB (Editor). *The Qur`an: Saheeh International Translation*. Maktabah Publications, 2009. Print.

Michelet, Jules. *History of France: From the Earliest Period to the Present Time,* Volume 1. London: Chapman and Hall, 1844. Print.

Miller, Peter N. *The Antiquary's Art of Comparison: Peiresc and Abraxas*. Tubingen, Germany: Max Niemeyer Verlag, 2001. Print.

Murdock, DM. "The Phallic 'Savior of the World' Hidden in the Vatican" Truth Be Known - Acharya S. 2012. Web.

Murray, Margaret Alice. *The God of the Witches*. London: Oxford University Press, 1970. Print.

Nettleton, Stuart. *The Alchemy Key: Unraveling the Single Tangible Secret In All Mysteries*. CreateSpace, 2008. Print.

New American Standard Bible. BibleHub.com. Web.

Nicolai, Christoph Friedrich. *Versuch uber die Beschuldigungen welche dem Tempelherrenorden gemacht worden, und uber dessen Geheimniß*. Berlin, Germany, 1782. Print.

Oates, Joan. *Babylon*. London, England: Thames and Hudson, 1979. Print.

Olsen, Oddvar. *The Templar Papers*. Pompton Plains, New Jersey: Career Press, 2010. Print.

"On the Baptism (A)—The Nag Hammadi Library." Gnosis.org. Web.

Orlov, Andrei A. *Dark Mirrors Azazel and Satanael in Early Jewish Demonology*. Albany, New York: State University of New York, 2011. Print.

Orlov, Andrei A. *Divine Scapegoats: Demonic Mimesis in Early Jewish Mysticism*. New York: State University of New York Press, 2015. Print.

Oursel, Raymonds (Editor). *Le Proces des Templiers*. Paris: Denoel, 1955.

Pagels, Elaine. *The Gnostic Gospels*. Random House, 1979. Print.

Parfrey, Adam and Craig Heimbichner (Editors). *Ritual America: Secret Brotherhoods and Their Influence on American Society*. China: Feral House, 2012. Print.

Partner, Peter. *The Murdered Magicians: The Templars and Their Myth*. Oxford, England: Oxford University Press, 1982. Print.

Pearson, Birger. *Gnosticism, Judaism, and Egyptian Christianity*. Augsburg Fortress Publishers, 1990. Print.

Petrement, Simone. *A Separate God: The Origins and Teachings of Gnosticism*. HarperCollins, 1993. Print.

Plancy, Jacques Albin Simon Collin de. *Dictionnaire Infernal*. Nabu Press, 2012. Print.

Plato. "Phaedo." Project Gutenberg. Web.

Plato, Harold North Fowler (Translator), WRM Lamb (Translator). *Statesman. Philebus. Ion.* Cambridge, Massachusetts: Harvard University Press, 1925. Print.

Plato. *The Republic*. Dover Publications, 2000. Print.

Plato. *Timaeus and Critias*. Penguin Classics, 1998. Print.

"La Peste Dans de Dioceses de Laon et Soissons." *Bulletin De La Societe Academique De Laon*. Vol. 21. Laon, France: Societe Academique de Laon, 1876. Print.

Picknett, Lynn and Clive Prince. *The Templar Revelation: Secret Guardians of the True Identity of Christ*. New York, New York: Simon & Schuster, Inc., 1997. Print.

Pike, Albert. *Morals and Dogma*. Richmond, Virginia: LH Jenkins, Inc., 1927. Print.

Pingree, David Edwin. *The Thousands of Abu Maļshar*. London, England: Warburg Institute, 1968. Print.

Pinkham, Mark Amaru. *Guardians of the Holy Grail: The Knights Templar, John the Baptist, and the Water of Life*. Kempton, Illinois: Adventures Unlimited, 2004. Print.

Pinkham, Mark Amaru. "The Templars' Biggest Secret & the Vatican." Gnostic Templars. Atlantis Rising Magazine. Web.

Platt, Rutherford H. (Editor). *The Forgotten Books of Eden*. New York: Bell Publishing Company. Print.

"Pliny the Elder, Natural History." Livius. Web.

Price, Robert M. "Review—A Survey on Some Recent Books on Gnosticism." Robert M. Price. Web.

"'Processus contra Templarios': Beautiful and full of typos." KnightsTemplarVault.com. Web.

Ragg, Lonsdale, and Laura Ragg. *The Gospel of Barnabus*. Cosimo Classics, 2010. Print.

Pearse, Roger. "Summing up the Ancient Accounts of the Borborites-Phibionites." Roger-Pearse.com. 12 Dec. 2013. Web.

The Royal Order of Jesters—Freemasonry's Animal House. Youtube. Michaelrose93, 11 Aug. 2014. Web. <https://youtu.be/VtgBdUtw26c>.

Rudolph, Kurt. *Mandaeism*. Leiden, Netherlands: Brill, 1978. Print.

Rudolph, Kurt. *Gnosis: The Nature & History of Gnosticism*. Edinburgh, Scotland: T & T Clark, Limited, 1984. Print.

Saint Ambrose. "De Sacramentis." Google Books. Web.

Salm, Rene. "The Mandeans and Christian Origins (R. Stahl)." Mythicist Papers. 12 Oct. 2012. Web.

Salm, Rene. "The Natsarene and Hidden Gnosis—Pt. 1." Mythicist Papers. 6 May 2013. Web.

Santos, Arysio. "The Atlantean Origin Of The Seven Sacraments." 2 Oct. 2014. Web.

Schwartz, Howard. *Lilith's Cave: Jewish Tales of the Supernatural*. New York: Oxford University Press, 1988. Print.

Scott, Walter. *Hermetica: The Ancient Greek and Latin Writings Which Contain Religious of Philosophic Teachings Ascribed to Hermes Trismegistus.* London, England: Dawsons of Pall Mall, 1968. Print.

Sebottendorff, Rudolf von. *Secret Practices of the Sufi Freemasons*. Rochester, Vermont: Inner Traditions, 2013. Print.

Shah, Idries. *The Sufis*. New York: Random House, 1971. Print.

Shakespeare, William, and RA Foakes. *A Midsummer Night's Dream.* Cambridge, England: Cambridge University Press, 1984. Print.

Shaw, Gregory. "Taking the Shape of the Gods: A Theurgic Reading of Hermetic Rebirth." Princeton University's Committee for the Study of Late Antiquity Colloquium: Hermetica: New Approaches to the Text and Interpretation of the Corpus Hermeticum. 6 May 2012. Lecture.

Simon, Maurice and Dr. Paul P. Levertoff. *The Zohar: An English Translation*, Volume Four. New York, New York: Soncino Press, 1984. Print.

Skinner, Dr. Stephen. *Techniques of Graeco-Egyptian Magic*. Llewellyn Publications, 2014. Print.

Smith, Morton. *Jesus the Magician.* San Francisco: Harper & Row, 1978. Print.

Sperling, Harry and Maurice Simon. *The Zohar: An English Translation*, Volume One. New York, New York: Soncino Press, 1984. Print.

Sperling, Harry and Maurice Simon. *The Zohar: An English Translation*, Volume Five. New York, New York: Soncino Press, 1984. Print.

Stapleton, HE, and GL Lewis. *The Sayings of Hermes Quoted in the Ma'al-Waraqi of Ibn Umail*. 1949. Print.

Stein, Murray and Carl Jung. *Jung on Christianity (Encountering Jung)*. Princeton, New Jersey. Princeton University Press, 1999. Print.

Stewart, Michael James Alexander. *The Forgotten Monarchy of Scotland: The True Story of the Royal House of Stewart and the Hidden Lineage of the Kings and Queens of Scots.* Shaftesbury, Dorset, England: Element, 1998. Print.

Stewart, Michael James Alexander and Walid Amine Salhab. *The Knights Templar of the Middle East: The Hidden History of the Islamic Origins of Freemasonry.* San Francisco, California: Red Wheel/Weiser, 2006. Print.

Stoker, Bram. *Dracula.* Charlottesville, Virginia: University of Virginia Library, 1996. Print.

"The Stromata." CHURCH FATHERS: (Clement of Alexandria). New Advent. Web.

Storey, Ian C. *Eupolis: Poet of Old Comedy*. Oxford, England: Oxford University Press, 2004. Print.

Stoyanov, Yuri. *The Other God: Dualist Religions from Antiquity to the Cathar Heresy*. New Haven, Connecticut: Yale University Press, 2000. Print.

Sykes, JB *The Concise Oxford Dictionary of Current English: Based on the Oxford English Dictionary and Its Supplements*. 6th edition. Oxford, England: Clarendon, 1976. Print.

"The Teachings of Silvanus—The Nag Hammadi Library." Gnosis.org. Web.

"The Testimony of Truth—The Nag Hammadi Library." Gnosis.org. Web.

"Third Book of Enoch." Archive.org. Web.

Tertullian. "On Baptism." Mb Soft. Web.

"Prescription against Heretics." CHURCH FATHERS: (Tertullian). New Advent. Web.

Twyman, Tracy R. *Clock Shavings*. Vancouver, Washington: Quintessential Publications, 2014. Print.

Twyman, Tracy R. *Hocus Pocus: The Magical Power of St. Peter*. Vancouver, Washington: Quintessential Publications, 2010. Ebook.

Twyman, Tracy R. "Interview with Prince Michael Stewart of Albany." *Dagobert's Revenge Magazine*, Vol. 2#1, 1999. Union City, New Jersey. Print.

Twyman, Tracy R. *The Judas Goat: The Substitution Theory of the Crucifixion*. Vancouver, Washington: Quintessential Publications, 2011. Ebook.

Twyman, Tracy R. *Money Grows on the Tree of Knowledge*. Vancouver, Washington: Quintessential Publications, 2011. Print.

Twyman, Tracy R. *The Merovingian Mythos and the Mystery of Rennes-le-Chateau*. Portland, Oregon: Dragon Key Press, 2004. Print.

Twyman, Tracy R. *Solomon's Treasure: The Magic and Mystery of America's Money*. Portland, Oregon: Dragon Key Press, 2005. Print.

Ustinova, Yulia. *The Supreme Gods of the Bosporan Kingdom: Celestial Aphrodite and the Most High God*. Leiden, Netherlands: Brill, 1999. Print.

"Vatican Book on Templars' Demise." BBC News. BBC, 5 Oct. 2007. Web.

Vere, Nicholas de. *The Dragon Legacy: The Secret History of an Ancient Bloodline*. San Diego, California: The Book Tree, 2004. Print.

Walbridge, John. "Explaining Away the Greek Gods in Islam." *The Journal of the History of Ideas*, Vol. 59, Issue 3, July 1998. Print.

Villers, Charles. "Some Account of the Researches of the German Literati on the Subject of Ancient Literature and History." London, England: AJ Valpy, 1812. Print.

Walker, Benjamin. *Gnosticism: Its History and Influence*. Wellingborough, Northamptonshire, England: Aquarian, 1983. Print.

Waddell, LA. *The Makers of Civilization in Race and History*. London, England: Luzac & Company, 1929. Print.

Wall, Otto Augustus. *Sex and Sex Worship (phallic Worship) a Scientific Treatise on Sex, Its Nature and Function, and Its Influence on Art, Science, Architecture, and Religion - with Special Reference to Sex Worship and Symbolism*. St. Louis, Missouri: Mosby, 1919. Print.

Ward, JSM *Freemasonry and the Ancient Gods*. London: Simpkin, Marshall, Hamilton, Kent, 1921. Print.

Wahshiyya, Ibn and Joseph von Hammer-Purgstall (Translator). *Ancient Alphabets and Hieroglyphic Characters Explained*. London, England: W. Bulmer and Company, 1806. Print.

Wasserman, James, and Nancy Wasserman. *To Perfect This Feast a Performance Commentary on the Gnostic Mass*. 3rd edition. Newburyport: Sekmet, 2013. Print.

Wasserman, James. *The Templars and the Assassins: The Militia of Heaven*. Rochester, Vermont: Inner Traditions, 2001. Print.

Webb, Al. "Prince Charles Praises Islamic Principles on Environment." National Catholic Reporter. 15 June 2010. Web.

Williams, Frank. *The Panarion of Epiphanius of Salamis*. 2nd edition. Leiden: Brill, 2009. Print.

Williams, Michael A. *Rethinking "Gnosticism" an Argument for Dismantling a Dubious Category*. Princeton, New Jersey: Princeton University Press, 1996. Print.

Willoughby, Harold R. *Pagan Regeneration: A Study of Mystery Initiations and Secret Rites In the Graeco-Roman World*. Kessinger Publishing, 2003. Print.

Wise, Michael, Martin Abegg, Jr., and Edward Cook. *The Dead Sea Scrolls: A New Translation* San Francisco, CA: HarperSanFrancisco, 1996. Print.

"The Testament of Solomon." Esoteric Archives. Web.

The Writings of Cyprian, Bishop of Carthage. Edinburgh, Scotland: T. & T. Clark, 1868. Print.

"The Works of Flavius Josephus." The Works of Flavius Josephus. 29 July 2015. Web.

Wright, Thomas. *The Worship of the Generative Powers During the Middle Ages of Western Europe*. Covina, California: Collectors Publications, 1967. Print.

Yarker, John. *The Arcane Schools*. Adamant Media Corporation, 2003. Print.

Yates, Giles F. "Horae Esotericae." *The American Quarterly Review of Freemasonry and Its Kindred Sciences*, Volume 1. New York: Robert Macoy, 1858. Print.

Yonge, Charles Duke. *The Works of Philo: Complete and Unabridged*. New Updated edition. Peabody, Massachusetts: Hendrickson Publishing, 1993. Print.

About the Authors

Tracy R. Twyman has been writing about the esoteric side of history and current events for over 20 years, dealing with topics like secret societies, ancient myths, demonology, ceremonial magic, divination, alchemy, mind control, mystical royal bloodlines, and the hidden history of money, to name just a few. Her major books include *Clock Shavings*, *Solomon's Treasure*, and *The Merovingian Mythos*. She has been a guest many times on numerous radio talk shows, including Coast to Coast AM and Ground Zero with Clyde Lewis. She has also been seen on several television shows, including National Geographic's "Is It Real?" and Jesse Ventura's "Conspiracy Theory." Her web presence is found at TracyRTwyman.com.

Alexander Rivera is the author of many short stories, novels and owner of the website TheAeonEye.com, which spans different topics regarding comparative mythology, the Holy Grail, esoterica, Gnostic texts and the Bible. He is a self-trained scholar, gathering primary sources and piecing it all together on his own or with the help of friends. He currently resides in Orlando, Florida, patiently waiting for the Baptism of Wisdom.

Lightning Source UK Ltd.
Milton Keynes UK
UKHW050829280822
407860UK00014BA/276/J